Applying Implementation Science
in Early Childhood Programs and Systems

Applying Implementation Science in Early Childhood Programs and Systems

edited by

Tamara Halle, Ph.D.
Child Trends
Washington, D.C.

Allison Metz, Ph.D.
National Implementation Research Network
Frank Porter Graham Child Development Institute
University of North Carolina at Chapel Hill

and

Ivelisse Martinez-Beck, Ph.D.
Division of Child and Family Development
Office of Planning, Research and Evaluation (OPRE)
Administration for Children and Families
Washington, D.C.

·P·A·U·L·H·
BROOKES
PUBLISHING C^O.®

Baltimore • London • Sydney

·P A U L·H·
BROOKES
PUBLISHING C.º ®

Paul H. Brookes Publishing Co.
Post Office Box 10624
Baltimore, MD 21285-0624

www.brookespublishing.com

Typeset by Cenveo Publisher Services, Columbia, Maryland. Manufactured in the United States by
Sheridan Books, Inc., Chelsea, Michigan.

Library of Congress Cataloging-in-Publication Data

Halle, Tamara.
   Applying implementation science in early childhood programs and systems / by Tamara Halle,
Ph.D., Allison Metz, Ph.D. and Ivelisse Martinez-Beck, Ph.D.
      pages   cm
   Includes bibliographical references and index.
   ISBN 978-1-59857-282-7 (alk. paper) — ISBN 1-59857-282-2 (alk. paper)
1. Early childhood education—Computer-assisted instruction.   2. Education—Effect of
technological innovations on.   3. Educational technology.   4. Children with disabilities—Education
(Early childhood)   5. Children with disabilities—Education (Early childhood)—Curricula.
6. Children with disabilities—Education (Early Childhood)—Evaluation.   I. Title.

   LB1139.35.C64H35 2013
   372.210785—dc23   2012046198

British Library Cataloguing in Publication data are available from the British Library.

2017   2016   2015   2014   2013

10   9   8   7   6   5   4   3   2   1

Contents

About the Editors... vii

Contributors ix

Foreword   *Samuel L. Odom* xii

Acknowledgments.. xv

Introduction: Where Is the New Frontier of Implementation
Science in Early Care and Education Research and Practice?
Ivelisse Martinez-Beck xix

Section I   Implementation Science: Defining the New Frontier

          Allison Metz 1

Chapter 1   Implementation Science: What Do We
            Know and Where Do We Go from Here?
            Robert P. Franks and Jennifer Schroeder 5

Chapter 2   The Key Components of Successful Implementation
            Allison Metz, Tamara Halle, Leah Bartley, and Amy Blasberg 21

Chapter 3   Readiness to Change: Effective Implementation
            Processes for Meeting People Where They Are
            Shira M. Peterson 43

Chapter 4   Innovative Methodologies to Explore Implementation:
            Whole-Part-Whole—Construct Validity, Measurement,
            and Analytical Issues for Intervention Fidelity
            Assessment in Education Research
            Chris S. Hulleman, Sara E. Rimm-Kaufman, and Tashia Abry 65

**Section II   Aligning Stage-Appropriate Evaluation with the Stages
            of Implementation: Formative Evaluation and Fidelity**

            Amy Blasberg 95

Chapter 5   Studying the Implementation of
            Coaching-Based Professional Development
            Douglas R. Powell and Karen E. Diamond 97

Chapter 6   Implementation of Getting Ready: A Relationship-
            Focused Intervention to Support Parent Engagement,
            Birth to 5
            Lisa L. Knoche..117

Chapter 7   An Eye to Efficient and Effective Fidelity
             Measurement for Both Research and Practice
             *Chrishana M. Lloyd, Lauren H. Supplee, and
             Shira Kolnik Mattera* 139

Chapter 8   Applying Lessons Learned from Evaluations
             of Model Early Care and Education Programs
             to Preparation for Effective Implementation at Scale
             Jason Downer 157

**Section III   Aligning Stage-Appropriate Evaluation
             with the Stages of Implementation:
             Ongoing Monitoring and Scale-Up/Replication**
             Amy Blasberg 171

Chapter 9   Lessons Learned in the Implementation of the
             TRIAD Scale-Up Model: Teaching Early Mathematics
             with Trajectories and Technologies
             Julie Sarama and Douglas H. Clements 173

Chapter 10   Improving Implementation of the Nurse–Family
             Partnership in the Process of Going to Scale
             Peggy Hill and David Olds 193

Chapter 11   Implementation and Replication of the
             Educare Model of Early Childhood Education
             Noreen Yazejian, Donna Bryant, and Portia Kennel 209

Chapter 12   Using Implementation Science to Support
             Replication, Scale-Up, and Ongoing Monitoring
             Carolyn Layzer 227

Section IV   Implementation Science at the Systems Level
             Tamara Halle 239

Chapter 13   Considering Statewide
             Professional Development Systems
             Kathryn Tout, Allison Metz, and Leah Bartley 243

Chapter 14   Evaluating Implementation of
             Quality Rating and Improvement Systems
             Diane Paulsell, Kathryn Tout, and Kelly Maxwell 269

Chapter 15   Applications of Implementation Science to
             Early Care and Education Programs and
             Systems: Implications for Research, Policy, and Practice
             *Tamara Halle, Martha Zaslow, Ivelisse Martinez-Beck,
             and Allison Metz* 295

Index 315

About the Editors

Tamara Halle, Ph.D., Codirector of Early Childhood Research and Senior Research Scientist, Child Trends, 7315 Wisconsin Avenue, Suite 1200 West, Bethesda, MD 20814

Dr. Halle is a developmental psychologist who codirects Child Trends's early childhood research practice. She conducts research on children's early cognitive and social development, children's school readiness, family and community supports for school readiness, and school characteristics associated with ongoing achievement and positive development. Her recent work focuses especially on implementation science; the well-being of dual-language–learning children; and evaluations of early childhood curricula, programs, and state and federal initiatives aimed at supporting children's school readiness.

Allison Metz, Ph.D., Associate Director and Scientist, National Implementation Research Network, Frank Porter Graham Child Development Institute, University of North Carolina at Chapel Hill, 521 South Greensboro Street, CB 8185, Chapel Hill, NC 27599

Dr. Metz is a developmental psychologist who specializes in the effective implementation and scaling-up of evidence-based and evidence-informed programs and strategies in a range of human service and early childhood settings. Her recent work has focused on implementation teams, implementation measures, and fidelity for child welfare programs and practices.

Ivelisse Martinez-Beck, Ph.D., Senior Social Science Research Analyst and Child Care Research Team Leader, Division of Child and Family Development at the Office of Planning, Research and Evaluation (OPRE), Administration for Children and Families, U.S. Department of Health and Human Services, 370 L'Enfant Promenade SW, Aerospace Building, 7th Floor West, Washington, DC 20447

Dr. Martinez-Beck is a developmental psychologist whose work involves coordinating the child care research team in OPRE; developing the child care policy research agenda, managing large research projects such as the National Survey of Early Care and Education, and representing OPRE and the child care policy research perspective in diverse federal interagency research work groups. A recent focus of her work has been on issues related to the quality of early care and education settings and links to young children's developmental outcomes and research on, and validation and evaluation of, quality rating and improvement systems.

Contributors

Tashia Abry, Ph.D.
Postdoctoral Research Associate
Arizona State University
P.O. Box 873701
Tempe, AZ 85287

Leah Bartley, M.S.W.
Implementation Specialist
National Implementation Research
    Network
Frank Porter Graham Child
    Development Institute
University of North Carolina at
    Chapel Hill
521 South Greensboro Street, CB 8185
Chapel Hill, NC 27599

Amy Blasberg, M.P.P.
Research Analyst
Child Trends
7315 Wisconsin Avenue,
    Suite 1200 West
Bethesda, MD 20814

Donna Bryant, Ph.D.
Senior Scientist
Frank Porter Graham Child
    Development Institute
University of North Carolina at
    Chapel Hill
105 Smith Level Road, CB 8180
Chapel Hill, NC 27599

Douglas H. Clements, Ph.D.
Kennedy Endowed Chair in Early
    Childhood Learning and Professor
University of Denver
Educational Research, Practice, and
    Policy
Morgridge College of Education
Katherine A. Ruffatto Hall 154
1999 East Evans Avenue
Denver, CO 80208

Karen E. Diamond, Ph.D.
Professor
Department of Human Development
    and Family Studies
Purdue University
1200 West State Street
West Lafayette, IN 47907

Jason Downer, Ph.D.
Research Associate Professor
Center for Advanced Study of Teaching
    and Learning
University of Virginia
350 Old Ivy Road, Suite 100
Charlottesville, VA 22903

Robert P. Franks, Ph.D.
Vice President and Director
Center for Effective Practice
Child Health and Development
    Institute
270 Farmington Avenue, Suite 367
Farmington, CT 06032

Peggy Hill, M.S.
Chief Operations Officer
Colorado Behavioral Healthcare
    Council
1410 Grant Street, Suite A-301
Denver, CO 80203

Chris S. Hulleman, Ph.D.
Research Associate Professor
Center for Advanced Study of Teaching
   and Learning
University of Virginia
2200 Old Ivy Road
Charlottesville, VA 22903

Portia Kennel, M.S.W.
Senior Vice President
Ounce of Prevention Fund
Educare Learning Network
33 West Monroe Street, Suite 2400
Chicago, IL 60603

Lisa L. Knoche, Ph.D.
Research Associate Professor
Nebraska Center for Research on
   Children, Youth, Families, and
   Schools
University of Nebraska
238 Teachers College Hall
Lincoln, NE 68588

Carolyn Layzer, Ph.D.
Senior Associate
Abt Associates, Inc.
55 Wheeler Street
Cambridge, MA 02138

Chrishana M. Lloyd, Ph.D.
Senior Research Associate
MDRC
16 East 34th Street, 19th Floor
New York, NY 10016

Shira Kolnik Mattera, Ph.D.
Research Associate
MDRC
16 East 34th Street, 19th Floor
New York, NY 10016

Kelly L. Maxwell, Ph.D.
Associate Director and Senior Scientist
Frank Porter Graham Child
   Development Institute
University of North Carolina at
   Chapel Hill
105 Smith Level Road, CB 8180
Chapel Hill, NC 27599

David Olds, Ph.D.
Director
Prevention Research Center for Family
   and Child Health
University of Colorado–Denver
Department of Pediatrics
13121 East 17th Avenue, MS 8410,
   Education 2 South, Room 5315
Aurora, CO 80045

Diane Paulsell, M.P.A.
Associate Director and Senior
   Researcher,
Mathematica Policy Research
P.O. Box 2393
Princeton, NJ 08543

Shira M. Peterson, Ph.D.
Independent Consultant
Children's Institute
274 N. Goodman Street, Suite D103
Rochester, NY 14607

Douglas R. Powell, Ph.D.
Distinguished Professor of Human
   Development
Department of Human Development
   and Family Studies
Purdue University
1200 West State Street
West Lafayette, IN 47907

Sara E. Rimm-Kaufman, Ph.D.
Associate Professor
University of Virginia
150 Ruffner Hall
405 Emmet Street
Charlottesville, VA 22904

Julie Sarama, Ph.D.
Kennedy Endowed Chair in Innovative
   Learning Technologies and
   Professor
University of Denver
Morgridge College of Education
Educational Research, Practice,
   and Policy
Katherine A. Ruffatto Hall 154
1999 East Evans Avenue
Denver, CO 80208

Jennifer Schroeder, Ph.D.
President
The Implementation Group
P.O. Box 1433
Broomfield, CO 80038

Lauren H. Supplee, Ph.D.
Senior Social Science Research Analyst
Administration for Children and
    Families
Office of Planning, Research and
    Evaluation
370 L'Enfant Promenade, SW
Aerospace Building, 7th Floor West
Washington, DC 20447

Kathryn Tout, Ph.D.
Codirector of Early Childhood
    Research and Senior Scientist
Child Trends
708 North First Street, Suite 333
Minneapolis, MN 55401

Noreen Yazejian, Ph.D.
Scientist
Frank Porter Graham Child
    Development Institute
University of North Carolina at
    Chapel Hill
105 Smith Level Road, CB 8180
Chapel Hill, NC 27599

Martha Zaslow, Ph.D.
Senior Scholar
Child Trends
7315 Wisconsin Avenue, Suite 1200
    West
Bethesda, MD 20814
and
Director
Office for Policy and Communications
Society for Research in Child
    Development
1313 L Street NW, Suite 140
Washington, DC 20005

Foreword

Simply stated, *Applying Implementation Science in Early Childhood Programs and Systems* is one of the most significant books published in early care and education (ECE) this year. Its significance lies in its goal of moving the field forward in using knowledge generated by developmental and education science to affect early child care practices for infants, young children, and families. The gap between science and practices has been widely lamented, often by developmental and education scientists and policy makers, but until recently, the reaction from the scientific and professional community has resembled the old saying about the weather: Everybody talks about it, but no one ever does anything about it.

In the field of medicine, the whole area of evidence-based practice emerged from a similar frustration, most notably by Cochrane Collaboration (2013), that health care practitioners in England were not utilizing the most current scientific knowledge in the care they provided to patients. Cochrane and other evidence-based medical scholars (Sackett, Straus, Richardson, Rosenberg, & Haynes, 2000) spurred on a national movement in the United States that now emphasizes "[lab] bench to bedside" translational research and utilization of that research in practice.

Within ECE, the same translational disconnect exists. The identification of developmentally appropriate practices in the 1980s (Bredekamp, 1986) provided some guidance, and the more recent emphasis on evidence-based practice (Buysse & Wesley, 2006) has anchored the field more directly in science and its translation. Currently, the ECE field is striving to fulfill the lofty mission of moving the most effective practices into common use in ECE programs. To support this mission, the emerging field of implementation science, with all its promise, is coming to the rescue, and this current volume is at the forefront of its application to ECE.

In this volume, Tamara Halle, Allison Metz, and Ivelisse Martinez-Beck move the reader from the abstract to the concrete. That is, they begin with chapters about the basic and foundational concepts in implementation science and then introduce chapters describing the application and evaluation to specific features of implementation. From this coverage of core implementation features—or drivers, as implementation scientists would call them—the editors provide illustrations of the use of implementation science principles in ECE. For this purpose, they have recruited a team of authors who describe the processes of scaling up evidence-based practices or programs with potential for use in larger numbers of programs and communities. These authors—many of whom participated in the September

2010 Working Meeting on Applications of Implementation Science to Early Care and Education Research sponsored by the Office of Planning, Research and Evaluation within the U.S. Department of Health and Human Services—describe examples ranging from case studies to major research projects.

If one goal of developmental and education science is to improve the human condition, then the processes of putting effective programs into common use, getting them out to the children and families who need them, and monitoring their effects are all logical next steps. The principles of implementation science have great promise in moving the field toward this "journal article to block corner" transmission of knowledge and action.

In the opening chapter, Robert P. Franks and Jennifer Schroeder note that one challenge for implementation science is that its theoretical base is relatively new. In this volume, the primary conceptual/theoretical framework cited is that of Fixsen, Blase, Metz, Duda, Van Dyke, and their colleagues from the National Implementation Research Network (Fixsen, Naoom, Blase, Friedman, & Wallace, 2005), but other frameworks also exist (e.g., Chen, 1998; Domitrovitch et al., 2008). In a chapter on implementation science and early childhood education, my colleagues and I (Odom et al., 2010) noted that these conceptual frameworks all were systems approaches, and for that we primarily have to thank Bronfenbrenner and his ecological systems theory of child development (Bronfenbrenner, 1979). In this volume, the authors do not always cite the microsystem-to-macrosystem continuum in their implementation models, but the features are there, sort of theoretical drivers of the processes.

A skeptic of the implementation science movement might speculate that there is very little "science" in implementation science. Science, as it needs to be, is a very conservative process. The principles and core concepts of implementation science (e.g., readiness, coaching, administrative support, etc.) should be, but rarely are, validated through randomized controlled trials (RCTs). Following a strict education science process, an implementation model like the one Carolyn Layzer proposes in Chapter 12 would require individual randomized studies of the linkage between variables to verify causal relationships. With a large enough sample, a structural equation model analysis would provide correlational information that could provide the bases for experimental verifications. I do not believe this is a "strawperson" argument.

A colleague of mine has observed that in the decades of the 1990s and 2000s, research in the field of education allowed itself to be "stolen" by psychology. By that, my colleague meant that the experimental design methodologies that actually originated in agricultural science and were adopted by psychologists for determining effects of psychological variables on outcomes (Campbell & Stanley, 1963) became the method of choice in education. RCTs became the gold standard in terms of research quality and efficacy. The National Academy of Sciences Committee on Scientific Principles for Education Research, as reported through Shavelson and Towne (2002), acknowledged that several questions were of interest in education (i.e., "What is happening" "Is there a systematic effect?" "How or why is it happening?") and acknowledged that different research methods are appropriate for different questions. Leadership in the field of education science elevated efficacy and its accompanying RCT methodology to the primary focus for the field. As the field has expanded its focus to the broader questions of scaling up and the science of implementation necessary to support such processes, the RCT (i.e., the methodological gold standard design for efficacy questions) has remained as the primary methodological approach (see, for example, the criteria for Goal 4 effectiveness research funded by the Institute of Education Science).

A question may exist, however, about whether the RCT methodology is sufficient for addressing broader, scale-up implementation science questions. In their chapter, Schroeder and Franks noted, "We may be on the threshold of a paradigmatic shift in how we understand program effectiveness and outcomes" (p. 17). It may well be that in the future we will need different methodologies (e.g., mixed methods research) to address such complicated implementation questions.

This volume is a step toward the paradigmatic shift. Authors in many chapters of this volume either reflect on how their research directly examines implementation drivers (e.g., Chapters 3 and 5) or state that the processes they followed in their evaluations of scaled-up programs "map onto" the principles of implementation science (e.g., Chapters 9–11). Many of the authors identify "lessons learned" from their work, and the lessons appear to replicate one another. Science is the work of recognizing patterns that repeat themselves in nature. The patterns one sees from these chapters may not be generating experimentally supported conclusions, but they are producing knowledge that may substantiate the principles of implementation science. In this way, I believe this volume is putting the science into implementation science as well as extending the application of implementation science to the ECE field. Both are highly valuable, scholarly, and practical contributions to the field.

Sam L. Odom, Ph.D.
Director
Frank Porter Graham Child Development Institute
University of North Carolina at Chapel Hill

References

Bredekamp, S. (1986). *Developmentally appropriate practice in early childhood programs.* Washington, DC: National Association for the Education of Young Children.

Bronfenbrenner, U. (1979). *The ecology of human development.* Cambridge, MA: Harvard University Press.

Buysse, V., & Wesley, P. W. (2006). *Evidence-based practice in the early childhood field.* Washington, DC: ZERO TO THREE.

Campbell, D.T, & Stanley, J.C. (1963). *Experimental and quasi-experimental designs for research.* Chicago, IL: Rand McNally.

Chen, H. (1998). Theory-driven evaluations. *Advance in Educational Productivity, 7*(1), 25–34.

Cochrane Collaboration. (2013). Background of the Cochrane Collaboration. Retrieved from http://www.cochrane.org/about-us/history/archie-cochrane#Back

Domitrovitch, C.E., Bradshaw, C.P., Poduska, J.M., Hoogwood, K., Buckley, J.A., Olin, S., … Ialongo, N.A. (2008). Maximizing the implementation quality of evidence-based prevention interventions in the schools. *Advances in School Mental Health Promotion, 1*(1), 6–28.

Fixsen, D.L., Naoom, S.F., Blase, K.A., Friedman, R.M., & Wallace, F. (2005). *Implementation research: A synthesis of the literature* (FMHI Publication No. 231). Tampa, FL: University of South Florida, Louis de la Parte Florida Mental Health Institute, National Implementation Research Network.

Odom, S.L., Hanson, M.J., Lieber, J., Diamond, K., Palmer, S., Butera, G., & Horn, E. (2010). Prevention, early childhood intervention, and implementation science. In B. Doll, W. Pfohl, & J. Yoon (Eds.), *Handbook of Youth Prevention Science* (pp. 413–433). New York, NY: Routledge.

Sackett, D.L., Straus, S.E., Richardson, W.S., Rosenberg, W., & Haynes, R.B. (2000). *Evidence-based medicine: How to practice and how to teach EBM.* Edinburgh, Scotland: Churchill Livingstone.

Shavelson, R.J., & Towne, L. (2002). *Scientific research in education.* Washington, DC: National Academy Press.

Acknowledgments

This volume was made possible in part by funding from the Office of Planning, Research and Evaluation (OPRE) of the Administration for Children and Families, U.S. Department of Health and Human Services, through Contract GS10F0030R, the Child Care and Early Education Policy and Research Analysis and Technical Expertise Project, to Child Trends.

This volume is an outgrowth of the Working Meeting on the Application of Implementation Science to Early Care and Education Research, which was sponsored by OPRE and held September 21–22, 2010, in conjunction with a federal interagency meeting, Improving Implementation Research Methods for Behavioral and Social Science, which was held September 20–21, 2010. Subsequent to these meetings, OPRE has supported an ongoing work group of early childhood researchers interested in implementation science and its applications to research and evaluation of early care and education programs and systems; this group is officially known as the Workgroup on Applications of Implementation Science to ECE Research and Practice, or the Implementation Workgroup for short. The editors thank OPRE for its ongoing support for furthering the science of early childhood and the science of implementation through sponsorship of the aforementioned Working Meeting, the production of this edited volume, and the ongoing facilitation of the Implementation Workgroup. The editors are particularly grateful to Naomi Goldstein and Mary Bruce Webb for their review and feedback on all of the chapters in this volume.

The structure of the Working Meeting, which also provided the framework for this volume, benefited from the thoughtful input of a planning group, which convened multiple conference calls over the months prior to the meeting. In addition to the staff members from Child Trends, the National Implementation Research Network, and OPRE who collaborated in the editing of this volume, the planning group included leading researchers in the field of early childhood research and implementation science and representatives from multiple federal agencies with research focused on effective implementation of early care and education programs and systems. The editors are grateful to the following members of the planning group for helping to shape both the format and content of the meeting: Donna Bryant, Celene Domitrovich, Jason Downer, Carolyn Layzer, Robert Pianta, Cybele Raver, Jennifer Schroeder, Susan Sheridan, Kathryn Tout, and Martha Zaslow. In addition, we wish to thank Ann Collins, Helen Raikes, Kate Anderson Simons, and Amy Susman-Stillman, who served as facilitators during breakout sessions. We are also grateful for the participants in the Working Meeting, whose contributions

during the breakout sessions helped to further our thinking about the challenges and benefits of incorporating implementation science principles and practices into early childhood research and practice. The feedback we received has guided a deeper exploration of these topics in this volume. Please see the complete listing of Working Meeting participants at the end of the Acknowledgments.

The editors want to express our deep appreciation for the authors who contributed such thoughtful and thought-provoking content to this volume. Many, but not all, of these authors were also presenters at the aforementioned Working Meeting. We thoroughly enjoyed working with the chapter authors as they developed and refined their ideas for presentation in this volume. The authors are exemplary in their commitment to applying implementation science to the study of early childhood programs and systems, and we look forward to following their work in the coming years.

We also wish to thank the staff from the Early Childhood Program Area at Child Trends for their critical support before and during the Working Meeting. In particular we thank Amy Blasberg, Sarah Daily, Shannon Moodie, Laura Rothenberg, and Shana Simkin for their assistance in assembling background readings, materials for the meeting, and taking notes during the meeting. Our deepest gratitude goes to Amy Blasberg, who played a leadership role in supporting the Working Meeting, who diligently tracked the chapters for this volume throughout multiple rounds of revisions, and who continues to play an important role in supporting the ongoing work of the implementation work group members. The production of this volume simply would not have been possible without Amy's competence and dedication.

Finally, we are extremely grateful to Astrid Zuckerman of Paul H. Brookes Publishing Co. for her support, patience, and enthusiasm throughout the development of this edited volume. Astrid attended the Working Meeting in September 2010 and encouraged us to develop the meeting content into this volume. Her expert editorial guidance and vision helped us throughout the process of completing this project.

A list of participants in the Working Meeting on the Application of Implementation Science to Early Care and Education Research, September 21–22, 2010, is listed below in alphabetical order:

Anne Bergan

Carol Bilbrey

Amy Blasberg

Catherine Bradshaw

Melissa Brodowski

Jennifer Brooks

Rachel Chazan-Cohen

Ajay Chaudry

Douglas Clements*

Sarah Daily

Catherine Darrow

Wendy DeCourcey

Celene Domitrovich

Jason Downer*

Kathleen Dwyer

Caroline Ebanks*

Robert P. Franks*

Naomi Goldstein

James Griffin

Tamara Halle*

Annemarie Hindman

Laura Hoard

Eboni Howard

Christopher Hulleman

---

*Participants who contributed as presenters during the meeting are denoted with an asterisk.

Molly Irwin
Susan Jekielek
Lynn Karoly
Lisa Knoche*
Chrishana Lloyd
Amy Madigan*
Nancy Margie
Ivelisse Martinez-Beck*
Joan McLaughlin
Allison Metz*
Shannon Moodie
Mary Mueggenborg
Jean Nussbaum
Carol O'Donnell
David Olds*
Diane Paulsell
Shira Peterson
Douglas Powell*
Helen Raikes
Laura Rothenberg

Heather Sandstrom
Shana Simkin
Kate Anderson Simons
Kyle Snow
Kam Sripada
Lauren Supplee
Amy Susman-Stillman
Louisa Tarullo
Kathryn Tout*
Shannon Wanless
Barbara Wasik
Mary Bruce Webb
T'Pring Westbrook
Christina Weiland
Anne Wolf
Maria Woolverton
Noreen Yazejian*
Martha Zaslow*
Astrid Zuckerman

To those in communities, states, and the federal
government who are working diligently to put research
into practice by actively pursuing the effective implementation
of early childhood interventions at local, state, and national levels

Introduction

Where Is the New Frontier of Implementation Science in Early Care and Education Research and Practice?

Ivelisse Martinez-Beck

To implement means to make something happen according to or by means of a definite plan or procedure. The science of implementation is the study of the process of implementing programs and practices that have research evidence suggesting they are worth replicating. It is *not* the act of validating a program as evidence based; instead, implementation science is the study of how a practice that is evidence-based or evidence-informed gets translated to different contexts in the "real world." In this way, it bridges the gap between science and practice. The purpose of this volume is to present current applications of implementation science in early childhood research and practice in order to highlight their key role in ensuring that early care and education initiatives are achieving their intended effects on their target populations.

The State of Implementation Science in Early Care and Education

The science of implementation has only recently gained widespread attention in the fields of health, mental health, and education, although researchers and practitioners have long recognized the importance of understanding the conditions that affect the delivery of effective programs. There is now a growing body of research looking at the processes and core components of implementing evidence-based practices in different settings and especially examining what it takes to move an evidence-based practice from the laboratory to the field (Berkel, Mauricio, Schoenfelder, & Sandler, 2010; Durlak & DuPre, 2008; Fixsen, Naoom, Blase, Friedman, & Wallace, 2005; Meyers, Durlak, & Wandersman, 2012). However, much of this research has focused primarily on adult services (Simpson, 2002), while few studies have focused on the implementation of evidence-based practice in the early care and education (ECE) field.

In a 2009 social policy report published by the Society for Research in Child Development (SRCD), Robert B. McCall called upon developmental scientists and others engaged in evaluating programs designed to improve outcomes of at-risk children and families to revise the research enterprise and integrate it with the community (McCall, 2009). In this report, McCall recognized that, increasingly, scholars in developmental science and related disciplines are asked by policy makers, practitioners, and funders to identify programs with demonstrated evidence of effectiveness, thus creating new opportunities for scholars to influence both policy and practice. However, McCall questioned the readiness of research scholars to provide evidence about the service programs and of service professionals to implement such programs in their communities, and he concluded that "the quality of implementation of a program is as important to achieving desired outcomes in society as the original demonstration of the program, but we do not have a well-developed science of implementation" (McCall, 2009, p. 3). This disconnect between research evidence and practice evidence explains "the paradox of non–evidence-based implementation of evidence-based programs" (Drake, Gorman, & Turrey, 2002, as cited in McCall, 2009).

Another recent SRCD social policy report by Vivian Tseng entitled *The Uses of Research in Policy and Practice* (Tseng, 2012) underscores the limitations of current research approaches to gather the evidence needed to implement effective programs. Tseng rightfully states that "while researchers have focused largely on questions of internal validity, the questions at the forefront of practitioners' minds are often questions of external validity and implementation.... Moreover, there is currently little empirical evidence on their questions" (2012, p. 11). She further acknowledges that "the research community has come a long way in strengthening standards of evidence on what works, but little progress has been made on critical questions for the would-be adopters of programs" (2012, p. 12). These realities about the state of the science of implementation in early childhood should make us reconsider our conceptual frameworks for studying both what works and what it takes to implement evidence-based programs, for which populations, and under which conditions and contexts.

Changing Conceptualizations of the Study of Implementation in Early Care and Education

New questions are surfacing about what it takes to bring to scale programs that have been proven to be efficacious or transport them to other locations, as well as about the articulation of model components that are essential for making the program a success. This is true of discrete models, such as language and literacy interventions, and also systems-level or statewide interventions such as initiatives to improve early childhood educators' professional development, children's school readiness, or child care quality (e.g., quality rating and improvement systems).

The most frequently used implementation evaluation methodologies in ECE have typically assessed whether program activities have been implemented as planned (often referred to as assessing "fidelity of implementation"). However, while making important progress, these methodologies 1) have failed to identify all of the elements required for effective implementation, 2) do not suffice to tell us fully how to replicate programs, and 3) tell us even less about strategies for improving the program. Furthermore, the lack of common implementation frameworks used in these types of implementation evaluations limit the generalizability of implementation findings across diverse programmatic and organizational settings, populations, or geographic locations. To advance implementation research evidence, early childhood researchers must reassess current conceptualizations of the study of implementation in the context of rigorous evaluations of programs and focused interventions.

As noted earlier, the history of implementation research in ECE is rather short, but new research, demonstration, and evaluation studies are incorporating more elements of implementation science as part of their focal activities. To illustrate how recent evaluation of early childhood interventions funded through agencies in the U.S. Department of Health and Human Services (HHS) have more fully incorporated implementation science in their logic models and conceptual frameworks, I offer here several examples of large evaluation studies funded from 2003 to the present. The examples are intended to illustrate how different waves of research have built on the insights and understandings of previous research teams.

The Partners for Inclusion Model

The first example involves the approach most frequently used in evaluations of initiatives in ECE that include an implementation component: an assessment of fidelity of implementation. It involves a recent evaluation of a quality-enhancement intervention in ECE: the evaluation of the Partners for Inclusion (PFI) model of on-site consultation conducted as part of the Quality Interventions for Early Care and Education (QUINCE) study, funded by the Administration for Children and Families (ACF) between 2003 and 2008 (Bryant et al., 2009). The PFI component of the QUINCE evaluation is noteworthy for its inclusion of an implementation as well as an impact evaluation. This was especially important because the intervention was put in place in multiple states and through multiple agencies.

After reflecting on the information provided through the implementation component of the evaluation, the authors of the PFI evaluation concluded that the implementation lens had been too narrow. By reviewing this evaluation team's reflections on what more was needed in order to fully understand implementation, we can learn a great deal about what kinds of information need to be collected in addition to fidelity of implementation for a full assessment of implementation. Such careful consideration is needed so that implementers of evidence-based models will be able to understand the conditions necessary to implement effective interventions on the ground, under different conditions, and in diverse contexts.

The PFI model of consultation was selected for this evaluation because its effectiveness had been established in two previous studies. The model was shown to enhance quality in both phases of its development: when delivered by highly trained university-based consultants with master's degrees and consultation experience (Wesley, 1994) and also when delivered by community-based child care consultants with varied levels of education and experience who were trained by the developers of the model (Palsha & Wesley, 1998). Both studies found significant gains in observed quality in infant/toddler and preschool classrooms and in a small number of family child care homes. The model developers had identified the core components of the intervention, had tested it in different early childhood settings and with diverse consultants, and had developed a standardized training system for consultants. They had also identified a set of conditions related to provision of supports for consultants that would be necessary to adequately implement the intervention. The model, at the time, seemed ready for a full random assignment evaluation, including assessment of implementation fidelity to the model, defined as the degree to which the intervention was implemented as intended.

The evaluation of the PFI model in the QUINCE study included a random assignment of consultants working in 24 agencies providing technical assistance (TA) to ECE providers in five states. Most of the TA delivered by these agencies was directed to supporting efforts to improve the quality of care and early education and the developmental outcomes of young children. Local agencies in the five states supplied consultants to be randomly assigned to the treatment and control groups. The control group would continue to deliver TA as usual; this meant that, in some cases, consultants in the control group were delivering other models of on-site consultation and coaching to the programs assigned to them. The agencies covered the consultants' salaries, supervised them, and encouraged them to implement the PFI model in the treatment group programs. Training of the consultants was delivered by the evaluation team under the leadership of the model developers. Thus, the goal of the study was to evaluate the efficacy of an evidence-based model of on-site consultation delivered under typical conditions of provision of TA to ECE programs in different sites across the country.

In addition to the study hypotheses related to the impact of the PFI intervention on quality of care and on developmental outcomes of children participating in those programs, the study team predicted that teachers and family child care providers who participated in a greater number of on-site consultant visits would make greater gains in child care quality than those who participated in fewer on-site consultation visits. Another set of hypotheses concerned the conditions under which the PFI model would work. The team hypothesized that 1) providers served by consultants who more closely adhered to the procedures of the PFI model would show greater benefits of participation in the intervention and 2) the PFI model would be an effective model for improving the quality of child care in both child care centers and family child care homes (regulated and unregulated), with providers from diverse cultural backgrounds, and in settings that served a range of children with special needs and diverse language and socioeconomic backgrounds. In short, PFI, a child care provider consultation model, was predicted to be effective in a broad range of circumstances (Bryant et al., 2009).

As acknowledged by the authors in their final evaluation report (Bryant et al., 2009), several factors have been linked in the literature to treatment fidelity, including intervention complexity, time required for implementation, availability of necessary resources, number and motivation of the people involved, support of administrators, prior training of participants, and the participants' perceptions of the intervention's effectiveness. Generally, the level of fidelity decreases as the intervention complexity, time requirements, necessary resources, and numbers of people needed to assist increase. Potential barriers to addressing fidelity include the cost of directly observing implementation, the lack of appropriate measurement tools, and the difficulty of operationalizing relationship-based interventions (such as PFI). All of these barriers were issues for the QUINCE team in documenting PFI fidelity.

In addition, the measurement of implementation fidelity in a study of consultation effectiveness is complicated by the multiple points of contact in the process. In the case of the PFI intervention, these included 1) the trainers who had to train the consultants, 2) the consultants who interact with the consultees and teachers in ECE programs, 3) the consultees who interact with the children they care for or teach, and 4) other adults involved in their programs.

> These multiple transactions and contextual variables increase the difficulty of implementing interventions with the intended strength and integrity, in terms of both the consultants' adherence to the (core) components of a consultation procedure and their consultees' follow through to address consultation goals. (Bryant et al., 2009, p. 82)

The project team anticipated challenges with measurement of fidelity, which were compounded by the need to collaborate with site liaisons in charge of the consultants in the evaluation and the need to use multiple methods of communication and documentation during implementation.

The study team aimed to assess the fidelity dimensions of exposure, adherence to the model's key components, and the quality of delivery. The dimensions of exposure and adherence were assessed and monitored through documentation completed by consultants (e.g., contact summary forms, action plans, final reports) and used to create a partial fidelity index. The quality of delivery was more difficult to assess, mostly because documentation was brief or silent as to quality and the project resources did not allow for direct observations of the consultation process to assess the quality of delivery.

The fidelity index revealed important information about the implementation of the PFI model in multiple contexts (Wesley et al., 2010). For example, it showed that consultants generally received high scores both on the key component of collaborative decision making with the classroom teachers and home-based providers with whom they were working and also on the total number of visits made to teachers and providers. However, the ratings demonstrated that it was challenging for consultants to organize their quality improvement efforts around the aspects of quality receiving the lowest scores on an observational measure of quality and to schedule their visits to teachers and providers on a regular basis. Perhaps of greatest concern, their accuracy of scoring of the appropriate environmental rating scale (for center-based or home-based care settings) was documented to be an issue.

With the environmental rating scale scoring providing a foundation for the joint planning for quality improvement with the teacher or home-based provider, the issues of accuracy of scoring and organizing efforts around the lowest scoring items clearly identified areas where further efforts in strengthening implementation of the intervention would be needed. In addition, only about 8% of the consultants scored high (3.5 or higher on a 4-point summary index) on the summary index of fidelity. While about 41% received scores between 3 and 3.45, fully half of the sample had summary scores below 3, clearly pointing to room for improvement in tightening adherence to the model.

Interestingly, the authors indicated both value and limitations in the use of the fidelity assessment (Bryant et al., 2009; Wesley et al., 2010). They concluded that while further work clearly would be needed in implementing core components of the model such as accuracy in scoring the environmental rating, full implementation of the PFI model would require attention to two further dimensions: time and context. They noted that evaluating impacts in the 1st year of full implementation may not have provided for a full test of the model and that allowing for a period to monitor and tighten implementation prior to evaluation would have been desirable. Indeed, analyses of implementation studies across several disciplinary fields suggests that it takes 2–4 years before a new practice model is fully operational and being used with fidelity in the field (Fixsen et al., 2005).

The authors also noted that aspects of the broader organizational context needed attention in order to more fully support implementation. For example, they observed that the degree to which agency directors supported the model varied, that agency directors sometimes felt pressed to deliver quality incentives to centers or home-based care sites before the assessment of quality could be completed and provide the basis of a full plan for quality improvement (thereby undermining the selection of priorities for quality improvement), and that caseloads varied substantially for consultants. Furthermore, there was an unresolved tension between the study team's provision of training and oversight for consultants providing the PFI model and the ongoing role of the agency directors. In summary, the authors of the QUINCE evaluation's PFI model underscored the need for taking into account organizational- and system-level variables in full implementation—an issue HHS has subsequently taken into account in further projects (see below).

It is important to note that even with the limitations on implementation fidelity and the issues of time and context for implementation, the PFI model was documented to have effects on quality (Bryant et al., 2009). Though slightly fewer than half of the treatment consultants were implementing PFI at an average level or higher on the summary index of fidelity and many were at the lower end of the range, the PFI intervention produced significant effects on multiple observed aspects of quality of care in the family child care homes (subscales of the Family Day Care Environmental Rating Scale) and on a measure of literacy and math stimulation (the Early Childhood Environment Rating Scale–Extension) in both center classrooms and family child care homes. Moreover, after controlling for children's characteristics and initial scores on measures of development, children in the center classrooms in the intervention group scored higher on measures of language development than children in control classrooms.

Through the QUINCE study, it became clear that future studies of quality improvement in ECE would not only need to take into account the enactment of the intervention and receipt of the intervention, they would also need to focus on the full complexity of the intervention delivery process over time and in the surrounding organizational and systems contexts. Section I of this volume seeks to provide a more fully articulated framework for what is needed in such work. Chapters 1–3 in this volume present descriptions of implementation science frameworks and principles to guide the design and collection of implementation data, the core components and drivers of good implementation, and constructs to determine readiness to change at the level of the system, programs, and individuals.

Head Start CARES

Based on the agency's experience with the QUINCE-PFI and similar evaluations, it became clear that incorporating a strong implementation study in ECE evaluation efforts is not only desirable but also necessary. Recent studies funded by ACF and other agencies in HHS are requiring comprehensive implementation studies as part of rigorous evaluations of interventions. One example is the study Head Start CARES (Classroom-based Approaches and Resources for Emotion and Social skill promotion), a large-scale, group-randomized trial of three social-emotional program enhancements within Head Start classrooms (Office of Planning, Research & Evaluation [OPRE], 2012). The project includes an impact and implementation study of three enhancements: the Incredible Years classroom management program, Preschool PATHS, and Tools of the Mind. The project is trying to answer both impact and implementation questions such as What is the effectiveness of specific social-emotional programs or practices within the Head Start population? Are specific social-emotional programs or practices more or less effective for certain populations? What characteristics of Head Start settings are necessary for effective implementation of different program or practices? And what factors are related to training, technical assistance, implementation, and fidelity of programs or practices within Head Start settings?

The project is intended to meet the needs of the national Office of Head Start and local Head Start settings by specifically addressing the implementation, effectiveness, and improvement of program options and practices within the Head Start community. In the short term, the research will provide the Office of Head Start with information regarding the appropriateness for use in Head Start settings of specific programs or practices nationwide, as well as information that can be used in TA efforts. In addition, the research will assist Head Start settings in deciding which programs or practices are most likely to improve children's social-emotional development, given the characteristics of their particular settings and the populations they serve. The study will also provide the field with a resource of quality research findings that practitioners can use to make decisions about program options and practices. Chapter 8 in this volume describes some of the components of the implementation evaluation in Head Start CARES.

The Maternal, Infant, and Early Childhood Home Visiting Program

Another example of an evaluation in ECE that incorporates strong implementation components is that of the Maternal, Infant, and Early Childhood Home Visiting Program (MIECHV; Health Resources and Services Administration, n.d.). The Affordable Care Act of 2010 established the MIECHV program, which is distributing $1.5 billion over 5 years to states to establish home visiting program models for at-risk pregnant women and children from birth to age 5. The Act stipulated that 75% of the funds must be used for home visiting programs with evidence of effectiveness based on rigorous evaluation research.

The Home Visiting Evidence of Effectiveness (HomVEE; U.S. Department of Health and Human Services, n.d.) review provided information about which home visiting program models have evidence of effectiveness as required by the legislation and defined by HHS, as well as detailed information about the samples of families who participated in the research, the outcomes measured in each study, and the implementation guidelines for each model. The legislation specified a number of program implementation requirements for models to be funded as evidence-based by the MIECHV program, including that models had to 1) have been in existence for at least 3 years prior to the start of the review, 2) be associated with a national program office that provides training and support to local program sites, and 3) have minimum requirements for the frequency of home visits and for home visitor supervision. Most home visiting programs included in the HomVEE review have preservice training requirements, implementation fidelity standards, a system for monitoring fidelity, and specified content and activities for the home visits.

The Affordable Care Act also specified that there should be an ongoing program of research to increase knowledge about home visiting implementation and effectiveness. Specifically, the legislation required a national evaluation of MIECHV to report findings to Congress in 2015. The Design Options for Home Visiting Evaluation (DOHVE; OPRE, 2010) project was tasked to design this national evaluation in order to gain information to strengthen future programs by systematically studying program implementation. The DOHVE project goes beyond issues of fidelity to include factors related to the context of implementation.

The implementation study designed as part of the evaluation of MIECHV will collect information on community context, influential organizations, the service model, the implementation system, home visitors, families, and actual service delivery.

> The implementation system includes the resources for carrying out the service model. It incorporates policies and procedures for staff recruitment, training, supervision and evaluation; assessment tools, protocols and curricula to guide service delivery; the use of administrative supports such as management information systems to monitor and promote staff adherence to the service model; organizational culture and climate regarding fidelity and the use of evidence-based practices; the availability of consultation to address issues beyond the home visitor's skills and expertise; and the home visiting program's relationships with other community-based organizations to facilitate referral and service coordination. (Michalopoulos et al., 2011, p. 21)

These components of the implementation study address most of the elements in the implementation science framework to be discussed in many chapters in this volume. In addition, the implementation study, in conjunction with the accompanying effectiveness study, is investigating which features of service models and implementation systems are associated with more positive effects for families.

A new project, the Maternal, Infant, and Early Childhood Home Visiting Evaluation (MIHOPE; OPRE, 2011), was launched in 2011 to conduct the evaluation designed through the DOHVE project. Chapter 10 in this volume provides some insights into efforts to improve implementation in the process of going to scale for one of the home visiting models in use by the MIECHV grantees and included in the MIHOPE evaluation: the Nurse–Family Partnership model.

Other Research Studies

Two other research efforts that involve critical implementation components were funded in September 2012 by the ACF's Office of Planning, Research and Evaluation (OPRE). One, known as the Head Start Professional Development: Developing the Evidence for Best Practices in Coaching, is a design-options project tasked with identifying effective coaching components that result in positive change in Head Start teachers' behaviors, as well as the conditions related to training, staffing, and supports that are needed to establish and maintain appropriate levels of fidelity to achieve the expected outcomes with efficiency. The other is the National Implementation Evaluation of the Health Profession Opportunity Grant, a program focused on cash assistance recipients and other low-income individuals. It will involve multiple tasks to assess implementation, systems change, and outcomes and will provide valuable information about the operations of these federally funded programs in improving education and employment opportunities for low-income people. This grant program was designed to yield information and lessons about operating such programs. In addition, the project evaluation will document the challenges faced and how these challenges were addressed during implementation of the program models as well as throughout their operation.

Addressing Gaps in the Research

Researchers, practitioners, and policy makers are recognizing the need to attend more closely to the implementation of evidence-based models in ECE programs to ensure that desired outcomes are achieved. To promote an understanding of the implementation frameworks that could be applied in the ECE field both in research and practice, OPRE sponsored the Working Meeting on the Application of Implementation Science to Early Care and Education Research in September 2010 to conduct an in-depth examination of the application of implementation science to ECE research (the meeting summary and proceedings are available at http://www.researchconnections.org/childcare/collaboration.jsp#Application). The meeting was held in conjunction with a federal interagency meeting entitled Improving Implementation Research Methods for Behavioral and Social Science, which focused on the topic of implementation research methodology in behavioral and social science research.

There were three main goals of the OPRE meeting:

1. To clarify the definitions and key concepts used in implementation science and thereby to develop a shared understanding of the role implementation science can play in ECE research

2. To explore the potential lessons learned from applying implementation science principles in ECE research and evaluation

3. To identify products that would assist early childhood program implementers, policy makers, and researchers in applying implementation principles in their work

The chapters in this volume are based on presentations and discussions held at the September 2010 meeting and have benefited from extended conversations among meeting participants and other experts on the science of implementation through convening of the Workgroup on Applications of Implementation Science to ECE Research and Practice. The purpose of this volume is to highlight how implementation science can improve the application and sustainability of evidence-based, effective practices in ECE. While recognizing that assessing fidelity to a particular model is an important component of implementation science, its authors underscore the fact that this component is not the *only* component of implementation that leads to successful transfer or transportability of effective ECE initiatives. A focus throughout this volume is on highlighting and exemplifying how the use of science-based implementation frameworks that are built on stages of implementation and core implementation components can improve the application of implementation findings to replicate effective ECE programs and systems.

The chapters are organized into four sections within the volume. Section I focuses on the definitions, frameworks, and methodologies related to implementation as a way to set the stage for an in-depth examination of the application of implementation science principles and practices to ECE research. In the first chapter, Robert P. Franks and Jennifer Schroeder discuss the importance of using an implementation framework as a conceptual guide to utilizing effective implementation practices. Chapter 2, by Allison Metz, Tamara Halle, Leah Bartley, and Amy Blasberg, explains in detail the core components associated with successful implementation and how these can contribute to the development of ECE programming. The authors also discuss the importance of aligning ECE research design with the stages of implementation. In the next chapter, Shira M. Peterson considers the theoretical and practical implications of "readiness to change" principles as they relate to implementation of ECE programs and practices in real-world contexts.

The final chapter in Section I is by Chris S. Hulleman, Sara E. Rimm-Kauffman, and Tashia Abry, who address the conceptualization of intervention fidelity and its implications for measurement, design, and analysis. As noted earlier in this introduction, the consideration of whether program activities have been implemented as planned (what Hulleman et al. refer to as "intervention fidelity" rather than the more commonly used "fidelity of implementation") is critical to obtaining the outcomes we hope to achieve for young children, their families, and early childhood programs. Chapter 4 provides excellent guidance on how to define, collect, and analyze this important program evaluation information.

Sections II and III of this volume build from the foundational information provided in Section I by offering examples of applications of these frameworks, principles, and analytic strategies in ECE interventions. Specifically, the chapters in Section II focus on formative evaluation and the exploration of intervention fidelity, while Section III highlights early childhood interventions that are at the stage of replication and scale-up.

Section II includes examples of the implementation of coaching-based professional development (Chapter 5), a relationship-based early childhood intervention called Getting Ready (Chapter 6), and early childhood interventions aimed at enhancing social-emotional development through the Head Start CARES project (Chapter 7). Section III features examples of replication and scaling up of an early math curriculum called Building Blocks (Chapter 9), a nurse home-visitation model called the Nurse–Family Partnership (Chapter 10), and an innovative public–private initiative aimed at closing the achievement gap for low-income children ages birth to 5 called Educare (Chapter 11). The authors of the chapters in these two sections demonstrate how program developers and researchers design evaluation studies that align with the appropriate stage of implementation and use frameworks and strategies that intentionally take into account key components of effective implementation.

Both Section II and III begin with an overview by Amy Blasberg that provides a helpful orientation to the content that is covered in the chapters that follow. In addition, both sections conclude with an integrative chapter (Chapter 8, authored by Jason Downer for Section II, and Chapter 12, by Carolyn Layzer for Section III) that provides additional, thoughtful discussion of the concepts raised in the individual chapters and their implications for future research and practice.

The programs and practices highlighted in Sections II and III of this volume are examples of ECE interventions enacted at the level of a classroom, home, or school. Can the principles and frameworks of implementation science be as easily applied to larger-scale early childhood initiatives? Section IV of this volume explores the use of an implementation lens as applied to system-wide early childhood initiatives such as professional development systems within states (Chapter 13) and quality rating and improvement systems (Chapter 14). This is a topic of particular interest to state policy makers as they work on developing and expanding statewide ECE systems. Section IV opens with an overview by Tamara Halle.

The volume concludes with Chapter 15 by Tamara Halle, Martha Zaslow, Ivelisse Martinez-Beck, and Allison Metz. This chapter addresses major themes presented throughout the volume and discusses various implications for research, policy, and practice.

Implementation science applied to the evaluation of ECE initiatives has experienced some growth during the past decade, as illustrated by the work included in this volume from many scholars in the field of ECE in support of better outcomes for at-risk children and families. But the field has a long way to go to achieve a common conceptualization of the role of implementation science research in evaluations of evidence-based interventions. Incorporating strong implementation components in studies of efficacy and effectiveness requires careful design, methodological approaches, and the development of measures that are able to capture the conditions necessary to fully implement interventions on the ground. A new research agenda needs to be developed to ensure that future studies include a strong focus on implementation and to allocate sufficient resources to accomplish the activities necessary to measure and document fidelity to program models as well as fidelity to the core components of an implementation science framework. The work included in this volume provides important information that can be used to shape this new research agenda on implementation science in ECE.

References

Berkel, C., Mauricio, A.M., Schoenfelder, E., & Sandler, I.N. (2010). Putting the pieces together: An integrated model of program implementation. *Prevention Science, 12,* 23–33.

Bryant, D., Wesley, P., Burchinal, P., Sideris, J., Taylor, K., Fenson, C., & Iruka, I. (2009). *The QUINCE-PFI Study: An evaluation of a promising model for child care provider training, final report.* Chapel Hill, NC: FPG Child Development Institute. Retrieved from http://www.researchconnections.org/childcare/resources/18531

Drake, R.E., Gorman, P., & Turrey, W.C. (2002). *Implementing adult "tool kits" in mental health.* Paper presented at the NASMHPD Conference on EBPs and Adult Mental Health, Tampa, FL.

Durlak, J.A. & DuPre, E.P. (2008). Implementation matters: A review of research on the influence of implementation on program outcomes and the factors affecting implementation. *American Journal of Community Psychology, 41,* 327–350.

Fixsen, D.L., Naoom, S.F., Blase, K.A., Friedman, R.M., & Wallace, F. (2005). *Implementation research: A synthesis of the literature* (FMHI Publication No. 231). Tampa, FL: University of South Florida, Louis de la Parte Florida Mental Health Institute, National Implementation Research Network.

Health Resources and Services Administration. (n.d.). Maternal, Infant, and Early Childhood Home Visiting Program. Retrieved from http://mchb.hrsa.gov/programs/homevisiting

McCall, R.B. (2009). Evidence-based programming in the context of practice and policy. *Social Policy Report 23*(3). Washington, DC: Society for Research in Child Development.

Meyers, D.C., Durlak, J.A., & Wandersman, A. (2012, May 30). The quality implementation framework: A synthesis of critical steps in the implementation process. *American Journal of Community Psychology.*

Michalopoulos, C., Duggan, A., Knox, V., Filene, J.L., Lundquist, E., Snell, E.K., ... Mello, M. (2011). *Design options for the home visiting evaluation: Draft final report* (ACF-OPRE Report 2011-16). Washington, DC: U.S. Department of Health and Human Services. Retrieved from http://www.acf.hhs.gov/programs/opre/resource/design-options-for-the-maternal-infant-and-early-childhood-home-visiting

Office of Planning, Research & Evaluation. (2010). *Design Options for Home Visiting Evaluation (DOHVE), 2010–2015.* Retrieved from http://www.acf.hhs.gov/programs/opre/research/project/design-options-for-home-visiting-evaluation-dohve-2010-2015.

Office of Planning, Research & Evaluation. (2011). *Maternal, Infant and Early Childhood Home Visiting Evaluation (MIHOPE), 2011–2015.* Retrieved from http://www.acf.hhs.gov/programs/opre/research/project/maternal-infant-and-early-childhood-home-visiting-evaluation-mihope-2011

Office of Planning, Research & Evaluation. (2012). *Head Start CARES (Head Start Classroom-based Approaches and Resources for Emotion and Social skill promotion), 2007–2013.* Retrieved from http://www.acf.hhs.gov/programs/opre/hs/cares/index.html

Palsha, S.A., & Wesley, P.W. (1998). Improving quality in early childhood environments through on-site consultation. *Topics in Early Childhood Special Education, 18*(4), 243–253.

Simpson, D.D. (2002). A conceptual framework for transferring research to practice. *Journal of Substance Abuse Treatment, 22*(4), 171–182.

Tseng, V. (2012). The uses of research in policy and practice. *Social Policy Report, 26*(2). Washington, DC: Society for Research in Child Development.

U.S. Department of Health and Human Services. (n.d.). *Home Visiting Evidence of Effectiveness.* Retrieved from http://homvee.acf.hhs.gov

Wesley, P.W. (1994). Providing on-site consultation to promote quality integrated child care programs. *Journal of Early Intervention, 18,* 391–402.

Wesley, P.W., Bryant, D., Fenson, C., Hughes-Belding, K., Tout, K. & Susman-Stillman, A. (2010). Treatment fidelity challenges in a five-state consultation study. *Journal of Educational and Psychological Consultation, 20*(3), 209–227.

Implementation Science

Defining the New Frontier

Allison Metz

There is a growing body of research that demonstrates the importance of implementation in improving outcomes for children and families. As such, a field dedicated to the science of implementation has emerged in recent years. The four chapters in the first part of this volume lay the groundwork for understanding the principles and frameworks of implementation science and provide a common language for key terms and constructs used throughout the entire book. Each chapter contributes to providing a foundation for the application of implementation science in early childhood research, practice, and policy.

In Chapter 1, Robert P. Franks and Jennifer Schroeder define implementation science and common terms associated with this new discipline, discuss shared themes across implementation frameworks, and explore the application of implementation science in an early childhood context. They begin by describing implementation as the pathway by which evidence is translated to practice. They note that the study of factors that contribute to effective implementation at the program, organization, and systems levels is central to building the science of implementation. The chapter includes definitions of commonly used terms such as *diffusion, replication, knowledge translation,* and *dissemination* and identifies how these processes are different from one another and how they relate to implementation. Other terms defined by the authors include *readiness, capacity, scalability, sustainability, fidelity,* and *quality improvement.* Creating a shared understanding of terminology will facilitate dialogue among researchers, practitioners, and policy makers regarding how to promote effective implementation.

The authors also synthesize common themes in implementation frameworks and identify elements that are present across various science-based implementation frameworks such as assessing readiness and capacity, engagement and buy-in, program installation, evaluation and fidelity, feedback loops, and innovation and adaptation. Lastly, the authors provide several examples of how implementation science has been applied in real-world early childhood settings.

In the next chapter, Allison Metz, Tamara Halle, Leah Bartley, and Amy Blasberg provide an overview of "active implementation frameworks" by describing the stages and core components of implementation. As a precursor to this description, they note that a prerequisite for engaging in active implementation strategies is a well-operationalized practice or program model, and they provide a multitiered description of what must be included in a fully defined practice model in order for implementation to commence.

The authors observe that there is substantial agreement in the implementation field regarding the idea that, while implementation is not always a linear process, there are discernible stages to implementation. They describe the structural components and activities that represent each stage—exploration, installation, initial implementation, and full implementation—and how completing each stage contributes to successful practice, organization, and system change.

The chapter continues by describing the implementation core components or "building blocks" of the infrastructure needed for effective change at multiple levels of the early childhood system. The authors define 1) core components that build the competency and capacity of practitioners to implement new innovations effectively, 2) core components that create the hospitable organization and systems environments needed for innovations to thrive, and 3) core components that build leaders' capacity to use appropriate leadership strategies for different challenges. The authors discuss how core implementation components are applied at different stages of implementation and provide key questions to ask at each stage. The chapter also provides a framework for "making implementation happen" through the development and use of implementation teams. The role of implementation teams at different stages is discussed. Finally, the authors note the implications that using active implementation frameworks in early childhood settings will have on practice and on research and evaluation.

Shira M. Peterson in Chapter 3 provides an in-depth look at the concept of readiness. She defines readiness to change in the context of promoting successful implementation, identifies common barriers to promoting readiness, and describes frameworks such as the Transtheoretical Model of change for assessing and facilitating readiness at staff and organizational levels. Key concepts such as collaboration, empathy, and reflective listening are explored in the context of increasing readiness.

Peterson goes on to describe how the core implementation components introduced in Chapter 2 can contribute to increasing readiness. In particular, she notes how staff selection, training, and coaching processes can be used during different stages of implementation to improve readiness of early childhood educators. The role of administrative supports and the importance of aligning policies and procedures with a new way of work also are explored. Finally, the author discusses implications for future research and practice application in an early childhood context.

Chapter 4, by Chris S. Hulleman, Sara E. Rimm-Kaufman, and Tashia Abry, presents a model of intervention fidelity assessment and discusses the implications this model could have on measurement, design, and analysis of early care and education programs. The authors define fidelity and provide distinctions between intervention fidelity (assessment of the core components of the practice model or intervention) and implementation fidelity (assessment of the supports that are needed to implement the intervention such as staff selection, training, and coaching).

Chapter 4 provides a detailed description of the five steps of an intervention fidelity assessment model: 1) developing an operational logic model that "represents program elements in practical terms" and describes the specific resources and activities that support implementation of the intervention, 2) identifying appropriate fidelity indicators for program elements, 3) establishing the reliability and validity of the fidelity measures, 4) combining fidelity indices where measures are found to be interrelated, and 5) conducting statistical analyses to link fidelity scores to outcomes. The authors then apply this five-step fidelity assessment process to Responsive Classroom, a model that focuses on integrating children's social and academic learning, to illustrate how these steps could be applied in an efficacy study.

Finally, Hulleman and colleagues examine how fidelity indices can address key questions in intervention fidelity assessments, including the extent to which a program model can be adapted before outcomes disappear, how best to weight fidelity indicators when creating composite scores for fidelity, whether and how the sequencing of program elements contributes to outcomes, how to match fidelity measures with different program elements, and how to align fidelity assessments with implementation trajectories (e.g., allowing practitioners enough time to achieve skillful implementation of new practices before assessing fidelity).

These four chapters provide a deep foundation for the full volume. This creates the basis to explore how the implementation science concepts and principles addressed in these chapters are applied in early childhood research and practice throughout the rest of the book.

CHAPTER 1

Implementation Science

What Do We Know and Where Do We Go from Here?

Robert P. Franks and Jennifer Schroeder

What is implementation science and why does it matter? In recent years, increasing attention has been given to the process of implementing programs and practices across a wide range of fields. It seems that it is no longer enough just to fund an innovation, but we also must devote resources to ensure that programs are successfully installed with fidelity to an identified model (Fixsen, Naoom, Blase, Friedman, & Wallace, 2005; Odom et al., 2010). As the importance of evidence-based practice (EBP) has grown, the science of implementation has also gained attention in health, mental health, education, and related fields. Research has demonstrated that fidelity to evidence-based models is related to outcomes and, further, that the process of implementation is related to fidelity (Fixsen, Blase, Timbers, & Wolf, 2001; Greenhalgh, Robert, MacFarlane, Bate, & Kyriakidou, 2004; Odom et al., 2010). In a major review of the literature, Durlak and DuPre (2008) showed that successful implementation can result in programs being 3 to 12 times more effective and concluded that "there is credible and extensive empirical evidence that the level of implementation affects program outcomes" (p. 334). Thus, implementation matters.

There is now a growing body of research that examines the implementation process in community-based settings; however, few studies have focused on the implementation of model programs in the field of early care and education (ECE). In this chapter, we will begin by introducing the concept of implementation science, define common terms, and identify shared themes across implementation models and theories. We will also explore the implications of implementation science for practice and research, in particular as it relates to the developing field of ECE. Subsequent chapters will explore these concepts in greater depth and identify applications of implementation science as a mechanism for successful installation of ECE programs and as a framework for sustainable child and family outcomes.

Implementation Science Defined

Implementation can be defined as a specified set of activities designed to put into practice an activity or program of known dimensions (Fixsen et al., 2005), such as an evidence-based program or practice. When considering the implementation process, we typically, but not always, examine the replication and dissemination of EBPs.

An EBP is commonly defined as a program or practice that, when implemented effectively, produces a statistically significant and positive outcome for the EBP recipient. Debate remains over the level of evidence required for an EBP to be considered evidence based. Often this involves the use of randomized control trials (research comparing the outcomes of program recipients with a randomly selected sample of individuals who did not participate in the program) in community-based settings that demonstrate that a program is ready to disseminate to participants in the community. Program developers typically strive to utilize consistent implementation procedures when establishing the evidence base for an EBP; however, the implementation activities required to reproduce an EBP in the community may or may not be explicitly described in the model.

Implementation can also include activities designed to put into practice an activity or program that may not be evidence based. In this case, program developers or researchers may be interested in investigating the utility of a pilot or model program, establishing evidence for a program that is thought to contribute to positive outcomes, or identifying implementation factors that may contribute to establishing an EBP that ensures positive outcomes. These programs are often considered "promising practices" or "recommended practices" rather than EBPs, depending on whether or not rigorous investigation of the program is already under way that is expected to establish the evidence base for the program.

One of the challenges of implementing EBPs and model programs is that when such practices are brought to community-based settings, the activities put into practice to implement the programs may not always be consistent or aligned with the original procedures used to establish the practice as evidence based and therefore may not produce the positive outcomes demonstrated in the research trial (Durlak & DuPre, 2008; Fixsen et al., 2001; Schorr, 1993). In these situations, it is possible that the program has not actually been implemented as intended and therefore is not likely to produce the expected results. This is referred to as a Type III error, an error that occurs when outcomes are evaluated from a program that was not implemented as intended (Dobson & Cook, 1980). Any outcomes that result are produced by factors other than the program of interest. The outcome of a Type III error is that children, families, and individuals will not benefit from a program they do not experience (Fixsen et al., 2005).

In some instances, when implementing model practices, adaptations are necessary to ensure successful implementation and help the practice fit the ecology and culture of the community; however, it is sometimes unclear what adaptations are acceptable and which can overly compromise fidelity to program models, resulting in compromised or negative outcomes. Despite these challenges, when implementing ECE programs in real-world settings, adaptation almost invariably becomes a consideration (Durlak & DuPre, 2008).

Implementation has been described as the "science, practice, and policy of getting science into practice and policy" (Fixsen, 2011). Factors associated with effective implementation are therefore crucial to ensuring that evidence-based programs—or for that matter any intervention, activity, or program—are implemented as intended in order to sustain changes in practice and policy. Attention should be given to factors that contribute to effective implementation, whether at the program, organization, or systems level. Under this premise, implementation science can be defined as *the scientific investigation of factors associated with effective implementation.* As will be described in this and subsequent chapters, there seem to be many factors that contribute to effective implementation. In addition, these factors seem to interact in a nonlinear and iterative manner and may affect multiple systems, including practice, policy, and research (Sung et al., 2003).

Due to the complexity of the implementation process, it can be argued that implementation science must capture the iterative and nonlinear nature of the various implementation components. This approach to empirical investigation differs from the more traditional method of research establishing the evidence base of EBPs, which typically involves the use of randomized control trials and research designs that measure participant outcomes from preprogram to postprogram implementation. As the major themes of implementation frameworks described in the next section will show, the implementation process involves multiple direct service activities, including training on the program model and monitoring fidelity to the program model (implementing the program model as intended), as well as service support activities such as data-driven decision making, ongoing coaching for practice improvement, and organizational or system policies that support quality implementation sustainability. The science of implementation must therefore not only focus on the components of fidelity to the program model but also address the organizational and system-level components that contribute to the quality implementation (including model fidelity) of the program, the continuous quality improvement at the individual and organizational level, and the quality implementation sustainability of the program over the long term. The benefit of a science that can account for a variety of components operating within a systemic framework is a more dynamic and individualized approach to service delivery and increases the likelihood of sustainability and high-quality outcomes.

Definitions of Commonly Used Terms

There is a range of terms often associated with implementation science and commonly used in the scientific, practice, and policy areas. Key terms include *diffusion, replication, dissemination, readiness, capacity, scalability, fidelity, coaching, training, technical assistance, quality improvement, sustainability,* and *purveyor and intermediary organizations.*

Diffusion, replication, dissemination, knowledge translation, and *implementation* are commonly used terms that refer to the process of bringing an established model from research to practice. These terms differ slightly in their meanings, particularly in how passive or active the process is. Diffusion usually tends to be a more passive process and can include the diffusion of knowledge. *Replication* usually refers specifically to re-creating a model program ("replicating" it) in another setting. *Dissemination* can refer to the spreading of knowledge, ideas, or practices. Similar to dissemination and diffusion, but focused more on the usability of research knowledge by users of an innovation, is *knowledge translation* (Grimshaw, Eccles, Lavis, Hill, & Squires, 2012; Lane, 2012). Implementation is the most active and intentional of these processes and is often differentiated from more passive approaches as "making it happen" (Fixsen et al., 2005; Greenhalgh, Robert, Bate, MacFarlane, &

Kyriakidou, 2005). The chapter by Metz, Halle, Bartley, and Blasberg (Chapter 2) provides an in-depth overview of what constitutes *active* implementation.

Readiness and capacity are often seen as critical elements in the early stages of the implementation process. *Capacity* can be defined as the host agency's available resources that can be dedicated to the implementation process, such as a well-trained workforce, knowledge and skills, physical space, ability to collect and use data, supporting policies, or other factors that can contribute to the successful implementation of new practices. *Readiness* refers to the ability of the host agency or organization to learn and assimilate new ideas, to engage in a change process, and to change practice that is critical to the host organization's ability to implement with quality and sustainability (Damschroder et al., 2009; Gulbrandsson, 2008; Weiner, 2009). The chapter by Peterson (Chapter 3) further explores the linkages between readiness to change and effective implementation.

Scalability is a term used to describe the potential for taking an individual model or pilot program and expanding it to fit some larger system. Fixsen, Blase, Metz, and Van Dyke (2013) define *scale* as "60% of the service units in a system… using the program with fidelity and good outcomes," meaning not only that the program has been adopted by most service providers in a large system but also that it is being implemented with quality.

For example, at some point in their early development, commonly recognized evidence-based treatment models such as Multisystemic Therapy (MST) were once localized, individual, structured programs developed to meet the needs of an identified population. As the model was researched and evidence was established, it was replicated in many settings. In this example, the scalability of MST—the potential for replicating it—was great, as it has been successfully replicated in settings around the world.

It is important to note that the process of bringing a program to scale in a larger system can encounter multiple challenges in terms of systems change and quality assurance; these challenges should be considered before initiating a scaling-up process (Chamberlain et al., 2011). The chapters in Part III of this volume highlight the replication and scale-up of several ECE practices and interventions, noting where applicable some of these challenges with regard to systems change and quality assurance.

Fidelity is a critical element to successful implementation, especially when replicating evidence-based models. *Fidelity* typically refers to how well the program is being implemented compared to the original program model or design. What we refer to here as fidelity to a program model is called by Hulleman, Rimm-Kaufman, and Abry in Chapter 4 "intervention fidelity," which they distinguish from "implementation fidelity," the latter denoting adherence to the core implementation components of an active implementation framework. Model drift can occur if sufficient attention is not paid to monitoring and supporting fidelity and can result in poor or even negative outcomes. Achieving fidelity also takes into account the complex organizational factors that may require minor adaptations while still replicating the core program components (Aarons et al., 2012; Mowbray, Holter, Teague, & Bybee, 2003). One of the challenges associated with implementing EBPs and other recommended-practice models is finding the adequate resources to support fidelity adherence in an ongoing manner once the program is installed.

Coaching, training, and *technical assistance* all refer to activities that support the implementation process. Coaching can be conducted by either trained internal staff or an outside "expert" who provides consultation and support to supervisory and frontline staff to ensure the model is being implemented correctly and any deficits in knowledge or skills are addressed. Research on the link between implementation activities and program outcomes has shown that the intended outcomes may not be achieved with training alone and that coaching and technical assistance are critical to successful program replication (Joyce & Showers, 2002; Rodriguez, Loman, & Horner, 2009). Coaching often has the goal of building the capacity of the providers so that they can ultimately do the work themselves without significant external support.

Training and technical assistance are typically provided or brokered by the treatment developer—an external expert entity, purveyor, or intermediary organization who brings knowledge and resources to address needs identified by the organization or through an external monitoring or evaluation process. Training and technical assistance can address very concrete issues, such as questions about billing or third-party reimbursement, or more complex issues such as organizational development, systems change, or sustainability planning. Coaching and training may or may not be explicit components of a program or intervention model, but they are understood as essential components of an intentional and active implementation model (see Chapter 2).

Quality assurance and *quality improvement* refer to processes that support the implementation, fidelity, and sustainability of model programs. These processes often play a critical role in ensuring that programs are being delivered with fidelity to an identified model and are resulting in expected outcomes. These processes work by collecting and using data to track and analyze performance, measure performance against established benchmarks, and create incentives and provide support for program improvement. Quality assurance and improvement activities can be seen as critical to the successful implementation of EBPs and model programs (Aarons et al., 2012).

Sustainability refers to the ongoing maintenance and successful implementation of a model program with good effect. In many cases, following initial stages of implementation that may include intensive financial, consultative, and technical support, model programs and practices have difficulty being sustained in the "real world." Sustainability planning has been identified as a critical component of the implementation process that should be considered from the outset of implementation activities (Johnson, Hays, Center, & Daley, 2004). The goals of sustainability planning are 1) establishing adequate policies and procedures to institutionalize the desired changes and 2) putting into place the necessary mechanisms to ensure the short- and long-term survival of the program following the intensive implementation process.

The intercession of purveyor and intermediary organizations—typically defined as external entities that facilitate the implementation process—may be necessary to ensure successful implementation (Durlak & DuPre, 2008; Fixsen et al., 2005; Greenhalgh et al., 2005). Fixsen et al. (2005) defined a purveyor organization as "an individual or group of individuals representing a program or practice who actively work with implementation sites to implement that program or practice with fidelity and good effect" (p. 14). They defined an intermediary organization more broadly, as "the specific agency that houses, supports, and funds the implementation of a program or practice...that will in turn help to develop, support and sustain one or more replication programs" (p. 82). The definition of an intermediary organization has been expanded to include the following functions: 1) consultation activities; 2) recommended-practice model development; 3) evidence-based practices purveyance; 4) quality assurance and improvement; 5) outcome evaluation and research; 6) training, public awareness, and education; and 7) policy and systems development (Franks, 2011). Purveyors and intermediary organizations could serve many functions, including a translational role between research and practice or a technical assistance provider to program implementers to ensure quality implementation and sustainability of programs (Fixsen, 2011).

Major Themes in Implementation Literature

Over the past decade, an increasing number of research studies and publications have focused on the topic of implementation; however, the field of implementation is still relatively new and comparatively small in relation to other research topics. Because implementation science is still an emerging field, few frameworks have accounted for the complex and dynamic nature of implementation.

Of note is the Fixsen et al. (2005) framework, which was developed through a comprehensive literature review of existing implementation studies published in the fields of health, mental health, education, and business and identified variables contributing to quality implementation, positive programmatic outcomes, and sustainability. The authors categorized six stages of implementation and core implementation components common to all fields: 1) exploration, 2) installation, 3) initial implementation, 4) full implementation, 5) innovation, and 6) sustainability. Core implementation components are addressed within the framework at the individual provider, organization, and systems levels. As a result, the authors point out that these stages may not progress in a linear fashion, but are often iterative and nonlinear, allowing for a program improvement feedback loop that includes strategic learning at the individual, organizational, and systems levels of program implementation in order to encourage policy changes that better support effective implementation over time. This framework is described in greater detail in Chapter 2.

From 2004 through 2012, several systematic reviews looked at features related to dissemination, diffusion of innovation, and implementation of model programs (e.g., Durlak & DuPre, 2008; Fixsen et al., 2005; Greenhalgh et al., 2004; Meyers, Durlak, & Wandersman, 2012; Stith et al., 2006). These reviews examined multiple factors related to implementation and evaluated hundreds of research studies to look for common themes and trends that emerge as common characteristics of implementation research. This research was not necessarily focused explicitly on implementation, but observations about issues related to implementation nevertheless often resulted from studies that examined efficacy, outcomes, program development, or innovations in practice (e.g., Durlak & DuPre, 2008; Meyers et al., 2012). In many instances, the common themes that emerged from these reviews were more numerous than their differences. Durlak and DuPre (2008) noted that of the 23 factors described in their review, a range of 13–21 common factors was observed by other authors. These factors included the importance of funding, a positive work climate, shared decision making, coordination with other agencies, formulation of tasks, leadership, program champions, administrative support, providers' skill proficiency, and training and technical assistance (Durlak & DuPre, 2008, p. 340). From this analysis, it seems that a common language for implementation science is emerging and converging factors are being explored that relate to the implementation process.

As we consider the range of potential themes and topics emerging in the growing field of implementation science, several key areas come to light as crosscutting themes in much of the literature. Many of these topics will be discussed in greater detail in subsequent chapters of this volume and have specific relevance for the early care and education field. Seven key areas that provide a foundational understanding of implementation science have been identified and are described in the following list:

1. *Assessing readiness and capacity.* Many researchers who have examined the developing field of implementation cite the importance of assessing the capacity for change and goodness of fit for implementing evidence-based and model programs in community-based settings (Durlak & DuPre, 2008; Fixsen et al., 2005; Greenhalgh et al., 2004; Meyers et al., 2012; Stith et al., 2006). Therefore, an important initial step in the implementation process is conducting a structured assessment, often one that assesses readiness to implement specific components and aspects of the identified model, before further investment is made in initiating a potentially costly implementation process.

2. *Structure of the implementation process.* Many of the articulated implementation processes are stage based and linear, with the ultimate goal of program installation and sustainability (Durlak & DuPre, 2008; Fixsen et al., 2005; Greenhalgh et al., 2004; Meyers et al., 2012; Wandersman et al., 2008). Although implementation methodologies vary, it is important to have a well-articulated methodology that is described up front so that the entities participating in the implementation process have a clear sense of the process and what is expected of them.

3. *Engagement and buy-in.* Buy-in is often considered to be important at every level (Durlak & DuPre, 2008; Greenhalgh et al., 2004; Meyers et al., 2012; Simpson, 2002). Agency or community leadership must provide sufficient support and assistance to create a climate for successful implementation. To achieve practice change, workers and line staff must be sufficiently engaged in the process to benefit from training and knowledge transfer. Ideally, participants in the implementation process should have a clear sense of what is expected of them and be willing to actively partake in the implementation process.

4. *Program installation.* What many people may consider the most active phase of the implementation process is what in the field is referred to as "installation" or "adoption" (Fixsen et al., 2005). During this process, knowledge is transferred and new skills are acquired through a structured process of training, coaching, and technical assistance (Durlak & DuPre, 2008; Greenhalgh et al., 2004; Meyers et al., 2012; Simpson, 2002; Wandersman et al., 2008). Most implementation models suggest that this process takes a considerable amount of preservice delivery time and effort.

5. *Outcome evaluation and fidelity monitoring.* Agencies learning a new model often need to build capacity not only to change practices and learn new skills but also to develop comprehensive data systems that allow the collection, analysis, and interpretation of various forms of data (Durlak & DuPre, 2008; Meyers et al., 2012; Stith et al., 2006). Model programs must also be monitored to ensure that they are being delivered with fidelity and resulting in expected outcomes.

6. *Feedback and quality improvement.* Ideally, data are not collected in isolation or for research purposes only but are used in a systematic way for quality improvement and skill development. Quality improvement can help increase the likelihood that model programs produce and sustain the outcomes as intended (Arthur & Blitz, 2000; Chinman et al., 2008; Schorr, 1993).

7. *Innovation and adaptation.* Many authors and researchers who study the implementation process address the issue of innovation and model adaptation (Durlak & DuPre, 2008; Fixsen et al., 2005; Greenhalgh et al., 2004; Meyers et al., 2012). When implementing a model practice, most agree that it is necessary to ensure that the model is compatible with the local culture, and context and accommodations must often be made to ensure buy-in and successful implementation. However, especially in the case of evidence-based models where fidelity is a consideration, care must be taken to ensure that innovations or adaptations do not compromise essential aspects of the model.

From these metareviews and syntheses of literature, it is evident that a shared language for the science of implementation is emerging. As a unified model continues to develop, the need to explicate the features through case examples and to further test components of the model through research and evaluation is needed. However, even at this early stage of development, treatment developers, purveyors and intermediary organizations, and agencies and funders can begin to use implementation frameworks as a road map for implementation of services and programs. A more in-depth consideration of the stages of implementation is presented in Chapter 2.

Challenges and Limitations

Although the availability of implementation frameworks provides a useful guide to quality implementation, there are also some challenges to using implementation frameworks to structure future implementation activities and related research. The following considerations highlight the potential challenges in using implementation frameworks:

- *The theoretical base for implementation is relatively new and needs to be tested and operationalized in real-world settings.* Many of the frameworks described above, as well as those that were not included in this chapter, were developed through a review of existing literature (see Meyers, Durlak, & Wandersman, 2012, for a more extensive description of existing implementation frameworks). Given the recent emergence of the field of implementation science, it is possible that the existing literature does not yet represent implementation practices in general, particularly since most if not all of the available frameworks have yet to be empirically tested in real-world settings.

- *Implementation frameworks may not neatly fit real-world ecology.* Given the iterative and nonlinear process of implementation, an emphasis on an organizing framework may risk overlooking the emergent qualities of practice improvement and the possible need to revisit earlier phases of implementation to improve program outcomes and sustainability.

- *Implementation frameworks may be better used as guides for organizing results than for driving research.* Implementation science may help to further inform implementation frameworks, but not necessarily the other way around. It would be informative to empirically test implementation frameworks, but implementation science may also be served by considering alternative hypotheses for empirical investigation.

- *Implementation frameworks may not be sufficiently articulated to identify and measure change.* Further refinement of processes, phases, and stages may be necessary to clearly define the empirical hypotheses needed to test implementation frameworks and related activities.

Despite these challenges, the field of early care and education can benefit from the integration of key implementation components into ECE practices by increasing the sustainability of quality practices and services and thereby enhancing the likelihood of positive outcomes for children and families. The implementation frameworks described above can be used as guideposts in the adoption and dissemination of evidence-based practices and even promising practices with the goal of establishing evidence of successful programmatic outcomes. As the field of ECE expands to incorporate implementation of EBPs, the dividends produced by an investment in offering quality programs and services will be greater if there exists an equal investment in quality implementation.

Case Examples: Applying Implementation Science in Real-World Settings

Although implementation science is a relatively new field, several examples illustrate how large-scale systems apply comprehensive implementation strategies to successfully disseminate model and recommended-practice programs. Although these strategies do not specifically operationalize previously described implementation frameworks, many of the features highlighted by these frameworks are evident in the following case examples. Several of these examples reflect the major themes in Meyers, Durlak, and Wandersman's (2012) synthesized model. In particular, the importance of assessing the capacity for change by utilizing a structured approach, identifying and engaging organizational and community leadership, developing implementation teams and a plan, collecting data, and providing ongoing training and technical assistance and quality assurance through the process of implementation can be seen in the following case examples.

The Learning Collaborative Approach:
Trauma-Focused Cognitive Behavior Therapy and Child FIRST

The importance of utilizing a structured implementation approach and relying on an external purveyor, intermediary, or technical assistance provider to facilitate the process of implementation has been often cited in the literature (Durlak & DuPre, 2008; Fixsen et al., 2005; Greenhalgh et al., 2004). The state of Connecticut has recently applied implementation strategies to bring two EBPs to scale across the state: 1) Trauma-Focused Cognitive-Behavior Therapy (TF-CBT) and 2) Child FIRST, an early childhood home visiting intervention. In both instances, through support from the Center for Effective Practice at the Child Health and Development Institute, the Learning Collaborative methodology was successfully utilized as the implementation strategy, with the Center for Effective Practice acting as an intermediary organization to facilitate the implementation (Franks, 2011).

The Learning Collaborative methodology was first developed by the Institute for Healthcare Improvement (IHI) as an approach to implementing practice improvements in community settings (Lang & Franks, 2011). IHI originally developed the methodology to provide a framework for creating improvements in health care (Institute for Healthcare Improvement, 2004), and the model was later adapted to the dissemination of trauma-focused mental health interventions by the National Center for Child Traumatic Stress and more recently to an early childhood intervention program in Connecticut. A learning collaborative differs from typical training and implementation strategies in that it typically involves a 6- to 15-month-long process that includes multiple phases of implementation and multimodal training for participants. Learning collaboratives involve multiple groups learning together from different communities or agencies. Through an interactive, collaborative process, participants learn from one another and overcome barriers to successful implementation.

Learning collaboratives include staff with diverse roles in a team-based approach, employ several in-person trainings and individual consultation throughout the year, emphasize the use of data for quality improvement, utilize active-learning techniques, and focus on organizational change and sustainability (Lang & Franks, 2011). An initial assessment of the site's capacity for change is assessed, and a "model for change" that targets areas in need of capacity building, training, and technical assistance is developed. Between in-person "learning sessions," participants engage in a variety of other implementation activities, including "action periods" in which they practice skills, apply small tests of change, and overcome obstacles to implementation. In addition, web-based learning, group consultation conference calls, site-based consultation, and affinity group meetings are utilized to help accelerate the process of implementation. The implementation process is closely monitored by the ongoing collection of metric and outcome data, which are continuously fed back to participants. Senior leaders at each agency actively participate in the training (along with supervisors, line staff, and others) to ensure that there is organizational buy-in and that any organizational barriers can be addressed and overcome.

Promising results have been found for the IHI Learning Collaborative model in health care fields, and learning collaboratives have also been used to improve health promotion practices in afterschool programs and to improve the quality improvement infrastructure of county mental health agencies (Lang & Franks, 2011). This methodical implementation process is particularly useful when attempting to bring model programs or EBPs to scale. Outcomes from the application of this model in Connecticut have yielded strong results indicating that the programs are being implemented with high fidelity and resulting in positive outcomes for children and youth participating in the program (Lang & Franks, 2011).

Child FIRST (Lowell, Paulicin, Carter, Godoy, & Briggs-Gowan, 2011) adapted this basic learning collaborative model to an early childhood home-visiting intervention for at-risk mothers and their young children, but several important adaptations were introduced. As Durlak and DuPre (2008) suggest, it was important to find the right balance between fidelity to the learning collaborative model and the adaptations necessary for this model to be used for a community-based home-visiting model. Further, minor adaptations to the original treatment model had to be considered by the model developer when disseminating across a state system of care.

Due to the intensive nature of the intervention, the "standard" learning collaborative timeline, which typically involved three or four in-person learning sessions punctuated by site-based action periods, had to be adapted to include both increased frequency and duration of learning sessions coupled with intensive site-based coaching and supervision. When working with the treatment developer, it became evident that the scope of the model, which includes a community-based care coordination component as well as an intensive home-based intervention, required a comprehensive implementation strategy that addressed the multiple needs of the participants. Ensuring buy-in and participation from communities, engaging senior leadership at participating agencies, and creating a sustainable learning community were all challenges faced by the implementation team. In addition, the use of metric and outcome data and continuous quality improvement continue to be ongoing critical components of the implementation process. This real-world example brings many of the previously described elements of implementation to life and highlights the importance of being flexible even when utilizing a highly structured approach to implementation.

Scaling of Evidence-Based Practice: The Incredible Years

The Incredible Years is a well-researched evidence-based behavioral improvement program for young children that is currently implemented by teachers in classroom settings in more than 400 classrooms in Colorado. The program was brought to the state by an intermediary purveyor, Invest in Kids, which served the role of bridging research and practice through the recognition of the need for a school-based behavioral health intervention that was evidence based, the identification of the EBP that matched this need, the engagement of local systems and schools interested in adopting the program, and the installation of the systems and processes necessary to implement the program with high quality.

Over the 7 years that The Incredible Years has been implemented in Colorado, the purveyor Invest in Kids has steadily monitored fidelity of program implementation, provided technical assistance when needed, addressed at the state and local levels policy issues that support quality implementation, and helped guide the scaling-up efforts to bring the program to an increasing number of classrooms each year. There are many factors that have supported the successful installation and initial implementation of the program, including the cultivation of new and ongoing funding sources, the establishment of data collection and fidelity monitoring processes, and an emphasis on local sustainability and community buy-in. Evaluation efforts are now aimed at investigating the implementation drivers that support sustainable and quality implementation of The Incredible Years in Colorado as well as related child outcomes.

Systems Change: Early Childhood Council Health Integration Initiative (Colorado)

In 2009, the Colorado Trust funded 20 Early Childhood Councils (ECCs) in the state to implement programs that integrate health with other systems relevant to the well-being of young children. This unique funding approach allowed for ECCs to focus not only on quality program implementation but also on systems-building activities that support program implementation sustainability. The evaluation of this initiative focuses on the process of systems building in ensuring quality implementation of programs. The implementation of programs, engagement of health system representatives in the implementation process, and related developmental evaluation are highly participatory in nature and focus on quality improvement practices to improve child and family outcomes. Section IV of this book discusses systems issues in more depth as they relate to the process of implementation.

Implications for Early Care and Education Program Evaluaton and Research

Based on the literature reviewed in this chapter, common themes are evident in areas for future evaluation and research. Greenhalgh et al. (2008) made multiple methodological recommendations for how research on diffusion and implementation of innovations should be conducted in the future. Based on their recommendations, future research should be 1) theory driven; 2) process oriented; 3) ecological (including a focus on the setting and context for implementation); 4) able to use common definitions, measures, and tools; 5) collaborative and coordinated; 6) multidisciplinary and multimethod; 7) meticulously detailed; and 8) participatory. Further, authors reviewed in this chapter have recommended a range of content areas to be considered in future implementation research, including:

1. Development of further consensus on the elements of implementation and shared definitions and frameworks in order to better operationalize, define, and describe factors associated with implementation (Durlak & DuPre, 2008; Fixsen et al., 2005; Greenhalgh et al., 2008; Schoenwald & Hoagwood, 2001)

2. Research to explore how contextual factors such as setting and capacity may affect successful implementation (Fixsen et al., 2005; Meyers et al., 2012; Schoenwald & Hoagwood, 2001; Wandersman et al., 2008)

3. Comparative research to determine how implementation factors influence outcomes (Durlak & DuPre, 2008; Fixsen et al., 2005; Greenhalgh et al., 2008; Meyers et al., 2012)

4. Research to explore the relative weight of implementation factors as they relate to outcomes and variability across similar implementation settings (Fixsen et al., 2005; Greenhalgh et al., 2008; Meyers et al., 2012)

5. Research to determine the relative influence of implementation structure and the impact of training and technical assistance (Durlak & DuPre, 2008; Durlak & Wandersman, 2012; Greenhalgh et al., 2008)

6. Research to explore the effects of adaptation and model fidelity on successful implementation and program outcomes (Durlak & DuPre, 2008; Durlak & Wandersman, 2012; Greenhalgh et al., 2008)

When considering early childhood and education implementation research, it is important to note that little research specific to the ECE field has been conducted. The recommendations above would certainly be applicable to the ECE field, with special consideration given to issues relevant to working with this population. Implementation frameworks highlight the need for organizational, community, and cross-system improvements in supporting quality program implementation. Unique factors associated with implementing ECE programs may be discovered in the future. Because traditional research tends to explore changes in time and causality between two points, examining ECE research through an implementation lens may yield new multidimensional and multidetermined approaches to better understand how implementation factors impact model fidelity and program outcomes.

Further, implementation factors should be examined continuously and repeatedly over time. ECE researchers can better explore what works for whom and under what conditions. In some cases, good measures of the implementation process do not yet exist or have not been sufficiently validated. Self-report measures can be unreliable, and objective measures are lacking and often difficult to operationalize (requiring intensive external observation by an objective party). In addition, many researchers may not be adequately trained or prepared to conduct implementation research. In sum, implementation research can be challenging and may not easily fit within our existing research paradigms.

Despite these challenges, it is imperative that ECE researchers continue to explore implementation as it relates to successful and sustainable program outcomes for young children and their families. Otherwise, we may continue to invest resources in ECE programs that lead to poor outcomes and erroneously conclude that it is a result of a flawed intervention. Instead, we should invest in developing and utilizing rigorous yet flexible implementation frameworks that can ensure that programs are implemented successfully with sufficient fidelity to program models. Only then can we accurately assess the impact of ECE programs in community settings and make informed decisions about program outcomes and investment of limited resources.

Summary

This chapter introduced the concept of implementation, defined key terms, reviewed implementation literature and frameworks, and set the stage for further description of the implementation process, models for change, and areas of future research. Although implementation science is an emerging field, it is evident that a great deal of attention and focus on implementation is under way. We may be on the threshold of a paradigmatic shift in how we understand program effectiveness and outcomes. No longer can we separate the intervention from the implementation process. This realization has significant implications for the early care and education field, especially during times of diminished resources. To make sound investments and ensure that resources are being utilized to their utmost potential, we must focus on how programs and services are implemented in community-based settings. Recognizing the value of implementation has implications for how programs are funded and replicated. This volume provides further in-depth analysis of implementation science as it relates to ECE initiatives and begins to provide a blueprint for policy makers, researchers, practitioners, and purveyors and intermediary organizations as they embark on developing and disseminating promising and model ECE programs in the hopes of yielding improved long-term outcomes for vulnerable young children.

References

Aarons, G., Green, A., Palinkas, L., Self-Brown, S., Whitaker, D., Lutzker, J., … Chaffin, M. (2012). Dynamic adaptation process to implement an evidence-based child maltreatment intervention. *Implementation Science, 7*, 32.

Arthur, M.W., & Blitz, C. (2000). Bridging the gap between science and practice in drug abuse prevention through needs assessment and strategic community planning. *Journal of Community Psychology, 28*(3), 241–255.

Chamberlain, P., Roberts, R., Jones, H., Marsenich, L., Sosna, T., & Price, J. (2011). Three collaborative models for scaling up evidence-based practices. *Administration and Policy in Mental Health, 39*(4), 278–290.

Chinman, M., Hunter, S.B., Ebener, P., Paddock, S.M., Stillman, L., Imm, P., & Wandersman, A. (2008). The Getting to Outcomes demonstration and evaluation: An illustration of the prevention support system. *American Journal of Community Psychology, 41*(3–4).

Damschroder, L., Aron, D., Keith, R., Kirsch, S., Alexander, J., & Lowery, C. (2009). Fostering implementation of health services research findings into practice: A consolidated framework for advancing implementation science. *Implementation Science, 4*, 50.

Dobson, L., & Cook, T. (1980). Avoiding Type III error in program evaluation: Results from a field experiment. *Evaluation and Program Planning, 3*, 269–276.

Durlak, J.A., & DuPre, E.P. (2008). Implementation matters: A review of research on the influence of implementation on program outcomes and the factors affecting implementation. *American Journal of Community Psychology, 41*, 327–350.

Fixsen, D. (2011, August). *Opening plenary remarks*. Presented at the Global Implementation Conference, Washington, DC.

Fixsen, D., Blase, K., Metz, A., & Van Dyke, M.V. (2013). Statewide implementation of evidence-based programs. *Exceptional Children, 79*(2), 213–230.

Fixsen, D., Blase, K., Timbers, G., & Wolf, M. (2001). In search of program implementation: 792 replications of the Teaching-Family Model. In G.A. Bernfeld, D.P. Farrington, & A.W. Leschied (Eds.), *Offender rehabilitation in practice: Implementing and evaluating effective programs* (pp. 149–166). London, England: Wiley.

Fixsen, D.L., Naoom, S.F., Blase, K.A., Friedman, R.M., & Wallace, F. (2005). *Implementation research: A synthesis of the literature* (FMHI Publication No. 231). Tampa, FL: University of South Florida, Louis de la Parte Florida Mental Health Institute, National Implementation Research Network.

Franks, R. (2011). Role of the intermediary organization in promoting and disseminating best practices. *Emotional and Behavioral Disorders in Youth, 10*(4), 87–93.

Greenhalgh, T., Robert, G., Bate, P., MacFarlane, F., & Kyriakidou, O. (2005). *Diffusion of innovations in health service organizations: A systematic literature review*. Oxford, England: BMJ Books, Blackwell.

Greenhalgh, T., Robert, G., MacFarlane, F., Bate, P., & Kyriakidou, O. (2004). Diffusion of innovations in service organizations: Systematic review and recommendations. *Milbank Quarterly, 82*(4), 581–629.

Grimshaw, J., Eccles, M., Lavis, J., Hill, S., & Squires, J. (2012). Knowledge translation of research findings. *Implementation Science, 7*, 50.

Gulbrandsson, K. (2008). *From news to everyday use: The difficult art of implementation*. Stockholm, Sweden: Swedish Department of Public Health.

Institute for Healthcare Improvement. (2004). The breakthrough series: IHI's collaborative model for achieving breakthrough improvement. *Diabetes Spectrum, 17*(2), 97–101.

Johnson, K., Hays, C., Center, H., & Daley, C. (2004). Building capacity and sustainable prevention innovations: A sustainability planning model. *Evaluation and Program Planning, 27*, 135–149.

Joyce, B., & Showers, B. (2002). *Student achievement through staff development*. Alexandria, VA: Association for Supervision and Curriculum Development.

Lane, J.P. (2012). Tracking evidence of knowledge use through knowledge translation, technology transfer, and commercial transactions. *FOCUS Technical Brief* (34). Austin, TX: SEDL, Disability Research to Practice Program.

Lang, J., & Franks, R. (2011). *Statewide implementation of best practices: The Connecticut TF-CBT learning collaborative*. Farmington, CT: Child Health & Development Institute.

Lowell, D., Paulicin, B., Carter, A., Godoy, L., & Briggs-Gowan, M. (2011). A randomized controlled trial of Child FIRST: A comprehensive home-based intervention translating research into early childhood practice. *Child Development, 82*(1), 193–208.

Meyers, D.C., Durlak, J.A., & Wandersman, A. (2012). The quality implementation framework: A synthesis of critical steps to the implementation process. *American Journal of Community Psychology, 50*(3-4), 462–480.

Mowbray, C., Holter, M., Teague, G., & Bybee, D. (2003). Fidelity criteria: Development, measurement, and validation. *American Journal of Evaluation, 24*(3), 315–340.

National Institute on Disability and Rehabilitation Research. (2005). *Knowledge translation planning: Background information for the June 9–10, 2005 panel meeting*. Paper presented at the meeting of the Knowledge Translation Planning Panel, June 9–10, 2005, Austin, TX.

Odom, S., Hanson, M., Lieber, J., Diamond, K., Palmer, S., Butera, G., & Horn, E. (2010). Prevention, early childhood intervention, and implementation science. In B. Doll, W. Pfohl, & J. Yoon (Eds.), *Handbook of youth prevention science* (pp. 413–433). New York, NY: Routledge.

Rodriguez, B., Loman, S., & Horner, R. (2009). A preliminary analysis of the effects of coaching feedback on teacher implementation fidelity of First Step to Success. *Behavioral Analysis in Practice, 2*(2), 11–21.

Schoenwald, S.K., & Hoagwood, K. (2001). Effectiveness, transportability, and dissemination of interventions: What matters when? *Psychiatric Services, 52*(9), 1190–1197.

Schorr, L. (1993). Effective strategies for increasing social program replication/adaptation. In *Seminar on Effective Strategies for Increasing Social Program Replication/Adaptation* (pp. 7–18). Washington, DC: National Association of Social Workers.

Simpson, D. (2002). A conceptual framework for transferring research to practice. *Journal of Substance Abuse Treatment, 22*(4), 171–182.

Stith, S., Pruitt, I., Dees, J., Fronce, M., Green, N., Som, A., & Linkh, D. (2006). Implementing community-based prevention programming: A review of the literature. *Journal of Primary Prevention, 27*(6), 599–617.

Sung, N., Crowley, W., Jr., Genel, M., Salber, P., Sandy, L., Sherwood, L., … Rimoin, D. (2003). Central challenges facing the National Clinical Research Enterprise. *Journal of the American Medical Association, 289*(10), 1278–1287.

Wandersman, A., Duffy, J., Flaspohler, P., Noonan, R., Lubell, K., Stillman, L., … Saul, J. (2008). Bridging the gap between research and practice: An interactive systems framework for building capacity to disseminate and implement innovations. *American Journal of Community Psychology, 41*, 171–181.

Weiner, B.J. (2009). A theory of organizational readiness for change. *Implementation Science, 4*, 67.

CHAPTER 2

The Key Components of Successful Implementation

Allison Metz, Tamara Halle, Leah Bartley, and Amy Blasberg

Implementation exists at the nexus between research and practice. Successful implementation is the mechanism by which young children and their families actually benefit from the practices and programs that research has identified as effective in a more limited context. This chapter will explain in detail the core components associated with successful implementation and how these can contribute to the development of effective early care and education practices, programs, and systems. Programs that have been implemented well have common, core implementation components that have recommended practices associated with them. This chapter will introduce and explain key terminology, with several concrete examples from the field of early care and education (ECE) used for illustration.

Since 2001, the science related to developing and identifying evidence-based programs and practices that lead to positive developmental outcomes for children and families has improved significantly. However, the science related to implementing these programs with high fidelity in real-world settings has lagged far behind. Several reports (Institute of Medicine, 2001; National Research Council and Institute of Medicine, 2009) have highlighted the gap between what we know about effective programs and what we know about how to actually provide effective programs consistently to populations that could benefit from them. In fact, the lag time between translating research into effective practice has been documented to be as long as 20+ years. This lag time, the "research-to-practice" gap, has garnered heightened attention in recent years.

New evidence is accumulating that points to implementation as the critical pathway between research and practice. Implementation is also important in systematic efforts to bring effective programs for children and families to scale in a way that will have meaningful effects on child well-being and key family outcomes. Researchers, funders, policy makers, and practitioners are paying more attention to the importance of implementation, defined as a specified set of activities designed to put into practice an activity or program of known dimensions (Fixsen, Naoom, Blase, Friedman, & Wallace, 2005).

The research-to-practice gap is a critical issue in the ECE field because we know that high-quality ECE has been shown to have significant benefits to children's developmental outcomes, particularly for children from economically disadvantaged backgrounds (Barnett, 2002; Dearing, McCartney, & Taylor, 2009; Loeb, Fuller, Kagan, & Carrol, 2004; McCartney et al., 2010; NICHD Early Child Care Research Network & Duncan, 2003; Tran & Weinraub, 2006). For example, there is longitudinal evidence indicating that high-quality early childhood programs reduce the likelihood of externalizing behaviors or delinquency (McCartney et al., 2010; Yoshikawa, 1995). However, many children and families who could benefit from high-quality ECE programs are not reaping the benefits of empirically proven interventions. Durlak and DuPre (2008) acknowledge the following:

> Social scientists recognize that developing effective interventions is only the first step towards improving the health and well-being of populations. Transferring effective programs into real-world settings and maintaining them there is a complicated, long-term process that requires dealing effectively with the successive, complex phases of program diffusion. (p. 327)

The field of implementation science has emerged with the purpose of closing the research-to-practice gap and is dedicated to building the evidence base for effective strategies regarding translating research to practice. From this burgeoning field, several *active* implementation processes have emerged that are based on a large and diverse research literature. In this chapter, we present an overview of implementation science and explain in detail the core components associated with successful implementation and how these can contribute to the development of effective ECE practices, programs, and systems. Not only do we highlight these core implementation components, but we also outline the associated recommended practices within each.

We begin the chapter with a section that addresses prerequisites for effective implementation, which include fully articulated and operationalized ECE program models, innovations, and initiatives. In this section, we provide a generic, operational definition of an ECE program model and strategies for assessing ECE interventions through an "implementation lens." In subsequent sections, we provide an overview of two overarching frameworks that are the foundation of active implementation frameworks (Fixsen et al., 2005) and inform implementation infrastructure: stages of implementation and implementation drivers. We then provide a description of the organized, expert assistance that must be in place to support effective implementation and increase staff and organizational readiness. Finally, we complete the chapter by discussing implications of implementation science for ECE practice and research.

Fully Operationalized Early Childhood Program Models, Innovations, and Initiatives

Before an ECE program model or initiative can be effectively implemented, it must first be well defined. Program developers or individuals establishing a larger early childhood initiative such as an ECE professional development system, a home visiting program, or a quality rating and improvement system must clearly articulate all the distinct parts of the program or initiative, starting with the goals, purposes, and target audiences, but also including the content of the program or initiative, the key activities of the program, the mode of service delivery, the duration and dosage of the program or initiative, and the expected outcomes. Hulleman, Rimm-Kaufman, and Abry (Chapter 4) note that this involves specifying the "who, what, where, how, and when" of a program (see also Hall & Hord, 2006). The accompanying text box describes what needs to be specified in a fully operationalized program or initiative (Metz, Bartley, & Blase, 2011).

Currently, there are few adequately defined programs, creating a major challenge for service providers who are considering using evidence-based program models in their agency. In addition to a paucity of well-articulated programs, Michie, Fixsen, Grimshaw, and Eccles (2009) noted there is little empirical evidence regarding which essential components contribute to positive outcomes for children and families. One way to begin to address this important research and policy question is to design research that measures various components of a well-defined program model and then examine empirically the faithfulness with

---

Requirements for a Fully Operationalized Program or Initiative

1. *Clear description of the ECE program*

   a. *Clear philosophy, values, and principles.* The philosophy, values, and principles that underlie the ECE program provide guidance for all program decisions and evaluations (a "lived" set of values) and are used to promote consistency, integrity, and sustainable effort across all provider organization units (e.g., classrooms).

   b. *Clear inclusion and exclusion criteria* that define the population for which the program is intended. The criteria define who is most likely to benefit when the program is used as intended.

2. *Clear description of the essential functions* that define the ECE program. The "essential functions" are the features that must be present to say that an ECE program exists in a given location. They sometimes are called core intervention components, active ingredients, or practice elements.

3. *Practice profiles* that operationally define the essential functions (Hall & Hord, 2010). Practice profiles describe the core activities that allow an ECE program to be teachable, learnable, and doable in typical ECE settings and promote consistency across early care educators at the level of actual service delivery.

4. *A practical assessment of the performance of early care educators* who are using the ECE program. The performance assessment relates to the program philosophy, values, and principles, essential functions, and *core activities* specified in the practice profiles; assessments are practical and can be done repeatedly in the context of typical ECE settings.

5. *Evidence that the program is effective* when used as intended. The performance assessment (sometimes referred to as "fidelity" or "adherence") is highly correlated (.70 or better) with intended outcomes for children and families (see Chapter 4 for further exploration of this concept).

(Reprinted from Metz, A., Bartley, L., & Blase, K.A. [2011]. *Developing practice profiles.* Retrieved from http://www.fpg.unc.edu/~nirn.)

which practitioners carry out those key program components, and how practitioners' execution of those program components is associated with the intended program outcomes (see Chapter 4 for further discussion of the evaluation of core program components). However, another important part of the rigorous investigation of program effects is to assess the degree to which the necessary supports are in place for effective execution of all of the program components in real-world settings. This latter focus on the essential conditions under which effective implementation of an ECE program or initiative can be supported over time is the basis of *active implementation frameworks* posited by implementation science.

Effective Implementation and Sustainbility Frameworks

A set of active implementation frameworks has been developed by the National Implementation Research Network based on an extensive review of the literature (Blase, Van Dyke, & Fixsen, 2012; Fixsen, Blase, Duda, Naoom, & Van Dyke, 2010; Fixsen, Blase, Metz, & Van Dyke, 2013; Fixsen et al., 2005). It includes elements that have been demonstrated to promote effective implementation in a wide range of settings. In particular, there are implementation and sustainability frameworks that can be used to install and improve the necessary implementation infrastructure and align the systems and functions that will support the full and effective use of ECE innovations. These frameworks include the following:

- *Stages of implementation:* Four discernible implementation stages, with accompanying structural components and activities needed for successful practice, organizational, and system change

- *Core implementation components* or *implementation drivers:* Implementation strategies and processes that result in the competent and sustained use of ECE program models and innovations and ensure continuous improvement through data-driven decision making and feedback loops

Implementation Stages

As noted by Franks and Schroeder in Chapter 1, the process of implementation can be iterative and nonlinear. Nevertheless, there is substantial agreement that planned change is a recursive process that happens in discernible stages. It is clear that implementation is not an event but a process, involving multiple decisions, actions, and corrections to change the structures and conditions through which organizations and systems support and promote new program models, innovations, and initiatives. Implementing a well-constructed, well-defined, well-researched ECE program can be expected to take 2–4 years (Bierman et al., 2002; Fixsen, Blase, Timbers, & Wolf, 2001; Panzano & Roth, 2006; Prochaska & DiClemente, 1982; Solberg, Hroscikoski, Sperl-Hillen, O'Conner, & Crabtree, 2004).

Four functional stages of implementation have been identified: 1) exploration, 2) installation, 3) initial implementation, and 4) full implementation (see Figure 2.1). Sustainability is embedded within each of the four stages rather than considered a discrete, final stage. Each stage of implementation does not cleanly and crisply end as another begins. Often they overlap, with activities related to one stage still occurring or reoccurring as activities related to the next stage begin. Furthermore,

Implementation stages

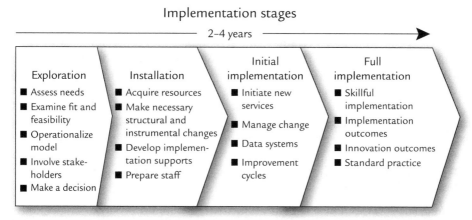

Figure 2.1.　Stages of implementation. (From Fixsen, D.L., & Blase, K.A. [2008]. *The National Implementation Research Network.* Chapel Hill: University of North Carolina, Frank Porter Graham Child Development Institute; reprinted by permission.)

depending on the factors and variables in the environment, implementation efforts may completely return to an earlier stage. For example, if there is significant staff turnover at the practitioner level, then an effort may move from being in the full implementation stage back to an initiative that is again in initial implementation. We describe each of the four stages in more detail below.

Exploration Stage　As a stage, exploration is often underutilized, and its importance to a successful implementation effort is not fully appreciated. In this first stage of implementation, ECE communities must assess the "goodness of fit" between potential ECE program models, innovations, and initiatives with the needs of the children and families they serve. Requirements for implementation must be carefully assessed and potential barriers to implementation examined. Decisions to adopt ECE innovations should involve assessments of need, level of evidence, readiness for replication, and resource availability. The overall goal of the exploration phase is to examine the degree to which a particular model, program, or approach meets the community's needs and whether implementation is feasible.

Systematically examining the requirements of ECE program models allows ECE providers and policy makers to better understand the criteria for selecting, training, and coaching staff; assessing fidelity; making the necessary organizational and system changes; and aligning policies, procedures, and data systems required by the potential model. The exploration stage draws to a close as a decision is made to either move forward with adoption and implementation of the examined program model or not move forward with that model and possibly explore other options.

Rogers (2003) provided a conceptual framework for the diffusion (i.e., widespread adoption) of innovations across social systems such as human services or education. Diffusion, or increased adoption, of a new innovation is dependent on the qualities of the innovation and the characteristics of those individuals who choose to adopt the new innovation. Rogers confirmed that there are stages related to how individuals make decisions about adopting (or not adopting) a new innovation, and attending to these stages is important to promoting the uptake of innovation over time. He also deduced that there are organizational characteristics that lead to early or late uptake.

This stage is characterized by frequent, iterative (or repeated) interactions among and between stakeholder groups, knowledgeable experts, and perhaps other sites or organizations that have already implemented the new way of work, the new program, or a similar plan. Interactions with purveyors are important during this stage. Purveyors are individuals or teams who have content knowledge of the new program or practice, understand the multilevel influences (e.g., regulations, funding, referral pathways) that affect implementation, and provide guidance on the implementation infrastructure needed to install, sustain, and scale up a program model or initiative (see Chapter 1 for further information on implementation terminology). Each stakeholder's perspectives, concerns, resources, and capacity are part of the equation that determines whether or not a particular approach will be adopted.

Installation Stage   Once a decision is made to adopt a program model, many structural and instrumental changes in a number of settings and systems must be made in order to initiate the new practices. Practical efforts to initiate the new program are central to the installation stage and include activities such as developing referral pathways (i.e., the means by which the target population is referred to services), ensuring that financial and human resources are in place, and finding physical space or purchasing equipment and technology. Often these critical, practical efforts are overlooked in the implementation process.

Developing the competence and confidence of ECE practitioners is a key component of this stage. Criteria and protocols for practitioner selection, training, coaching, and performance assessments are developed. In addition, steps are taken to ensure hospitable organizational and systems environments are created that support the new program model. For example, policies and procedures are developed and put in place that will facilitate uptake of the program model, and data systems are developed to measure fidelity and outcomes.

During installation, resources are being consumed in active preparation for actually doing things differently in keeping with the tenets of the new model, program, or plan. These installation stage activities and their associated start-up costs are necessary first steps to begin any new early care and education endeavor. As noted earlier, too often this stage is overlooked and a new program is simply inserted into the existing system without making the necessary infrastructure changes to support the new program model, leading to compromised implementation, low fidelity, and consequently disappointing outcomes for targeted populations.

Initial Implementation Stage   During the initial implementation stage, the new program model or initiative is put into practice. Attempts to implement a new program or innovation often end or seriously falter during the installation stage or early in the initial implementation stage. During initial implementation, the full brunt of influences at the practice, organization, and system levels are felt by everyone involved in launching the new program effort. Buy-in achieved during the exploration and installation stages may wane as individuals from every level of the ECE system (e.g., early childhood educators, supervisors, provider agency administrators, state leaders, stakeholders, service system partners) take on new roles and responsibilities to support the new program model or initiative. The overarching goal is to survive this "awkward stage" of high expectations and unavoidable challenges.

The key activities of the initial implementation stage involve strategies to promote continuous improvement and rapid-cycle problem solving. Using data to assess implementation, identify solutions, and drive decision making is a hallmark of this stage. It is critical to address barriers and develop system solutions quickly rather than allowing problems to reemerge and reoccur. Continuous improvement may call for changes in practice or policy, as well as dealing with some instrumental issues that were not apparent in early stages (e.g., how will teachers with limited access to the Internet actively participate in web-based professional development strategies?). Several chapters in this volume provide additional examples of how ECE practices and programs navigated this initial implementation stage.

A continued focus on buy-in is also a key feature of the initial implementation stage. New leaders, new community members, and new family, caregivers, and early childhood advocates are always entering the scene, and the need to provide them with information and discuss their contributions and concerns is ongoing. Overall, the change processes at all levels need to be managed. Managing change means anticipating issues, maintaining high rates of communication, solving problems, and creating systemic solutions whenever possible. It also helps to maintain an optimistic but realistic perspective.

Full Implementation Stage Full implementation occurs as the new learning becomes integrated into practice at the individual, organizational, and systems levels. The new program or innovation is now more skillfully provided by more experienced early childhood educators and supervisors. In addition, the processes and procedures to support the new way of work are in place. The system, while never completely stable, has largely been "recalibrated" to accommodate and hopefully fully support the new ways of work.

The time it takes to move from initial implementation to full implementation will vary depending on the complexity of the new program model, the baseline infrastructure, the availability of implementation supports and resources, and other contextual factors. But, as noted earlier, achieving full implementation may take anywhere from 2 to 4 years.

While data on fidelity to the core program components and fidelity to the core implementation components, as well as outcome data, must be collected from initiation of new practices or services (initial implementation), summative judgments about the effectiveness of the new program model can be made only when the full implementation stage has been reached. Benchmarks should be established early on as to what constitutes full implementation. Variables for the determination might include average length of early childhood educator experience, degree of fidelity, and functioning of the infrastructure and system components (e.g., funding and referral streams, training, coaching, or fidelity systems in place) or the amount of time that has elapsed since the new program or practice was initiated. Examples of specific indicators could be 80% of early care educators trained; 60% of early care educators implementing the new program model with fidelity; and data systems fully operating in 100% of ECE provider agencies.

Sustainability As noted above, sustainability is not a discrete stage but is considered a part of every stage. Sustainability planning and activities need to be an active component from the initial stages of implementation. To sustain an initiative, both financial and programmatic sustainability are required. Financial sustainability involves ensuring that the funding streams for the new practice are established, reliable, and adequate. In addition, there must be adequate funding for the infrastructure to maintain fidelity or maintain protocols. Programmatic sustainability is related to ensuring that sustainable supports are in place to continue effective training, coaching, and performance assessment protocols; to measure fidelity and make data-driven decisions for continuous improvement; and to ensure that facilitative policy making and procedural decisions continue to support full implementation.

Summary of Implementation Stages   There are several overall messages related to stages of implementation. First, each stage is critical to the overall process. Failure to attend to activities that are stage appropriate may result in conflicts, challenges, and issues that inhibit full implementation and positive outcomes. Second, it is important to engage in activities that match the stage of development of a new early childhood practice or initiative. For example, during the exploration stage, program staff and evaluation staff should focus on assessing issues related to fit and feasibility, readiness, and capacity, rather than measuring outcomes. Third, sustainability is not a separate stage that occurs only after full implementation; rather, the programmatic and financial considerations related to sustainability should be integrated into each stage and assessed throughout the implementation process.

Core Implementation Components: Implementation Drivers

Implementation drivers are the core components or "building blocks" of the infrastructure needed to support practice, organizational, and systems change. The implementation drivers emerged based on the commonalities among successfully implemented programs and practices across disciplines (Fixsen et al., 2005). The structural components and activities that make up each implementation driver contribute to the successful and sustainable implementation of programs, practices, and innovations (see Figure 2.2).

In the ECE context, implementation drivers are the essential components for implementing the ECE program or innovation, while core program or intervention components (described above) are the essential elements required for achieving desired outcomes for children and families. It should be noted that some ECE interventions may include or focus exclusively on outcomes for ECE providers or ECE systems rather than having explicit outcomes targeted at children and families, as noted in Figure 2.2. However, it is understood that the purpose of implementing these ECE initiatives is ultimately to benefit children and families.

According to Fixsen et al. (2005), there are three types of implementation drivers, and when used collectively, these drivers ensure high fidelity of the intervention and sustainable program implementation. *Competency drivers* are mechanisms to develop, improve, and sustain early childhood educators' and supervisors' ability to implement an ECE program model or innovation to benefit children and families. *Organization drivers* intentionally develop the organizational supports and systems interventions needed to create a hospitable environment for a new ECE program model by ensuring that the competency drivers are accessible and effective and data are used for continuous improvement. *Leadership drivers* are methods to distinguish

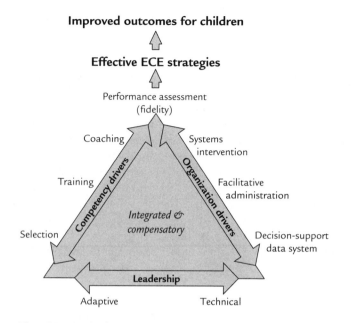

Figure 2.2. Core implementation drivers as they relate to early care and education practices, programs, and innovations. (From Fixsen, D.L., & Blase, K.A. [2008]. *The National Implementation Research Network*. Chapel Hill: University of North Carolina, Frank Porter Graham Child Development Institute; reprinted by permission.)

and manage technical problems where there are high levels of agreement about problems and high levels of certainty about solutions and to constructively deal with adaptive challenges where problems are not clear and solutions are elusive (Heifetz & Laurie, 1997). Effective leaders are continually assessing the functioning of competency and organization drivers to ensure the full and effective use of these drivers to support implementation and achieve desired outcomes and goals.

Whether implementing an ECE program model, practice, innovation, or initiative at the local, state, or federal level, it is critical that systematic attention be paid to ensuring an effective, sustainable implementation infrastructure. Operationalizing, developing, and installing each implementation driver enables the infrastructure to be built and eventually taken to scale if and when the innovation is replicated.

Below, we describe the individual drivers in more detail and identify recommended practices associated with each. Recommended practices were identified through an extensive review of the literature (Fixsen et al., 2005), intensive concept mapping, and nominal group processes with a number of successful purveyors of evidence-based and innovative program models (Blase, Fixsen, Naoom, & Wallace, 2005) and structured interviews with a random sample of evidence-based program developers (Naoom et al., 2010).

Competency Drivers The purpose of the competency drivers is to develop the confidence and competence of early childhood educators engaged in a new program or practice to ensure high-fidelity implementation of the new program or practice. Competency is built through the selection, coaching, and training of staff that is reflective of the knowledge, skills, and abilities needed to implement the new program or practice. Competency is then improved and sustained through ongoing staff performance assessments that measure early childhood practitioners' fidelity to the new model. The four competency drivers are selection, training, coaching and supervision, and performance assessment.

Selection Staff selection is the foundation for developing practitioner competency to implement a new ECE program or practice with fidelity. Basic selection criteria include the knowledge, skills, and abilities to carry out the new ECE program or practice with benefits to children and families. These criteria may include levels of education and experience. However, it is also critical to consider program-specific attributes and characteristics that are not easily trained or coached and therefore must be considered predetermined selection criteria. For example, selection prerequisites for an early childhood home visiting program might include the ability to consider family strengths in service planning, as well as the ability to engender trust and engage the family in service planning. Selection criteria (including when staff are reassigned) should be informed by the ECE program's guiding theory and philosophical underpinnings, core program model components, and practitioner roles and responsibilities. Recommended practices in staff selection (NIRN, 2011) include the following:

- Specification of required skills, abilities, and other model-specific prerequisite characteristics
- Methods for recruiting likely candidates who possess these skills and abilities
- Protocols for interviewing candidates
- Criteria for selecting practitioners with those skills and abilities

Training High-fidelity and sustainable implementation of a new ECE program or practice will require behavior change in early childhood practitioners. During the early stages of implementation, training and coaching are the primary mechanisms for changing practitioner behavior. Model-specific training helps practitioners (and others) in an organization learn when, where, how, and with whom to use (and not to use) new approaches and new skills. Implementation-informed training will provide more than an orientation to the new practice or approach. It will also provide staff with opportunities to practice new skills and receive constructive feedback. Regardless of the specific ECE model or practice, there are common strategies for effective training, including skill-based demonstrations, behavior rehearsals, and the opportunity to practice to a set of predetermined criteria (Joyce & Showers, 2002; Schoenwald, Brown, & Henggeler, 2000). Recommended practices for training (NIRN, 2011) include the following:

- Providing knowledge related to the history, theory, philosophy, and values of the program
- Introducing the components and rationales of key practices
- Providing opportunities to practice new skills to a criterion and receive feedback in a safe and supportive training environment

Coaching and Supervision While implementation-informed training models provide the foundation for behavior change among practitioners, training alone will not sustain high-fidelity implementation over time (Joyce & Showers, 2002).

Coaching early childhood practitioners is essential because most skills needed by successful practitioners can be assessed during selection and introduced in training but really are learned on the job with the help of a coach (Bertram, Blase, Shern, Shea, & Fixsen, 2011). Denton, Vaughn, and Fletcher (2003) examined the factors that facilitate maintenance of the practices teachers learn in professional development experiences. Foremost among these factors is the provision of coaching and mentoring, delivered either by an expert or a peer or group of peers. The authors estimate that teachers need to engage in about 25 teaching episodes implementing the new practice before the integration of the practice into their repertoire of strategies is complete and maintenance is likely. Further practice helps refine and maintain implementation of the new strategy. Recommended practices for coaching (NIRN, 2011) include the following:

- Developing and implementing a coaching service delivery plan that stipulates where, when, with whom, and why coaching will occur
- Using multiple sources of data to provide feedback to practitioners, including direct observation
- Using coaching data to improve practice and organizational fidelity

Performance Assessment   The final competency driver related to successful implementation is performance assessment. Each competency driver is linked to the others. Performance assessment is designed to assess the use and outcomes of the skills that are reflected in the selection criteria, taught in training, and reinforced and expanded in coaching processes. Assessments of practitioner performance are directly related to measures of practitioner fidelity and provide feedback useful to key staff implementing the new ECE program or practice. Measures of practitioner performance are an indicator of how the overall organizational system is functioning and provide opportunities for each level of the system (practitioners, program managers, administrators, leadership) to make changes to support practitioners' ability to use new skills with high fidelity. Performance assessment data are used to reinforce strengths and build the competency and confidence of practitioners. Data can also be used to assess strategies for improving selection, training, and coaching methods. Recommended practices for performance assessment (NIRN, 2011) include the following:

- Developing and implementing transparent staff performance assessments
- Using multiple sources of data to assess performance, including direct observation
- Instituting positive recognition so assessments are seen as an opportunity to improve performance
- Using performance assessment data to improve practice and organizational fidelity

Organization Drivers   The purpose of organization drivers is to create and sustain hospitable organizational and systems environments for effective services. Organization drivers support the effective use of the competency drivers, ensure data-driven decision making and feedback loops are in place, and use data for continuous improvement. The three organization drivers are facilitative administration, systems interventions, and decision-support data systems.

Facilitative Administration In early childhood programs, every administrative decision is also a decision about children and families. Facilitative administration makes use of a range of data inputs to inform decision making, support the overall programmatic and implementation processes, and keep practitioners organized and focused on the desired program outcomes. In an organization with facilitative administrators, careful attention is given to policies, procedures, structures, culture, and climate to assure alignment of these aspects of an organization with the needs of practitioners. When using an implementation-informed approach, the goal of facilitative administration is to realign, repurpose, and restructure existing organizational functions to support the new way of work. In order to accomplish this, facilitative administration requires clear communication and feedback loops within the entire organization and the use of data to monitor program functioning and improve implementation supports. Recommended practices for performance assessment (NIRN, 2011) include the following:

- Ensuring leadership is committed to the new program or practice and available to address challenges and create solutions
- Developing clear communication protocols and feedback loops
- Adjusting and developing policies and procedures to support the new way of work
- Reducing administrative barriers to ensure a hospitable environment for high-fidelity program (or practice) implementation

Systems Interventions Fidelity, outcomes, and sustainability are all directly or indirectly influenced by multiple systems—local, state, federal, provider, and organization. Alignment of external systems to specifically support the work of practitioners is an important aspect of systems interventions. Systems interventions are strategies for leaders and staff within an organization to work with external systems to ensure the availability of the financial, organizational, and human resources required to support the work of the practitioners. They are designed to help create a generally supportive context in which effective services can be provided, maintained, and improved over the years. Recommended practices for systems interventions (NIRN, 2011) include the following:

- Forming and supporting an early childhood leadership team
- Developing formal processes to ensure policy–practice feedback loops and bidirectional communication across and within levels of a system
- Engaging and nurturing champions and opinion leaders

Decision-Support Data Systems Decision-support data systems provide data to guide decisions about practitioner performance, organizational and system changes, and child and family outcomes. Data systems should provide information on fidelity and the correlation between fidelity and child outcomes. These data should be relevant, available, accessible, and collected at actionable levels so that all levels of the system (practitioners, managers, administrators, communities) can make use of these data for continuous improvement. "Data systems truly become *decision support data systems* by creating conditions under which data can be understood and used" (Bertram et al., 2011). Recommended practices for the data systems driver include the following:

- Collecting fidelity data (performance assessment)
- Collecting short-term, intermediate, and long-term outcome data
- Ensuring data are reliable, reported frequently, built into practice routines, accessible at actionable levels, and used to make decisions
- Instituting feedback loops so that the organization can use data to adjust aspects of the system to improve effectiveness and efficiency

Leadership Drivers   The purpose of the leadership drivers is to attend to both technical and adaptive leadership strategies and to ensure that appropriate methods are used to address different types of challenges. Heifetz and Laurie (1997) discriminated between technical and adaptive leadership strategies and provided an overall framework for the leadership drivers.

Technical Leadership   Technical leadership is appropriate when there are high levels of agreement about problems and high levels of certainty about solutions. Technical challenges are best solved by traditional leadership approaches where the primary locus of responsibility for organizing the work is a single individual who can provide specific guidance on processes that will result in good outcomes. Technical leaders are good at providing specific recommendations and rationales for changes in policies or procedures. They are involved in decision making at every level of the system and focused on issues that affect implementation, and they are fair, considerate, and inclusive.

Adaptive Leadership   Adaptive leadership is appropriate when legitimate yet competing perspectives emerge, the definition of the problem is unclear, the solution is unclear and requires learning, or the primary locus of control is not one individual. Problem solving involves changes in philosophy, values, and beliefs; methods of interaction; and approaches to accomplishing goals. Solutions may be experimental, take a long time to implement, and face resistance. Adaptive leaders convene groups and work to build consensus, align practices with the overall mission and values of an organization, actively and routinely seek feedback from practitioners, and ensure policy–practice feedback loops are in place and open lines of communication exist.

Driver Integration   Implementation drivers must be integrated and compensatory to make full and effective use of new program models, practices, and innovations. Driver functioning must be intentionally aligned to promote practitioner fidelity and achieve optimal child and family outcomes. For example, the facilitative administrative driver should promote policies and procedures that align with effective training and coaching strategies. Driver functioning must also be compensatory, so that weaknesses in one driver are compensated by another. For example, if training resources are limited, strengthening the coaching driver or performance assessment driver would be necessary to help ensure practitioner fidelity.

Intersection of Core Implementation Components and Stages of Implementation

The implementation drivers play a critical role at each stage of implementation. Stage-based activities include operationalizing and analyzing driver functioning

Table 2.1.   Key questions about implementation drivers as they emerge at each stage of implementation

Stages	Competency drivers	Organization drivers
	Selection, training, coaching, and performance assessments	*Facilitative administration, systems intervention, and decision-support data system*
Exploration	How well does the potential program model align with current staffing structures and procedures? Does the new program model seem feasible to implement, given the staffing structure in the organization? Who is qualified to carry out this practice? How many staff are needed? Are there workforce development issues? Is training available and affordable? Will training provide practitioners with foundational skills prior to implementation? Have coaching and supervision activities been defined? Are there resources available to support coaching and performance assessments?	How well does the potential program model align with the organization's mission, leadership priorities, and community needs? Does the new program model seem feasible to implement, given the organization's structure and priorities? What process and outcome data will need to be collected and analyzed to support high-fidelity implementation? What data system and technology requirements exist? Who will evaluate data? What policies or procedures will need to be changed or developed to support implementation? Has the "fit" and interface with external systems been assessed? What partnerships may need to be developed or strengthened?
Installation	Have new interview protocols and hiring criteria been developed? Are these protocols attracting staff with the desired skills and abilities? Is there a process established to feed interview information into training and coaching content? Have training plans been developed that are aligned with new practices and needs based on the interviews? Is there a plan for feeding training data backward to staff in charge of recruitment and selection? Have coaching service delivery plans been developed based on the program model and information from hiring interviews?	Have appropriate fidelity and outcome measures been identified? Have policies, procedures, organizational structures, and finances adjusted to support the new way of work? Is there a process for monitoring these policies, procedures, organizational structures, and financial changes as they relate to the program model? Are plans under way to build partnerships and work with external systems to support implementation? What external partners are not involved but should be? Will multiple data sources be used to assess staff performance? Have these sources been identified? Is there a plan to collect short-term, intermediate, and long-term outcome data? Is there a plan to collect fidelity data?
Initial Implementation	Have appropriate staff been recruited and hired? Has preservice training been conducted? Has coaching commenced with staff? Are coaching and performance assessment data reviewed at least quarterly to promote fidelity? Is there a process for ensuring that staff receive positive recognition and reinforcement for participation in the new service? Is there a process in place to feed back performance assessment with staff and used in coaching?	Are data provided on a regularly scheduled basis for practitioners, coaches, and administrators? Are policies and procedures implemented and monitored to support implementation? Have key external partnerships been formed? Are champions engaged and nurtured? Are adaptive and technical problems identified, discussed, and unraveled by facilitative administration and implementation teams?

Table 2.1.   *(continued)*

Stages	Competency drivers	Organization drivers
	Selection, training, coaching, and performance assessments	*Facilitative administration, systems intervention, and decision-support data system*
Full Implementation	Are recruitment and interview protocols effective? Do selection criteria need to be changed? Is training delivered with fidelity? Is training effective? Is coaching delivered with fidelity? Is coaching correlated with improved practitioner fidelity? Are there performance assessment issues that are being experienced across staff that may warrant a policy or procedural change? Is staff performance related to improvement in expected outcomes?	Are data reviewed regularly? Are data used to inform decision making? Are identified individuals accountable? Are organizational changes in policies and procedures supporting implementation? What administrative barriers exist? How can these barriers be addressed? Are systems partnerships actively supporting implementation? Is leadership at every level constantly working to identify and tackle technical and adaptive challenges?

throughout the implementation process. Table 2.1 contains key questions to guide discussion around stage-based driver work.

Implementation Support

Traditional approaches to disseminating and implementing evidence-based programs, practices, and innovations for children and families have not been successful in closing the research-to-practice gap. In extensive reviews of the dissemination and diffusion literature (Hord & Hall, 1997; Greenhalgh, Robert, MacFarlane, Bate, & Kyriakidou, 2004), past efforts to support implementation have been characterized as "letting it happen" or "helping it happen." Approaches that let implementation happen leave it to state leaders, practitioners, and policy makers to make use of research findings on their own. Approaches that help it happen provide manuals or websites to "help" implementation happen in real-world settings. Both of these approaches have been found to be insufficient for promoting the full and effective use of innovations (Balas & Boren, 2000; Clancy, 2006).

Greenhalgh et al. (2004) identified a new category they called "making it happen," which involves expert implementation teams using evidence-based implementation strategies to actively support implementation of a new innovation or initiative with demonstrated greater success than traditional dissemination methods. Blase et al. (2005) provided qualitative reviews of recommended practices in use by successful implementation teams and have helped to operationalize the "making it happen" category identified by Greenhalgh and colleagues.

Implementation teams can take on different forms and structures. Some implementation teams utilize external expert assistance. For example, program developers and purveyors of individual ECE program models actively work to help communities and states implement ECE innovations with fidelity and good effect. Purveyors are often affiliated with researchers and training and technical assistance centers. As another example, implementation teams may use intermediary organizations that help others implement a variety of evidence-based and innovative ECE programs and practices. Intermediary organizations help communities and states build an infrastructure to facilitate the adoption, implementation, and sustainability of a number of innovations by 1) broadly educating and stimulating interest, 2) assessing the "evidence," 3) connecting program developers and purveyors with implementing agencies, 4) ensuring effective implementation and fidelity, 5) building capacity and integrating efforts, 6) managing "scale-up shifts," and 7) assisting with alignment (Franks et al., 2010).

Other implementation teams are developed on site with support from groups outside the organization or system. Local implementation teams are accountable for making it happen and assuring that effective interventions and effective implementation methods are in use to produce intended outcomes for children and families. Implementation teams provide a structure to move programs and practices through stages of implementation. They focus on 1) increasing buy-in and readiness, 2) installing and sustaining the implementation drivers, 3) assessing fidelity and outcomes, 4) building linkages with external systems, and 5) problem solving and sustainability.

An advantage of relying on implementation teams is that the team collectively has the knowledge, skills, abilities, and time to succeed. Collectively, the core competencies of the implementation team include 1) knowledge and understanding of core program components and linkages to outcomes, 2) knowledge of implementation science and recommended practices for implementation (e.g., stage-based work, installation of implementation drivers), and 3) applied experience in using data for program improvement and instituting continuous improvement cycles.

There is evidence that using implementation teams to make it happen produces higher rates of success more quickly than traditional methods of implementation. For example, Fixsen, Blase, Timbers, and Wolf (2001) reported 80% success in about 3 years with implementation teams using the active methods for implementation. By contrast, Balas and Boren (2000) report just 14% success after about 17 years without the use of implementation teams. While there is evidence to demonstrate that such teams are important ingredients to successful implementation, teams with the requisite ECE innovation and implementation expertise are not common. To produce socially significant impacts for children and families, it is important to include implementation teams throughout the implementation stages.

Implementation Teams During Exploration   Creating readiness for individuals and organizations is an important part of the work and effectiveness of implementation teams. Prochaska, Prochaska, and Levesque (2001) found that about 20% of individuals and organizations in their studies were "ready for change." Thus, creating readiness is an essential function for implementation teams during the first stage of implementation. This stage is complete only when the necessary buy-in and support for the new ways of work have been achieved. (See Chapter 3 for further consideration of readiness to change.)

Implementation Teams During Installation   Implementation teams help organizations and communities, and states amass the resources needed ensure that new procedures work fully and effectively. Implementation teams ensure that implementation drivers have been defined and installed for the new ECE program model or practice. They play a role in developing implementation resources such as new job descriptions and hiring protocols, training and coaching guidelines, data systems, administrative supports, and external partnerships.

Implementation Teams During the Initial Implementation Stage   As ECE professionals are implementing new programs and practices, the implementation team members are actively using and assessing the implementation drivers to ensure full and effective use of the new program models. Implementation teams are helping to develop the staff competencies required by the new ECE program model, helping administrators and leaders adjust organization functions to align with the new program, and promoting ongoing buy-in and readiness of practitioners and leaders. Implementation teams are actively using data for continuous improvement, instituting clear communication protocols, promoting policy–practice feedback loops, and helping to intervene in external systems when barriers are encountered.

Implementation Teams During the Full Implementation Stage   As the new way of work becomes routinized and institutionalized, implementation teams remain an essential contributor to the success of using a new ECE program model or practice. As turnover takes place among ECE practitioners, staff, administrators, and leaders, the implementation team ensures that new staff develop the competencies to carry the ECE program model or practice and that organizational supports are in place to facilitate the work of ECE practitioners.

Implications for Early Care and Education Practice, Research, and Evaluaton

Science-based implementation strategies promote the full and effective use of ECE program models, practices, and initiatives so that child and family outcomes are improved. To summarize, the key ingredients to implementation success include the following:

- The purposeful selection of an effective and feasible ECE program model or practice that is well defined with clearly articulated fidelity measures, expected outcomes, and guidelines for adaptation if necessary

- A conceptual framework to support the change process so that effective ECE practitioner practices can become embedded and sustained in socially complex settings; this conceptual framework consists of stage-matched activities that guide the implementation process and implementation drivers that build the infrastructure necessary to promote and sustain the new way of work

- Continuous improvement processes and data feedback loops between the policy and practice levels to ensure that changes are made at every level of the system to support the new program model or practice

- Organized expert implementation support in the form of implementation teams that serve as an accountable structure to move through the stages of implementation successfully

Examples of Implementation Frameworks in Action with Early Care and Education Practices and Programs

While in this chapter we have gone to great lengths in explicating the various frameworks and components of effective implementation, the core features of effective implementation can essentially be summarized by three concepts: the *what,* the *how,* and the *who* of implementation. The *what* is the clearly defined ECE practice or program to be installed in real-world settings for particular populations. The *how* is the implementation strategies and frameworks that lead to hospitable organizational environments and competent practitioners who support the effective installation and sustainability of innovative ECE practices or programs. The *who* is the individuals who make successful delivery of an intervention possible—that is, the implementation teams. To fully appreciate the way effective implementation practices and frameworks can inform the field of ECE research and practice, it is helpful to consider a few concrete examples of these frameworks and principles in action. We therefore offer here one example of an early childhood practice for consideration: the appropriate use of child assessments.

The What: *Effective Use of Early Childhood Assessments in Head Start*   All good implementation starts with a clearly defined practice or program. With regard to the effective use of early childhood assessments, clearly defined research-based guidelines on how to select and use early childhood assessments have been outlined by a National Research Council (NRC; 2008) report. For example, one of those critical guidelines is that assessments should be chosen based on the purpose for which they will be used. Other guidelines include choosing child assessments that are developmentally appropriate, valid, and reliable for the populations being assessed.

The reauthorization of Head Start through the Improving Head Start for School Readiness Act of 2007 (PL 110-134) required Head Start programs to follow the NRC report's recommendations. Specifically, Head Start programs are now required to choose child assessments that are developmentally appropriate, valid, reliable, and culturally and linguistically appropriate for the populations they serve. More recently, the Designation Renewal System (instituted through passage of Federal Regulation 1307) also included Head Start requirements related to assessment. According to this regulation, programs must use child assessment data for individualization (which has always been part of Head Start performance standards) and for informing program-level planning. Thus, the selection and use of early childhood assessments in Head Start programs is guided by research-based recommended practices.

The How: *Effective Use of Early Childhood Assessments*   Both the NRC report and the framework of implementation drivers assert that selecting an appropriate tool is only the beginning of ensuring that children benefit from the effective use of child assessment tools. For children and early childhood programs to benefit, one needs to select not only the appropriate tool for the purpose and population but also the *appropriate staff* to administer the tool. In most cases, Head Start teachers and home visitors are the individuals administering the assessments. Appropriate and adequate *training of the staff* in the child assessment tool must also occur, and *ongoing support and coaching* should insure that there is no "drift" in the use of the tool. *Performance assessments* should be carried out both for those who train the Head Start teachers in the use of the tool and for those teachers who are using the tool. In this way, the competency of the individuals carrying out the child assessments (i.e., the competency drivers) is insured.

In addition, the appropriate *institutional infrastructure* must be in place to support the appropriate use of child assessments. This may include time and funding for staff to be trained in the use of the tool, providing an adequate amount of time for teachers or home visitors to administer the assessment (which may include one-to-one time with the children), additional staff to provide appropriate ratios in the classroom while teachers work one-on-one with children or parents (if that is the type of assessment selected by the program), and time and resources for staff (who may be managers or administrators) to enter data and meet with teachers, home visitors, and parents to reflect on the results of the assessment. These represent the organization drivers noted earlier in this chapter.

Of course, there will likely be both technical and adaptive challenges to the appropriate use of child assessments. An example of a *technical challenge* may be building a computer-based reporting system to store the child assessment data and link those data to other programmatic information; another could be addressing the skills Head Start teachers need to upload data using such a reporting system. An *adaptive challenge* may emerge when Head Start administrators and teachers don't agree on the primary purpose for collecting the child assessment data. Another adaptive challenge for Head Start programs is determining how to use data for multiple purposes—for example, for individualized instruction of children as well as for making progress toward school readiness goals, informing professional development, and curriculum planning, as newly required by the Designation Renewal System.

These competency drivers, organization drivers, and leadership issues around technical and adaptive challenges will function dynamically across all stages of implementation, from exploring the use of child assessments to installation, initial implementation, and full implementation of the research-based practice.

Implementation Teams: Supporting Effective Use of Early Childhood Assessments in Head Start   In terms of the individuals who are intentionally supporting the effective use of child assessments in Head Start programs, there are different implementation teams at various levels of the system. For example, at the *program level*, the implementation team may include the Head Start director and the education coordinators/managers, and perhaps also mental health consultants. These are the individuals who are supporting the actual implementers (i.e., the teachers and home visitors who are being asked to change their behaviors around child assessment or use a new child assessment instrument). The director can provide the funds to purchase assessment tools, the professional development time to train teachers on their appropriate use, and the staff to provide adequate classroom ratios while either training on the tool or assessment administration is taking place. Education coordinators/managers and mental health consultants can craft the training and provide ongoing supervision and oversight, as needed.

At the *state or regional level*, regional program managers and state-based technical assistance providers offer technical assistance or professional development activities around child assessment. Some of the training may be offered through the local resource and referral agency or local community colleges.

At the *national level*, the Office of Head Start has created a Training and Technical Assistance Network that intentionally provides support for those who are tasked with fulfilling the child assessment requirements for Head Start programs.

All five national centers are involved in issues related to assessment. Finally, federal staff also play a role by providing guidance on regulations. As with the implementation drivers, implementation teams will also be active at each stage of implementation, although their roles and functions may vary depending on the stage of implementation.

Implications for Early Care and Education Research and Program Evaluation

There are several key takeaway messages from the information shared in this chapter. First, implementation science can be integrated into early childhood programs and systems as well as the evaluation of those programs and systems. Furthermore, these implementation frameworks and principles can be successfully applied to implementing evidence-based and evidence-informed ECE programs and practices.

The implementation of early childhood *systems* (e.g., professional development systems, quality improvement systems) is complex, but it can benefit from applying an implementation perspective. In particular, implementers of early childhood programs and systems need to pay attention to scaling up the infrastructure that will support the effective implementation of their activities just as much as implementing the program itself. As a part of this work, implementation teams must be ready to support programs and individuals through the scaling process. Furthermore, these teams can offer this support by staying engaged at each stage of implementation. The chapters in Section IV of this volume explore this issue in further detail.

We posit that developing a shared framework for implementation will increase the generalizability of implementation findings beyond immediate ECE projects or initiatives, enhance communication among key stakeholder groups with a vested interest in the quality implementation of ECE interventions and programs, and increase the relevance of lessons learned for the ECE community. Furthermore, a common implementation framework will increase the awareness of what it takes to implement a well-defined ECE approach with fidelity, provide a frame by which implementation can be evaluated for the purposes of program improvement, and provide a useful lens through which implementation of ECE programs may be studied empirically.

References

Balas, E.A., & Boren, S.A. (2000). Managing clinical knowledge for health care improvement. In J. Bemmel & A.T. McCray (Eds.), *Yearbook of medical informatics 2000: Patient-centered systems* (pp. 65–70). Stuttgart, Germany: Schattauer Verlagsgesellschaft.

Barnett, W.S. (2002). Early childhood education. In A. Molnar (Ed.), *School reform proposals: The research evidence* (pp. 1–26). Greenwich, CT: Information Age.

Bertram, R., Blase, K., Shern, D., Shea, P., & Fixsen, D. (2011). *Policy Research Brief: Implementation opportunities and challenges for prevention and promotion initiatives*. Alexandria, VA: National Association of State Mental Health Programs.

Bierman, K.L., Coie, J.D., Dodge, K.A., Greenberg, M.T., Lochman, J.E., McMahon, R.J., & Pinderhughes, E. (2002). The implementation of the fast track program: An example of a large-scale prevention science efficacy trial. *Journal of Abnormal Child Psychology, 30*, 1–17.

Blase, K.A., Fixsen, D.L., Naoom, S.F., & Wallace, F. (2005). *Operationalizing implementation: Strategies and methods*. Tampa, FL: University of South Florida, Louis de la Parte Florida Mental Health Institute.

Blase, K., Van Dyke, M., & Fixsen, D. (2012). Implementation science: Key concepts, themes, and evidence for practitioners in educational psychology. In B. Kelly & D. Perkins (Eds.), *Handbook of implementation science for psychology in education: How to promote evidence-based practice.* London, England: Cambridge University Press.

Clancy, C. (2006). The $1.6 trillion question: If we're spending so much on healthcare, why so little improvement in quality? *Medscape General Medicine, 8,* 58.

Dearing, E., McCartney, K., & Taylor, B.A. (2009). Does higher quality early child care promote low-income children's math and reading achievement in middle childhood? *Child Development, 80,* 1329–1349.

Denton, C.A., Vaughn, S., & Fletcher, J. (2003). Bringing research-based practice in reading intervention to scale. *Learning Disabilities Research & Practice, 18,* 201–211.

Durlak, J.A., & DuPre, E.P. (2008). Implementation matters: A review on the influence of implementation on program outcomes and the factors affecting implementation. *American Journal of Community Psychology, 41,* 327–350.

Fixsen, D.L., & Blase, K.A. (2008). *The National Implementation Research Network.* Chapel Hill: University of North Carolina, Frank Porter Graham Child Development Institute.

Fixsen, D.L., Blase, K., Duda, M., Naoom, S., & Van Dyke, M. (2010). Implementation of evidence-based treatments for children and adolescents: Research findings and their implications for the future. In J. Weisz & A. Kazdin (Eds.), *Implementation and dissemination: Extending treatments to new populations and new settings* (2nd ed., pp. 435–450). New York, NY: Guilford Press.

Fixsen, D., Blase, K., Metz, A., & Van Dyke, M.V. (2013). Statewide implementation of evidence-based programs. *Exceptional Children, 79*(2), 213–230.

Fixsen, D.L., Blase, K.A., Timbers, G.D., & Wolf, M.M. (2001). In search of program implementation: 792 replications of the Teaching-Family Model. In G.A. Bernfeld, D.P. Farrington, & A.W. Leschied (Eds.), *Offender rehabilitation in practice: Implementation and evaluating effective programs* (pp. 149–166). London, England: Wiley.

Fixsen, D.L., Naoom, S.F., Blase, K.A., Friedman, R.M., & Wallace, F. (2005). *Implementation research: A synthesis of the literature* (FMHI Publication No. 231). Tampa, FL: University of South Florida, Louis de la Parte Florida Mental Health Institute, National Implementation Research Network.

Franks, R.P. (2010). Role of the intermediary organization in promoting and disseminating mental health best practices for children and youth: The Connecticut Center for Effective Practice. *Emotional & Behavioral Disorders in Youth, 10,* 87–93.

Greenhalgh, T., Robert, G., MacFarlane, F., Bate, P., & Kyriakidou, O. (2004). Diffusion of innovations in service organizations: Systematic review and recommendations. *Milbank Quarterly, 82,* 581–629.

Hall, G.E., & Hord, S.M. (1987). *Change in schools: Facilitating the process.* Albany, NY: SUNY Press.

Hall, G.E., & Hord, S.M. (2010). *Implementing change: Patterns, principles and potholes.* Upper Saddle River, NJ: Pearson.

Hall, G.E., & Hord, S.M. (2011). *Implementing change: Patterns, principles and potholes* (3rd ed.). Boston, MA: Allyn & Bacon.

Hall, G.E., Hord, S.M., Stiegelbauer, S.M., Dirksen, D.J., & George, A.A. (2006). *Measuring implementation in schools.* Austin, TX: Southwest Educational Development Laboratory.

Heifetz, R.A., & Laurie, D.L. (1997). The work of leadership. *Harvard Business Review, 75,* 124–134.

Improving Head Start for School Readiness Act of 1007 § 1307, 42 U.S.C. § 9801 (2007).

Institute of Medicine. Committee on Quality of Health Care in America. (2001). *Crossing the quality chasm: A new health system for the 21st century.* Washington, DC: National Academy Press.

Joyce, B., & Showers, B. (2002). *Student achievement through staff development.* Alexandria, VA: Association for Supervision and Curriculum Development.

Loeb, S., Fuller, B., Kagan, S.L., & Carrol, B. (2004). Child care in poor communities: Early learning effects of type, quality, and stability. *Child Development, 75,* 47–65.

McCartney, K., Burchinal, M.R., Clarke-Stewart, A., Bub, K.L., Owen, M.T., Belsky, J., & NICHD Early Child Care Research Network. (2010). Testing a series of causal propositions relating time in child care to children's externalizing behavior. *Developmental Psychology,* *46,* 1–17.

Metz, A., Bartley, L., & Blase, K.A. (2011). *Developing practice profiles.* Retrieved from http://www.fpg.unc.edu/~nirn

Mitchie, S., Fixsen, D., Grimshaw, J.M., & Eccles, M.P. (2009). Specifying and reporting complex behaviour change interventions: The need for a scientific method. *Implementation Science, 4,* 1–6.

Naoom, S.F., Van Dyke, M., Fixsen, D.L., Blase, K.A., & Villagomez, A.N. (2012). Developing implementation capacity of organizations and systems to support effective uses of family literacy programs. In B. Wasik (Ed.), *Handbook of family literacy* (2nd ed.) (pp. 447–464). New York, NY: Routledge.

National Research Council. (2008). *Early childhood assessment: Why, what, and how.* Committee on Developmental Outcomes and Assessments for Young Children, C.E. Snow, & S.B. Van Hemel (Eds.). Washington, DC: National Academies Press.

National Research Council and Institute of Medicine. (2009). *Preventing mental, emotional and behavioral disorders among young people: Progress and possibilities.* M.E. O'Connell, T. Boat, & K.E. Warner (Eds.). Washington, DC: National Academies Press.

NICHD Early Child Care Research Network, & Duncan, G. (2003). Does quality of child care affect child outcomes at age 4 1/2? *Developmental Psychology, 39,* 451–469.

NIRN. (2011). Additional evidence for staff selection. Retrieved from http://nirn.fpg.unc.edu/sites/nirn.fpg.unc.edu/files/resources/NIRN-AdditionalEvidence-StaffSelection.pdf

Panzano, P.C., & Roth, D. (2006). The decision to adopt evidence and other innovative mental health practices: Risky business? *Psychiatric Services, 57,* 1153–1161.

Prochaska, J.O., & DiClemente, C.C. (1982). Transtheoretical therapy: Toward a more integrative model of change. *Psychotherapy, 19,* 276–287.

Prochaska, J.M., Prochaska, J.O., & Levesque, D.A. (2001). A transtheoretical approach to changing organizations. *Administration and Policy in Mental Health and Mental Health Services Research, 28,* 247–261.

Rogers, E.M. (2003). *Diffusion of innovations.* New York, NY: Free Press.

Schoenwald, S.K., Brown, T.C., & Henggeler, S.W. (2000). Inside multisystemic therapy: Therapist, supervisory and program practices. *Journal of Emotional and Behavioral Disorders, 8,* 113–127.

Solberg, L.I., Hroscikoski, M.C., Sperl-Hillen, J.M., O'Conner, P.J., & Crabtree, B.F. (2004). Key issues in transforming health care organizations for quality: The case of advanced access. *Joint Commission Journal on Quality and Safety, 30,* 14–24.

Tran, H., & Weinraub, M. (2006). Quality, stability, and multiplicity in nonmaternal child care arrangements during the first 15 months of life. *Developmental Psychology, 42,* 566–582.

Yoshikawa, H. (1995). Long-term effects of early childhood programs on social outcomes and delinquency. *Future of Children, 5,* 51–75.

CHAPTER 3

Readiness to Change

Effective Implementation
Processes for Meeting People Where They Are

Shira M. Peterson

W hen it comes to implementing evidence-based practices in early care and education (ECE), why is it important to talk about readiness to change? The reason is that the concept of readiness to change—defined here as "the combination of internal and external resources that are available to support meaningful and sustained change in a particular behavior" (Peterson & Baker, 2011, p. 34)—helps us see that implementation is a matter not only of "making things happen" but also of understanding what is happening and why and of engaging in collaborative processes to "meet people where they are."

Many behavior change initiatives assume that most people are ready to engage in immediate behavior change; however, it is compelling to learn that, across a range of behaviors, typically only about one out of five people is ready to engage in immediate change (Prochaska & Velicer, 1997). A large body of research has demonstrated that when programs are tailored to match individuals' readiness to change, participants are more likely to stay in the program, demonstrate openness to receiving new information, and make positive behavior change (Noar, Benac, & Harris, 2007; Prochaska, DiClemente, Velicer, & Rossi, 1993). The National Institutes of Health's Behavior Change Consortium has recommended that all behavior change programs be tailored to participants' readiness to change (Ory, Jordan, & Bazzarre, 2002).

It is becoming clear that these findings are relevant for implementation efforts in the context of early childhood programs. It seems likely that many implementation efforts in our field have failed because there was not sufficient time and effort invested to recognize and respond to the readiness to change of the people expected to be doing the implementation. In an interview, William Miller (n.d.) described how our understanding of readiness to change has changed since the 1990s: In the past, he observed, "If people didn't seem to have the motivation for change, they were blamed for it. We even said things like, 'Come back when you're motivated.'" But the field has progressed. "What's changed," Miller explained, "is the sense that motivation is part of our job in helping people. It's part of our job to help people find motivation, that's already there inside the person."

Today, assessing and responding to readiness to change is recognized as a key aspect of the work that is done in the early stages of implementation. During the *exploration* stage, in particular, conducting formal and informal assessments of staff and organizational readiness provides a picture of the readiness to change of staff. Assessing readiness at this earliest point can shape all other implementation processes that take place from that moment forward, including the choice of what and when to implement, the type and intensity of support required, and the timeline for implementation. This step is also crucial for reducing implementation costs: By identifying appropriate supports for staff based on their readiness to change, initiatives can avoid the waste of resources that results from offering the same "one-size-fits-all" type of support to those who are not ready to benefit.

Readiness is also considered during subsequent stages of implementation. During *installation*, support strategies to increase readiness are put in place. Staff readiness can then be assessed once again to determine whether further efforts are needed to increase readiness or whether staff are sufficiently ready to begin implementation. During *initial* and *full implementation*, readiness is monitored so that support staff can continue to bolster the necessary internal and external supports for the planned implementation. These strategies remain ongoing throughout the later stages of implementation so that new staff are supported and new challenges are addressed as they arise.

This chapter will address theoretical and practical implications of readiness to change principles as they relate to implementation of programs and practices in real-world contexts in early care and education. These principles will be discussed in terms of readiness to change in the ECE workforce; what theory and research tell us about what makes change difficult and what makes change possible; the typical stages of change; the "spirit and skills" that are effective for working with people who are not ready to change; and strategies for supporting readiness to change in implementation initiatives, with examples currently being used in ECE practice. The chapter concludes with recommendations for furthering research in this emerging field.

What Is Readiness to Change?

Readiness to change refers to the developmental process in which a person, organization, or system increases the capacity and willingness to engage in a particular activity. This topic provides a frame for understanding how human beings experience any type of intentional change in our lives. Think of any behavior change you have made in the past—anything from starting a diet or organizing your work space to adjusting to a divorce or changing the way you interact with your children—and it becomes apparent that changing our own behavior is no simple matter.

While some change is relatively easy (driving a new route to work or switching phone providers), other kinds of change are harder to make. We may have experienced trepidation or anxiety to find ourselves in situations that challenged our beliefs, values, or aspects of our upbringing or cultural identity. We may have felt guilty or ashamed when change meant acknowledging ways in which our behaviors might have caused harm to others or otherwise did not live up to our ideals. The prospect of change can bring up fear, resentment, or anger when we experience criticism from others who wish (or demand) that we would change our behavior to meet their expectations. Even when we would like to make a change, taking the first step can feel daunting and overwhelming. Most of us can recall a time when we reacted with resistance, ambivalence, hostility, or hopelessness at one or more of these kinds of situations.

At the same time, you probably have had many experiences of success in changing your own behavior. Call to mind one such experience, and you might remember the hopeful and encouraging sense of possibility that came from recognizing your own inner power and autonomy and facing your obstacles with courage. You may have experienced the sense of belonging and collaboration that came from being part of a decision-making team, or the sense of relief that came with finding friends or coworkers or groups to whom you could reach out for moral support, encouragement, or advice when you needed it.

Another way to describe being "ready to change" is the state of being "willing and able." Being *willing* implies freedom of choice. It means having reasons for change that come from within, that are aligned with our values and goals, and that are relatively free from both external control and internal resistance. Even when we are responding to external standards or demands, willingness implies that we do so with a perceived sense of choice (e.g., we are choosing to act in alignment with our own needs and values) and not by coercion. Being *able* implies having access to resources that will enable us to persist in doing the hard work of change. Such resources include forms of support, both internal (e.g., knowledge, skills) and external (e.g., friends to support us, a collaborative work environment), that will help us weather the tough times when we feel like giving up. Being able also implies having confidence that we can overcome obstacles to change. When we are both willing and able to change, it is more likely that we will commit to change—in other words, that we will set goals for our behavior and recommit to these goals in the face of inevitable setbacks.

Aarons, Horowitz, Dlugosz, and Ehrhart (2012) have described key aspects of readiness in terms of three types of "change beliefs." The first is *valence*, which refers to the degree to which people think the change is worthwhile for them personally. The second is *efficacy*, the degree to which people think they are capable of implementing change. The third is *discrepancy*, the belief that change is needed due to a gap between the current and the desired state.

What is common in each of these definitions is that readiness to change is viewed as the necessary foundation for behavior change that is meaningful, intentional, and sustainable. In a sense, readiness to change is like the foundation of a house: you can have high-quality materials, a knowledgeable builder, and a hardworking contractor, but without a solid foundation to build upon, the house may eventually succumb to the forces of time and weather. This is also a key principle for implementation science: You can have a high-quality, evidence-based intervention with knowledgeable leaders and support staff, but without a willing and able workforce, the intervention is unlikely to be implemented and sustained as designed.

Readiness to Change in the Early Care and Education Context: An Illustration

The concept of readiness to change has been widely theorized, researched, and applied in the field of health behavior and mental health counseling, and it is now beginning to be incorporated into other domains of practice. Rather than directly importing this knowledge into our field, our understanding of readiness to change will be more meaningful if it is embedded within what we know about the ECE workforce and the nature of ECE work itself.

Recognizing readiness to change requires that we first seek to understand a person's experiences, perceptions, and feelings around the behavior change in question. Let's look at a fictional example of an early educator who we might describe as "not ready to change."

Case Study

Sonia is an assistant teacher at an urban Head Start center. She has worked in ECE for 15 years and has been at her current center for 5 years. For the most part, Sonia has been happy with her chosen job. She loves children and is proud of "all my little success stories." She gets a sense of competence and fulfillment from helping prepare young children for school, especially helping them learn preacademic skills like recognizing and writing letters. Sonia was involved in developing the curriculum in her classroom and is pleased to be part of the decision-making process at her center.

This year, the local Head Start agency has mandated that all Head Start centers begin implementing (the fictional) Growing Learners, an evidence-based preschool curriculum. While some teachers were involved in focus groups to help select the curriculum, Sonia was not able to attend because she was taking care of her ill mother at the time. She learned about the new curriculum just two months before she was expected to implement it in her classroom.

Sonia has been very frustrated and unhappy since her center adopted the new curriculum. She is particularly upset with the feedback she receives from her director and from the coach assigned to work with her this year. In her words, "They're so focused on what I need to change. They don't see the good that I've been doing with the kids." Sonia also does not like the structure of the curriculum, particularly the requirement that teachers follow children's interests rather than use direct instruction. "We are not allowed to teach the children their letters," she says. "It doesn't make any sense."

For Sonia, not only does this philosophy go against what she is most proud of in her work, it also goes against her values as a mother. Sonia describes her Puerto Rican culture as one that "values excellence and hard work." She teaches her children to take responsibility for themselves and to go beyond others' expectations of them, as she has always tried to do in her own life. Despite her life's challenges, she is proud of her efforts to make a good life for herself and her children. Yet because of her stressful and discouraging experience at her job this year, Sonia is considering early retirement; this will likely be her last year at this job.

It is clear that describing Sonia as "not ready" to implement the new curriculum does not come close to capturing the depth of her experience. Nonetheless, it is human nature to categorize, and we may find ourselves judging or labeling individuals like Sonia as "resistant," "hard to reach," or "difficult to work with." If we define success in our work in terms of getting people to change, we may find it extremely frustrating to interact with individuals who seem uninterested in taking in new information, reflecting on their behavior, or trying new practices. We may quickly come up with ideas to "fix" Sonia's situation or construct explanations to try to convince her of our perspective. Yet the lens of readiness to change provides us with a different way of looking at the people with whom we work, a different way of communicating, and even a different way of viewing ourselves.

The nature of ECE work, with its central focus on responsive relationships with children, means that implementing evidence-based practices often includes shifting one's attitudes, beliefs, and reflective capacities that underlie the way one interacts with young children. Changing such aspects of oneself is never as simple as learning the "how-to"; this kind of change can often require nothing short of a journey of self-discovery and personal development. Recognizing and responding to readiness to change means that we seek to understand a person's current situation and experiences so that we can collaboratively identify *what is possible*, rather than focusing on *what should happen*. Importantly, when implementation processes are responsive to adults' readiness to change, they create a parallel process with the central feature of high-quality early care and education: responsive adult–child relationships. Far from a one-size-fits-all approach focused on transmitting new information and skills, responding to adults' readiness to change entails a shift away from the how-to and toward the why of change: Why do people do what they do, and what would make it possible for them to change? Before exploring these questions further, let's look at what we know about readiness to change in the context of the ECE workforce.

Realities of the Early Care and Education Workforce

The current state of the ECE workforce is characterized by a number of factors that may affect readiness to change, including low pay, high turnover, low levels of formal education (particularly among "assistant" positions; infant/toddler caregivers; family child care providers; and family, friend, and neighbor caregivers), low levels of perceived support in the work environment, low job satisfaction, and low levels of professional identity (see Peterson & Valk, 2010). These factors imply that readiness to change is likely to be lower in the ECE context than in other work domains such as K–12 education or mental health services.

Administrative support may also be lower in the field of early childhood than in other fields of practice. Despite the fact that administrative support is associated with intrinsic motivation for professional development (Wagner & French, 2010), work satisfaction, and job retention (Jorde-Bloom, 1989), only two universities in the United States offer degree programs in early childhood administration (D. Schaack, personal communication, January 2012), and many administrators lack the time and skills for supervision. One study found that only 34% of child care staff had ever experienced reflective supervision (Howes, James, & Ritchie, 2003).

Early educators are also likely to experience discord between the practices they experienced in their own family or with their children and the practices they are asked to adopt in their work. Many evidence-based programs and practices in ECE have been derived from middle-class American cultural norms, and these can be unfamiliar, threatening, or alienating for individuals raised with different cultural traditions. Our field must be prepared to look carefully at how we can ensure that the design and implementation of evidence-based programs and practices are respectful and inclusive of the diverse cultural traditions in our country.

Regardless of the reasons why early educators are not willing or able to implement new practices, it remains the case that supervisors and support staff will not be able to work effectively with such individuals unless they recognize that educators may be at different levels of readiness to change.

In two studies that my colleagues and I conducted, we asked mentors and home visitors to rate the educators they served in terms of their readiness to make a change in their child care practices or program. Our first study involved a mentoring intervention for center-based infant/toddler caregivers and preschool educators. We asked mentors to rate each educator on a pilot version of the Stage of Change Scale for Early Education and Care (see Peterson, 2012). At the time of the first assessment, 34% of educators were rated by their mentor as being "not ready to change"; one year later, the figure was 19%. It is unclear to what extent this change was a result of growth in educators' readiness to change or a result of attrition of educators due to a "mismatch" with the program goals; mentors did indicate that some educators left or were dropped from the program by their mentor due to lack of interest in working toward changes in practice. Educators who were not ready to change were described by their mentors as people who did not have anything they wanted to change, seemed easily overwhelmed by obstacles, or were signed up to participate in the mentoring program by their administrator. Mentors described some of these educators as "quarter-hearted" (not even halfhearted) or as people who "talk the talk, but don't walk the walk." Some of these educators seemed to make no observable changes in practice despite working with a mentor for up to 2 years.

Our second study was conducted with data from a home visiting program for family child care providers (Peterson & Weber, 2011). Providers were rated by their home visitor on the Stage of Change Scale for Early Education and Care, version 2.0 (Peterson, Baker, & Weber, 2010). At the time of the first assessment, 16% of providers were rated by their home visitor as not ready to change; at the end of the intervention, the figure was 8%. Analyses also showed that providers' baseline readiness to change significantly predicted the amount of growth observed in the quality of their child care literacy environment, as measured by the Child/Home Early Language and Literacy Observation (Neuman, Dwyer, & Koh, 2007). Providers who began the program at the later stages of change made gains in the quality of the literacy environment, while providers who began at the earlier stages of change in fact showed decreases in quality. This finding suggests that professional development interventions may be most likely to result in changes in practice for participants who begin the program at a higher level of readiness to change.

Together, these studies suggest what is known to many of us intuitively: Many educators in the workforce may not be ready to make immediate changes in their practices, even after participating in high-quality, one-on-one professional development programs. The findings also support the conclusion that key change beliefs are necessary before educators can be expected to implement changes in behavior.

What Makes Change Difficult

Why is it so difficult for human beings to intentionally change our behavior? In many ways, our context shapes our willingness and ability to take steps toward change.

This section provides a brief description of contextual factors that can affect readiness to change, including cultural beliefs and attitudes, social systems and relationships, current and persistent stressors, and enduring personal characteristics.

Cultural Beliefs and Attitudes

Cultural beliefs and attitudes play an especially large role in the early stages of change. People who are considering (or being asked to consider) a behavior change that challenges the assumptions of their culture or family of origin are unlikely to be ready to change unless they are able to reconcile their sense of identity and cultural values with the new behavior. Values for community and belonging within one's cultural group often mean that supports for change must be culturally responsive, that is, based on cultural norms and practices that are familiar to the individual (Gay, 2010). People from cultures with a strong value for community also may benefit from thinking about ways that change will benefit their community, rather than just themselves or another individual (DiClemente, 2004).

Social Systems and Relationships

The structure of social systems and organizations such as the workplace, social service system, or other social network can affect whether people will experience support for their needs that would allow them to engage in change. Self-determination theory (Ryan & Deci, 2000) provides a model for understanding how motivation to change is impacted by support for our universal human needs, in particular *autonomy* (e.g., giving people choice, freedom, and control in how they act), *competence* (e.g., giving people specific positive feedback on the progress they are making toward their own goals), and *relatedness* (e.g., conveying a sense of belonging and support from supervisors and coworkers). Organizations that provide support for universal human needs are more likely to have staff who are motivated and ready to change (Fullan, 2008; Gagné & Deci, 2005). Organizations that do not support staff needs, or that employ an authoritarian style that dictates the standards from the top (Lunenburg & Ornstein, 2012), frequently create resentment and even deception and an underground culture of resistance.

Relationships with family, friends, coworkers, and others can also be vitally important factors in whether a person will undertake an intentional behavior change. Experiencing social support, or the lack thereof, can especially figure into one's ability to integrate and sustain change over time (Wagner, Burg, & Sirois, 2004).

Current and Persistent Stressors

Current and persistent stressors include major life transitions (e.g., divorce, a new baby) as well as ongoing sources of stress (e.g., financial strain, domestic violence). People experiencing high levels of stress may be much less likely to be able to take on the challenge of change than are those who experience more stability and safety.

Attachment experiences earlier in life also play an important role in our ability to change our behavior. As we know from research on early childhood development, our secure attachments to primary caregivers in the earliest years of life have significant and long-term impacts on our development. Children who experience insecure attachments tend to develop an internal working model of the world that says "My needs are not important." As a result, adults with insecure attachment histories tend to have an underdeveloped reflective function. That is, they are weak in their ability to recognize thoughts, feelings, and needs in themselves and others (Fonagy, Steele, Steele, Moran, & Higgitt, 1991). Adults who experienced insecure attachments as children may be less able to empathize with the children in their care and may also have more difficulty seeing a situation from another person's point of view.

Trauma history is another factor that can affect our readiness to change. Trauma refers to a subjective experience of an extremely stressful event or series of events (e.g., violence, natural disasters, injury, illness, separation, loss) in which a person feels an overwhelming sense of helplessness, vulnerability, fear, or horror (Robinson, Smith, & Segal, 2011). It can also stem from long-term exposure to personal or collective stressors such as poverty, community violence or war, abuse, neglect, or discrimination. Trauma results in a disruption of the body's natural equilibrium in response to stress, promoting increased cortisol levels even when threat is only imagined, which can persist over time as a tendency toward hyperarousal, fear, and lack of a sense of trust. Trauma and other adverse events experienced in childhood have many long-term consequences in adulthood, such as increased likelihood of depression, drug abuse, and health problems (Felitti et al., 1998).

Enduring Personal Characteristics

Finally, behavior change is clearly shaped by enduring individual differences in temperament, personality, and learning style. These differences can affect not only the rate at which a person tends to move through the stages of change but also the types of supportive strategies that work best to support movement through the stages. Responding sensitively to temperamental differences in children is an important aspect of high-quality caregiving; likewise, understanding adult temperament is one of the ways we can respond effectively to differences in readiness to change. Temperament can affect the rate of change; for example, people low on the "approach to novelty" dimension may be generally slower to move through the stages of change, regardless of the behavior or situation. Temperament can also impact the types of strategies that will be effective to support people in thinking about change; people high on the "regularity" dimension, for instance, may have a stronger need for order (e.g., schedules, regular feedback) than would people rated low on this dimension.

Stages of Change

The Transtheoretical Model (TTM) of change was developed in the field of health behavior as a way to capture what appear to be common stages and processes that people experience when making any type of behavior change (Prochaska, DiClemente, & Norcross, 1992). While originally developed in the context of smoking and drug addiction programs, the model has been applied to a wide range of domains, including exercise, diet, stress management, organizational change, and parenting behaviors. Regardless of the type of behavior, people seem to progress through five common stages of change. The stages of change are best thought of as a spiral—people may progress through the stages, regress back to earlier stages, and resume progress over the course of months, weeks, or even within a day. Table 3.1 presents key characteristics of each stage, what you might hear an educator say in this stage, and the purpose of support services at each stage.

Table 3.1. Five stages of change

Stage	A person in this stage...	What you might hear	Purpose of support services
Stage 1: Precontemplation	Does not intend to make any change; is unaware or unconcerned about his or her behavior and its effects	"My director is making me..." "No one's ever complained about my work before." "I don't really care."	Raise awareness Raise importance
Stage 2: Contemplation	Would like to improve his or her behavior, but is overwhelmed by obstacles	"I would like to, but..." "I can't do it." "I'll try it." (But when you come back next month, he or she hasn't tried it.)	Weigh pros and cons Raise confidence
Stage 3: Preparation	Has an active intent to make a change; is devising a plan of action; is aware of resources to support change	"I want to try..." "What will it look like?" "What do I need in order to do this?"	Raise commitment Set goals and create action steps
Stage 4: Action	Is actively engaged in change; persists with the new behavior over time; seeks help when challenges occur	"I've been doing this for a few weeks and I've noticed..." "What could I do when... happens?"	Implement changes Problem-solve challenges as they arise
Stage 5: Maintenance	Works to maintain changes and integrate them into his or her lifestyle; continually reflects on the new behavior	"I've found a new way to..." "I'm wondering how I can make this work even better" "How can I share what I have learned?"	Integrate changes Support other learners

In the earlier stages of change, people are most likely to benefit from *experiential processes* (the "why") focused on increasing internal motivation (reasons for change), confidence, and commitment. In the later stages, people are more likely to benefit from *behavioral processes* (the "how to") that focus on goal setting, problem solving, and coming up with strategies to support persistence in sustaining the behavior. Tailoring interventions to individuals' stage of change involves supporting the processes that are most likely to benefit people in their particular stage (Prochaska & Velicer, 1997).

Spirit and Skills for Increasing Readiness to Change

Coaches, instructors, and other support staff who work directly with educators and center administrators may benefit from learning research-based strategies specifically designed to increase readiness to change *before* people can begin working on behavioral change. These strategies include a particular set of attitudes (spirit) and communication techniques (skills) that can be developed through training and ongoing practice.

The following principles are drawn from the Transtheoretical Model of change, as well as from person-centered models of communication, including nonviolent communication (Rosenberg, 2003; see also http://www.cnvc.org) and motivational interviewing (Miller & Rollnick, 2002, 2009; Rosengren, 2009; see also www.motivationalinterview.org); both are widely disseminated and implemented and can be learned and practiced through in-person and online trainings, videos, readings, and websites. These principles also draw upon research on mindfulness, which is now widely used in the medical and helping professions (Irving, Dobkin, & Park, 2009) as well as in organizations (Carroll, 2007). Examples in the following discussion relate to how coaches can support early educators' readiness to change, but the same principles could be used by purveyors of innovations, researchers, evaluators, program administrators, and anyone else who plays a role in the implementation process.

The Spirit of Empathy and Collaboration

Demonstrating a spirit of empathy and collaboration is crucial for reducing defensiveness and fostering a safe environment for people to be open to exploring their own experience of change.

Empathy   A spirit of empathy entails attention to and compassion for the educator's inner experience. Validating the speaker's experience helps to create a "secure base"—especially crucial for those with insecure attachment or trauma histories—to explore feelings about change. Empathy has been shown to increase self-efficacy and perceived autonomy and to predict later behavior change (Holmes, 2009; Sellman, Sullivan, Dore, Adamson, & MacEwan, 2001).

A key principle is "empathy before education": People will more likely be able to take in new information after they are heard and validated themselves (Rosenberg, 2003). Some of the ways empathy is conveyed are through listening for understanding and reflecting the learner's feelings and needs. A spirit of empathy means we try to avoid habitual communication patterns that get in the way of connection (e.g., advice, blame, judgment, exaggeration).

The fundamental stance of empathy is a nonjudgmental, accepting attitude. Although it is human nature to want to fix, an empathic spirit means that we "resist the righting reflex" (Rosengren, 2009) and accept people the way they are. Accepting a person does not necessarily mean we approve of or condone their behavior; rather, it means we validate that every choice they make is an attempt to meet their needs in some way.

Empathy is related to mindfulness, which is the state of being nonjudgmental and aware of the present moment (Nhat Hanh, 1992). Mindfulness entails acceptance of what is, instead of wishing or expecting things to be different in some way. Even when our purpose is to support people's readiness to change, we can acknowledge that it is impossible to know how our presence or words will affect someone. In any given moment, there is an infinite number of factors that might affect a person's motivations and actions. Being mindful means we can maintain a sense of purpose in our goal of helping someone become more open to change, while at the same time letting go of our expectations of what the outcome will look like.

In order to be present and empathic toward others, we need to be present and empathic toward ourselves. Mindfulness requires that our awareness extend 360 degrees: to the situation, to the other person, and to our own internal experience. When we attend to our own reactions in a particular situation, we inevitably find that our own judgments, triggers, and unmet needs can get in the way of our ability to be fully present in the moment. Identifying and attending to our own needs can bring us back to a state of calm alertness that increases our ability to extend empathy to others.

Collaboration Collaboration entails doing things *with* people, rather than *to* them, *for* them, or *without* them. A spirit of collaboration means working toward creating a trusting partnership based on choice and mutuality, rather than hierarchy. It necessitates avoiding many of the techniques that are commonly used to try to persuade or coerce people to change (e.g., giving rationales that are not tailored to the individual's interests or needs, threatening punishment, offering reward for compliance), which are likely to stimulate defensiveness. In a collaborative spirit, everyone's needs matter, and we work toward finding strategies that work for everyone involved.

One of the critical aspects of collaboration is autonomy. A sense of autonomy, the ability to make choices on one's own behalf, is an essential ingredient for change. Especially for individuals with insecure attachment or trauma histories, a perceived sense of autonomy is critical for creating a sense of safety and trust (Elliott, Bjelajac, Fallot, Markoff, & Glover Reed, 2005). When people sense that someone is attempting to control them, they will often assert their sense of independence by resisting or rebelling against what they perceive as external demands.

One way we can foster a sense of autonomy is by asking, rather than telling, the educator how he or she would like the relationship to proceed. This conveys the message that "what is important to me is what will make this relationship work for you." Other ways of fostering autonomy include providing choices whenever possible, explicitly reflecting on what the person has choices about, and affirming the choices that the person has already made.

For people to experience a sense of collaboration, it is critical that they experience a sense of autonomy not only in relationships with coaches or support staff but in their work environment as well. Part of our role in supporting individuals' readiness to change may be working with center administrators and supervisors to create a workplace that embodies the spirit of collaboration and provides support that is matched to educators' readiness to change (Prochaska, Prochaska, & Levesque, 2001).

Another critical element of collaboration is honesty. Genuine collaboration means that we are honest about our values and responsibilities to our job, while at the same time emphasizing that what we care about most is what would work best for the educator. Honest, authentic communication sends the message "This is where I'm coming from, and I'm curious what it's like for you to hear that."

The Skill of Reflective Listening

The key to reflective listening is conveying a genuine interest in the learner's perspective. When we allow educators plenty of time to talk, we provide the opportunity for them to become empowered to understand their experience in relation to change. A rule of thumb is that when working with people who are not ready to change, we should be listening 80% of the time. And in the 20% of the time when we are speaking, 80% of what we say should be reflecting back what we heard.

Reflective listening entails listening for understanding and then verbalizing our reflections of the learner's experience, including the feelings, needs, values, and thoughts underlying what the learner says. By reflecting what we hear a person say, we hold up a mirror for them to become aware of their own experience and see their situation realistically. The language of reflective listening is observational and nonjudgmental, offering a sense of acceptance and compassion for the person exactly the way they are. Examples of reflections include repeating the speaker's own words, paraphrasing ("It sounds like..."), complex reflections ("On the one hand...but on the other hand..."), over- and understating, and summaries of the conversation.

Affirmations are a form of reflection that focuses on the educator's capacity to take steps in the direction of change. Examples of affirmations include the following:

- "It sounds like you've given this a lot of thought."

- "You know what works best for you."

- "I appreciate your willingness to speak honestly with me about this."

People who experience low self-esteem or a negative overall self-concept may have trouble noticing or appreciating their own abilities or positive qualities. As with children who are still developing a well-rounded self-concept, adults with a negative self-concept may continue to develop a more balanced sense of self when they hear specific, positive feedback about how their actions have contributed to their own needs or to the needs of others. A balanced self-concept allows us to accept our strengths as well as our limitations, enabling us to see a clearer picture of what would make change possible.

The Skill of Open-Ended Questioning

Open-ended questions invite honest dialogue about the target behavior and express genuine curiosity about the educator's perspective and experience. As conversation starters, open-ended questions can be a way to build a relationship and develop a sense of trust, so that the learner can feel safe to talk about their experience. In the phrasing of open-ended questions, it is important to keep in mind that it is more effective to ask people questions that elicit "change talk" ("What would it take for you to use finger paint with children?") rather than eliciting "sustain talk" ("Why don't you want to use finger paint with children?"). Research suggests a causal pathway between questions that elicit change talk and eventual behavior change; in other words, the more one asks about reasons for change, the more change talk the person is likely to express, and the more likely the person is to change his or her behavior (Moyers & Martin, 2006).

Support Strategies Designed to Increase Readiness to Change

Three support strategies that can increase readiness to change are raising awareness, raising importance, and raising confidence.

Raising Awareness   Our main task in dealing with people in the precontemplation stage (see Table 3.1) is to help them develop an awareness of their situation and their experience of it. This can be stimulated by eliciting stories of personal experience, whether about the educator's experience in her work, at home, or in her upbringing. For educators who may have insecure attachment histories, asking questions about childhood experiences may be especially beneficial in supporting compassion for one's own feelings and needs. While some of us may perceive this topic to be inappropriate in a work context or may feel hesitant to talk about such personal and potentially sensitive topics, the nature of early care and education work suggests that this kind of conversation may be precisely the type of mechanism needed to transform the quality of classroom practices. In light of estimates that about one third of educators may have experienced insecure attachments as children, this kind of empathy work may very well be the "missing link" in our ability to support adults to change their practices with children. This explicit focus on educators' personal experience is highlighted in WestEd's Program for Infant/Toddler Care (PITC), which emphasizes uncovering the beliefs, attitudes, and experiences that underlie the way we interact with young children. Examples of open-ended questions to raise awareness include the following:

- "What's it like to think about play?"

- "When you were a child, what would have made playtime more enjoyable for you?"

- "Would it be okay if I tell you some information about why children play? [Give information.] What's it like for you to hear that?"

Raising Importance When we experience change as important—that is, when a new behavior is aligned with our values, needs, or interests—we are more likely to think about taking steps toward change. Internal motivation, also known as "buy-in," refers to a sense that a behavior change is important for reasons that are internal, rather than external, to the individual. Table 3.2 presents the continuum of motivation described by Ryan and Deci (2000), ranging from more external to more internal, with examples of what you might hear an educator say in regard to a target behavior—in this case, engaging in music activities with children.

Table 3.2. Continuum of motivation

	More external				More internal
Amotivation (nonvaluing)	External regulation (compliance)	Introjection (ego-involved)	Identified (conscious valuing)	Integrated (synthesis with self)	Intrinsic (inherent satisfaction)
"It's not important to me to do music activities with children."	"If I don't do music activities with children, I'll get fired." "If I do music activities with children, I'll get a good score on my observation."	"If I don't do music activities with children, I'll see myself as a bad teacher." "If I do music activities with children, I'll see myself as a good teacher."	"I want to do music activities with children because it's important to me to help children develop a love of music."	"I want to do music activities with children because I enjoy seeing children develop a love of music."	"I just enjoy doing music activities with children."

One way to help raise importance and internal motivation is to ask questions that clarify an educator's values and highlight discrepancies between his or her values and current behavior. Examples of questions that clarify values include the following:

- "What is the most important thing for you in this job?"

- "What is the most important thing you want for children?"

- "What makes that important to you?"

- "You said it's important to you that children are encouraged to play, but at the same time you said you're not comfortable playing along with them. What's it like to think about that?"

- "What's the worst thing that could happen if you never played with the children again?"

- "What's the best thing that could happen if you continue to play with the children?"

A key point here is that educators may have very different internal motivations for the same behavior. For example, some educators may be internally motivated to do music activities with children because they value helping children develop a love of music, while others more highly value giving children opportunities to learn rhythm and rhyme, using recommended practices in their work, or simply feeling like they are part of a team in their workplace. The important thing is not that educators value change for the reasons *we* want them to, but that each person value change for the reasons that are important to himself or herself.

Raising Confidence   A sense of confidence in our own abilities makes it more likely that we will be ready and committed to take steps toward behavior change. Confidence in one's ability regarding a specific behavior is known as *self-efficacy*. Self-efficacy is typically low in the early stages of change and increases as people begin to create a realistic plan, implement changes, and observe the positive effects of their behaviors on themselves and those around them. Examples of questions to raise confidence include the following:

- "What makes it possible for you to play with children?"

- "What has worked for you in the past?"

- "What would make it work better for you?"

Implementation Processes that Support Readiness to Change

So what does it take to build a strong foundation? What does it take to ensure that our implementers are ready to change? Support for educators' readiness to change comes from the same core implementation components, or implementation drivers, that support all the other elements of implementation (Fixsen, Naoom, Blase, Friedman, & Wallace, 2005). *Competency drivers*—selection, training, and coaching—that develop, improve, and maintain staff competency and confidence can play a key role in increasing readiness, and *organization drivers*—particularly, facilitative administration—that develop hospitable environments for change can also promote readiness to change throughout an organization. Let's look at each of these in turn.

Selection

It is critical that supervisors' and administrators' readiness to change be assessed before any further supports for staff competency are put into place. Buy-in at these levels is crucial if implementation is to be supported at the level of staff. If it is determined that supervisors are ready for implementation, staff readiness can be assessed next. For a particular intervention, it might be useful to establish a threshold for staff readiness that must be reached before implementation begins; but in some cases, there may be no feasible way to establish such a threshold, so support for readiness to change would remain ongoing during implementation. Important factors to consider are whether the intervention can be implemented by some staff or must be implemented by all, and whether time and resources can be allocated to increasing readiness to change.

There are several reliable and valid tools for measuring individual readiness to change. The Stage of Change Scale for Early Care and Education is one such tool that was developed specifically to assess a home- or center-based educator's readiness to change his or her child care practices or program (Montes, Peterson, & Weber, 2011; Peterson, Baker, & Weber, 2010). The seven-item scale takes 5–10 minutes to be completed by a coach or supervisor; this has the benefits of reducing the paperwork required of educators and providing a potentially more objective picture than a self-report. (A pilot self-report version of the scale showed low internal reliability and resulted in ratings on average one stage higher than the coach report.) The professional manual accompanying the scale describes strategies that coaches and supervisors can use to respond to individuals at each stage of change. The Stage of Change Scale is currently being used in the Getting Ready program, an initiative to support child care providers who are thinking about enrolling in Parent Aware, Minnesota's quality rating and improvement system.

An example of a generic individual survey of readiness is the University of Rhode Island Change Assessment (URICA; McConnaughy, Prochaska, & Velicer, 1983), which has been adapted for a variety of health and mental health contexts, including parenting behaviors (Brestan, Ondersma, Simpson, & Gurwitch, 1999). Measures of readiness in organizational settings include the Evidence-Based Practice Attitude Scale (Aarons, 2004) and the Stages of Concern Questionnaire (George, Hall, & Stiegelbauer, 2006). These latter two instruments were developed for mental health professionals and K–12 educators, respectively, who typically have higher education levels and higher levels of professional identity than staff in ECE settings; therefore, caution must be used in adapting these measures in the ECE context.

Informal assessments of early educators' readiness can range from simple "readiness rulers" that rate importance, confidence, and commitment (e.g., "On a scale of 1–10, how important is this change to you?") to complex center-wide assessments, such as that developed by Kentucky's Stars for Kids Now quality rating system, used by technical assistance providers to document staff skills, readiness, and commitment to making improvements in quality.

Training

Once it is decided that implementation will proceed to the installation stage, training may be designed to increase staff's readiness to change. For example, a child care center may dedicate one full year to raising staff's motivation and confidence for implementing continuity of care of infants and toddlers. Training may take the form of monthly small group "listening meetings" to invite staff to talk about their experiences, concerns, needs, and strategies for making a continuity-of-care approach work for them. Using a "circle process"—inviting each participant to take a turn to tell his or her story without interruption (Pranis, 2005)—may convey the message that everyone is respected and equal. Facilitators of such groups should be experienced and skilled in working with individuals who are not ready to change, drawing on the spirit and skills described above.

If the readiness of staff is mixed, an assortment of training opportunities may be offered. For example, a school district in the installation phase of implementing a new curriculum may offer two forms of professional development that educators can select based on their readiness to change: a series of facilitated small group meetings for educators who are concerned or overwhelmed about the new curriculum, and standard trainings for educators who are ready to increase knowledge and skills and problem-solve about how to respond to challenges of implementation.

Children's Institute is currently piloting an initiative that provides targeted training support to family child care providers who have not demonstrated an interest in making changes in their child care practices. A small group intervention was designed by Amy Baker with the goal of increasing providers' sense of safety and trust, willingness to consider another person's point of view, and willingness to reflect on the reasons why you do what you do. Providers were selected and recruited by phone by one of the facilitators who is well known in the local family child care community. The facilitators have experience as family child care home visitors and describe themselves as people who have experienced major changes in their lives and can reflect openly on the personal, often difficult, experiences that accompany change.

The model is "psycho-educational," designed not as education and not as therapy, but as something in between. It draws from various approaches, including group therapy, counseling, and circle processes. Features of the model include

- Participants come up with guidelines for the meetings as well as with topics for discussion.

- Each meeting includes one or more "rounds," going around the room so each person is invited to speak in turn without interruption.

- Facilitators encourage participants to use "I" messages and to listen with an open mind.

- Facilitators and participants explicitly discuss group processes, especially conflicts and challenges, as needed.

- Facilitators model and encourage participants to offer each other acceptance, affirmation, and support.

- Facilitators debrief after each session, looking at group processes, themes, and content.

Initial anecdotal evidence suggests that the program is working as intended. By the fifth meeting, the facilitators observed that trust and openness in the group was growing. One provider commented, "I have been a provider for 15 years and this is the first [class in which] I'm really learning something!" Discussions in the group have explored issues related to confidence, professional identity, and autonomy—key principles relating to readiness to change. For example, one caregiver talked about a preschool child who seemed to be beyond her expertise. The first day he was in care, he jumped into the crib, knocked over the furniture, and so scared the other children that the caregiver sent them out of the room with her assistant. The caregiver told the mother she couldn't care for him, and he didn't return to the program. The group talked at length about the situation, focusing on the importance of a probationary period that would give the caregiver and the family time to determine whether or not the child will be a good match. At the end of the discussion, the caregiver questioned herself for being unable to care for this child and put the question to the group. The consensus was that it was up to each individual caregiver to decide who he or she could care for, affirming this caregiver's role as a business owner and a professional.

Coaching

Coaching and other individualized models of professional development are used in a variety of different implementation initiatives, including statewide quality rating and improvement systems (Isner et al., 2011). The typical model of coaching used in many implementation efforts is based on the premise that educators will be ready to change their practices once they can set appropriate goals for themselves and take steps toward those goals. However, educators who are not ready to change may not benefit from such models; in fact, many coaches and mentors express frustration when educators "resist" their suggestions and fail to demonstrate behavior change (Norman & Feiman-Nemser, 2005; Peterson, Valk, Baker, Brugger, & Hightower, 2010; Ryan & Hornbeck, 2004).

There are two possible ways to remedy this situation. One is to limit coaching programs to individuals who are in the later stages of readiness. This has the benefit of maintaining the structure of current coaching programs and saving resources by offering these intensive behavior-oriented services only to individuals who are likely to benefit from them.

This approach is being carried out in the Partners in Family Child Care project, a home visiting program designed by Children's Institute, with services delivered by the Family Child Care Satellite Network of Greater Rochester (New York). In the original design of this project, home visiting services were available to any family child care provider who wanted them. However, after 3 years of implementation, evaluation results showed that providers who began the program at an earlier level of readiness were less likely to show improvements in child care quality. The decision was made to limit eligibility for services to providers who demonstrate willingness and ability to successfully implement the behaviors targeted in the program. Providers were required to complete an application form prior to enrollment, asking questions such as: *What are you working on changing in your program? What resources are you already using to support these changes?*

Based on anecdotal records, the quality of participation in the intervention seemed substantially different in the 4th year compared to previous years. Provider group meetings saw higher attendance rates: 50% compared to approximately 33%. Home visitors commented that this cohort of providers seemed more engaged in the program, more open to taking in new information, and more committed to making changes in their practices. One home visitor commented, "[My providers] say, 'I learned something!' That's what I like to hear and I'm hearing a lot of it."

A second approach to the problem is to significantly alter the structure of coaching programs so that services are tailored to match educators at all levels of readiness to change. While this requires intensive training and support for coaching staff in the spirit and skills described above, as well as structural adjustments that must be created by coaching program administrators and supervisors, the benefits are that educators who are not ready to change are more likely to receive effective supports for increasing their motivation, confidence, and commitment, thereby allowing behavior change to take place.

This approach is being used in a Parents as Teachers home visiting program offered through the Family Resource Centers of Crestwood Children's Center in Rochester, which serves both families and home-based family child care providers. Through a local grant, Children's Institute is providing yearlong consultation with the home visiting team to support the team's ability to work effectively with people who are not ready to change. The program manager initially demonstrated a high level of interest and motivation for the topic, and this has been critical in supporting the home visitors' buy-in for this initiative. Still, learning a new set of strategies is challenging, and we have found that it took almost a full year for some of the home visitors to feel confident in their ability to use these new skills in their work. Continuing support for home visitors is planned for the future to ensure the sustainability of these efforts. Future efforts may include booster sessions in motivational interviewing (offered by a local trainer through the county office of mental health), discussion of challenging cases and group supervision during team meetings, and increased supervisory support to increase staff's own readiness to change their practices.

Administration

Organization drivers are program and organizational structures that create hospitable environments for implementation. Facilitative administration is a key element that pertains to supporting educators' readiness to change. It is the responsibility of program administrators to review timelines, policies, procedures, and paperwork to ensure that programs are responsive to the readiness to change of educators.

An example of facilitative administration that supports readiness to change can be seen in the South Carolina Infant/Toddler Specialist Network (SCITS). SCITS is a statewide program that offers intensive professional development services to home- and center-based child care providers serving children from birth to 3 years old. Services are based on WestEd's PITC in California and are delivered by certified Infant/Toddler Specialists (ITSs). Several processes are in place to ensure that SCITS services are responsive to educators' readiness to change. Program monitors at South Carolina's ABC system (the state's voluntary tiered reimbursement system) conduct an initial assessment of a program's readiness and commitment to change. The ABC monitor's endorsement of a program's readiness is required for a program to receive SCITS services. Once enrolled in services, regular evaluations measure the degree to which staff are embracing concepts presented by the ITSs. These measures, completed by the ITSs, program administrators, and staff, capture evidence not only of the participants' ability to follow through with concrete responsibilities that are expected of them but also of the extent to which a participant is demonstrating openness to change. It is at these benchmarks in the service plan that the opportunity to discontinue services is presented if any of the parties feel that the investment of time and effort is not fruitful.

Monthly ITS team meetings include discussions about the challenge of obtaining participants' buy-in and other issues related to providers' readiness to change. ITSs offer each other support with strategies to open up conversations and build the relationship with child care providers. However, it seems that frequently when the ITSs are mired in a relationship with providers who are not open to following their recommendations, they sometimes have trouble "seeing out" of the situation and can forget their own strategies.

In July 2011, all the ITSs participated in a two-day seminar entitled *The Stage of Change Approach to Early Education Professional Development*, offered by Children's Institute. At a subsequent team meeting, a proposal was put forward to formalize some of the readiness-to-change strategies in a tool kit, which would include a formal assessment using the Stage of Change Scale, an informal evaluation of common obstacles to readiness to change, and a listing of common strategies used to approach participants at the earlier stages of change. The ITSs were very receptive to the proposed tool kit. One commented: "I think it would be beneficial. It will help me to have realistic expectations for what I can accomplish. And for the director, too, so she has realistic expectations." It was important for the ITS team to acknowledge that the proposed tool kit would serve only as a guide and would not discount the fact that relationships are complicated, requiring many nuanced interactions that may not necessarily be captured in the strategies included in the tool kit.

Conclusions and Future Research Directions

The following is a summary of the recommendations for implementation processes to support readiness to change in ECE contexts:

- Assess the readiness to change of supervisors, administrators, and staff, either formally or informally, on a regular basis.

- Provide trainings designed to increase awareness, importance, and confidence in educators who are not ready to make immediate behavior change.

- Limit coaching support to educators who are ready to make behavior changes, or draw on existing resources to train coaches in the "spirit and skills" for effectively working with educators who are not ready to change.

- Review program and organizational structures to ensure that they are supportive of educators at all levels of readiness to change.

The field of ECE will be greatly served by further research on how to effectively support readiness to change in the context of implementation efforts. The following are just a few possible questions for future research that have the potential to inform policy and practice:

- What factors (e.g., cultural background, professional identity, attachment history) are associated with educators' readiness to implement new initiatives?

- What practices are effective in working with educators who are not ready to change?

- What kind of preparation and training is necessary for support staff to work effectively with educators who are not ready to change?

- What are the ethical dilemmas raised by using readiness-to-change principles in ECE settings (e.g., when participation in a change initiative is not voluntary, or when educators are involved in implementation processes that affect them yet they are not included in decision-making processes)?

References

Aarons, G.A. (2004). Mental health provider attitudes toward adoption of evidence-based practice: The Evidence-Based Practice Attitude Scale (EBPAS). *Mental Health Services Research, 6*, 61–74.

Aarons, G.A., Horowitz, J.D., Dlugosz, L.R., & Ehrhart, M.G. (2012). The role of organizational processes in dissemination and implantation research. In R.C. Bronson, G.A. Colditz, & E.K. Proctor (Eds.), *Dissemination and implantation research in health* (pp. 128–153). New York, NY: Oxford University Press.

Brestan, E.V., Ondersma, S.J., Simpson, S.M., & Gurwitch, R. (1999, April). *Application of Stage of Change Theory to parenting behavior: Validating the Parent Readiness to Change Scale.* Poster presented at the Florida Conference on Child Health Psychology, Gainesville, FL.

Carroll, M. (2007). *The mindful leader.* Boston, MA: Trumpeter Books.

DiClemente, C.C. (2004). *Stages of change and addiction: Clinician's manual.* Center City, MN: Hazelden.

Elliott, D.E., Bjelajac, P., Fallot, R.D., Markoff, L.S., & Glover Reed, B. (2005). Trauma-informed or trauma-denied: Principles and implementation of trauma-informed services for women. *Journal of Community Psychology, 33*(4), 461–475.

Felitti, V.J., Anda, R.F., Nordenberg, D., Williamson, D.F., Spitz, A.M., Edwards, V., … Marks, J.S. (1998). Relationship of childhood abuse and household dysfunction to many of the leading causes of death in adults: The Adverse Childhood Experiences (ACE) study. *American Journal of Preventive Medicine, 14*, 245–258.

Fixsen, D.L., Naoom, S.F., Blase, K.A., Friedman, R.M., & Wallace, F. (2005). *Implementation research: A synthesis of the literature* (FMHI Publication No. 231). Tampa, FL: University of South Florida, Louis de la Parte Florida Mental Health Institute, National Implementation Research Network.

Fonagy, P., Steele, M., Steele, H., Moran, G.S., & Higgitt, A.C. (1991). The capacity for understanding mental states: The reflective self in parent and child and its significance for security of attachment. *Infant Mental Health Journal, 12*, 201–218.

Fullan, M. (2008). *The six secrets of change: What the best leaders do to help their organizations survive and thrive.* San Francisco, CA: Jossey-Bass.

Gagné, M., & Deci, E.L. (2005). Self-determination theory and work motivation. *Journal of Organizational Behavior, 26*, 331–362.

Gay, G. (2010). *Culturally responsive teaching: Theory, research, & practice* (2nd ed.). New York, NY: Teachers College.

George, A.A., Hall, G.E., & Stiegelbauer, S.M. (2006) *Measuring implementation in schools: The Stages of Concern Questionnaire.* Austin, TX: SEDL.

Holmes, J. (2009). *Exploring in security: Towards an attachment-informed psychoanalytic psychotherapy.* New York, NY: Routledge.

Howes, C., James, J., & Ritchie, S. (2003). Pathways to effective teaching. *Early Childhood Research Quarterly, 18*(1), 104–120.

Irving, J.A., Dobkin, P.L., & Park, J. (2009). Cultivating mindfulness in health care professionals: A review of empirical studies of Mindfulness-Based Stress Reduction (MBSR). *Complementary Therapies in Clinical Practice, 15*(2), 61–66.

Isner, T., Tout, K., Zaslow, M., Soli, M., Quinn, K., Rothenberg, L., & Burkhauser, M. (2011). *Coaching in early care and education programs and quality rating and improvement systems (QRIS): Identifying promising features.* Report submitted to Children's Services Council of Palm Beach County. Washington, DC: Child Trends.

Jorde-Bloom, P. (1989). Professional orientation: Individual and organizational perspectives. *Child and Youth Care Quarterly, 18*(4), 227–242.

Lunenburg, F., & Ornstein, A. (2012). *Educational administration: Concepts and practices* (6th ed.). Belmont, CA: Wadsworth/Thompson Learning.

McConnaughy, E.A., Prochaska, J.O., & Velicer, W.F. (1983). Stages of change in psychotherapy: Measurement and sample profiles. *Psychotherapy, 20,* 368–375.

Miller, W. (n.d.). A brief (8-minute) interview with William Miller about the background of motivational interviewing. Retrieved from http://www.motivationalinterview.org/quick_links/about_mi.html

Miller, W.R., & Rollnick, S. (2002). *Motivational interviewing: Preparing people for change* (2nd ed.). New York, NY: Guilford Press.

Miller, W.R., & Rollnick, S. (2009). Ten things that motivational interviewing is not. *Behavioural and Cognitive Psychotherapy, 37,* 129–140.

Montes, G., Peterson, S.M., & Weber, M. (2011). *Reliability and validity of the Stage of Change Scale for Early Education and Care 2.0: Mentor/coach form* (Technical Report T11-008). Rochester, NY: Children's Institute.

Moyers, T.B., & Martin, T. (2006). Therapist influence on client language during motivational interviewing sessions: Support for a potential causal mechanism. *Journal of Substance Abuse Treatment, 30,* 245–251.

Neuman, S., Dwyer, J., & Koh, S. (2007). *Child/Home Early Language and Literacy Observation (CHELLO).* Baltimore, MD: Paul H. Brookes Publishing Co.

Nhat Hanh, T. (1992). *Peace is every step: The path of mindfulness in everyday life.* New York: Bantam.

Noar, S.M., Benac, C., & Harris, M. (2007). Does tailoring matter? Meta-analytic review of tailored print health behavior change interventions. *Psychological Bulletin, 133*(4), 673–693.

Norman, P.J., & Feiman-Nemser, S. (2005). Mind activity in teaching and mentoring. *Teaching and Teacher Education, 21*(6), 679–697.

Ory, M., Jordan, P.J., & Bazzarre, T. (2002). The Behavior Change Consortium: Setting the stage for a new century of health behavior change research. *Health Education Research, 17,* 500–511.

Peterson, S.M. (2012). Understanding early educators' readiness to change. *National Head Start Association Dialog, 15*(1), 95–112.

Peterson, S.M., & Baker, A.C. (2011). Readiness to change in communities, organizations, and individuals. In J.A. Sutterby (Ed.), *Early childhood professional development: Research and practice through the early childhood educator professional development grant: Advances in early education and day care* (pp. 33–59). Bingley, England: Emerald.

Peterson, S.M., Baker, A.C., & Weber, M.R. (2010). *Stage of Change Scale for Early Education and Care 2.0: Professional manual.* Rochester, NY: Children's Institute. Available at http://www.childrensinstitute.net/store/assessment-measures

Peterson, S.M., & Valk, C. (2010). Beyond babysitting: Challenges and opportunities for early childhood education. In S.B. Neuman & M.L. Kamil (Eds.), *Preparing teachers for the early childhood classroom: Proven models and key principles* (pp. 49–64). Baltimore, MD: Paul H. Brookes Publishing Co.

Peterson, S.M., Valk, C., Baker, A.C., Brugger, L., & Hightower, A.D. (2010). "We're not *just* interested in the work": Social and emotional aspects of early educator mentoring relationships. *Mentoring and Tutoring, 18*(2), 155–175.

Peterson, S.M., & Weber, M. (2011). *Partners in Family Child Care, 2008–2011 summary report* (Technical Report T11-015). Rochester, NY: Children's Institute.

Pranis, K. (2005). *The little book of circle processes: A new/old approach to peacemaking.* Intercourse, PA: Good Books.

Prochaska, J.O., DiClemente, C.C., & Norcross, J.C. (1992). In search of how people change: Applications to addictive behaviors. *American Psychologist, 47*(9), 1102–1114.

Prochaska, J.O., DiClemente, C.C., Velicer, W.F., & Rossi, J.S. (1993). Standardized, individualized, interactive and personalized self-help programs for smoking cessation. *Health Psychology, 12*(5), 399–405.

Prochaska, J.M., Prochaska, J.O., & Levesque, D.A. (2001). A transtheoretical approach to changing organizations. *Administration and Policy in Mental Health and Mental Health Services, 28*(4), 247–261.

Prochaska, J.O., & Velicer, W.F. (1997). The Transtheoretical Model of health behavior change. *American Journal of Health Promotion, 12,* 38–48.

Robinson, L., Smith, M., & Segal, J. (2011). Healing emotional and psychological trauma: Symptoms, treatment, and recovery. Retrieved from http://www.helpguide.org/mental/emotional_psychological_trauma.htm

Rosenberg, M.B. (2003). *Nonviolent communication: A language of life.* Encinitas, CA: PuddleDancer Press.

Rosengren, D.B. (2009). *Building Motivational Interviewing skills: A practitioner's workbook.* New York, NY: Guilford Press.

Ryan, R.M., & Deci, E.L. (2000). Self-determination theory and the facilitation of intrinsic motivation, social development, and well-being. *American Psychologist, 55,* 68–78.

Ryan, S., & Hornbeck, A. (2004). Mentoring for quality improvement: A case study of a mentor teacher in the reform process. *Journal of Research in Childhood Education, 19*(1), 79–96.

Sellman, J.D., Sullivan, P.F., Dore, G.M., Adamson, S.J., & MacEwan, I. (2001). A randomized controlled trial of motivational enhancement therapy (MET) for mild–moderate alcohol dependence. *Journal of Studies on Alcohol, 62*(3), 389–396.

Wagner, B.D., & French, L. (2010). Motivation, work satisfaction, and teacher change among early childhood teachers. *Journal of Research in Childhood Education, 24*(2), 152–171.

Wagner, J., Burg, M., & Sirois, F. (2004). Social support and the Transtheoretical Model: Relationship of social support to smoking cessation stage, decisional balance, process use, and temptation. *Addictive Behaviors, 29,* 1039–1043.

CHAPTER 4

Innovative Methodologies to Explore Implementation

Whole-Part-Whole—Construct Validity, Measurement, and Analytical Issues for Intervention Fidelity Assessment in Education Research

Chris S. Hulleman, Sara E. Rimm-Kaufman, and Tashia Abry

In the early 20th century, structuralism was a popular approach in psychology. Structuralists sought to understand human behavior by deconstructing the conscious experience into progressively smaller pieces. Their key methodology was introspection, which required researchers to report on discrete aspects of their own thoughts and feelings. Although the structuralist approach was defined by methodological rigor, a group of German psychologists, the Gestaltists, took issue with its fundamental principle of breaking the whole into parts. Their viewpoint, led by Wertheimer (e.g., see Weiner, 1972, for a review), was that the whole was more than the sum of its parts. These Gestaltists believed that consciousness was best studied in its entirety, rather than by breaking it into finite pieces as advocated by the structuralists. By breaking consciousness into smaller pieces, the Gestaltists argued, the essence was lost.

This fundamental disagreement between structuralists and Gestaltists is more than a historical footnote—it resurfaces as a contemporary measurement problem: How do we develop fine-grained measures that capture the breadth and depth of a construct, often by breaking it into pieces, without losing its essence? For example, by defining school quality in terms of domain-specific aspects (e.g., curriculum, environment, assessment, diversity; Tout et al., 2010) and developing measures that focus on these aspects, do we lose the essence of what it means to have a quality learning environment?

This measurement challenge, which is most often associated with the assessment of constructs such as personality traits (e.g., extraversion) or affective states (e.g., test anxiety), is also relevant to implementation science in general, and assessment of intervention fidelity in particular. That is, measuring the extent to which an early care and education program is implemented as intended (i.e., intervention fidelity) requires the same construct and psychometric validity as do measures of personality constructs. For fidelity assessment, establishing construct validity means breaking down an intervention model into its core components (whole-part) and ensuring that the fidelity indices, when administered individually, sum to represent full-scale implementation (part-whole) without losing the essence of the intervention.

This chapter presents a model of intervention fidelity assessment in the context of a school-based intervention, with the aim of demonstrating to researchers and evaluators that this measurement challenge can be overcome by developing valid measures of intervention fidelity. To achieve this aim, we selected an intervention— the RC approach—focused on the improvement of elementary school classrooms, that exemplifies some distinct challenges associated with measuring whole-part and part-whole construct validity.

The same principles and challenges apply to all types of interventions, including those focusing on early care and education, such as community-based home health care and school-based behavioral health programs (Lang & Franks, 2011; Lowell et al., 2010), and to the measurement of key implementation supports (i.e., implementation drivers). Although this chapter uses an elementary education example to examine issues of construct validity in intervention fidelity assessment, linkages to early care and education environments and implementation science in general will be explicated throughout.

Are Schools Ready for Kids? The RC Approach

Developed by the Northeast Foundation for Children (NEFC), the RC approach is designed for K–6 classrooms and is widely disseminated in the United States, with more than 90,000 teachers trained. The approach focuses on integrating children's social and academic learning in elementary school through 7 core principles and 10 practices (see Table 4.1). Examples of principles include: "the social curriculum is as important as the academic curriculum; how children learn is as important as what children learn; and knowing the children we teach—individually, culturally, and developmentally—is as important as knowing the content we teach" (Northeast Foundation for Children, 2007, p. 3).

RC practices provide a set of steps designed to help teachers enact the developmentally oriented recommendations embodied in the RC principles.

For example, the *Morning Meeting* consists of a daily gathering as a class when the teachers and children greet each other, share personal news in an orderly way, engage in a fun and playful activity together, and prepare for the day ahead. *Rule Creation* involves a set of practices that engage students in the process of creating the classroom rules so that all children can meet their classroom learning goals. *Academic Choice* is an approach to instruction in which the teacher determines the learning objectives and then provides students some choice as to how to meet those objectives. Teachers implement Academic Choice by having students choose from several approaches to conduct their work within a particular lesson, describe their plan to their teacher, engage in their work, and then reflect (in writing or to the group) upon their new learning. *Guided Discovery* is an approach to introducing materials in an organized manner that fosters creative and careful use of those materials.

In essence, the RC approach is designed to offer teachers a set of principles and strategies to build teacher capacity and support the quality of their interactions

Table 4.1.   Responsive Classroom core principles and practices (Northeast Foundation for Children, 2007, 2009)

Core principles	Core practices
1. The social curriculum is as important as the academic curriculum.	The following 10 practices emanate from the 7 principles:
2. *How* children learn is as important as *what* children learn.	1. Morning Meeting
3. The greatest cognitive growth occurs through social interaction.	2. Academic Choice
	3. Interactive Modeling
4. Cooperation, assertion, responsibility, empathy, and self-control are needed to be successful socially and academically.	4. Rule Creation
	5. Positive Teacher Language
	6. Logical consequences
5. Knowing the children individually, culturally, and developmentally is as important as knowing the content.	7. Guided Discovery
	8. Classroom Organization
	9. Working with families
6. Knowing the children's families is as important as knowing the children.	10. Collaborative problem solving
7. How the adults at school work together to accomplish their mission is as important as their individual competence.	

From Northeast Foundation for Children (NEFC). (n.d.). *Principles and practices of Responsive Classroom*. Retrieved from http://www.responsiveclassroom.org/principles-and-practices-responsive-classroom; adapted by permission.

with children. Two hallmark characteristics stand out in describing teachers who fully implement the RC approach: 1) Teachers foster the development of a caring classroom community, and 2) Teachers emphasize proactive rather than reactive approaches to classroom management and discipline. A core premise of the RC approach is that an environment where children's social-emotional needs are recognized and met sets the stage for academic learning. This framework aligns well with early childhood theory and resembles programmatic efforts, such as Head Start, that emphasize emotional and cognitive development and focus broadly on the needs of the whole child.

The RC approach offers some unique challenges to measuring intervention fidelity with validity. First, many of the practices have features that resemble those used in typical classrooms. For example, many early childhood teachers use a class meeting format at the beginning of the day. Although elements of such class meetings may resemble the RC Morning Meeting, there are important differences that differentiate high from low intervention fidelity of the RC approach. As an example, many Morning Meetings offer routine approaches to discussing the date, weather, and plan for the day. In contrast, the RC Morning Meeting involves a greeting in which each child is greeted by name and a group activity designed to be fun and engaging and help children feel a connection toward their peers and toward school.

Second, the RC approach, at its core, is comprised of a set of practices. However, simply implementing those practices without adhering to the core beliefs about children represented in the RC principles may not represent the intended effect of the RC approach. For instance, a Morning Meeting that is rushed and mechanical, as opposed to one that draws teachers and children together as a community, represents a different level of intervention fidelity. This illustrates the challenge of obtaining construct validity in fidelity assessment. In addition, by measuring RC practices with very exact language and precise measures, we may not adequately reflect comparable practices that are present in control groups. If we break apart assessment of the RC approach into key pieces, then we may lose the essence of creating a warm, safe learning environment to maximize learning for all children. For these and other reasons, the RC approach offers a useful exemplar for understanding issues of construct validity when measuring intervention fidelity.

Fidelity Definitions and Construct Validity

In intervention research, the primary research question is usually whether the program had its intended effects. In a randomized field trial, this is the intent-to-treat analysis: Did the program work for those who were assigned to the treatment compared to those who were not assigned to the treatment? Policy decisions are often made at this level of analysis. What this evaluation misses, however, is whether any effects (or lack thereof) were due to the program as *intended* versus the program as *implemented*. To the extent that a program is implemented with less than complete fidelity, the causal inference about program effectiveness is in regard to the program as implemented, particularly as contrasted with the comparison condition. Attributing a lack of program impact to a program that was not well implemented is a Type III error (Dobson & Cook, 1980) and risks discarding a potentially effective intervention. Thus, critical questions to be answered when evaluating program effectiveness include: To what extent was the program implemented as intended, and did variations in implementation impact the outcomes?

Intervention fidelity is the extent to which the program, as designed, was actually implemented. Crucial to fidelity assessment is the identification of the *intervention core components* that comprise the intervention model (also called *essential functions* or *active ingredients*). These are the key conceptual aspects of the intervention that must be in place for the intervention to be implemented. Intervention components are defined through the use of conceptual logic models (discussed later). For example, in the RC approach, the 10 practices outlined in Table 4.1 are the core intervention components.

Our definition of intervention fidelity is different from *implementation fidelity*, which involves the contextual factors that support the implementation of the intervention core components, such as staff selection, administrative training, and the provision of resources. These *implementation core components* (Fixsen et al., 2005) are not part of the intervention model per se, but rather help support the implementation of the intervention core components. In the case of the RC approach, creating a schoolwide time for the Morning Meeting is not one of the 10 RC practices outlined in Table 4.1, but could facilitate the implementation of the these practices. Thus, planning time facilitates implementation of RC practices, but is not an intervention core component because planning time is not explicitly part of the program model.

The distinction between intervention fidelity and implementation fidelity nearly parallels the differentiation between core components that have direct versus indirect effects on children. For example, teachers play the primary role in the implementation of the RC approach as defined by the core components of using RC practices in the classroom. As such, we are focusing on the *direct* effects of RC practices (implemented by the teacher) on children. At a broader, contextually based level are implementation core components that create essential conditions that support teacher implementation of RC practices but are not core components of the theorized model. These implementation core components (Fixsen et al., 2005), which include administrative support and training, selection of staff, and consulting, have an *indirect* effect on children as mediated by the intervention core components. That is, administrative support can provide a facilitative condition for the implementation of RC practices, but it is the RC practices themselves that are theorized to directly enhance student outcomes. Thus, the implementation core components can be referred to as *implementation drivers* (Fixsen, Blase, Naoom, & Wallace, 2009). The caveat to this distinction is the case in which the contextual level is specifically a part of the intervention model; then, those aspects become intervention core components (see Chapter 8 for an example of coaching as a core intervention component of ECE models).

Drivers of effective implementation are important to understanding whether interventions work in a variety of settings and are the focus of other work (e.g., Chapter 2; Wanless, Patton, Rimm-Kaufman, & Deutsch, 2012). In contrast, we focus on the assessment of intervention core components. Intervention fidelity assessment helps us understand how much *actual* difference in causal elements exists after implementation. The actual difference in core intervention components, or *achieved relative strength* of the intervention (Cordray & Pion, 2006; Hulleman & Cordray, 2009), determines intervention outcomes and is what needs to be measured in both treatment and control conditions. In the case of the RC approach, one treatment teacher may implement 6 of the 10 practices as intended by the developer, whereas 3 of the 10 practices may be present in control classrooms. This would mean that the achieved relative strength of the intervention for this RC teacher was only 3 components, instead of a possible 10. Due to our focus on intervention fidelity and intervention core components, in the remainder of the chapter any reference to core components will refer to intervention core components.

Although definitions of intervention fidelity vary throughout the literature (for a review, see O'Donnell, 2008), fidelity is generally composed of five dimensions:

1. Exposure—To what extent are participants exposed to the treatment?

2. Adherence—Were treatment components delivered as designed?

3. Quality—How well was the treatment implemented?

4. Responsiveness—To what extent are participants engaged and involved in the treatment?

5. Differentiation—Are critical program components that differentiate treatment from control present?

Responsibility for treatment fidelity within the five dimensions can lie with implementers of the intervention (e.g., early care providers or teachers), participants (e.g., children in an intervention with teachers as implementers), or both (Hulleman & Cordray, 2009). Importantly, these five dimensions are meant to provide a framework for fidelity assessment that enables the evaluator to capture the whole of the intervention and not simply disjointed pieces. Other fidelity frameworks that use slightly different language can be equally helpful—the important point is to measure fidelity across different dimensions of implementation.

There is ample evidence within health efficacy and effectiveness studies that variation in treatment fidelity accounts for variability in outcomes (e.g., Dane & Schneider, 1998; Mitchel, Hu, McDonnell, & Swisher, 1984; Tortu & Botvin, 1989). Increasingly, evidence within early care and education research demonstrates that intervention fidelity can explain some of the variation in treatment effectiveness (e.g., Chapter 1; Durlak & DuPre, 2008; Durlak et al., 2011; McIntyre, Gresham, DiGennaro, & Reed, 2007; Nunnery et al., in press).

To be able to assess whether a program was implemented, the conceptual foundation of the program must be elucidated, along with the essential components required for proper implementation. This involves breaking down an intervention model into its core components and ensuring that the fidelity indices, when administered individually, can be combined to represent full-scale classroom implementation without losing the essence of the intervention. Thus, the measurement of fidelity is, at its core, an exercise in construct validity.

In essence, this is the whole-part-whole tension present between the structuralists and Gestaltists. Our aim in this chapter is to demonstrate that this measurement challenge can be overcome by developing valid measures of intervention fidelity within the context of a school-based intervention. We do this by applying the five-step model of fidelity assessment developed by Nelson, Cordray, Hulleman, Darrow, and Sommer (2012) to the RC approach. The first step of this process is to develop systematic and detailed representations of the program (i.e., logic models) to guide fidelity assessment.

The First Step in Fidelity Assessment: Logic Models

Logic models are a common method for explicating program elements. As defined by the W.K. Kellogg Foundation (2004), a logic model visually represents the relationships between the resources required, activities to be put in place, and outcomes that occur as a result of program implementation. Knowlton and Phillips (2009) further differentiate logic models into two distinct types that pertain to fidelity assessment: a conceptual model and an operational model. The *conceptual logic model,* or theory of change, represents program elements in conceptual terms by describing the constructs that underlie activities and resources. The *operational logic model* represents program elements in practical terms by describing the activities and resources involved in implementing the intervention.

First, the core intervention components that form the foundation of the theory of change are specified (see Figure 4.1). The theory of change lays out the *sequence* of intervention components and subsequent outcomes expected under ideal conditions. Each intervention component is described in terms of constructs, and the sequence of how constructs are related to each other, as well as to proximal and distal outcomes (i.e., outputs and outcomes, respectively; Lugo-Gil et al., 2011), corresponds to the theoretical intervention model.

Figure 4.1 presents the conceptual logic model for the RC approach. The initial step in creating change is the *training* teachers receive in how to use RC practices

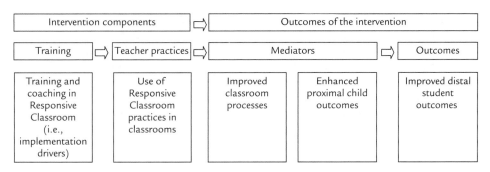

Figure 4.1. The conceptual logic model for the Responsive Classroom approach.

in the classroom. Next, teachers need to implement the *practices* in the classroom. These two intervention components, training and practices, set into motion two classroom-level mediators: improved classroom processes and enhanced student engagement in school. These mediators result in student outcomes such as improved social skills and achievement.

Next, the operational logic model specifies program implementation (i.e., who, what, where, how, and when) and describes how program activities are mapped onto the conceptual intervention core components from the theory of change. These operational core components are the specific teacher behaviors that represent the theorized core intervention components. As presented in Figure 4.2, RC implementation begins with the planned work, including *resources and inputs, activities,* and *school and classroom outputs.* The presence of resources and inputs occurs first and includes elements of the NEFC training infrastructure, including

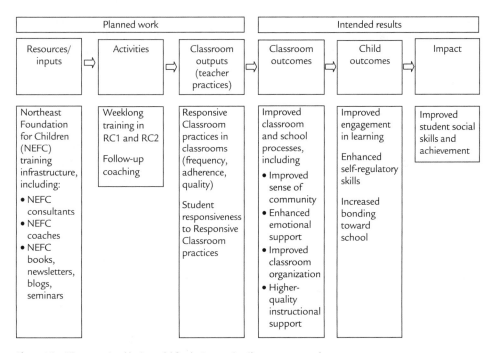

Figure 4.2. The operational logic model for the Responsive Classroom approach.

consulting teachers and coaches, manuals and books, as well as other multimedia resources. Next, activities include training in the RC approach. Training sessions involve certified RC consulting teachers who provide weeklong training work-shops in the first and second summers, along with in-school, follow-up coaching. The final part of implementation, school and classroom outputs, refers to the use of RC practices in classrooms—specifically, teachers' frequency of use and adherence to the 10 RC practices of Morning Meetings, Rule Creation, Interactive Modeling, Positive Teacher Language, and so forth.

The planned work should ideally lead to intended results, including school and classroom outcomes, child outcomes, and impact. School and classroom outcomes are processes induced by the use of RC practices, such as enhanced sense of community in the school, improved emotional support (i.e., more warmth, caring, and responsiveness among teachers and children), improved quality of classroom management, and higher quality instruction. These processes should then increase children's engagement in learning, self-regulatory skills, and school bonding. Finally, under ideal conditions, program impact will be evidenced by improved student social skills and achievement.

When specifying the model, it is important to consider the level at which the intervention is enacted. Many school-based interventions, including the RC approach, can be enacted district-wide, schoolwide, or by an individual teacher (Greenberg, 2010). Schoolwide implementation implies that virtually all adminis-trators, teachers, and other school staff receive some training in the RC approach. Subsequently, the RC approach is leveraged to build community and improve the climate within the whole school through schoolwide meetings, with consistency in discipline across all of the adults who interact with children (e.g., music teach-ers, art teachers, cafeteria staff). Thus, schoolwide change results from synergis-tic effects that emerge when RC administrators and RC teachers come together to create changes in school culture. In fact, school-level change can be viewed as an outcome unto itself for schools using RC practices to achieve improvement to the school climate, guided by coaching and materials aimed at school administrators (Casto & Audley, 2008; Northeast Foundation for Children, 2006).

Similar to measuring implementation of an evidenced-based practice on a large scale, intervention fidelity would be measured in relation to efforts to change the broader adult community, such as interactions among implementers or between implementers and administrators. However, the difference between implementa-tion assessment and fidelity assessment is that the former is focused on the drivers of implementation at scale, whereas the latter is focused on measuring core compo-nents of the intervention model.

In contrast, many school-based interventions are enacted almost exclusively by individual teachers. As a result, the processes and behaviors most pertinent to fidelity assessment shift to the classroom. Several options are available for measur-ing intervention fidelity when teachers are implementers (i.e., when individual teachers at the school become RC teachers). On the one hand, intervention fidelity can be measured by considering the quality of the summer workshops and the frequency and quality of the follow-up coaching (i.e., activities that are a part of the planned work; see Figure 4.2). On the other hand, intervention fidelity can be measured by assessing the teachers' use of practices in the classroom (i.e., school and classroom outputs).

This discussion of level of implementation highlights an important first objective in considering measurement of intervention fidelity with validity: defining the implementers and the outcome(s) of interest. One of the core premises of the RC approach is that student change occurs through the experience of RC practices. Intervention fidelity at this level assesses RC teaching practices or student responsiveness to classroom practices. This localizes the main thrust of intervention fidelity assessment at the classroom level. Other interventions that are enacted at the school or district level will focus fidelity assessment accordingly. However, this does not mean that the RC approach does not have school- or district-level components. Rather, it means that fidelity measurement will focus on teachers and the practices they use to interact with children. For brevity, we focus on teachers' implementation of RC practices in this chapter. Other work (e.g., Wanless et al., 2012) considers school-level predictors of the use of the RC approach.

A Five-Step Model of Intervention Fidelity Assessment

We advocate a five-step process for assessing intervention fidelity with construct validity (Cordray & Hulleman, 2009; Nelson et al., 2012):

1. Specify the core conceptual and operational program components.

2. Identify appropriate fidelity indicators.

3. Determine index validity (including reliability).

4. Combine indices where appropriate.

5. Link fidelity to outcomes where possible.

In Step 2, the conceptual and operational logic models focus the assessment on the specific actions required to implement the intervention core components. Common methods used to measure fidelity include surveys, observations, and interviews. To capture a comprehensive and rich picture of implementation, we recommend that measures of each core component include as many dimensions of fidelity—exposure, adherence, quality, responsiveness, and differentiation—as possible. If some core components are measured mainly with adherence measures while others include primarily measures of quality, then any differences in their relationship with outcomes may be due to the content of the items, the type of fidelity, or both. In the RC example below, the fidelity measures were equivalently focused on exposure and adherence across core intervention components.

Before being incorporated within the analysis of treatment variation, reliability and validity evidence should be gathered for the different fidelity measures (Step 3). Reliability involves the extent to which the fidelity measures intercorrelate. For instance, we would expect that teacher self-reports of RC practices would correlate with classroom observations. Validity involves the extent to which the fidelity instruments measure what is intended (i.e., construct validity). For instance, assessing the frequency of the Morning Meeting (adherence) but not the quality of delivery (quality) may fail to cover the breadth of the construct (Shadish, Cook, & Campbell, 2002).

If several fidelity measures are highly interrelated, they can be combined into composite fidelity indices (Step 4). Composite fidelity indices are useful, as they can be more easily utilized to determine achieved relative strength of the intervention (Abry, Rimm-Kaufman, Hulleman, Thomas, & Ko, 2012; Hulleman & Cordray, 2009). That is, composite indices more succinctly quantify overall fidelity, which can then be used to link fidelity to outcomes in a simpler fashion. In addition, creating indices that represent individual core components is helpful in assessing the extent to which individual components have been implemented.

Once the appropriate fidelity measures have been combined, fidelity can be linked to outcome measures using both descriptive and inferential statistics (Step 5). It is possible that fidelity is more strongly linked to outcomes for some core components than for others. This can help identify core (versus ancillary) intervention components and provide clues as to how best to adjust the intervention to be more effective and adjust the theoretical model. For example, if fidelity measures of 2 of the 10 RC practices were strongly related to outcomes whereas the others were unrelated, this might lead to changes in the RC model and how heavily some components are emphasized compared to others.

Application of the Five-Step Model of Fidelity Assessment: The Responsive Classroom Efficacy Study

In this section, we use results from the Responsive Classroom Efficacy Study (RCES; Rimm-Kaufman et al., 2012) to highlight various issues involving model specification (Step 1), fidelity measurement (Step 2), determining indices of intervention fidelity (Steps 3 and 4), and linking fidelity to intervention outcomes (Step 5). For brevity, we have limited our scope to examining intervention fidelity of teachers' use of RC practices in the classroom, thus considering the direct effect of the intervention on students.

Step 1: Model Specification

The RCES research team began by developing intervention fidelity measures meeting construct validity and data collection feasibility objectives. RCES was the second study of the RC approach conducted by Rimm-Kaufman and colleagues, and thus the research group leveraged lessons learned in the earlier efficacy study (Rimm-Kaufman & Sawyer, 2004; Rimm-Kaufman, Fan, Chiu, & You, 2007) to hone the measures. The research team, comprising independent evaluators of the RC approach, was able to take an objective stance toward assessing the intervention. However, being independent evaluators posed a challenge in understanding intervention fidelity, requiring the team to become immersed in the approach and establish a collaborative relationship with NEFC while also maintaining its objective stance.

Several steps were necessary to articulate the logic model and develop our measures. First, researchers on the measurement development team attended RC workshops. Second, the researchers engaged in a thorough review of RC practices through the RC books and materials available. Third, we engaged several people from the NEFC to provide feedback to us on measurement development. Fourth, realizing that measurement development would be an iterative process, we held weekly conversations with the NEFC developers to be sure that we were measuring the presence of RC practices without losing the essence of the RC approach.

Finally, we coordinated our efforts with existing efforts at NEFC. Specifically, the NEFC team was developing a measure designed to be used in schools so that school administrators could measure the presence or absence of RC practices (Wilson, Freeman-Loftis, Sawyer, & Denton, 2009), and thus our dialogue was effective in both directions. Throughout the process, the research team considered the feasibility of the proposed measurement process in relation to resources available through the study.

Step 2: Developing Fidelity Indicators

Our research team developed three distinct measures of intervention fidelity, focusing mainly on exposure and adherence. The Classroom Practices Teacher Survey (CPTS; Nathanson & Rimm-Kauffman, 2007b) is a 46-item teacher-report measure ($\alpha = .91$) measuring teachers' perception of their use of RC practices. The CPTS was designed to measure exposure and adherence. Teachers rate their use of a specific classroom practice on a five-point Likert scale, ranging from 1 (not at all characteristic) to 5 (extremely characteristic). Each item asks about the use of RC practices, but the items are phrased carefully to avoid use of RC language. Further, seven of the items are reverse-scored to further reduce biased responding. For example, to measure use of Morning Meetings, teachers are asked to rate the statement "In the morning, we have a class meeting where we sit in a circle facing one another." To measure Academic Choice, teachers are given "When my students are working on activities of their own choosing, I have structures in place that assist them in planning their activity."

The Classroom Practice Frequency Survey (CPFS; Nathanson & Rimm-Kauffman, 2007a) is an 11-item teacher-report measure ($\alpha = .89$) assessing the frequency of teachers' use of RC practices, thus assessing students' exposure to the intervention. Teachers are asked to recall their use of specific practices. Again, the practices are described avoiding the use of RC language. For example, to measure Academic Choice, teachers evaluate the statement "I provide opportunities for students to choose how to do work, what kind of work to do, or both (e.g., in studying marine biology, students may choose the animal they want to study and/ or students can demonstrate knowledge about this animal through writing a report, drawing a picture book, crafting a clay model)." Teachers report their responses on an eight-point scale ranging from 1 (almost never) to 8 (more than once per day).

The Classroom Practices Observation Measure (CPOM; Abry, Brewer, Nathanson, Sawyer, & Rimm-Kauffman, 2010) is a 16-item observational measure ($\alpha = .88$) of exposure and adherence to the intervention core components. The measure describes RC practices without using RC terminology to ensure that the measure can be used in intervention and control classrooms and because the classroom observers have not necessarily been trained in the RC approach. For example, for the RCES, an assessment item to measure Rule Creation stated, "Three to five general, positively worded rules are posted in the classroom." To measure Positive Teacher Language, one item stated, "Teacher asks questions or makes statements that invite students to remember expected behaviors." Each item was coded on a three-point Likert scale, ranging from not at all characteristic to very characteristic. A 16-item version was administered during morning observations and an abbreviated 10-item version that excluded Morning Meeting items was used during observations conducted during mathematics instruction. Two items were reverse-scored. An extensive training process was developed to establish and maintain coder reliability (see Abry, Rimm-Kaufman, Larsen, & Brewer, 2011).

Table 4.2 lists the 10 RC intervention core components and the total number of indicators across the three types of measures developed by Rimm-Kaufman and colleagues (Rimm-Kaufman, Berry, Fan, McCracken, & Walkowiak, 2008).

Once the measures have been developed, it is essential to work backward from the indicators to the construct (i.e., the intervention model) to determine whether these constructs fully capture the treatment. Crucially, the essence of the intervention needs to be represented. If not, it is possible that by breaking the intervention model into pieces the big picture, or gestalt, of the intervention will be lost.

Table 4.2. Responsive Classroom fidelity indicators

Core components	Subcomponents	Total number of indicators	Indicators per component
Morning Meeting	General	5	25
	Greeting	3	
	Sharing	4	
	Group activity	6	
	Morning message	7	
Academic Choice	Plan	4	11
	Work	4	
	Reflect	3	
Interactive Modeling	Teacher demonstration	2	7
	Student observations	2	
	Student practice	3	
Rule Creation	Students generate hopes and dreams	2	11
	Students brainstorm rules	4	
	Rules consolidated	3	
	Rules posted	2	
Positive Teacher Language	Reinforcing	1	4
	Reminding	2	
	Redirecting	1	
Logical consequences	Respectful	0	7
	Relevant	3	
	Realistic	0	
	Time-out	4	
Guided Discovery	Introduce material	0	3
	Generate and model ideas for use and care	2	
	Explore and experiment with material	1	
Classroom Organization	Arrangement	1	4
	Materials	2	
	Displays	1	
Working with families	General communication	1	2
	Involve parents in goal setting	1	
	Involve parents in classroom and school activities	0	
Collaborative problem solving	Conferencing	0	0
	Role play	0	

One way of ensuring that this validity check occurs is for the instrument developers to check back with program developers (or implementers) after the fidelity instrument has been developed. Not only can program developers consider whether any important components are missing or if there are extraneous components that could be eliminated, but they can also consider two different scenarios. First, developers or implementers could consider whether a teacher who scores highly on these measures would be considered an RC teacher, whereas a teacher who scores low would not be. Conversely, they could envision the practices of the ideal RC teacher and consider the extent to which the measure adequately taps these practices. The answers to these questions will help instrument developers understand whether their fidelity measures adequately map back not only to the individual core components but also to the entirety of the intervention they are intending to measure.

Steps 3 and 4: Determining Index Validity and Reliability

The research team combined items and indices to measure fidelity to core intervention components and to quantify achieved relative strength of the intervention. Indices were then created to correspond to several core components.

First, we determined how to combine items across different types of measures. There are several possible methods to combine indicators into indices. The most basic is to create composite fidelity indices by taking a variety of different measures (teacher report, self-report) and combining them into one overall indicator of intervention fidelity. A second approach would be to create indices based on the measure. That would involve creating one fidelity index for the teacher self-report measure and a second for the classroom observation measure. A third method would be to combine items in meaningful ways across the different types of measures. This would mean taking all items pertaining to a specific core component and combining them into an index that represents fidelity to that core component. We recommend the third approach for several reasons (cf. Abry et al., 2012). Creating indices by core components allows the researcher to examine fidelity to each core component as well as overall fidelity (if the separate indices are combined). Core component indices support efforts to diagnose features of the intervention model that are easier or more difficult to implement. The core component approach allows the researcher to examine the construct validity of the intervention model and its core components rather than only providing a diffuse measure of overall fidelity as produced by the first two approaches.

In the RC data, there is one observational measure (CPOM) and two teacher self-report measures (CPFS, CPTS). Because the measures were on different scales, items were first standardized across the sample, and then relevant items from across the measurement instruments were combined to form the index for each core component. For this chapter, we focus on three core RC practices: Morning Meeting (10 items), Academic Choice (8 items), and Interactive Modeling (5 items). Importantly, these measures quantified the levels of adherence and exposure of the intervention—as opposed to quality, responsiveness, and differentiation—which constrains our inferences about implementation to these dimensions of fidelity.

Table 4.3 presents the number of items from each type of measure that contributed to the fidelity indices for each core component. Each RC practice (i.e., intervention component) was broken down further into subcomponents. For Interactive

Table 4.3.   Responsive Classroom intervention fidelity indicators by intervention core component, subcomponent, and type of measure

Core Responsive Classroom component	Subcomponent	Number of indicators			Total indicators
		CPOM	CPTS	CPFS	
Morning Meeting	General	1	3	1	5
	Greeting	1	1	1	3
	Sharing	1	2	1	4
	Group activity	1	4	1	6
	Morning message	2	4	1	7
Academic Choice	Plan	2[a]	1	1	4
	Work	2[a]	1	1	4
	Reflect	0	2	1	3
Interactive Modeling	Teacher demonstration	1[a]	0	1	2
	Student observations	1[a]	0	1	2
	Student practice	1[a]	1	1	3

Key: CPOM, Classroom Practices Observation Measure; CPTS, Classroom Practices Teacher Survey; CPFS, Classroom Practices Frequency Survey.

[a]Single item that addresses multiple subcomponents.

Modeling, key subcomponents of this practice include the teacher demonstrating the skill or activity, students observing the teacher demonstrations, and students practicing the skill or activity. It should be noted that not every subcomponent was analyzed with each type of measure, nor was every core component measured with an equal number of items. This resulted in some fidelity indices containing more of one type of measure than another, and with some core components containing significantly more items than others (e.g., 25 items for Morning Meeting compared to 7 for Interactive Modeling).

Once indices for each core component have been created, they can be used to compare the relative strength in intervention components between treatment and counterfactual conditions. As mentioned earlier, *achieved relative strength* refers to the difference between the actual implementation of the intervention in the treatment group and in the control group. Using achieved relative strength means that "the estimates of effects on the outcome are the result of the achieved relative strength of the contrast between treatment and control, not the theoretically expected difference" (Hulleman & Cordray, 2009, p. 91). The achieved relative strength values correspond to effect size values to aid interpretation. One of the challenges of ensuring construct validity is that many RC practices resemble practices used in typical classrooms. For instance, many teachers provide instructional choice to their students and may be creating the same advantages for children as RC teachers. Furthermore, within RC classrooms, some teachers are not fully implementing the RC approach as intended. In this section, we outline two types of achieved relative strength indices (ARSI): the average index and the binary complier index.

The average ARSI is computed by standardizing the average difference between fidelity indices from each condition (subtracting the mean scores and dividing by the pooled standard deviation; see Hulleman & Cordray, 2009, for details). Table 4.4 presents the average ARSI values for intervention and control teachers for 84 fourth-grade teachers at 24 schools (13 intervention, 11 control). Because the items were standardized across the entire sample, positive values are

Table 4.4.   Achieved relative strength values for fourth-grade teachers in the Responsive Classroom Efficacy Study

RC practice	N	Overall mean (*SD*)	Treatment mean (*SD*)	Control mean (*SD*)	Min	Max	ARSI
MM	84	−0.13 (1.00)	0.65 (0.58)	−0.95 (0.61)	−1.49	1.10	2.19
IM	84	0.00 (0.74)	0.19 (0.76)	−0.20 (0.65)	−2.09	1.46	0.47
AC	84	−0.04 (0.86)	0.33 (0.84)	−0.42 (0.71)	−1.64	2.23	0.80

Key: RC, Responsive Classroom; MM, Morning Meeting; IM, Interactive Modeling; AC, Academic Choice; ARSI, Achieved Relative Strength Index.

Note: N = 43 (treatment) and 41 (control).

above the mean of the sample and negative values are below the mean. The ARSI column reveals that although intervention teachers are implementing all four components to a higher degree than control teachers on average, the achieved relative strength values differed across core components.

The Morning Meeting practice shows the largest ARSI, greater than two standard deviations. It comprises four subcomponents: greeting, group activity, sharing, and morning message. Aside from the sharing subcomponent, these practices are very characteristic of RC classrooms and are seldom apparent in control classrooms.

The Academic Choice practice was substantially different between RC and control conditions, corresponding to roughly 4/5 of a standard deviation. This practice involves the teacher creating the learning objective and letting the student choose how to engage in the work. Academic Choice has subcomponents of planning, working, and reflecting. Although these subcomponents are carefully articulated in the NEFC manuals (NEFC, 2007, 2009), the subcomponents have similar characteristics to practices following from the theory of multiple intelligence and differentiated instruction (Tomlinson, 2001).

Psychometrically, the variation in ARSIs across the three core components can be interpreted in relation to the approach to measurement. Teacher-reported measures, though designed to tap exposure and adherence, also detect aspects of teachers' underlying belief system, as well as their day-to-day practices. In contrast, observed measures of RC reflect observed evidence of exposure and adherence to the intervention. In thinking through the process of teacher change, it may be easier to produce change in adherence to classroom practices than it is to change underlying beliefs (Rimm-Kaufman, Storm, Sawyer, Pianta, & La Paro, 2006). For example, it may be easier for teachers to adjust their daily routine to include the Morning Meeting four days a week than to change their philosophy about how and why students should be disciplined. Consider the following quotes from two RC coaches:

> Although the teachers at [my school] are very excited about Morning Meeting, they have many doubts about whether the rest of the RC approach, especially discipline and teacher language, will work for the students at their school. They seem somewhat discouraged that they still have behavior issues with which to deal. Many struggle with basic management issues and attribute much of their difficulties to the students.

> I met with the three RC teachers about logical consequences and problem-solving conferences. They are still having some difficulty separating proactive approaches to discipline from reactive. Some also continue to question whether logical consequences are tough enough, perhaps because they still have a basically punitive philosophy.

The disconnect between measurement of teacher change and actual teacher change may be more present for some RC practices than others, particularly for the observational measures. Teachers are observed only five times per year, and thus the observed behaviors represent a sampling of what occurs during the year. On any given day, only a subset of RC practices can be observed within the classroom. For instance, an observer can notice and code the teachers' use of Morning Meeting components, the presence of posted rules and the extent to which they follow RC recommendations, and use of student choice in the classroom. However, observers may not be privy to classroom practices that occur only occasionally. Furthermore, an observer in the classroom five days a year is unlikely to observe disciplinary practices used only several times per year to address very disruptive behavior. Also, without frequent observations conducted toward the beginning of the year, observers may be less able to report the full extent that teachers use the Interactive Modeling practices when introducing new materials to the class. Perhaps as a result of the approach to sampling for the observational measure, teachers are observed when they are engaged in the day-to-day practices that best differentiate between intervention and control conditions. However, the actual practices that make the RC approach the most effective are not as easily observed or are not present frequently enough to be observed by sampling only five times per year.

In terms of recommended practices of fidelity assessment, these issues are not easily rectified post hoc. Rather, they are most effectively addressed by creating measurement instruments that reflect the breadth of core intervention components and are calibrated to the types of information that are best measured using observational versus self-reported measures. This will ensure that the measures of the intervention core components are being captured with construct validity. When this is accomplished, the average achieved relative strength helps intervention evaluators ensure construct validity by indexing the relative difference in intervention core components between treatment and control conditions. Because the average ARSI can be calculated on a familiar metric (i.e., Cohen's d), it provides a useful measure to communicate the strength of the intervention as implemented.

A second type of ARSI, the binary complier index (Hulleman & Cordray, 2009), refers to a dichotomous index, or threshold, that represents whether or not students are receiving sufficient treatment to create change. In essence, the binary complier index can be determined by choosing practices and setting a level of those practices regarded as an adequate dose of the intervention to create change. Cutoff values for the binary complier index can be derived theoretically or empirically, based on their ability to discriminate between RC teachers and non-RC teachers. In this section, we focus on the binary complier index for the Morning Meeting and Academic Choice practices.

In relation to the Morning Meeting, two thresholds were set by the NEFC based on theoretical grounds—one to capture exposure and frequency of the practice, and a second that also included aspects of adherence. The initial threshold was to hold a Morning Meeting at least four times a week. To capture adherence, there were several questions on the teacher survey (CPTS) that reflected subcomponents of the practice, including having the students greet each other, sharing thoughts and feelings, having a community-building activity, and displaying a message of the day. Thus, the second Morning Meeting threshold was set such that a teacher needed to indicate that he or she completed each of the additional aspects of the Morning Meeting four or more times per week in order to be considered an RC teacher.

For Academic Choice, the threshold was set based on conceptual grounds. Specifically, we set the threshold for being a high-fidelity RC teacher at once per week on each of three indicators from teacher self-reports. This decision reflected the notion that using the Academic Choice practice once a week is the minimum use to be considered an RC teacher.

The Morning Meeting exposure criterion indicated that nearly all (85%) treatment teachers would be classified as RC teachers, whereas the adherence criterion designated just over half (58%) the treatment teachers as RC teachers. The percentage of teachers who were classified as RC teachers in the control condition can be thought of as the extent to which RC practices represent commonly used practices in the school. Interestingly, for the Morning Meeting practice, this also depended on whether the exposure (29%) or adherence (6%) criterion was used. In this case, the difference reflects the construct breadth that the measure captures—the single-item measure captured whether Morning Meetings occurred at all (exposure), whereas the additional items helped capture adherence to specific subcomponents of the Morning Meeting. For Academic Choice, 67% of teachers in the treatment group were classified as high-fidelity RC teachers, compared to 49% of teachers in the control group.

As outlined in the conceptual model, changes in RC practices are designed to shift classroom social processes and enhance children's engagement in learning. Such changes require repeated exercise and practice at sufficient frequency for teachers and children to develop new habits. In theory, holding a Morning Meeting four or more times per week gives opportunities for teachers to teach and children to practice specific social skills (e.g., cooperation, turn taking, empathy toward peers). Further, the Morning Meeting offers each child an opportunity to be part of a positive social activity at school, thus promoting children's engagement in learning and supporting their positive feelings about school.

The binary complier index provides a very useful tool for understanding construct validity in intervention fidelity. By setting a benchmark for intervention implementation, program developers are operationally defining what it takes to implement the intervention. Thus, implementers have a specified target to aim for when implementing the program that allows for some imperfection in implementation. Additionally, this assessment indicates aspects of the intervention in which implementation drivers could facilitate higher levels of RC practices (cf. Chapter 2).

Measuring achieved relative strength in both intervention and control conditions raises questions about how much intervention is *enough* to create the intended impact of the intervention, as specified by the logic models (i.e., improved school, classroom, and child outcomes; see Figure 4.3). One way to determine this threshold is to empirically examine the relationship between intervention fidelity and outcomes. There is a hierarchy of approaches, from descriptive to inferential, that can be used to incorporate measures of intervention fidelity and achieved relative strength when analyzing program impacts.

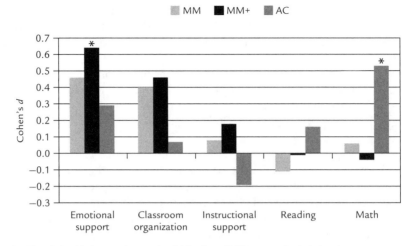

Figure 4.3. The relationship between intervention fidelity (i.e., the binary complier index) and program outcomes in the Responsive Classroom Efficacy Study. In computing the binary complier index, teachers in the study were categorized as either meeting the threshold for implementing that specific program core component (compliers) or not (noncompliers). The RC practices presented here are as follows: MM, Morning Meeting measured with a single item (exposure); MM+, Morning Meeting measured with multiple items (adherence); and AC, Academic Choice. The outcome variables are listed along the x-axis and include emotional support, classroom organization, and instructional support (classroom outcomes), and reading and math (intervention impacts; see Figure 4.2). The bars represent differences between compliers and noncompliers in standard deviation units of the outcomes on the y-axis. *Compliers significantly different from noncompliers at $p < .05$.

Step 5: Linking Fidelity Measures to Outcome Measures

There are numerous approaches that could be used to incorporate fidelity assessment into impact analyses, from descriptively comparing levels of implementation in treatment and control (e.g., Snyder et al., 2010), computing indices of achieved relative strength (Hulleman & Cordray, 2009), and correlational analyses between fidelity indices and outcomes in both treatment and control conditions, to more sophisticated approaches such as replacing the treatment indicator with the fidelity indicator or complier index (Schochet & Burghardt, 2007; Peck, 2003) and instrumental variables (Bloom, 2005). Various analytical frameworks can be employed, including ordinary least squares multiple regression (Unlu et al., 2011), multilevel modeling (e.g., Justice, Mashburn, Pence, & Wiggins, 2008), and structural equation modeling (e.g., Abry et al., 2012; Kopp, Hulleman, Rozek, & Harackiewicz, 2012). Analyses can also be conducted to understand the sources of variation in intervention fidelity (e.g., Hulleman & Cordray, 2009).

Importantly, all of these analytic approaches deviate, to a greater or lesser extent, from the causal inference framework produced by random assignment (Holland, 1986; Rubin, 1974). That is, even if construct validity of our fidelity measures has been secured, we are sacrificing some of our ability to infer cause and effect with these approaches because fidelity has been measured and not manipulated (cf. Imai, Keele, Tingley, & Yamamoto, 2011; Shadish et al., 2002). It is within this more limited causal inference context that the results of these analytic approaches can be understood. Given these limitations, we turn to the utility of linking these fidelity indices to outcomes.

First, descriptive and correlational analyses of fidelity measures within both treatment and control conditions can be used to examine presence and relationships among intervention core components. This approach allows us to examine, as directly as possible, whether the construct we theorized to impact outcomes was actually implemented. In essence, this is our test of construct validity: Did we successfully actualize our theorized model within the educational context?

These initial questions are best examined through descriptive statistics of fidelity measures within both treatment and control conditions. Calculating ARSIs then provides an index of how strong the intervention was in comparison to the control (or counterfactual) condition. In addition, zero-order correlations among core components provide evidence regarding the consistency of implementation core components. The higher the correlations among core components, the more uniformly the intervention was implemented across core components. Furthermore, zero-order correlations between core components and outcomes provide us with two important pieces of information. First, correlations that are significant (statistically, practically, or both) provide information regarding the correlational aspect of causality: Does the supposed cause correlate with the outcome? If the cause (the intervention and associated core components) does not correlate with the outcome, then our ability to infer that the intervention causes changes in the outcome is seriously undermined. Second, correlations between core components and outcomes provide information about the impact of intervention strength: Does a higher amount of implementation lead to better outcomes?

A recommended practice is to table fidelity indices of core components in both treatment and control conditions. Included within these tables, or in a separate table, could be the ARSIs based on these values (e.g., Table 4.4). Formulas for calculating the ARSIs can be found in Hulleman and Cordray (2009) and are derivations of Cohen's *d* and Hedges's *g* adjusted for the type of index.

In addition, presentations of correlation matrices containing fidelity indices of intervention core components, mediational variables, and outcomes need to be standard. Preferably, these correlation matrices should have the treatment condition values on one side of the diagonal and control condition values on the other side. This provides the opportunity to examine how relationships with intervention core components vary by condition. For example, Table 4.5 presents the correlation matrices among RC core components, classroom outcomes, and student outcomes. Correlations for the control group are above the diagonal, and those for the treatment group are below the diagonal.

Next, we can turn attention toward further analyses to examine the relationships between fidelity indices and outcomes. At the most basic level, comparing differences in program outcomes using the binary complier index is straightforward. Once the complier index is calculated, this analysis can be as simple as computing t-tests between the groups using the outcomes as dependent variables. Hulleman and Cordray (2009, p. 99) presented the results of a motivation intervention in both the laboratory and the classroom using the binary complier index. Using the RCES data, we conducted similar analyses. As shown in Table 4.6, we computed binary complier indices for the RC core components of Morning Meeting and Academic Choice. Note that the Morning Meeting core component related more to classroom outcomes, whereas the Academic Choice component related more to student outcomes. Also note that the index created from the Morning Meeting adherence threshold showed larger contrasts on classroom outcomes than the index based on the exposure-only threshold.

Table 4.5. Correlations for core intervention components and selected outcomes by experimental and control groups

	1	2	3	4	5	6	7	8
RC practice								
1. MM	—	.43**	.19	.16	.23	.10	-.10	-.02
2. IM	.39**	—	-.06	.39*	.15	.22	-.03	.02
3. AC	.16	.49**	—	-.03	-.11	-.20	.36*	.36*
Classroom outcome								
4. ES	.32*	.16	.29	—	.54***	.69***	.26	-.16
5. CO	.23	.18	.47***	.67***	—	.59***	-.16	-.05
6. IS	.22	.18	.28	.72***	.67***	—	.03	-.26
Student outcome								
7. Mathematics	-.26	.08	.24	.10	.32	.07	—	.10
8. Reading	-.24	-.16	.25	-.05	.08	-.10	.69***	—

Key: RC, Responsive Classroom; MM, Morning Meeting; IM, Interactive Modeling; AC, Academic Choice; ES, emotional support; CO, Classroom Organization; IS, instructional support.

Note: ES, CO, and IS are domains of the Classroom Assessment Scoring System: $N = 43$ (treatment) and 41 (control). Mathematics and reading achievement are aggregated at the classroom level. Correlations for the control group are presented above the diagonal. Correlations for the experimental group are presented below the diagonal.

$*p < .05$; $**p < .01$; $***p < .001$.

Table 4.6. Example weighting of Responsive Classroom practices for child social and academic outcomes

	Social outcomes		Achievement outcomes	
	Weight assuming equal importance	Weight based on logic models	Weight assuming equal importance	Weight based on logic models
Morning Meeting	.2	.3	.2	.15
Creating rules with children, modeling rules, and approaching discipline	.2	.3	.2	.15
Positive Teacher Language	.2	.2	.2	.3
Interactive Modeling and Guided Discovery	.2	.1	.2	.1
Academic Choice	.2	.1	.2	.3

Another approach is to utilize the framework described by Schochet and Burghardt (2007), which involves several variations of the complier index within a broader analytic framework. Within the context of clustered data, which are quite common in early care and education research, this means using a multilevel modeling or random effects framework. The treatment indicator can then be replaced with the binary complier index or even the fidelity indicator itself (cf. Justice et al., 2008; Unlu et al., 2011).

If the goal is to understand the role that intervention fidelity plays in explaining the treatment effect, it is possible to conduct path modeling to estimate the mediated or indirect effects of the intervention through the fidelity indices. This approach involves adding intervention fidelity indices into the statistical model used to predict program outcomes (e.g., Abry et al., 2012; Kopp et al., 2012). For example, within the context of the RC approach, Abry et al. (2011) computed multi-item indices of four core RC practices: Morning Meeting, Classroom Organization, Interactive Modeling, and Academic Choice. Utilizing a multilevel modeling framework, they found that Academic Choice accounted for unique variance in student math and reading test scores, whereas the other practices did not.

Although we focus on analysis of fidelity within randomized experiments, fidelity can also be incorporated within quasi-experimental designs. Although quasi-experimental designs have weaker claims to causal inference than do experimental designs, valuable information about levels of program fidelity can still be made, particularly if fidelity was assessed within the comparison condition. In those cases, the analyses would be quite similar: overall descriptive statistics that capture the degree of fidelity in treatment and control conditions, indices of achieved relative strength, correlations between level of fidelity and outcomes, and the treatment indicator could be adjusted for the level of fidelity in both treatment and control conditions. Measuring fidelity in quasi-experiments can even strengthen internal validity claims, because more is known about the level of fidelity in the nontreated group.

Applications of Fidelity Indices to Address Important Questions in Intervention Fidelity Assessment

In this section, we outline several issues within the measurement of intervention fidelity and its application to understanding early childhood interventions, including how much adaption is too much (i.e., the zone of tolerable adaptation), weighting and combining fidelity indices, sequencing of core intervention components, the interactions among components (and between components and program implementers), matching measures to core components, and the development of implementation skills.

Zone of Tolerable Adaptation

How much can program implementers change an intervention before treatment effects disappear? Is it more important for implementers to follow a very specific protocol established by the developers, or are interventions more effective when adapted to local conditions (cf. Dusenbury, Brannigan, Falco, & Hansen, 2003)? These questions are raised repeatedly as ECE settings adopt new interventions and strive to maintain their presence in a district (Dusenbury et al., 2003; Greenberg, 2010; Stringfield, Reynolds, & Schaffer, 2008). In essence, these questions speak to the issue of the zone of tolerable adaptation, defined as the extent to which an intervention can be modified and tailored before the accompanying treatment effects disappear. On the one hand, modifications to an intervention may help make the intervention well suited for local conditions (Datnow & Stringfield, 2000). For example, teachers may adapt the intervention to be more culturally sensitive or tailor the intervention activities to meet the developmental level of the students in the classroom. In fact, Stringfield et al. (2008) report that schoolwide reform interventions are most effective only when such mutual adaptation, or co-construction, of the intervention occurs. On the other hand, adaptation of program components may result in dropping components of the intervention demonstrated to be critically important to its effectiveness.

The need to adapt interventions to local conditions has become an accepted condition of scale-up efforts (Dusenbury et al., 2003), particularly so that the intervention is sustained in early childhood programs or initiatives such as home-based or center-based early childhood programs, home visitation programs, local ECE professional development programs, or statewide ECE professional development systems (Greenberg, 2010; Stringfield et al., 2008). As a result, intervention developers have increased the flexibility of their programs so that teachers can use, integrate, and take ownership of the programs and their implementation. Adaptations can be conducted, however, only when implementers adhere to core principles of the intervention, knowing which elements can and cannot be adapted (Dusenbury et al., 2003). Crucially, applying the key supports of successful implementation, or implementation drivers, when adapting interventions can facilitate successful adaptation (Fixsen et al., 2005).

Knowledge of systematic research that links intervention outcomes to fidelity of core intervention components, grounded within the conceptual framework of the intervention, is necessary in order to ascertain which components are crucial and which are adaptable. The conceptual framework identifies the scope of practices that are—and those that are not—consistent with core components that combine to construct the intervention. Research support for the relationship between implemented core components and outcomes guides an understanding of which components are crucial for intervention impact. In this way, the gestalt of the intervention is retained (thus maintaining construct validity), yet guidance in terms of intervention adaptation is provided.

Within the RC approach, tolerable adaptation of the Morning Meeting might involve having the students move chairs or desks out of the way for a Morning Meeting, rescheduling the Morning Meeting later in the day to create time for art or music, or having meetings be student led later during the school year. In contrast, adaptations that are not tolerable might include a regular Morning Meeting conducted in rows so that children cannot see one another, a meeting that engages in straightforward rehearsal and memorization tasks instead of an activity, or a meeting in which children are being unkind to one another and the teacher does not intervene. In relation to Academic Choice, a tolerable adaptation might be having children engage in a working phase that is tailored to students' individual ability levels or having students reflect on their learning through conversation or in writing. Intolerable adaptations might include limiting choice within activities to letting children decide where they will sit in the room during reading or dropping the planning and reflection RC core subcomponents from the Academic Choice activity. The analytic methods described earlier could assist in determining which adaptations are or are not tolerable in a planned variation model (Yeh, 2000), where variations of the intervention are implemented and connected to variations in outcomes.

Weighting and Combining Components

Once fidelity indicators have been developed, an important issue during the analytic phase is to consider how best to weight each indicator when creating indices, either to specific intervention components or to the overall model. The first step in the process is to link the measurement of fidelity back to the logic models and not simply to create indices based on the method of data collection.

In the RCES, three measures of fidelity were utilized. One option for creating fidelity indices is to sum the scores on each measure to create three distinct fidelity measures: the CPOM, CPTS, and CFTS. However, each of these instruments contains items from some or all of the core components, often not equally weighted. For example, 64% of the items on the CPTS measure the Morning Meeting, compared to only 43% of the items on the CPOM. The approach we recommend, in contrast, is to create indices based on core components. Not only does this approach enable the researcher to evaluate fidelity to intervention core components separately, but it also has more power empirically. As demonstrated by Abry (2012), fidelity indices created by core components account for more variance in child outcomes than those created by method of measurement.

In addition, some components might be weighted more heavily than others when creating indices and conducting analyses. This emphasis might be introduced because, at the conceptual level, some components are thought to be more crucial or because prior research demonstrated their primacy, or due to other considerations such as measurement precision or frequency. The program logic models should be our first point of reference in this process. In the RC model, not all RC practices are equivalently likely to produce changes in children's achievement outcomes. For example, the Morning Meeting is the foundation from which all other RC practices emanate, and as such it might be weighted more heavily when predicting social outcomes. On the other hand, Academic Choice is expected to be a more prominent driver of academic outcomes, and it is weighted more heavily on that basis.

Table 4.6 assigns approximate weights to the various components in relation to RC program outcomes. Because some of the RC practices were not measured adequately, we include only the practices for which we have strong measures. This weighting will then have implications for the development of indices and incorporation into data analyses. For example, in the creation of an overall fidelity index, the measures of each of the core components could be multiplied by their respective weights when computing a total fidelity score.

Sequencing of Components

Does the theory of change specify that some components should be implemented before others, either as part of a developmental sequence or to set the foundation for later instruction? What does this mean for measurement and analyses? The RC practice of Morning Meetings occurs early in the day, and early in the year, which provides the facilitative social-emotional context for optimal learning later in the day and later in the year. Thus, measuring its presence in the beginning of the year may have a different meaning—giving it more importance in terms of construct validity—than later in the year. A second RC example is that Guided Discovery offers a structure for introducing students to the use and care of new materials. Teachers use this more in the beginning of the year and the beginning of new lessons. Therefore, observing its presence in the beginning of the year or as teachers introduce new lessons would reflect the highest construct validity.

Matching Measures and Core Components

From a measurement standpoint, researchers and evaluators need to consider the extent to which the type of measure might be better suited for some core components than for others. In general, program implementers (e.g., health care providers, coaches, teachers) are probably better at reporting whether they did certain aspects of the program, and in what order, than they are at reporting how engaged children were during the learning activity or how many off-task behaviors occurred during a learning session (suggesting that children may not have been exposed to the intervention). The latter two are probably better suited for observational measures. In the RC approach, teachers are generally good at reporting their use of a Morning Meeting and the Morning Meeting components. However, they may be less effective at assessing the quality of the social interactions during that Morning Meeting because they are participants in the meeting.

In contrast, there are other instances when self-reports are likely to be a more valid measure of the intervention than observation. This may be particularly true for behaviors that occur infrequently during the year. RC teachers may set up school–family activities where families articulate and represent what they hope for their children during the year (i.e., Hopes and Dreams). Another example is the rare but salient negative situation that can swamp months of teacher effort toward high implementation. Imagine the high-implementing RC teacher who "loses it" with her students and gets angry. This kind of very negative behavior may have long-lasting consequences, but it can be very hard to measure via observation. The most valid way to get at these low-frequency events is probably through teacher report.

A different example pertains to teacher beliefs about schooling, which are an important part of the theory of change in most educational interventions, including the RC approach. It is relatively straightforward to observe whether a teacher has a Morning Meeting or not, but it is less plausible that an observational measure can directly capture a teacher's beliefs about how children learn. Measures of beliefs are typically measured best through teacher self-report (Rimm-Kaufman et al., 2006).

The above discussion highlights the fact that there are no perfect measures. One way to address this challenge is by triangulating among several different types of measures. For example, on-site coaches could report on teacher level and quality of implementation, as could independent observers. When combined with teacher reports, this variety of measures strengthens the breadth and depth of the assessment of fidelity to intervention core components.

Timing and the Implementation Dip

Becoming a high-implementing practitioner reflects a process of human change (Evans, 2001). For example, when practitioners initiate their training, the intervention likely produces a disruption in normal practice and may actually decrease the effectiveness of new practices, not increase it. This "implementation dip" (Fullan & Miles, 1992) is important to recognize and consider analytically (Borman, Gamoran, & Bowdon, 2008). As noted earlier in Chapter 2, reaching full implementation may take a period of 2–4 years, depending on the complexity of the intervention model, the availability of implementation supports and resources, and characteristics of the individual practitioners and contexts in which they are intervening.

Within the RC approach, for example, setting aside time for a Morning Meeting may be relatively easy; however, adhering to the multiple aspects of a Morning Meeting, and doing so with quality, may take time. Initially, it may take longer to run a Morning Meeting than intended, thus reducing the amount of instructional time. However, once the Morning Meeting routine has been established, increases in efficiency and quality may occur, boosting learning in other areas. In contrast, the effects of Academic Choice on student motivation and engagement to learn particular content may have more immediate effects. Thus, RC teachers may need more time to develop the social-emotional foundation of the classroom, whereas some aspects of the instructional environment may be quicker to become fully implemented. These principles hold true regardless of the intervention.

These examples demonstrate that the development of practitioners' skills in implementing a particular intervention's core components needs to be considered when evaluating the effectiveness of an intervention. This big-picture perspective on the intervention, which should be incorporated within the logic models, reinforces the whole-part-whole challenge that evaluators and researchers face when assessing intervention fidelity. The process is not as simple as developing indicators of each core component and averaging them together to form an index of intervention fidelity. Such issues as sequencing, timing, development of implementers' skills, and tolerable adaptation can all influence the construct validity of intervention fidelity measures.

Conclusions and Implications for Early Childhood Education Program Evaluation and Research

One of the goals of measuring intervention fidelity with careful attention to construct validity is to contribute needed information at various points in the intervention development cycle. Furthermore, the methods have different utility depending on the various stages of implementation (i.e., exploration, installation, initial implementation, and full implementation; see Chapter 2) and stages of evaluation (e.g., efficacy trials, impact evaluation). For instance, achieved relative strength values may be necessary in examining the feasibility of an intervention and whether the training actually produces changes in implementation. Measuring the sequencing of components and interactions between components and implementers may play an important role in building a feasible intervention that can be used by a variety of implementers in a broad range of settings. The binary complier index may be particularly relevant in efficacy trials as a way of conducting treatment-on-the-treated analyses. Given the unevenness in intervention uptake, thresholds that establish sufficient and insufficient use of the intervention may direct intervention developers and researchers to return to an earlier stage of implementation or to replication and scale-up. Understanding the zone of tolerable adaptation may be particularly relevant to addressing questions that rise from scale-up studies (Yeh, 2000). Specifically, mixed-method techniques can be used to assess the adaptations to the approach that are present and subsequently evaluate the point at which those adaptations no longer fit with the definition or intention of the intervention.

Breaking down intervention fidelity into its essential elements helps to identify practices that are central to the effectiveness of the intervention compared to those practices that may be less essential. As a consequence, new, more streamlined interventions can be developed that focus more attention on training in the more important practices compared to the less important ones. By linking fidelity indices to core components, implementation drivers can be added for core intervention components that were not implemented well. However, in conducting these analyses, it is important to remember that the whole is not merely a sum of its parts, and analyzing the relationship between individual core components and outcomes might not fully represent the intervention model or its effectiveness. Thus, researchers and evaluators would be wise to take a step back from their analytic framework to ensure they are capturing the whole and not merely the sum of the parts.

Indeed, early childhood interventions discussed later in this volume should be considered in terms of the time it takes practitioners to acquire new skills and the alignment of the evaluation with the stage of implementation. The various analytic methods introduced in this chapter (e.g., creating overall fidelity indices as well as those representing individual core components) can assist researchers and evaluators in this endeavor.

References

Abry, T., Brewer, A.J., Nathanson, L., Sawyer, B., & Rimm-Kaufman, S.E. (2010). *Classroom Practices Observation Measure*. University of Virginia, Unpublished measure.

Abry, T., Rimm-Kaufman, S.E., Hulleman, C.S., Thomas, J.B., & Ko, M. (2012, March). *The how and for whom of program effectiveness: Dissecting the Responsive Classroom approach in relation to academic achievement*. Paper presented at the spring conference of the Society for Research on Educational Effectiveness, Washington, DC.

Abry, T., Rimm-Kaufman, S.E., Larsen, R.A., & Brewer, A.J. (2011, September). *Applying new methods to the measurement of fidelity of implementation: Examining the critical ingredients of the Responsive Classroom approach in relation to mathematics achievement*. Poster presented at the Society for Research on Educational Effectiveness, Washington, DC.

Abry, T.D.S. (2012). *The what, how, and for whom: Unpacking the mechanisms of a social and emotional learning intervention* (Unpublished doctoral dissertation). University of Virginia, Charlottesville, VA. Retrieved from http://search.proquest.com/docview/1041294261?accountid=14678

Bloom, H. (2005). *Learning more from social experiments: Evolving analytic approaches*. New York, NY: Russell Sage Foundation.

Borman, G.D., Gamoran, A., & Bowdon, J. (2008). A randomized trial of teacher development in elementary science: First-year achievement effects. *Journal of Research on Educational Effectiveness, 1*, 237–264.

Casto, K., & Audley, J. (2008). *In our school: Building community in elementary schools*. Turner Falls, MA: Northeast Foundation for Children.

Cordray, D.S., & Hulleman, C.S. (2009, June). *Assessing intervention fidelity in RCTs: Models, methods and modes of analysis*. Invited panel session at the Institute of Education Sciences Research Conference, Washington, DC.

Cordray, D.S., & Pion, G.M. (2006). Treatment strength and integrity: Models and methods. In R.R. Bootzin & P.E. McKnight (Eds.), *Strengthening research methodology: Psychological measurement and evaluation* (pp. 103–124). Washington, DC: American Psychological Association.

Dane, A.V., & Schneider, B.H. (1998). Program integrity in primary and early secondary prevention: Are implementation effects out of control? *Clinical Psychology Review, 18*(1), 23–45.

Datnow, A., & Stringfield, S. (2000). Working together for reliable school reform. *Journal of Education for Students Placed at Risk, 5*(1–2), 183–204.

Dobson, L., & Cook, T. (1980). Avoiding Type III error in program evaluation: Results from a field experiment. *Evaluation and Program Planning, 3,* 269–276.

Durlak, J.A., & DuPre, E.P. (2008). Implementation matters: A review of research on the influence of implementation on program outcomes and the factors affecting implementation. *American Journal of Community Psychology, 41,* 327–350.

Durlak, J.A., Weissberg, R.P., Taylor, R.D., & Dymnicki, A.B. (2011). The impact of enhancing students' social and emotional learning: A meta-analysis of school-based universal interventions. *Child Development, 82,* 405–432.

Dusenbury, L., Brannigan, R., Falco, M., & Hansen, W. (2003). A review of research on fidelity of implementation: Implications for drug abuse prevention in school settings. *Health Education Research, 18,* 237–256.

Evans, R. (2001). *The human side of school change.* San Francisco, CA: Jossey-Bass.

Fixsen, D.L., Blase, K.A., Naoom, S.F., & Wallace, F. (2009). Core implementation components. *Research on Social Work Practice, 19,* 531–540.

Fixsen, D.L., Naoom, S.F., Blase, K.A., Friedman, R.M., & Wallace, F. (2005). *Implementation research: A synthesis of the literature.* Tampa, FL: University of South Florida, Louis de la Parte Florida Mental Health Institute, National Implementation Research Network (FMHI Publication No. 231).

Fullan, M., & Miles, M. (1992, September). Getting reform right: What works and what doesn't. *Phi Delta Kappan,* pp. 745–752.

Greenberg, M.T. (2010). School-based prevention: Current status and future challenges. *Effective Education, 2,* 27–52.

Holland, P.W. (1986). Statistics and causal inference. *Journal of the American Statistical Association, 81,* 945–960.

Hulleman, C.S., & Cordray, D.S. (2009). Moving from the lab to the field: The role of fidelity and achieved relative intervention strength. *Journal of Research on Intervention Effectiveness, 2*(1), 88–110.

Imai, K., Keele, L., Tingley, D., & Yamamoto, T. (2011). Unpacking the black box of causality: Learning about causal mechanisms from experimental and observational studies. *American Political Science Review, 105*(4), 765–789.

Justice, L.M., Mashburn, A., Pence, K.L., & Wiggins, A. (2008). Experimental evaluation of a preschool language curriculum: Influence on children's expressive language skills. *Journal of Speech, Language, and Hearing Research, 51,* 983–1001.

Knowlton, L.W., & Phillips, C.C. (2009). *The logic model guidebook: Better strategies for great results.* Washington, DC: Sage.

Kopp, J., Hulleman, C.S., Harackiewicz, J.M., & Rozek, C. (2012, March). *Applying the five-step model of fidelity assessment to a randomized experiment of a high school STEM intervention.* Paper presented at the spring conference for the Society of Research on Educational Effectiveness, Washington, DC.

Lang, J., & Franks, R. (2011). *Statewide implementation of best practices: The Connecticut TF-CBT learning collaborative. IMPACT series.* Farmington, CT: The Child Health & Development Institute.

Lowell, D., Paulicin, B., Carter, A., Godoy, L., & Briggs-Gowan, M. (2011). A randomized controlled trail of Child FIRST: A comprehensive home-based intervention translating research into early childhood practice. *Child Development, 82,* 193–208.

Lugo-Gil, J., Sattar, S., Ross, C., Boller, K., Kirby, G., & Tout, K. (2011). *The quality rating and improvement system (QRIS) evaluation toolkit* (OPRE Report 2011–31). Washington, DC: Office of Planning, Research and Evaluation.

McIntyre, L.L., Gresham, F.M., DiGennaro, F.D., & Reed, D.D. (2007). Treatment integrity of school-based interventions with children in the *Journal of Applied Behavior Analysis, 1991–2005. Journal of Applied Behavior Analysis, 40,* 659–672.

Mitchel, M.E., Hu, T.W., McDonnell, N.S., & Swisher, J.D. (1984). Cost-effectiveness analysis of an educational drug abuse prevention program. *Journal of Drug Education, 14*(3), 271–292.

Nathanson, L., Sawyer, B., & Rimm-Kaufman, S.E. (2007a). *Classroom Practices Frequency Scale.* Unpublished instrument. University of Virginia.

Nathanson, L., Sawyer, B., & Rimm-Kaufman, S.E. (2007b). *Classroom Practices Teacher Survey.* Unpublished instrument. University of Virginia.

Nelson, M.C., Cordray, D.S., Hulleman, C.S., Darrow, C.L., & Sommer, E.C. (2012). A procedure for assessing intervention fidelity in experiments testing educational and behavioral interventions. *Journal of Behavioral Health Services and Research, 39*(4), 374–396.

Northeast Foundation for Children (NEFC). (n.d.). *Principles and practices of Responsive Classroom.* Retrieved from http://www.responsiveclassroom.org/principles-and-practices-responsive-classroom

Northeast Foundation for Children (NEFC). (2007). *Responsive Classroom Level I Resource Book.* Turner Falls, MA: Author.

Northeast Foundation for Children (NEFC). (2009). *Responsive Classroom Level II Resource Book.* Turner Falls, MA: Author.

Nunnery, J.A., Slavin, R.E., Madden, N.A., Ross, S.M., Smith, L.J., Hunter, P., & Stubbs, J. (in press). Effects of full and partial implementations of Success for All on student reading achievement in English and Spanish. *American Educational Research Journal.*

O'Donnell, C.L. (2008). Defining, conceptualizing, and measuring fidelity of implementation and its relationship to outcomes in K–12 curriculum intervention research. *Review of Educational Research, 78,* 33–84.

Peck, L.R. (2003). Subgroup analysis in social experiments: Measuring program impacts based on post-treatment choice. *American Journal of Evaluation, 2*(24), 157–187.

Rimm-Kaufman, S.E., Berry, R., Fan, X., McCracken, E., & Walkowiak, T. (2008, June). *The efficacy of the responsive classroom approach for improving teacher quality and children's academic performance.* Paper presented at the Institute of Education Sciences Research Conference, Washington, DC.

Rimm-Kaufman, S.E., Fan, X., Chiu, Y.I., & You, W. (2007). The contribution of the Responsive Classroom approach on children's academic achievement: Results from a three-year longitudinal study. *Journal of School Psychology, 45,* 401–421.

Rimm-Kaufman, S.E., Larsen, R., Curby, T., Baroody, A., Merritt, E., Abry, T., ... Thomas, J. (2012, September). *Efficacy of the Responsive Classroom approach: Results from a three-year, longitudinal randomized controlled trial.* Paper presented at the annual conference of the Society for Research in Educational Effectiveness, Washington, DC.

Rimm-Kaufman, S.E., & Sawyer, B.E. (2004). Primary-grade teachers' self-efficacy beliefs, attitudes toward teaching, and discipline and teaching practice priorities in relation to the Responsive Classroom approach. *Elementary School Journal, 104*(4), 321–341.

Rimm-Kaufman, S.E., Storm, M., Sawyer, B., Pianta, R.C., and La Paro, K. 2006. The Teacher Belief Q-Sort: A measure of teachers' priorities and beliefs in relation to disciplinary practices, teaching practices, and beliefs about children. *Journal of School Psychology, 44,* 141–165.

Rubin, D.B. (1974). Estimating causal effects of treatments in randomized and nonrandomized studies. *Journal of Educational Psychology, 66,* 688–701.

Schochet, P.Z., & Burghard, J. (2007). Using propensity scoring to estimate program-related subgroup impacts in experimental program evaluations. *Evaluation Review, 31,* 95–120.

Shadish, W.R., Cook, T.D., & Campbell, D.T. (2002). *Experimental and quasi-experimental designs for generalized causal inference.* Boston, MA: Houghton Mifflin.

Snyder, F., Flay, B., Vuchinich, S., Acack, A., Washburn, I., Beets, M., & Li, K.-K. (2010). Impact of a social-emotional and character development program on school-level indicators of academic achievement, absenteeism, and disciplinary outcomes: A matched-pair, cluster-randomized, controlled trial. *Journal of Research on Educational Effectiveness, 3,* 26–55.

Stringfield, S., Reynolds, D., & Schaffer, E.C. (2008). *Improving secondary students' academic achievement through a focus on reform reliability: Four- and nine-year findings from the High Reliability Schools project.* Reading, UK: CfBT Education Trust. Retrieved from http://www.cfbt.com/evidenceforeducation/pdf/high%20reliability_v5%20final.pdf

Tomlinson, C.A. (2001). *Differentiate instruction in mixed-ability classrooms* (2nd ed.). Upper Saddle River, NJ: Merrill Prentice Hall.

Tortu, S., & Botvin, G.J. (1989). School-based smoking prevention: The teacher training process. *Preventive Medicine, 18,* 280–289.

Tout, K., Starr, R., Soli, M., Moodie, S., Kirby, G., & Boller, K. (2010). *Compendium of quality rating systems and evaluations.* Washington, DC: Office of Planning, Research and Evaluation.

Unlu, F., Bozzi, L., Layzer, C., Smith, A., Price, C., & Hurtig, R. (2011). *Linking implementation fidelity to impacts in an RCT: A matching approach.* Bethesda, MD: Abt Associates.

Wanless, S.B., Patton, C.S., Rimm-Kaufman, S.E., & Deutsch, N.L. (2012). Setting-level influences on implementation of the Responsive Classroom approach. *Prevention Science.* Advance online publication. doi: 10.1007/s11121-012-0294-1

Weiner, B. (1972). *Theories of motivation: From mechanism to cognition.* Chicago, IL: Markham.

Wilson, M.B., Freeman-Loftis, B., Sawyer, B., & Denton, P. (2009). *The Responsive Classroom assessment guide.* Turner Falls, MA: Northeast Foundation for Children.

W.K. Kellogg Foundation. (2004). *Logic model development guide.* Battle Creek, MI: W.K. Kellogg Foundation.

Yeh, S.S. (2000). Improving educational and social programs: A planned variation cross-validation model. *American Journal of Evaluation, 21*(2), 171–184.

Aligning Stage-Appropriate Evaluation with the Stages of Implementation

Formative Evaluation and Fidelity

Amy Blasberg

The first part of this volume focused on definitions, frameworks, and methodologies to orient the reader to the concepts of implementation science. The chapters in Section II share researchers' experiences in applying the concepts of implementation science to their work in the field of early care and education during the early stages of implementation.

In Chapter 5, Douglas R. Powell and Karen E. Diamond examine the implementation of coaching models embedded in professional development programs. Although coaching can be a component of implementation (i.e., coaching is considered a "competency driver" that facilitates an intervention being implemented with fidelity), in this instance the coaching itself is the intervention. The authors stress the importance of collecting data on coaching interventions in general and share examples of collecting these data from their own extensive body of research.

The chapter starts by describing the significance of coaching and explains three key features of different coaching models: structure, process, and content. According to the authors, collecting implementation data is so crucial because it can "determine the feasibility of particular elements of coaching, interpret program outcomes, identify meaningful patterns of variation in program implementation, predict the strength and type of coaching outcomes, and identify factors associated with variations in coaching implementation" (p. 113).

In Chapter 6, Lisa L. Knoche highlights the core implementation components of an efficacy trial of Getting Ready, a parenting program focused on promoting school readiness for families with young children who are participating in early childhood intervention and prevention programs such as Head Start and Early Head Start. Knoche explores the core components during the stage of initial implementation and illustrates the compensatory nature of the implementation components by showing that a weakness in one area can be supplemented by a strength in

95

another area. For example, the implementers of Getting Ready did not have control over staff selection, one of several competency drivers. However, by individualizing the training that staff members received, they were able to compensate for the inability to select staff according to certain qualifications.

As a result of this efficacy trial, four main lessons were learned about evaluating an intervention during the initial stages of implementation:

1. It is challenging to measure the implementation of individualized interventions.

2. The context (i.e., the program or setting in which the intervention is implemented) of any intervention should be a key consideration.

3. Collecting data from both the treatment and control groups enhances the ability to draw conclusions from the data.

4. If the intervention resembles existing practices, it is important to be intentional about how the intervention is presented in order to highlight the distinction for practitioners and achieve buy-in.

The next chapter, by Chrishana M. Lloyd, Lauren H. Supplee, and Shira Kolnik Mattera, describes the development of a measure to track fidelity of three different curricula in Head Start classrooms using a comparable measurement tool in order to capture "the gap between the intended evidence-based practice and the actual implementation of the practice" (p. 139). The authors elaborate on measurement issues for collecting fidelity data, including how to develop general versus specific measures for interventions and how to reconcile results when multiple raters collect data. The use of the new measure(s) to support the implementation process is also discussed. Specifically, data on fidelity were collected throughout the year, and these data were used to monitor classroom practices, identify issues with implementation, and target support to teachers who were not implementing their respective curricula with fidelity. Several lessons learned are presented for both researchers and practitioners, and a key point is the emphasis on moving away from intervention-specific fidelity measurement in order to advance the field.

At the end of Section II, an integrative chapter by Jason Downer raises important issues and implications from the three preceding chapters.

CHAPTER 5

Studying the Implementation of Coaching-Based Professional Development

Douglas R. Powell and Karen E. Diamond

Individualized approaches to professional development (PD) are increasingly viewed as a highly promising strategy for improving the outcomes of early childhood programs. Compared to group-based methods of PD such as workshops, the presumed advantage of coaching and related forms of one-on-one work with teachers is the provision of tailored guidance on how to adopt evidence-based practices within the context of a teacher's existing pedagogical practices, content knowledge, and classroom resources.

The proliferation of interest in coaching-based PD programs far exceeds available research knowledge on coaching with early childhood teachers. A small yet growing corpus of studies points to positive effects of coaching-based PD on early childhood teachers' instructional practices (e.g., Hsieh, Hemmeter, McCollum, & Ostrosky, 2009) and on children's outcomes (e.g., Powell, Diamond, Burchinal, & Koehler, 2010; Wasik & Hindman, 2011). The ways in which coaching is carried out in prekindergarten settings are mostly an ignored topic in the scholarly literature, however. There is a paucity of descriptive studies of coaching practices, and published reports on outcomes of coaching-based PD often do not include empirical information on whether coaching was implemented as intended. This is an unfortunate state of affairs because prudent advances in the design and scaling up of coaching-based PD require a rigorous scientific understanding of how coaching is implemented.

In this chapter, we describe approaches to and issues in measuring the implementation of a coaching-based PD program for early childhood teachers of at-risk children. Attention is given to the state of research on the implementation of coaching-based PD in early childhood settings, the identification and measurement of dimensions of coaching with early childhood teachers, and uses of implementation data for improving the design and outcomes of coaching-based PD programs. We approach implementation research primarily with a focus on intervention

The authors' research was supported by Grants R305B070605, R305M040167, and R305B050030 from the Institute of Education Research and Grant S349A010162 from the Early Childhood Educator Professional Development Program, U.S. Department of Education, to Purdue University.

fidelity, traditionally defined as the extent to which an intervention or program was implemented as intended (Cordray & Pion, 2006; Hulleman & Cordray, 2009).

The chapter draws on a program of research spanning more than a decade and involving three consecutive coaching-based PD programs carried out with Head Start teachers regarding strategies for promoting children's literacy and language development. The first program, Project Literacy, combined coaching in teachers' classrooms with a three-credit course offered across one academic semester. Coaching was conducted approximately every third week during the program (Powell, Steed, & Diamond, 2010).

The second PD program, Classroom Links to Early Literacy, conducted with a different set of Head Start programs, involved an introductory 2-day workshop followed by seven coaching sessions conducted across one semester. A goal of research on the second PD program was to determine whether there were differences in the effectiveness of coaching delivered through on-site visits to classrooms and coaching delivered remotely through innovative uses of video technology (Powell, Diamond, et al., 2010). The on-site coaching visits entailed approximately 90 minutes of coach observation of targeted teaching practices, followed by about 30 minutes of consultation with the teacher focused on the coach's feedback about the observed practices. The technologically mediated delivery of coaching involved individualized feedback to a teacher based on a teacher-submitted video of targeted instruction plus teacher access to a hypermedia resource that included video exemplars of teaching practices aimed at supporting children's literacy and language growth (Powell, Diamond, & Koehler, 2009). Coaches used a computer software system to generate feedback on coach-selected segments of the teacher-submitted video. The feedback received by teachers paired the coach-selected segments of the teacher-submitted video (left side of screen) with coach comments that included embedded links to pertinent video exemplars in the hypermedia resource.

Our third coaching-based PD program, Classroom Links to Sounds and Words, was a significant revision of the second program. The changes were driven in part by findings of our research on the second PD program. The research included a random-assignment outcome study of program effects on teaching practices and children's literacy and language outcomes plus data on implementation of the PD program (Powell, Diamond, et al., 2010). This chapter includes a description of how the implementation and outcome findings contributed to revision decisions.

Status of Research on Coaching in Early Childhood Programs

The typical goal of coaching is to help teachers adopt a new curriculum (e.g., Bierman et al., 2008) or specific evidence-based teaching practices (e.g., Wasik & Hindman, 2011) proven or hypothesized to lead to improved child outcomes. The coach's task can involve myriad roles and functions. The International Reading Association (2004), for example, cites 18 different activities for reading coaches that vary in level of intensity from providing materials to analyzing videotaped lessons of teachers. To promote positive change in teachers' behaviors, coaches may model or demonstrate recommended practices in the teacher's classroom or provide access to live (e.g., demonstration classroom) or recorded exemplars of practice. Coaches may use a checklist or rating scales to observe a teacher's adherence to recommended practices and share results of the observation with a teacher in an effort to identify compliance and needed changes (e.g., Assel, Landry, Swank, & Gunnewig, 2007). Alternatively, instead of emphasizing evaluations of teachers' performances, coaches may seek to promote change in teaching practices by encouraging teachers to reflect on their own behaviors (e.g., Neuman & Wright, 2010). Coaching is commonly offered in conjunction with one or more additional resources for teachers such as a course (e.g., Neuman & Cunningham, 2009) or tools for monitoring children's progress (Landry, Anthony, Swank, & Monseque-Bailey, 2009). In these arrangements, the coach may function as an intermediary agent in promoting a teacher's appropriate understanding and use of additional information (Powell, Steed, et al., 2010).

To date, the small number of studies of coaching in early childhood settings generally have sought to determine whether individualized work with teachers is an effective form of PD (Powell, Diamond, & Cockburn, 2013). Coaching has been examined as a unitary construct, often in comparison to alternative forms of PD such as course work (Neuman & Cunningham, 2009), access to videos of teaching exemplars (Pianta, Mashburn, Downer, Hamre, & Justice, 2008), and tools for monitoring children's progress (Landry et al., 2009). Some reports of coaching-based PD research simply describe procedures for ensuring the fidelity of coaching implementation (e.g., periodic meetings with supervisors) but do not specify the extent to which the coaching oversight plans were implemented or report whether coaching sessions in fact were carried out as intended. When coaching-based PD outcome studies include measures of coaching implementation, the information seldom transcends basic indicators of coaching delivery (e.g., number of coaching contacts with teachers). As noted above, there is a dearth of descriptive research on coaching processes in early childhood settings, and it appears that no research has systematically compared different approaches to or dimensions of coaching.

In addition to a small number of studies on effects of coaching-based PD, coaching is included in some research aimed at determining the effects of a curriculum or targeted instructional practices. Many of the 12 projects involved in the Preschool Curriculum Evaluation Research Consortium (2008) study, for example, included a coach or mentor to support teachers' implementation of the intervention as intended. Curriculum or instructional intervention studies that involve coaching with teachers often shed little if any light on the coaching process, however, because the key question regarding implementation fidelity is teachers' compliance with an intervention protocol, not the fidelity of coaching implementation.

High levels of teachers' implementation fidelity significantly diminish an interest in measuring the implementation of coaching, because presumably the coaching and other supports for teachers' practices (e.g., workshops) "worked" in achieving the desired outcome of teacher compliance with an intervention protocol. A recent study of effects of a school readiness intervention illustrates this orientation to implementation fidelity. In addition to participation in group training, teachers received detailed manuals and kits of materials for implementing the intervention plus weekly mentoring that was to involve modeling, coaching, and ongoing feedback regarding program delivery. The mentors collected data monthly on the fidelity of teachers' implementation of program components. The investigators did not report data on the implementation of coaching or other PD components (Bierman et al., 2008).

The use of coaches is not a guaranteed path to a consistently high level of fidelity of teacher implementation of desired classroom practices. For example, one study found that coaching (mentoring) was associated with positive child effects for a curriculum that emphasized letter knowledge and phonological awareness, but not for a curriculum that emphasized language skills. At midyear of the intervention study, about 71% of teachers using the letter knowledge curriculum received high implementation scores, whereas only about 60% of teachers using the language curriculum scored at the highest levels of fidelity (Assel et al., 2007). These patterns are consistent with a general finding that, when taken to scale, the fidelity of implementation of a manualized intervention is typically about 60% and rarely reaches 80% (Durlak & DuPre, 2008). Specifically, an analysis of implementation studies of more than 540 prevention and health promotion programs for children and adolescents found no studies indicating perfect or near-perfect implementation of the intervention as intended, and few studies identified intervention implementation levels greater than 80% (Durlak & DuPre, 2008).

Teachers' less-than-optimal implementation of a curriculum or targeted practices raises questions about the quality and quantity of coaching supports that obviously cannot be answered if no data are available on the implementation of coaching. Research data on the implementation of coaching are essential to the consideration of possible improvements in teachers' implementation of a new curriculum or instructional practices via coaching. This especially is the case when teacher practices are conceptualized as the outcome of an intervention (e.g., Pianta et al., 2008) rather than a mediator of intervention effects on children.

While the limited effort to measure coaching implementation may seem curious in the context of widespread interest in coaching-based PD, there is a long history of degradation of the treatment variable in intervention research (e.g., Powell & Sigel, 1991). A typical outcome study allocates considerably more resources to collecting and analyzing outcome data than information on intervention implementation. With regard to coaching-based PD, then, a consequence of this research tradition is that existing depictions of effective coaching (e.g., Shanklin, 2006) are informed mostly by professional insights, ideological or theoretical views, and/or results of interviews or surveys conducted with coaches and/or teachers (e.g., Garet, Porter, Desimone, Birman, & Yoon, 2001), not rigorous and direct study of coaching as it is enacted. Increasingly, there are indications that "black box experiments are out" (Cook & Payne, 2002, p. 160), however. The evidence-based practice movement has intensified interest in "what works" in education (Slavin, 2004), including programs for young children and their families (e.g., Powell, 2005). The appearance of the current volume on implementation science is among the tangible signs of growing appreciation of program implementation processes.

Identifying Dimensions of Coaching

Decisions about the dimensions of coaching to measure in an examination of coaching implementation are most appropriately informed by a PD program's theory of change. A good theory of change identifies the elements of coaching that program designers hypothesize are active ingredients in improving the quality of teaching practices. Below we describe coaching dimensions that are often emphasized in descriptions of individualized work with teachers. We organize the dimensions into a conceptual framework of coaching that includes structural, process, and content domains of coaching.

Structure

The structural domain of coaching pertains to organizational arrangements for the delivery and receipt of coaching. This includes the number, duration, and frequency or interval of coaching sessions, as well as coaching session components (e.g., observation of teacher in classroom, consultation with teacher) and their lengths (e.g., 60 minutes of observation, 30 minutes of consultation). Structural aspects of technologically mediated coaching might include teacher submission of a videotape of classroom practices and coach commentary on same (e.g., Powell, Diamond, et al., 2010). Data collected in this domain of implementation can address such basic questions about teacher participation in a PD program as the proportion of the intended coaching session actually conducted with a teacher. Data on intervals between coaching sessions would be important to collect if a PD program's theory of change posited that a regular spacing between sessions (e.g., once every 2 weeks) is conducive to incremental change in teachers' practices (e.g., receiving feedback on attempts to implement practices recommended in a prior coaching session).

The structure of a coaching-based PD program may also include components related to coaching that are provided as a primary or supplemental source of information about desired teaching practices. Examples include workshops, group trainings, a course, printed materials, and web resources. In our research on technologically mediated delivery of coaching, for example, we examined the number of web-based video exemplars accessed by a teacher as a percentage of the exemplars recommended by a coach in feedback to a teacher (Powell et al., 2009).

Process

The process domain of coaching encompasses actions aimed at promoting change in teaching practices. Earlier in this chapter, we noted a distinction between a coach asking questions aimed at facilitating a teacher's reflection on her or his practice versus offering evaluative comments on a teacher's observed practices. PD programs that view a coach's evaluative comments as an active ingredient of the coaching process generally emphasize two types of feedback to teachers: 1) practices that are appropriately implemented and 2) practices that need improvement or implementation. For example, Landry and colleagues (2009) developed and evaluated a PD program in which coaches used a "glows and grows" mentoring tool to provide written feedback to teachers on instructional practices that were appropriately implemented ("glows") and practices that needed attention ("grows"); from that, a ratio of affirmations-to-recommendations could be computed, for instance.

Recommendations for practice improvement or implementation may be examined with regard to their content (see below) as well as the extent to which they show progress over time (e.g., coding whether a recommendation is a new, repeated, or expanded recommendation from prior coaching sessions; Powell, Steed, et al., 2010). The coaching process also could include demonstrations of desired instructional practice via a coach modeling the practice in a teacher's classroom or providing the teacher with a link to a video exemplar of the desired practice (Powell et al., 2009).

The quality of the interpersonal relationship between coach and teacher is commonly viewed by PD programs as central to supporting change in teaching practices. Pertinent variables here might include the teacher's contributions (active vs. passive) to coaching sessions and views of the extent to which the coach is supportive of and interested in the teacher's situation. While teacher–coach relationship quality may be a key dimension of coaching implementation, relationship attributes such as mutual respect and good rapport may not lead to the intended improvements in teaching quality if teacher–coach exchanges give insufficient attention to the content of the PD program.

Content

The substantive focus of coaching sessions represents a separate domain of the coaching process that a PD program's theory of change is likely to address. It is common for curriculum fidelity measures to assess the percentage of curriculum content delivered by a teacher (e.g., Pence, Justice, & Wiggins, 2008). In a similar manner, indicators of content coverage in coaching sessions can be developed from the actual and intended content of the PD program. For example, in a study of our first coaching-based PD program, we coded the instructional improvement plans developed in coaching sessions with regard to the child knowledge and skills targeted in specific instructional practices (e.g., vocabulary, letters, letter-sound associations, print conventions). We also coded the pedagogical emphasis of the instruction (e.g., instructional materials, teaching behaviors, whole or large group, individual or small groups of children). In total, 18 different codes were used to describe the content of coaching sessions, including a code for content unrelated to the literacy and language focus of the PD program (Powell, Steed, et al., 2010).

Measuring the Implementation of Coaching

Information about what happens in coaching sessions may be secured through existing program records as well as measures or data systems created for research purposes. The few available studies on coaching implementation tend to emphasize the quantity (i.e., frequency counts) of various coaching features. Collecting data on the quality of coaching implementation is a promising albeit time-intensive approach to describing coaching. A largely ignored measurement issue in the coaching literature is the reliability of self-report information on coaching sessions. Data sources, measurement strategies, and reliability issues are discussed below.

Data Sources

Carefully completed records of coaching sessions developed for program management purposes (e.g., documenting supports provided to teachers) or for facilitating a coach's work with a teacher (e.g., providing a summary of recommended actions) may be used for the research purpose of measuring one or more of the three dimensions of coaching implementation specified earlier (structure, process, and content). Typically, the records are completed by the coach. For example, Neuman and Wright (2010) created an online coaching log to examine coaches' use of their time during language and literacy coaching sessions with child care teachers. The log was designed as a 15-minute activity diary that coaches were to complete within 48 hours of each coaching session. The log included 65 items pertaining to such information as the coaching technique used by the coach (e.g., coplanned lesson) and goals for the session.

It also seems common for coaching-based PD programs to develop record-keeping systems for research purposes, such as collecting information from coaches regarding teacher participation in the program. For instance, one study of teachers' responses to web-based PD resources employed a six-item measure completed by coaches regarding teacher responsiveness to the program (Downer, Locasale-Crouch, Hamre, & Pianta, 2009).

In our PD research, data on the implementation of on-site coaching sessions came from coding a written record of each coaching session prepared by the literacy coach as part of the coaching session. The record was signed by both the coach and teacher, and a copy was left with the teacher at the conclusion of the session (the form was a no-carbon-required triplicate). The form included four sections: highlights of the coach's classroom observation, a review of observed progress in implementing instructional improvement plans generated at a previous coaching session, teacher reflections on the observation and/or progress to date, and instructional improvement plans. Coaches also completed a second form to document their actions at the session (e.g., modeled a practice in the teacher's classroom). In the technologically mediated delivery of coaching employed in two of our three PD programs, transcripts of coach feedback to teachers on segments of a videotape submitted by the teacher provide a complete record of coach inputs. We coded the transcripts for purposes of describing the remote coaching condition. We also maintained records of when teacher-submitted videotapes arrived and when coach feedback was released.

Efficiency in record keeping is an advantage of our use of coaching session documents shared with teachers as part of individualized work with a teacher. From the perspectives of both teacher and coach, the record provides a summary of key points of the coaching session, including recommended instructional improvements. It serves as a reminder of needed actions and a reference point for a subsequent coaching session.

From a research perspective, the document is amenable to coding basic information about coaching sessions. The main cost of securing in-depth information about coaching implementation, of course, is the time required for coding each record, including procedures for establishing and maintaining high levels of intercoder reliability. This time factor is reduced somewhat when coaching visits are expected to follow a tightly scripted protocol for teacher actions, as is often the case when coaching is used to support teachers' implementation of a specific curriculum. In this approach, implementation of the coaching protocol could be documented with a checklist completed by the coach and/or teacher, with appropriate provisions for establishing reliability (see below). The online coaching log created by Neuman and Wright (2010) was intended as a scalable and cost-efficient method for quickly securing records from geographically different sites and making the information instantly accessible to researchers. Regardless of the nature of the record, upfront training on how to complete forms and frequent monitoring of completed logs are recommended strategies for ensuring compliance with data collection procedures.

Questionnaires are an efficient way to collect some types of coaching implementation data. As indicated earlier in this chapter, teachers' views of the helpfulness of a PD program, including the quality of the relationship with a coach, provide a valuable perspective on program implementation. We adapted a measure developed by Dunst, Trivette, and Hamby (1996) to assess teachers' views of the strength of the professional helping relationship with the coach. The Dunst et al. scale includes 25 items that measure different aspects of help-giving practices.

Growing interest in web-based PD provides new opportunities to employ technologies to measure the implementation of coaching (e.g., Whitaker, Kinzie, Kraft-Sayre, Mashburn, & Pianta, 2007). With teacher consent, we installed software on project-provided laptop computers used by teachers in two of our PD interventions to log teachers' browser actions regarding uses of the case-based hypermedia resource noted earlier. (The PD program provided laptop computers because most teachers did not have broadband Internet to accommodate streaming video.) For each page visit, for example, we coded the uniform resource locator (URL), whether the visit time interval was less than 5 seconds, the time and day of the visit, and whether the action was a first-time visit to the page (Powell et al., 2009). A summary of selected findings is offered later in this chapter.

Quality

The handful of studies that report coaching implementation data tend to give greater attention to the quantity than to the quality of coaching dimensions, for the pragmatic reason that quantity indicators are relatively inexpensive to measure. Also, there is not an empirical literature to guide measurement decisions for coaching quality. The relationship between coaching quality and quantity is largely unknown, and there is no scientific understanding of the relative impact of coaching quality and quantity on teaching practices and children's outcomes. Moreover, the quality of implementation has a tenuous role in conceptualizations of implementation in the scholarly literature. Some frameworks include quality as an important aspect of implementation (e.g., Dane & Schneider, 1998; Durlak & DuPre, 2008), whereas other conceptual treatments view quality of program delivery as a potential moderator of implementation (e.g., Carroll et al., 2007).

Both qualitative and quantitative research methods are appropriate to studying the quality of coaching implementation. One of the few qualitative studies of coaching in the extant scholarly literature was conducted by Gersten, Morvant, and Brengelman (1995) with 12 teachers in an urban elementary school (Grades 1–6). The investigators employed a multifaceted approach to data collection, including audiotapes and live observations of coaching sessions, periodic semistructured interviews with teachers, and reviews of logs and field notes maintained by the coaches.

With regard to quantitative methods, finer grained coding of actions of coach and teacher during a coaching session could yield indicators of implementation quality. The act of a coach modeling a recommended practice in a teacher's classroom could be assessed with regard to the coach's commentary on the modeled practice, for instance. Did the coach draw attention to key practices by describing their primary features and purposes? Did the coach analyze children's reactions to the practice with the teacher? Did the coach elicit and discuss the teacher's reactions to the modeled practice, including perceived facilitators or barriers to trying out the practice?

Reliability Considerations

The reliability of information reported by coaches or teachers is a key issue in the use of self-report data. We consider the signatures of both teacher and coach on the report that documents key aspects and outcomes (i.e., instructional improvement plans) of a coaching session as providing a modest level of assurance regarding the accuracy of coaching records. With teacher and coach consent, we also have audiotaped about one fifth of coaching sessions across an intervention semester and systematically compared the coach feedback included in transcripts of the audiotaped session to the corresponding record signed by coach and teacher. Across all coaches, we have found a strong correspondence between audiotape transcripts and written records regarding the coach's recommendations for practice improvements. As expected, the transcript includes more detail than the one-page written record and thus is a better (though labor-intensive) data source for detailed coding of coaching sessions.

Investigators who view nonverbal behaviors as important indicators of coaching implementation may wish to adopt the practice of videorecording interactions between professionals and parents in home visiting programs (e.g., Knoche, Sheridan, Edwards, & Osborn, 2010). It is possible that coach awareness of the taping procedure prompts greater attention to the completeness and accuracy of the written record. A strategy to address this possibility is to record all coaching sessions and code randomly selected sessions for corroboration purposes.

The potential problem of relying on a self-report measure of coaching implementation without any form of corroboration is underscored in findings of an evaluation of an early childhood professional development intervention that included a time-sampling observation of in-classroom coaching (Simons, Agnamba, Halle, & Zaslow, 2010). Investigators found that for 36% of the observed coaching time, the coach was interacting with children when the teacher was not attending to the coach's actions (i.e., teacher was not in close proximity to the coach or was engaged in another activity), but coaches reported that they were modeling for the teacher. Coaches modeled teaching strategies while teachers observed for approximately 6% of the observing coaching time. The researchers suggested that coaches may benefit from clear definitions of modeling and practical guidance on how to model for a teacher in a classroom (Simons et al., 2010).

We note tangentially that reliability concerns about coach- or teacher-reported measures of coaching implementation extend to the aforementioned practice of using coaches or teachers as the sole reporters of teachers' implementation of practices targeted in a PD program. The potential for teacher bias in reporting his or her practices is obvious. Coaches may view a teacher's use of practices promoted in a PD program as an indirect assessment of the coach's efficacy. The Assel et al. (2007) research is among the PD studies that used coaches to complete fidelity measures to document the extent to which teachers were implementing a curriculum. To partially address the potential problem of bias, the coaches ("mentors" in the Assel et al. study) did not complete fidelity measures on teachers with whom they were mentoring.

Uses of Information on Coaching Implementation

Data on the implementation of coaching-based PD may be used to determine the feasibility of an approach to coaching, interpret program outcomes, and identify patterns of variation in program implementation. We provide illustrations of each of these purposes from findings of our research on coaching with Head Start teachers regarding strategies to strengthen children's literacy and language development. We also recognize and briefly discuss uses of coaching implementation data to predict the strength and type of coaching outcomes and to identify factors associated with variations in coaching implementation.

Determining Feasibility

Information on the implementation of coaching sessions enabled our research group to determine the feasibility of providing in-depth attention to different aspects of literacy and language development in individualized work with teachers. Coaching implementation data also informed decisions about the content and structure of our PD programs. Each of these uses of implementation data is described below.

Teachers pursue a wide range of goals for children in their classroom, including social, academic, and physical outcomes. In the early period of our PD work, we wondered whether it would be possible for coaching sessions with teachers to maintain a content focus on literacy and language outcomes in the context of teachers' interests in multiple domains of children's development. Our interest in this matter was heightened by results of interviews with Head Start teachers regarding their perspectives on how children develop early literacy and language competence. The interviews were conducted by our research group prior to launching a PD program. While teachers communicated a common view of the importance of early literacy, their views varied considerably with regard to the timing of literacy instruction, particularly in relation to other domains of child development. Many teachers viewed children's mastery of social-emotional skills (e.g., self-regulation) as a prerequisite to literacy learning, with instructional attention to literacy and other academic skills appropriately delayed until a child displayed socially competent behaviors (Powell, Diamond, Bojczyk, & Gerde, 2008). In response to teachers' comments, we revised the PD materials to call teachers' attention to the ways in which literacy and social-emotional skills could be integrated in a single lesson (e.g., by defining words such as "patience" or writing about children's feelings in different situations).

Coaching implementation data collected in each of our three PD studies indicate there was minimal "mission drift" in the content of coaching sessions and thereby point to the feasibility of maintaining a clear focus on literacy and language instruction in coaching sessions. In our first coaching-based PD intervention, 90% of instructional improvement plans pertained to early literacy and language outcomes (Powell, Steed, et al., 2010), and implementation data from our second PD program indicated that less than 3% of coaching sessions included one or more coach suggestions for instructional improvement that were not directly related to the content of the PD program (Powell, Diamond, et al., 2010).

Although coaching implementation data across our three PD programs indicate adherence to specified content, findings from our first program suggested that the important content domain of phonological awareness may receive insufficient attention when teachers and coaches have the opportunity to pursue improvements in a broad range of early literacy and language domains. Our analysis of coaching implementation data indicated that less than 5% of the 1,504 instructional improvement plans generated during coaching sessions addressed phonological awareness, and 13% of classrooms developed no plan explicitly focused on children's phonological awareness skills. Our interpretation of this pattern was that a PD program that affords considerable content flexibility regarding the literacy and language domains addressed in coaching sessions may provide inadequate exposure to instructional practices that teachers and perhaps coaches view as low-priority outcomes in early childhood programs (Powell, Steed, et al., 2010).

More broadly, PD interventions in content areas such as literacy or mathematics in which multiple related competencies are important components of early learning may benefit from a targeted approach to coaching (e.g., to ensure that a mathematics PD intervention addresses skills such as geometry and measurement as well as number recognition and counting; National Association for the Education of Young Children and National Council of Teachers of Mathematics, 2002). As an extension of this interpretation, we designed the subsequent (second) PD program with stronger attention to phonological awareness within a narrower set of literacy and language content boundaries. The outcome study of this subsequent coaching-based PD program found positive effects on teachers' phonological awareness instruction and children's phonological awareness skills, as described in the next section (Powell, Diamond, et al., 2010).

Coaching implementation data were central to a set of sequential, small-scale studies we conducted as part of an iterative approach to the development of our third coaching-based PD program, Classroom Links to Sounds and Words (Diamond & Powell, 2011). Our goal in developing this third program was to strengthen the intensity and targeted focus of our second one, Classroom Links to Early Literacy. Each small-scale study was carried out to inform the content or structure of an element of the third PD program. Each element entailed a substantial revision of a component of the predecessor program. For example, we hypothesized that successive attention to the same instructional practice in two or three consecutive coaching sessions would yield stronger outcomes than the one-time attention to an instructional practice commonly pursued in the predecessor program (Powell & Diamond, 2011).

We wondered if teachers would follow a coaching protocol that targeted the same teaching practice (e.g., teaching compound words) in several consecutive coaching sessions, with the expectation that teachers would make use of coach feedback on an initial implementation of the practice in their repeated, follow-up implementation of the targeted practice (e.g., implement a coach recommendation based on observation of the first attempt to teach compound words). Teacher accountability in a PD program presumably is intensified when teachers provide repeated attention to an instructional practice in the context of explicit recommendations for improvement. We implemented the revised coaching plan with five teachers and collected detailed information about their adherence to the planned content and schedule of coaching sessions. We also conducted in-depth interviews with the teachers about their reactions to the coaching protocol, including the organization of written comments in the coach's feedback (Diamond & Powell, 2011).

An important lesson of the small-scale studies noted above was that a higher level of intervention specificity regarding teachers' instruction and the focus of coaching sessions did not lead to a regimented, one-size-fits-all approach to coaching. Even with a narrower set of content boundaries, coaching can and should be individualized for each participating teacher. For example, evidence-based practice in teaching novel words to young children emphasizes the provision of child-friendly definitions (Powell & Diamond, 2012). Helping teachers implement this basic practice in vocabulary instruction may entail different types of coaching strategies across teachers. Some teachers may benefit from help in generating child-friendly definitions, others may need recommendations on how to improve their use of child-friendly definitions, and still other teachers may welcome a discussion of the rationale for child-friendly definitions.

Interpreting Outcomes

Data on program implementation can be particularly helpful in interpreting results of an intervention outcome study. In a study of effects of a coaching-based PD program with early childhood educators, for example, Neuman and Wright (2010) found positive effects on structural features of learning centers (e.g., arrangement of a book area) in intervention classrooms but no significant improvement in early childhood educators' instruction. The researchers speculated that these results were a function of coaching sessions that gave considerably more attention to characteristics of learning centers than to quality of instruction, a pattern identified in an analysis of coaching session records.

We used data on the implementation of coaching sessions to interpret two key findings of our study of our second PD program (Classroom Links to Early Literacy). Recall that one of the goals of this study was to determine whether there were differential effects of on-site and technologically mediated (remote) delivery of coaching. Our random assignment comparison of on-site and remote-delivery coaching found no consistent differences in the effectiveness of one delivery method compared to the other. The findings led us to conclude that technologically mediated delivery of literacy coaching is a promising alternative to in-person coaching in teachers' classrooms (Powell, Diamond, et al., 2010).

Data on coaching implementation strengthened our confidence in the results and our conclusion regarding on-site versus remote delivery of coaching. There were similar levels of intended implementation of on-site and remote delivery of coaching. The average number of coaching sessions in the on-site and remote coaching conditions was similar, although there was slightly more variability in the remote condition than in the on-site delivery of coaching. Teachers in both conditions observed on average a similar number of demonstrations of evidence-based practices. Specifically, teachers in the remote condition watched an average of 17 video exemplars of evidence-based practice, while teachers in the on-site delivery of coaching watched an average of 11 video exemplars and 6 instances of the coach modeling an evidence-based practice in their classroom. Further, there were no significant differences between on-site and remote conditions in the main content focus of coaching sessions. A similar number of different literacy topics were pursued in coaching sessions conducted in the on-site and remote conditions. In addition to helping us interpret our results regarding on-site versus remote delivery of coaching, these program implementation data provide evidence on the feasibility of technologically mediated coaching with teachers.

A second key finding of our Classroom Links to Early Literacy outcome study was that the coaching-based PD program had significant positive effects on the language and literacy environments provided by classroom teachers ($d = .92$) and on children's code-focused skills, including blending, letter-sound association, and print awareness (d's ranging from .17 to .29). There were no significant gains in teachers' oral language instruction, including strategies to promote children's vocabulary knowledge, and children's receptive vocabulary skills. Children in both intervention and control conditions made significant gains on a standardized measure of receptive vocabulary (Powell, Diamond, et al., 2010).

Our coaching implementation data helped us interpret the pattern of program effects on teachers and children. The design of the PD program called for relatively equal attention to code-focused instruction and to practices aimed at promoting oral language outcomes. However, the coaching implementation data indicated that code-focused practices were the primary content focus of 60% of coaching sessions (36% letter knowledge, 24% phonological awareness) and instructional strategies for promoting children's oral language skills were the primary focus of 36%; 4% of coaching sessions had an equal focus on both outcome domains (Powell, Diamond, et al., 2010). Information on the content of coaching sessions led us to speculate that the intervention did not help teachers significantly move their oral language teaching practices into closer proximity with evidence-based practices because there was insufficient attention to oral language instruction in coaching sessions (Powell & Diamond, 2011).

The data on coaching implementation also led us to design a successor PD program, our third coaching-based intervention with teachers, to include more coaching sessions (12 vs. 7) and to give primary focus to vocabulary instruction in the first six coaching sessions (with secondary attention in the latter six sessions). Results of a preliminary study of effects of that program (Classroom Links to Sounds and Words) found that intervention teachers defined significantly more words and also provided more labeling statements and/or questions about an object or action than control group teachers at the conclusion of the intervention (Powell, Diamond, & Burchinal, 2012).

Identifying Patterns of Variation

A third use of program implementation data is to discern meaningful patterns in the ways a program is delivered and received. Information on distinct profiles of program delivery or receipt can inform decisions about program design features that facilitate or accommodate program engagement. For example, an analysis of teachers' use of a website regarding quality instruction in early childhood class-rooms led Downer, Kraft-Sayre, and Pianta (2009) to suggest strategies for increasing website use levels and for replicating patterns of use on a wider scale.

An analysis of teachers' engagement of the hypermedia resource developed and offered in our second PD intervention illustrates some benefits of examining patterns of participation in a PD program (Powell et al., 2009). The hypermedia resource provided teachers with a library of nearly 100 video exemplars of evidence-based teaching practices. Each video was paired with bulleted comments that efficiently described key features of the instructional practice shown in the video. The videos were typically about 2 minutes in length and highlighted the practices of Head Start teachers who successfully participated in a prior PD program. The hypermedia resource also included more than 30 professional articles that offered rationales for recommended practices. The hypermedia resource had a two-tiered organizational structure. Sixteen cases that were focused on specific aspects of evidence-based instruction in early literacy and language development (e.g., interactive book reading) were organized into five modules (reading, writing, conversations with children, phonological awareness, and individualization). As described earlier, we collected data on teachers' browser actions through the use of software on each individual laptop in order to depict uses of the hypermedia resource.

Several general patterns in teachers' use of the hypermedia resource (video library) were consistent with original expectations. For example, we found that a majority of teachers used the resource in late afternoon and evening hours. This was consistent with our intention of providing teachers with flexibility in when and where they viewed their coach's feedback and used the hypermedia resource. Also, teachers' visits were not evenly distributed across the 16 cases, with half of the cases receiving 75% of all visits. Cases focused on strategies for supporting children's phonological awareness were among the most popular. The attention to this content is aligned with the level of attention to phonological awareness instruction in coaching sessions (Powell, Diamond, et al., 2010).

Some other patterns in teachers' uses of the hypermedia resource differed from our expectations. Resource pages that offered practice rationales, particularly the articles, were infrequently visited, whereas the video exemplars and their accompanying text received significantly more visits. We were surprised by the exceptionally limited use of the articles, all of which had been published in periodicals targeted to practitioners and were included, where appropriate, as links in coach feedback to teachers. Data on teachers' use of the hypermedia resource revealed that they viewed on average about 20% of the videos that their coach recommended and included as links in feedback to the teacher. On the other hand, teachers also viewed videos they found independently of their coach's recommendation. Of the videos teachers viewed, only about half were those suggested by the coach. This suggests a second pattern of hypermedia use—one that was not mediated by the coach and perhaps reflected a more proactive search for concrete guidance on how to improve classroom supports for children's literacy and language development.

Predicting the Strength and Type of Outcomes

Variations in the delivery and receipt of a coaching-based PD program likely affect the type and strength of program outcomes. This idea is fundamental to our interpretation of outcomes of our second PD program. As noted earlier, we surmised that the higher level of attention to code-focused instruction than to oral language instruction in coaching sessions may account for the PD program's positive effects on teachers' code-focused instruction and children's code-focused skills and for the absence of the PD program's effects on teachers' oral language instruction and children's language skills (Powell, Diamond, et al., 2010). This interpretation is a logical speculation and not a statement based on research that examined relations between indicators of coaching implementation and outcomes of the PD program.

To date, it appears that studies of the implementation of coaching with early childhood teachers have not examined associations between dimensions and outcomes of coaching. Addressing this void in the empirical literature across a range of coaching-based PD programs holds promise of identifying the active ingredients of coaching. Conceptual and methodological lessons from early childhood curriculum research may provide helpful guidance to investigations of coaching-based PD.

For example, Odom et al. (2010) examined indicators of the quantity (e.g., proportion of curriculum completed) and quality (e.g., ratings of the skill with which teachers delivered lessons) of preschool teachers' implementation of a comprehensive school readiness curriculum in relation to children's outcomes. The investigators' decision to measure both quantity and quality variables stemmed from an interest in the effects of different scenarios of implementation (e.g., high level of curriculum coverage at a lower quality, high level of curriculum coverage at a high level of quality). Analyses involved a composite score of the quantity and quality of curriculum implementation, computed by multiplying the proportion of curriculum completed by the average quality for each of the curriculum areas. Odom and colleagues found significant associations between the quality and quantity of curriculum implementation and children's outcomes, with different patterns of implementation–child outcome associations across outcome domains.

In another example from early childhood curriculum research, Hamre et al. (2010) assessed three aspects of curriculum implementation—dosage (frequency of curriculum use), adherence (following prescribed lesson plans), and quality of delivery (use of evidence-based practices)—in relation to children's language and literacy growth. The investigators found that children in classrooms in which activities had a higher dosage (lasted longer) and in which teachers exhibited a higher quality in delivering literacy lessons made significantly greater gains in early literacy skills across the preschool year.

Identifying Correlates of Coaching Implementation

A fifth use of information on coaching with early childhood teachers addresses the question of why there are variations in the implementation of coaching-based PD programs. Similar to other education and human service programs, it seems that PD programs are seldom implemented in full alignment with original plans. Data on correlates of implementation variations may help policy makers and program designers enact provisions that facilitate PD delivery and receipt. Little research has been done on predictors of variations in coaching-based PD implementation in early childhood settings. In the larger scientific literature on program implementation, research on predictors of program delivery and receipt is a relatively new line of investigation that faces the challenge of considering a plethora of predictor variables. Twenty-three ecological factors (Durlak, 2010) have been linked theoretically or empirically to implementation processes.

Several levels of predictor variables seem especially promising to pursue in research on factors that shape coaching-based PD implementation. Teacher variables are an obvious starting point, including teacher background characteristics such as education and years of teaching experience (Downer, Locasale-Crouch, et al., 2009). Early childhood educators' implementation of a new curriculum has been linked to teachers' openness to consultation regarding a school readiness curriculum (Domitrovich, Gest, Gill, Jones, & DeRousie, 2009) and to teachers' eagerness to learn new teaching strategies (Lieber et al., 2009). There appears to be no research on teacher reactions to a coach's suggestions, particularly the criteria used by a teacher to determine whether a coach's recommendations are credible and worthy of implementation in their classroom (Powell & Diamond, 2011). A counterpart to the level of teacher engagement in a coaching arrangement is the coach's level of confidence in recommendations offered to the teacher. Coaches who distance themselves from practices promoted in a PD program (e.g., "The curriculum manual says you're supposed to do this") may send an implicit message about their regard for the heart of a PD program.

Another level of possible predictors of coaching implementation is situated in the organizational context of a PD program. Teachers may be more eager to embrace practices promoted in a PD program if the practices are also valued by their program agency or sponsor. For instance, the greater attention to code-focused instruction than to oral language practices in our second PD program, as described earlier, may have been influenced in part by the press of congressionally mandated outcomes for Head Start programs, including children's identification of 10 letters of the alphabet (Powell et al., 2008). This possible link is based on speculation, however. The empirical literature would benefit from studies on the relation of coaching implementation to the goals of the host agency.

In addition to substantive alignment with agency priorities, coaching-based PD programs may fare better in positive organizational settings. Research suggests that a constructive (e.g., humanistic, supportive) organizational culture (Aarons & Sawitzky, 2006) and early childhood teachers' perceptions of their center directors as supportive and collegial (Baker, Kupersmidt, Voegler-Lee, Arnold, & Willoughby, 2010) are related to implementation of new practices.

Summary

Coaching and similar forms of individualized work with teachers currently command keen interest in decisions about approaches to early childhood PD as policy makers and early childhood program leaders search for ways to bolster young children's school readiness through improvements in teaching practices. Providing tailored support to teachers regarding the implementation of evidence-based practices in their classrooms is increasingly considered to be superior to the more common strategy of conducting workshops for groups of teachers. A fledgling research literature provides some promising results, as well as numerous unanswered questions about the outcomes and process of coaching with early childhood educators. Many of the unanswered questions reflect the dearth of research on the implementation of coaching.

Productive studies of intervention implementation begin with a conceptual framework that represents an intervention's theory of change. An examination of intervention fidelity—that is, the extent to which an intervention is implemented as planned—requires a careful specification of how the intervention is expected to influence its targeted outcomes. This chapter draws on a 10-year program of research on coaching-based PD to suggest that three dimensions of coaching are central to individualized work with teachers:

1. Structure (e.g., number, duration, frequency, or interval of coaching sessions)

2. Process (e.g., feedback on appropriately implemented practices and practices that need improvement or implementation)

3. Content (e.g., coverage of evidence-based practices and information)

Credible studies of coaching implementation employ valid and reliable measures. While this basic condition of good research may seem unnecessary to mention, the prevalence of self-report data in extant studies of intervention implementation leaves open the possibility of potential bias that few studies have addressed through systematic safeguards (e.g., corroboration) or by independently gathering data on coaching sessions (e.g., recording, live observation). Still, existing records of coaching, such as written feedback to teachers, may be used as an efficient source of information on coaching implementation in the context of data reliability provisions, as described in this chapter.

Findings of research on coaching implementation may be used in five different ways that collectively contribute to progress in the design and possible scaling up of individualized approaches to PD. Specifically, implementation data can determine the feasibility of particular elements of coaching, interpret program outcomes, identify meaningful patterns of variation in program implementation, predict the strength and type of coaching outcomes, and identify factors associated with variations in coaching implementation. Illustrations of each of these uses of coaching implementation data are offered in this chapter.

Although our PD research program pertains to literacy and language outcomes, the conceptual framework, methodological issues, and uses of intervention data described in this chapter may be applicable to other content domains in early childhood. Our hope is that the coaching-based PD research literature will grow to the point that narrative literature reviews and meta-analyses may be conducted on coaching dimensions across different substantive areas. To this end, the intervention research agenda must include rigorous implementation studies that broaden and deepen our understanding of what works in supporting effective teaching and strong outcomes for young children.

References

Aarons, G.A., & Sawitzky, A.C. (2006). Organizational culture and climate and mental health provider attitudes toward evidence-based practice. *Psychological Services, 3*, 61–72.

Assel, M.A., Landry, S.H., Swank, P.R., & Gunnewig, S. (2007). An evaluation of curriculum, setting, and mentoring on the performance of children enrolled in pre-kindergarten. *Reading and Writing, 20*, 463–494.

Baker, C.N., Kupersmidt, J.B., Voegler-Lee, M.E., Arnold, D.H., & Willoughby, M.T. (2010). Predicting teacher participation in a classroom-based integrated preventive intervention for preschoolers. *Early Childhood Research Quarterly, 25*, 270–283.

Bierman, K.L., Domitrovich, C.E., Nix, R.L., Gest, S.D., Welsh, J.A., Greenberg, M.T., ... Gill, S. (2008). Promoting academic and social-emotional school readiness: The Head Start REDI program. *Child Development, 79*, 1802–1817.

Carroll, C., Patterson, M., Wood, S., Booth, A., Rick, J., & Balain, S. (2007). A conceptual framework for implementation fidelity. *Implementation Science, 2*, 40.

Cook, T.D., & Payne, M.R. (2002). Objecting to the objections to using random assignment in educational research. In F. Mosteller & R. Boruch (Eds.), *Evidence matters: Randomized trials in education research* (pp. 150–178). Washington, DC: Brookings Institution Press.

Cordray, D.S., & Pion, G.M. (2006). Treatment strength and integrity: Models and methods. In R.R. Bootzin & P.E. McKnight (Eds.), *Strengthening research methodology: Psychological measurement and evaluation* (pp. 103–124). Washington, DC: American Psychological Association.

Dane, A.V., & Schneider, B.H. (1998). Program integrity in primary and early secondary preventions: Are implementation effects out of control? *Clinical Psychology Review, 18,* 23–45.

Diamond, K.E., & Powell, D.R. (2011). An iterative approach to the development of a professional development intervention for Head Start teachers. *Journal of Early Intervention, 33,* 75–93.

Domitrovich, C.E., Gest, S.D., Gill, S., Jones, D., & DeRousie, R.S. (2009). Individual factors associated with professional development training outcomes of the Head Start REDI program. *Early Education and Development, 20,* 402–430.

Downer, J.T., Kraft-Sayre, M.E., & Pianta, R.C. (2009). Ongoing, web-mediated professional development focused on teacher–child interactions: Early childhood educators' usage rates and self-reported satisfaction. *Early Education and Development, 20,* 321–345.

Downer, J.T., Locasale-Crouch, J., Hamre, B., & Pianta, R. (2009). Teacher characteristics associated with responsiveness and exposure to consultation and online professional development resources. *Early Education and Development, 20,* 431–455.

Dunst, C.J., Trivette, C.M., & Hamby, D.W. (1996). Measuring the helpgiving practices of human services program practitioners. *Human Relations, 49,* 815–835.

Durlak, J.A. (2010). The importance of doing well in whatever you do: A commentary on the special section "Implementation research in early childhood education." *Early Childhood Research Quarterly, 25,* 348–357.

Durlak, J.A., & DuPre, E.P. (2008). Implementation matters: A review of research on the influence of implementation on program outcomes and the factors affecting implementation. *American Journal of Community Psychology, 41,* 327–350.

Garet, M., Porter, A., Desimone, L., Birman, B., & Yoon, K.S. (2001). What makes professional development effective? Results from a national sample of teachers. *American Educational Research Journal, 38,* 915–945.

Gersten, R., Morvant, M., & Brengelman, S. (1995). Close to the classroom is close to the bone: Coaching as a means to translate research into classroom practice. *Exceptional Children, 62,* 52–66.

Hamre, B.K., Justice, L.M., Pianta, R.C., Kilday, C., Sweeney, B., Downer, J.T., & Leach, A. (2010). Implementation fidelity of MyTeachingPartner literacy and language activities: Association with preschoolers' language and literacy growth. *Early Childhood Research Quarterly, 25,* 329–347.

Hsieh, W.-Y., Hemmeter, M.L., McCollum, J.A., & Ostrosky, M.M. (2009). Using coaching to increase preschool teachers' use of emergent literacy teaching strategies. *Early Childhood Research Quarterly, 24,* 229–247.

Hulleman, C.S., & Cordray, D. (2009). Moving from the lab to the field: The role of fidelity and achieved relative intervention strength. *Journal of Research on Educational Effectiveness, 2,* 88–110.

International Reading Association. (2004). *The role and qualifications of the reading coach in the United States.* Newark, DE: Author.

Knoche, L.L., Sheridan, S.M., Edwards, C.P., & Osborn, A.Q. (2010). Implementation of a relationship-based school readiness intervention: A multidimensional approach to fidelity measurement for early childhood. *Early Childhood Research Quarterly, 25,* 299–313.

Landry, S.H., Anthony, J.L., Swank, P.R., & Monseque-Bailey, P. (2009). Effectiveness of comprehensive professional development for teachers of at-risk preschoolers. *Journal of Educational Psychology, 101,* 448–465.

Lieber, J., Butera, G., Hanson, M., Palmer, S., Horn, E., Czaja, C., … Odom, S. (2009). Factors that influence the implementation of a new preschool curriculum: Implications for professional development. *Early Education and Development, 20,* 456–481.

National Association for the Education of Young Children (NAEYC) and the National Council of Teachers of Mathematics. (2002). *Position statement on early childhood mathematics: Promoting good beginnings.* Washington, DC: NAEYC.

Neuman, S.B., & Cunningham, L. (2009). The impact of professional development and coaching on early language and literacy instructional practices. *American Educational Research Journal, 46*, 532–566.

Neuman, S.B., & Wright, T.S. (2010). Promoting language and literacy development for early childhood educators: A mixed-methods study of coursework and coaching. *Elementary School Journal, 111*, 63–86.

Odom, S.L., Fleming, K., Diamond, K., Lieber, J., Hanson, M., Butera, G., … Marquis, J. (2010). Examining different forms of implementation and in early childhood curriculum research. *Early Childhood Research Quarterly, 25*, 314–328.

Pence, K., Justice, L.M., & Wiggins, A.K. (2008). Preschool teachers' fidelity in implementing a comprehensive language-rich curriculum. *Language, Speech, and Hearing Services in Schools, 39*, 329–341.

Pianta, R.C., Mashburn, A.J., Downer, J.T., Hamre, B.K., & Justice, L. (2008). Effects of web-mediated PD resources on teacher–child interactions in pre-kindergarten classrooms. *Early Childhood Research Quarterly, 23*, 431–451.

Powell, D.R. (2005). Searches for what works in parenting interventions. In T. Luster & L. Okagaki (Eds.), *Parenting: An ecological perspective* (2nd ed., pp. 343–373). Mahwah, NJ: Erlbaum.

Powell, D.R., & Diamond, K.E. (2011). Improving the outcomes of coaching-based professional development interventions. In S.B. Neuman & D.K. Dickinson (Eds.), *Handbook of early literacy research* (Vol. 3, pp. 295–307). New York, NY: Guilford.

Powell, D.R., & Diamond, K.E. (2012). Promoting early literacy and language development. In R.C. Pianta, W.S. Barnett, L.M. Justice, & S.M. Sheridan (Eds.), *Handbook of early childhood education* (pp. 194–216). New York, NY: Guilford.

Powell, D.R., Diamond, K.E., Bojczyk, K.E., & Gerde, H.K. (2008). Head Start teachers' perspectives on early literacy. *Journal of Literacy Research, 40*, 422–460.

Powell, D.R., Diamond, K.E., & Burchinal, M.R. (2012). Using coaching-based professional development to improve Head Start teachers' support of children's oral language skills. In C. Howes, B. Hamre, & R. Pianta (Eds.), *Effective professional development in early childhood education* (pp. 13–29). Baltimore, MD: Paul H. Brookes Publishing Co.

Powell, D.R., Diamond, K.E., Burchinal, M.R., & Koehler, M.J. (2010). Effects of an early literacy professional development intervention on Head Start teachers and children. *Journal of Educational Psychology, 102*, 299–312.

Powell, D.R., Diamond, K.E., & Cockburn, M. (2013). Promising approaches to professional development for early childhood educators. In O. Saracho & B. Spodek (Eds.), *Handbook of research on the education of young children* (pp. 385–392). London, England: Routledge/Taylor & Francis.

Powell, D.R., Diamond, K.E., & Koehler, M.J. (2009). Use of a case-based hypermedia resource in an early literacy coaching intervention with pre-kindergarten teachers. *Topics in Early Childhood Special Education, 29*, 239–249.

Powell, D.R., & Sigel, E.I. (1991). Searches for validity in evaluations of young children and early childhood programs. In B. Spodek & O. Saracho (Eds.), *Yearbook of early childhood education* (Vol. 2, pp. 190–212). New York, NY: Teachers College Press.

Powell, D.R., Steed, E.A., & Diamond, K.E. (2010). Dimensions of literacy coaching with Head Start teachers. *Topics in Early Childhood Special Education, 30*, 148–161.

Preschool Curriculum Evaluation Research Consortium. (2008). *Effects of preschool curriculum programs on school readiness (NCER 2008–2009).* National Center for Education Research, Institute of Education Sciences, U.S. Department of Education. Washington, DC: U.S. Government Printing Office.

Shanklin, N.L. (2006). *What are the characteristics of effective literacy coaching?* Urbana, IL: Literacy Coaching Clearinghouse, National Council of Teachers of English.

Simons, K.A., Agnamba, L.A., Halle, T.G., & Zaslow, M.J. (2010). *Evaluation of the implementation of the Excellence-in-Teaching initiative: Year 3 report.* Prepared for the U.S. Department of Education, Policy and Programs Studies Service. Washington, DC: Child Trends.

Slavin, R.E. (2004). Education research can and must address "what works" questions. *Educational Researcher, 33*, 27–28.

Wasik, B.H., & Hindman, A.H. (2011). Improving vocabulary and pre-literacy skills of at-risk preschoolers through teacher professional development. *Journal of Educational Psychology, 103*, 455–469.

Whitaker, S., Kinzie, M., Kraft-Sayre, M.E., Mashburn, A., & Pianta, R.C. (2007). Use and evaluation of web-based professional development services across participant levels of support. *Early Childhood Education Journal, 34*, 379–386.

CHAPTER 6

Implementation of Getting Ready

A Relationship-Focused Intervention to
Support Parent Engagement, Birth to 5

Lisa L. Knoche

This chapter describes the Getting Ready intervention, a dynamic and individualized intervention targeting children's school readiness through enhanced parent engagement for children from birth to age 5 years. Getting Ready was implemented within Early Head Start (EHS) and Head Start (HS) programs. The chapter specifically focuses on *how* the Getting Ready innovation was embedded into service settings with the anticipated outcomes of improving parent engagement and subsequent child school readiness skills. It uniquely describes how core implementation components are realized in a highly individualized and dynamic intervention with families, particularly at the beginning stages of an intervention, and chapter includes 1) a description of the Getting Ready intervention, 2) relevant performance site characteristics and delivery agents, 3) details on core implementation components that were realized in the efficacy trial, and 4) lessons learned, including related recommendations for practice and research.

The Getting Ready Intervention

The Getting Ready intervention (Sheridan, Marvin, Knoche, & Edwards, 2008) provides an integrated, ecological, strengths-based approach to supporting school readiness for families with children up to 5 years of age who are participating in early childhood intervention and prevention programs. The intervention is constructed on the foundational belief that optimal school readiness for children and their families occurs through the development of positive relationships within the multiple interacting ecological systems of the home (i.e., parent–child relationships) and between the home and other supportive environments and programs (i.e., parent–professional relationships). For the Getting Ready intervention, "school readiness" is understood to mean that children must develop certain capacities to be "ready" to participate in formal schooling; these capacities are enhanced via the parent–child relationship. However readiness does not reside in the child alone; families must also be ready to develop positive partnerships with educators and other school personnel to 1) ensure consistent cross-setting supports and messages,

2) integrate efforts at providing learning opportunities, and 3) promote positive developmental outcomes in children.

The intervention's distinctiveness lies in its joint emphasis on 1) guiding parents to engage in warm and responsive interactions, encourage their children's autonomy, and participate in children's learning (i.e., parent engagement) and 2) supporting parents and early childhood professionals in individualized, collaborative interactions (i.e., partnerships) to jointly facilitate children's school readiness. Family-centered principles (Dunst, Trivette, & Deal, 1988) that are focused on promoting family strengths and building positive relationships for enhanced parenting skills (Mirenda, MacGregor, & Kely-Keough, 2002) and family engagement (Trivette, Dunst, & Hamby, 2010) are guiding principles for the Getting Ready model. It is culturally sensitive (responsive to values, priorities, and interaction styles of families), developmentally responsive (appropriate to children's needs across the developmental spectrum), intentional (focused on specific objectives), strengths based (building on family and child competencies and interests), and collaborative (structured around mutual—parent and professional—goals).

Research Support for the Parent–Child Relationship

Because parental behavior has long been associated with specific social and cognitive outcomes in young children (Knitzer, Steinberg, & Fleisch, 1993; NICHD Early Child Care Research Network, 2002; Pan, Rowe, Singer, & Snow, 2005), it is an obvious target for interventions aiming to enhance young children's school readiness. Parent engagement is comprised of three dimensions of parental behaviors that are valued cross-culturally and facilitate optimal school readiness and success: 1) parental warmth, sensitivity, and responsiveness; 2) support for children's emerging autonomy; and 3) participation in learning and literacy (Morrison, Connor, & Bachman, 2006; Sheridan & Kratochwill, 2008). The research of our team, along with others', indicates these dimensions are predictive of children's later social-emotional, language, and cognitive development (Chazan-Cohen et al., 2009; Sheridan, Knoche, Edwards, Bovaird, & Kupzyk, 2010; Sheridan, Knoche, Kupzyk, Edwards, & Marvin, 2011).

Parental warmth and sensitivity that includes encouragement and support lay the foundation for secure behavior and exploration (Hirsh-Pasek & Burchinal, 2006; Parker, Boak, Griffin, Ripple, & Peay, 1999; Shonkoff & Phillips, 2000). Parental interactions that include displays of affection, physical proximity, contingent positive reinforcement, and sensitivity are associated with children's positive cognitive growth over time (Bradley, Corwyn, Burchinal, McAdoo, & Coll, 2001; Burchinal, Campbell, Bryant, Wasik, & Ramey, 1997; Landry, Smith, Swank, Assel, & Vellet, 2001; Pungello, Iruka, Dotterer, Mills-Koonce, & Reznick, 2009; Rao et al., 2010). During the preschool period, parental warmth, sensitivity, and responsiveness are associated with children's improved short-term cognitive, social-emotional, and language skills (Dunst & Kassow, 2008; Dunst et al., 2007; Hirsh-Pasek & Burchinal, 2006; Trivette, Dunst, Hamby, & Pace, 2007), long-term positive academic performance (Downer & Pianta, 2006), and positive social-emotional outcomes, such as strong prosocial orientations, numerous and high-quality friendships, and high levels of peer acceptance in kindergarten (Kerns, Klepac, & Cole, 1996). Alternatively, intrusive parenting is predictive of later academic, social-emotional, and behavior problems, with some variation by ethnic group (Egeland, Pianta, & O'Brien, 1993; Feldman & Masalha, 2010; Pungello et al., 2009).

Parental support for children's autonomy is known to be critical for fostering the skills that are essential for child well-being and future success in school (Clark & Ladd, 2000). Parents' abilities to provide developmentally sensitive support for autonomous problem solving have been associated with increased levels of cognitive competence in young children (Mulvaney, McCartney, Bub, & Marshall, 2006); communication with peers (Martinez, 1987); self-regulatory skills, including task persistence (Grolnick & Farkas, 2002; Kelley, Brownell, & Campbell, 2000; Neitzel & Stright, 2003); and adaptive levels of social assertiveness and self-directedness in social and play interactions (Denham, Renwick, & Holt, 1991; McNamara, Selig, & Hawley, 2010).

Finally, parental participation in learning has been shown to be positively related to young children's later academic performance (Foster, Lambert, Abbott-Shinn, McCarty, & Franze, 2005; Hill, 2001; Weigel, Martin, & Bennett, 2006a, 2006b). Parents who frequently engage in responsive language and literacy interactions with their children and who provide a home environment rich in opportunities for learning through shared book reading, constructive play, and exploration have children who display higher language and cognitive skills in toddlerhood, preschool, and the primary years (e.g., Chazan-Cohen et al., 2009; Hood, Conlon, & Andrews, 2008; NICHD Early Child Care Research Network, 2002; Raikes et al., 2006; Tamis-LeMonda & Bornstein, 2002).

Research Support for Parent–Professional Partnerships

The parent–professional relationship is another important component of intervention (Clark & Ladd, 2000). Furthermore, partnership practices yield a greater provision of services in natural learning settings for children, greater cultural sensitivity, and a community-based system of care and education (Knitzer et al., 1993; Mendoza, Katz, Robertson, & Rothenberg, 2003). In potentially challenging or high-risk situations, the establishment of positive, constructive relationships among parent–professional partners provides an opportunity for dialogue and problem solving, a "window of opportunity" not present when home and early childhood services operate in isolation from or counter to one another.

Collaborative partnerships among parents and professionals correlate with positive outcomes for children and families and bolster the efficacy and efficiency of interventions in advancing young children's development (Caspe & Lopez, 2006; Epstein & Sanders, 2002; Grolnick & Slowiaczek, 1994; Masten & Coatsworth, 1998; Turnbull, Turnbull, Erwin, Soodak, & Shogren, 2011). Interventions that focus on promoting family strengths and building constructive partnerships produce changes in the family environment, the parent–child relationship, parenting skills, and family involvement in children's learning (Caspe & Lopez, 2006). When families report a positive perception of the relationship with the professional with whom they work, more positive outcomes are reported (Korfmacher, Green, Spellmann, & Thornburg, 2007). Parental competence and self-efficacy appear to be influenced by helpgiving that is highly participatory and individualized (Dunst et al., 2007). A meta-analysis of studies of helpgiving practices indicates that family-centered programs and practices, including efforts to support the self-efficacy of families, have indirect effects on both children and parents (Trivette et al., 2010).

Key Features of the Getting Ready Intervention

The Getting Ready intervention takes place within structured early childhood preschool or infant/toddler programs, augmenting existing curricula and services. This enhances the typical EHS and HS services that are offered to families. Getting Ready is not an "add-on" curriculum, but an individualized, integrated process for conducting "business-as-usual" program activities and programming. The use of Getting Ready strategies in concert with the established early childhood programs strengthens the ongoing interactions with families in support of child and family school readiness. The Getting Ready intervention offers opportunities for professionals to support and enhance the quality of parent–child interactions in daily routines and creates a shared responsibility between parents and early childhood professionals (ECPs)—including home visitors, teachers, and other early interventionists—to influence child developmental success and school readiness.

The Getting Ready intervention integrates principles of *triadic intervention* (McCollum & Yates, 1994) as a means of supporting the parent–child relationship and *collaborative (conjoint) consultation models* (Sheridan & Kratochwill, 2008; Sheridan, Kratochwill, & Bergan, 1996) in an effort to guide the parent–professional interaction. The integrated triadic and collaborative Getting Ready intervention strategies are described in Table 6.1, and the dynamic relation between these strategies is depicted in Figure 6.1. This collective set of strategies is used in a fluid, dynamic, and individualized way to 1) support parents in establishing warm and sensitive interactions with their children, promoting children's emerging autonomy, and participating actively in their children's learning; and 2) promote parent–professional partnerships for guiding children's development, all in ways that are culturally comfortable to them (Edwards, Sheridan, & Knoche, 2010). By focusing on these targets, the ultimate goal of Getting Ready is to promote children's healthy social-emotional, cognitive, communicative, and behavioral development in support of school readiness and future learning.

The Getting Ready intervention takes place during home visits or group socializations with families scheduled as part of regular program activities (monthly or weekly). ECPs establish working partnerships with parents and used triadic and collaborative strategies (Table 6.1) to increase effective parent engagement in planned and routine activities and to support the parent–child relationship. ECPs share and discuss observations about children with their families and affirm parents' competence in supporting or advancing children's abilities. Furthermore, they discuss developmental expectations and appropriate targets by sharing developmental information and focusing parents' attention on their children's strengths. ECPs and parents brainstorm collaboratively around problems or issues related to children's social, motor, cognitive, or communicative development and learning. ECPs ask parents for their reflections and ideas related to the children's recent learning needs and interests. When appropriate, ECPs make suggestions for possible modifications to intervention plans, which might include new learning opportunities or developmental targets, and they may also interact directly with the child to serve as a model for the parent.

Table 6.1. Getting Ready model triadic and collaborative intervention strategies and objectives

Establish parent–child and parent–professional relationships

· Establish a context for positive parent–child interaction by positioning them in close, face-to-face proximity with one another; encourage reflective communication; highlight child strengths.

· Use communication strategies to build the parent–early childhood professional (ECP) relationship (e.g., listen actively to a parent's challenges/concerns, use open-ended questions, request parents' opinions and ideas, and affirm parents' competence); encourage positive parent–child interactions.

Share observations and knowledge of child over time

· Exchange information about what parents and ECP observe about the child's developmental progress.

· Share screening data, including areas of delay; focus parent's attention on the child's strengths and needs; solicit parental perspectives on day-to-day child interests and activities; clarify developmentally relevant observations.

· Share observations continuously to ensure ongoing attention to child strengths and areas of need.

· Affirm parents' insights and competent observations.

Identify mutually agreed-upon developmental expectations for the child

· Focus parents' attention on child strengths and developmental needs.

· Engage in open discussions of family and program goals for the child and the child's development; establish an agreed-upon set of desired targets toward which the child will progress, as responsive to observations and data.

· Share developmentally appropriate information.

· Assist parents in identifying appropriate targets by focusing attention on the child's current challenges, needs, strengths, and emerging abilities.

Share ideas and brainstorm methods for helping the child meet expectations

· Discuss the contexts that best elicit and support the child's growth; discuss means for monitoring changes in the child's learning and development.

· Assist parents to identify everyday opportunities for the child to support developmental tasks.

· Identify current and potential parent behaviors that can support targeted learning.

· Suggest developmentally appropriate activities; model adult behaviors (e.g., nodding, commenting, elaborating, praising, questioning) that maintain a child's interest and scaffold his or her learning.

· Make suggestions when necessary.

Observe parent–child interactions and provide feedback

· Provide parents an opportunity to practice interactions and skills with their child during home visits.

· Observe the parent–child interaction; adjust the manner in which parents support skill learning by modeling with the child or providing suggestions, if necessary. Provide parental validations and affirmation to support the development of parenting skills.

· Identify current strengths related to developmental expectations.

· Provide developmental information.

Monitor the child's skill development and determine directions for continued growth

· Engage in ongoing discussions regarding the child's response to learning opportunities or new parenting behaviors.

· Discuss needed adjustments in interactions and/or learning opportunities.

· Use data to determine progress and areas in need of modification.

· Cycle to new developmental expectations and learning opportunities as needed.

· Cocreate specific plans for maintaining the child's progress and parents' skills at collaboration.

From Knoche, L.L., Edwards, C.P., Sheridan, S.M., Kupzyk, K.A., Marvin, C.A., Cline, K.D., & Clarke, B.L. (2012). Getting Ready: Results of a randomized trial of a relationship-focused intervention on parent engagement in rural Early Head Start. *Infant Mental Health Journal, 33,* 442; reprinted by permission.

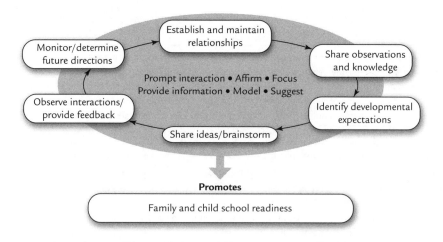

Figure 6.1. The Getting Ready intervention. The outer oval depicts the collaborative consultation structure that supports the parent–professional relationship, while the set of triadic strategies (parent–child–professional) indicated in the middle of the model are used by the early childhood professional to simultaneously support the parent–child relationship during the collaborative parent–professional interactions. It is the tandem use of these triadic and collaborative strategies (further specified in Table 6.1) that characterizes the Getting Ready intervention. (From "Getting Ready: Promoting School Readiness through a Relationship-Based Partnership Model," by S.M. Sheridan, C.A. Marvin, L L. Knoche, & C.P. Edwards, 2008, *Early Childhood Services, 2*[3], pp. 149–172. Copyright 2008 by Plural Publishing, Inc. Reprinted with permission.)

During home visits and family socializations, ECPs observe the parent–child interaction and provide feedback to draw the parents' attention to specific exhibited parental actions that resulted in positive responses from their children and provide suggestions when necessary. ECPs also support families in noting progress toward developmental targets, help to determine necessary modifications and learning opportunities to support the child's ongoing development, and share developmental information as appropriate in a targeted and intentional fashion.

The Getting Ready intervention promotes a joining of expertise of parents with that of the ECP, bringing together family contributions about relevant experiences and professional contributions about developmentally important activities. The collaborative nature of the process encourages parents and ECPs to share their respective observations and knowledge to support the child's development. The strategies are highly individualized; as part of the professional development efforts (described below), ECPs are trained to use the strategies in a targeted and intentional manner. It is this strategic, focused, and integrated use of the Getting Ready strategies that is essential for the success of the model. Use of the strategies in this way requires a high level of observational skill and ability on the part of the ECP.

Site and Participant Characteristics

Assignment to Condition

Families involved in the efficacy trial of Getting Ready were enrolled in home-based Early Head Start programming or center-based Head Start programming; a total of 451 families (234 EHS and 217 HS) participated in the trial. At the start of the Getting Ready intervention activities, agency administrators at participating sites were contacted by research staff and informed of the Getting Ready intervention. Sites were randomly assigned to treatment or control conditions. All families who were enrolled in programming and still eligible for a minimum of 12 months of EHS services or 2 years of HS services were recruited for participation. Both English- and Spanish-speaking families were recruited. The families' assignments to treatment or control conditions reflected a nested design, in that the condition assignment of each family matched that of their agency-assigned ECP, who was randomized based on their site location.

Early Head Start Settings

The EHS programming took place within three rural community service agencies in a Midwestern state. Agencies housed between 5 and 21 ECPs (also referred to as "home visitors"). ECPs in the rural EHS agencies provided services to pregnant women and families with children under age 3 years via weekly home visits scheduled to last up to 90 minutes and monthly family group activities held at the community agency (socializations). The average size of ECPs' caseloads in EHS was 10 families. Home visits were conducted weekly and lasted 60–90 minutes based on EHS performance standards (Administration on Children and Families, 2010). Home visitation services focused on child development and parenting skills using published developmental curricula such as Beautiful Beginnings (Raikes & Whitmer, 2006) or Parents as Teachers (PAT; Parents as Teachers National Center, 2008). This model of EHS service delivery is in line with EHS program guidelines and was characteristic of both treatment and control conditions.

Early Head Start Early Childhood Professionals

Sixty-four EHS ECPs provided programming to enrolled EHS families (n = 33 in control and n = 31 in treatment samples). Key demographic characteristics were not statistically significantly different between treatment and control participants. Ninety-nine percent were female and 1% male. The average age of EHS ECPs was 31.9 years (SD = 9.4). The average number of years of experience working in early childhood services was 5.2 (SD = 4.9), and the ECPs had been employed in their current position an average of 2.0 years (SD = 3.6). Thirty-nine percent of the ECPs reported being Hispanic/Latino. The educational level of the participants varied: 4% had a high school diploma, 33% reported some training beyond high school, 8% earned a 1-year vocational training certificate, 37% earned a 2-year college degree, 17% reported earning a 4-year college degree, and 1% reported receiving graduate training.

Head Start Settings

The HS programming took place in 29 HS classrooms housed in 21 different public elementary school buildings. The HS program was in session during the academic year, 5 days each week, for 4 hours each day. All classrooms were accredited by the National Association for the Education of Young Children and utilized the High/Scope curriculum (Hohmann & Weikert, 2002). Each classroom comprised 18 to 20 children, from ages 3 to 5 years. Each classroom had at least one full-time, state-certified lead teacher and one full-time paraprofessional classroom aid. Standard (i.e., business-as-usual) programmatic services offered to all children included an average of five home visits by the teacher each academic year, parent–teacher conferences twice each year, and monthly parent–child (socialization) activities at the school and/or in the community.

Head Start Early Childhood Professionals

Thirty-six HS ECPs provided programming to enrolled HS families ($n = 15$ in control and $n = 21$ in treatment samples). There were no statistically significant differences between treatment and control groups on key demographic variables. All HS ECPs held state-certified teaching endorsements in early childhood. All had at least a bachelor's degree, with 34.2% reporting some graduate coursework and 15.8% an advanced graduate degree. All were female, and their mean age was 33.5 years ($SD = 10.0$). Ninety-two percent self-reported to be non-Hispanic Caucasian; 8% were Hispanic/Latino. ECPs had an average of 8.3 years of experience working in early childhood ($SD = 7.6$) and had been employed in their position for 2.5 years ($SD = 3.4$).

Effectiveness of Getting Ready: Significant Outcomes

Data indicate that the Getting Ready intervention is effective at supporting both child and family outcomes. The intervention yielded enhanced social-emotional competencies (Sheridan et al., 2010) for preschool children. ECPs reported that children demonstrated increased attachment behaviors with adults, improved initiative, and reduced anxiety/withdrawal behaviors (Sheridan et al., 2010). Similarly, in the area of language and early literacy, children in the treatment group demonstrated significantly greater rates of positive change in oral language, early reading, and early writing skills relative to controls (Sheridan et al., 2011). Furthermore, language and literacy outcomes were moderated by teacher- or parent-reported concerns. Specifically, when concerns were noted by parents or ECPs regarding children's development upon preschool entry, the effects of the intervention on direct language assessments and teacher reports of language and literacy were greater than for their peers without concerns and for controls (Sheridan et al., 2011).

Results also indicated positive treatment effects on parenting behaviors (Knoche et al., 2012). Parents who participated in the Getting Ready intervention demonstrated higher quality interactions with their children, including enhanced quality of warmth and sensitivity and support for their children's autonomy, than parents in the control group. They were also more likely to use appropriate directives with their children and to demonstrate appropriate supports for their young children's learning.

Level of Intervention and Stage of Implementation

The level of intervention delivery and the stage of implementation are important considerations for the study of implementation. The Getting Ready study was conducted as part of the Interagency School Readiness Consortium—an interagency initiative funded through the Department of Health and Human Services's National Institute of Child Health and Human Development (NICHD), Administration for Children and Families, and Office of the Assistant Secretary for Planning and Evaluation and the Department of Education's Office of Special Education and Rehabilitative Services—to identify efficacious interventions for promoting school readiness for young children at developmental risk. This study was the first efficacy trial of the Getting Ready intervention wherein the triadic and collaborative strategies (see Table 6.1) were integrated as supports for general cognitive, behavioral, and social-emotional school readiness indicators for children from birth to age 5 years. Consequently, this first efficacy trial is characterized as an initial implementation of the Getting Ready intervention, with a movement toward full operation (Fixsen, Naoom, Blase, Friedman, & Wallace, 2005). In accordance with recommended practice, at this initial stage of implementation, we embedded implementation research questions and methodology into study activities in an effort to produce data that would ultimately support implementation and inform the iterative evaluation process.

In Getting Ready, the intervention was targeting multiple levels. The Getting Ready strategies were implemented by ECPs, who in turn worked directly with families to support positive parent–child interaction, enhance family engagement, and build parent–professional partnerships. Thus, the staff training and coaching components of the intervention were implemented at the ECP level, while the ECPs in turn focused on family-level implementation.

At this initial implementation stage, it was important to consider a range of variables that have been shown to impact successful implementation (Fixsen et al., 2005). As indicated by other researchers (e.g., Panzano et al., 2007), contextual variables (e.g., EHS/HS guidelines), organizational variables (e.g., work environment characteristics, employee satisfaction, perceived levels of administrative support and dedicated resources), and purveyor variables (e.g., background and level of experience, dedicated time and resources, evaluation/research activities and data collection needs) interacted to influence the success of implementation at this stage. For example, organizational variables were particularly salient given that the study was conducted in existing programs.

As described in Chapter 1, purveyors are the group of individuals who actively work to help implement a program with fidelity and effectiveness. In the case of Getting Ready, the purveyor was the research team. The experience of the research team in working with this group of ECPs and programs was relevant, along with the time and resources devoted by the research team to support implementation of the intervention.

Our Getting Ready research team was a secondary entity working in partnership with several community agencies and school districts. These partnerships created unique dynamics for focusing on implementation issues given that characteristics of the respective agencies and schools interacted with components of the intervention and with characteristics of the purveyor (the research team). Since the intervention was being embedded within existing agency settings, our research team had to carefully consider implementation features and integrate systems and practices of the existing programs into the intervention. The process was one of collaboration and mutual give-and-take, in which the Getting Ready intervention was not exclusively manipulated to accommodate the unique organizational environments. Rather, the organizational environments, including existing program processes and expectations, were modified or adjusted slightly to accommodate the intervention.

This accommodation required a foundational level of trust and confidence in the implementation partnership. For example, several of the EHS programs were implementing Parents as Teachers (Parents as Teachers National Center, 2008) for their universal home visiting curriculum. This curriculum includes a prescribed sequence of activities that are initiated by the ECP during weekly home visits. In contrast to the predetermined activity focus of PAT, the Getting Ready intervention includes family involvement in topic selection for home visits. Therefore, our research team had to negotiate with our partner agencies for a degree of flexibility that would allow some variation in the order of PAT curriculum delivery. Our research team was concerned with fidelity of implementation of the Getting Ready intervention, just as our partners were concerned with fidelity to their respective curricula. These competing yet complementary needs required flexibility on the part of both teams. Fortunately, there was a shared belief among both partners about the importance of meaningful family engagement (see the discussion of organizational selection below).

During the course of this efficacy trial, sustainability was a key consideration. The research team worked to develop and support the capacity and structure within agencies to ensure the activities would be sustained once grant funding was expended and supports provided by the research team were removed. Specific sustainability efforts included ongoing training to staff nearing the end of the project and the involvement of new agency personnel and management. In addition, we incorporated and embedded documentation needed for the intervention with required programmatic paperwork.

Core Implementation Components

The core implementation components have been previously mentioned and defined in this volume. As identified by Fixsen et al. (2005), these components include 1) staff selection, 2) preservice and in-service training, 3) ongoing consultation and coaching, 4) staff and program evaluation, 5) facilitative administrative support, and 6) systems interventions. These components are integrated and compensatory, resulting in interplay among components. This connectedness of the components was an essential feature for the component characterization in the Getting Ready intervention.

Three of these core implementation components, characterized as *competency components*, were particularly salient in the efficacy trial of the Getting Ready intervention: two that represented the professional development model in Getting Ready—in-service staff training and ongoing staff consultation and coaching—and a third that represented fidelity, staff performance assessment. While the other core organizational components were certainly important and relevant to the efficacy trial, systematic data were not collected on them, and therefore this summary specifically highlights the core competency components.

Professional Development

The primary purpose of professional development in Getting Ready was to support ECPs developing competence and confidence in their interactions with parents, so as to support parents' own competence and confidence in their interactions with children. Therefore, the model of professional development was relationship based and highly individualized. The primary components of professional development in the Getting Ready trial were a training institute, individual coaching, and group coaching. This combination of training and support activities has been found to be an optimal form of professional development (Joyce & Showers, 2002).

In-service Training Prior to initiating the Getting Ready intervention during home visits, ECPs in the treatment group participated in a 2-day interactive in-service session at which they were introduced to the triadic and collaborative strategies and their use in home visits, socializations, and other interactions with families. A 1-day refresher training was provided approximately 1 year following initial training. These sessions were intended to provide the essential background knowledge and information on the intervention strategies, as well as the theoretical foundation of the intervention, including the rationale for the planned approach. Furthermore, these sessions included demonstrations and videos of strategies in use and also provided some limited opportunities for role play and behavioral rehearsal experiences.

Coaching Following the in-service training, ECPs received ongoing support twice monthly in both group sessions (two to five ECPs and a project coach), lasting 90 minutes on average, and individual 60-minute sessions. The purpose of Getting Ready coaching was to support the initial training and promote the effective and intentional use of triadic and collaborative strategies in home visits with families. The coaching sessions were led by a project coach experienced in consultation, parent education, and early childhood intervention and education services. The coaching process was relationship based and paralleled the ECPs' efforts with parents. That is, coaches worked to support the confidence and competence of ECPs in their interactions with families and ECPs in turn worked to support these same characteristics for parents as they interacted with their children.

The coaching sessions were driven by the Coaching Families and Colleagues model (Hanft, Rush, & Shelden, 2004). Consistent with past literature, coaches provided teaching, feedback, and emotional support (Spouse, 2001). Specifically, the coach provided information and taught skill use as needed; the Getting Ready strategies were new to the ECPs, and coaches were responsible for helping move the ECPs from "letting it happen" to "making it happen." ECPs' strengths and needs informed the content of coaching sessions (Brown, Knoche, Edwards, & Sheridan, 2009). Each individual and group session had a primary focus on a single triadic/collaborative strategy. Group sessions provided the opportunity for peers to share ideas for interventions, develop cohesive relationships around specific professional goals, and learn with and from each other.

A variety of strategies and approaches was embedded into the coaching. Select home visits were captured on video by coaches and were then edited and used in coaching sessions to reinforce desired professional and parent behaviors and to extend self-awareness about the significance of those behaviors, reflective of a "self-as-a-model" cognitive–social learning approach (Dowrick, 1994; Hosford, 1980). Additionally, the coaching strategies of role play and behavioral rehearsal were also incorporated into the coaching sessions to support ECPs' use of the triadic/collaborative strategies. ECPs acted out scenarios that were designed to provide them with an opportunity to practice strategy use "in the moment." Over time, this approach was viewed favorably by ECPs, though use of role play and behavioral rehearsal was challenging in the early stages of implementation; there was reluctance on the part of many ECPs to engage in these types of practice.

Our experience in providing coaching to ECPs reinforces the necessity of an iterative process in the implementation of core competency components. Some ECPs were responsive to video examples, while others responded more favorably to behavioral rehearsal; there was a progression of acceptance in the use of these coaching strategies to support practice improvement and effective implementation of Getting Ready strategies. A single model of coaching support would not have yielded the desired implementation outcomes. Coaching strategies were attempted and, if unsuccessful at one point in the professional development course, were reintroduced at a later point. This iterative process in coaching support evolved out of necessity to maximally support the ECPs as they worked to implement Getting Ready.

In each coaching session, the project coach included reflective questions to guide the discussions with ECPs, highlight professional strengths in the use of the triadic/collaborative strategies, and set the stage for ECPs to use information in their work between coaching sessions. In addition to reminding ECPs of appropriate strategy use, they provided positive reinforcement and emotional support for the ECPs. Finally, and perhaps of most importance in this individualized intervention, was the support coaches were able to offer around adaptations of the Getting Ready model. The Getting Ready strategies are dictated by situational variables, both contextual and personal, and thus their use requires professionals to be reflective and confident in their ability to utilize varying strategies as the situation demands. Unlike a curriculum with a specific scope and sequence, the Getting Ready strategies are tailored to individual family needs. Given this variation, professionals demand a high level of support from their respective coaches to effectively implement the intervention.

ECPs who engage with families sometimes meet resistance and pushback or, in some cases, apathy and disengagement. This is a particular challenge as it relates to the goal of Getting Ready in actively engaging parents in the learning and development of their children. The Getting Ready coaches therefore served a countercontrol function (Bierman et al., 2002). The coach continued to provide support to ECPs as they were learning and attempting to implement the Getting Ready strategies with families; this was particularly important given the individualized nature of the intervention. The protocol of strategy use varied family to family and situation to situation. For example, one challenge commonly experienced by ECPs was the use of "affirmations" with families. The coaches had to reinforce the ECPs' use of affirmations, because in many instances parents did not readily acknowledge the positive statements being offered in a way that was affirming to the ECPs. ECPs were anticipating positive feedback after issuing a statement of affirmations to parents; however, the behavior of parents did not always meet this expectation. Coaches helped the professionals work through these challenges and persist in the use of the Getting Ready strategies.

The coaching sessions in Getting Ready were not supervisory in nature. Coaches were not affiliated with the implementing organizations, but were employed by the research team. This separation was a helpful feature of implementation, providing a clear division of responsibilities and roles. ECPs could freely share concerns, hesitations, and frustrations without fear of it reflecting on their paid position. Readers are referred to Brown et al. (2009) for additional details on the professional development model.

Component Compensation

The core implementation components (Fixsen et al., 2005) are compensatory and integrated. This means that weaknesses or gaps in some components can be reinforced, or even salvaged, by other core implementation components. The compensatory nature of the components was essential for the Getting Ready PD model, particularly in offsetting limits in staff selection. That is, the individualized PD approach allowed for coaches to differentiate levels of support based on the varied backgrounds of ECPs.

Under ideal intervention implementation circumstances, the delivery agents would be vetted via observational assessment or other skill-based information and evaluated to be appropriate and prepared candidates for carrying out intervention activities. But because our research team was not able to target, observe, and select staff to implement the Getting Ready intervention and was working with existing agency staff who possessed varied educational backgrounds and work experiences (see the demographic characteristics reported above), an individualized PD approach was particularly important. The trainers and coaches were able to appropriately target information specifically to meet individual professional needs. The Getting Ready intervention presupposes a foundational knowledge in child development; in this case, the coach team sometimes had to provide additional child development information before moving into the targeted intervention strategies. Our individualized model of professional development made this compensatory work feasible.

Furthermore, organizational selection was also a key consideration in implementation of the Getting Ready intervention. Though our research team did not have a role in staff selection, we did have a choice in the organizations within which the intervention was being implemented. The targeted service agencies and school districts were dedicated to putting high-quality parent engagement activities in place and to supporting their staff in acquiring skills that would support their work with families. Thus, organizational selection also helped compensate for staff selection and made performance assessment (described below) more feasible. This is yet another example of the compensatory nature of the core implementation components.

Staff Performance Assessment

Another core implementation component that was a key feature of this initial implementation project was staff performance assessment. Performance of ECPs was assessed via 1) PD activities, 2) observational assessments of ECP behavior with families, and 3) review of family communication documents.

Performance assessment was integrated into the PD model in Getting Ready; coaches used video-mediated feedback to provide performance feedback to ECPs on their use of the triadic and collaborative strategies. Additionally, the coaches attended home visits with ECPs and completed checklists on behaviors observed in the moment with families. These behavioral checklists were then shared with ECPs and used to reinforce staff strengths. Coaches also prompted ECPs to reflect on their strategy use as a form of self-assessment. Through feedback and self-assessment, ECPs set professional goals to improve their use of strategies in supporting parent engagement. The performance assessment data that were embedded in the PD model were used intentionally to support program improvement.

In addition, observational data records of home visits were collected to investigate fidelity of use of the Getting Ready strategies by ECPs (Knoche, Sheridan, Edwards, & Osborn, 2010). Data included measures of participant responsiveness, adherence, quality, and dosage and were collected across treatment and control conditions to define unique program differences (Dane & Schneider, 1998; Durlak & DuPre, 2008). Twice-yearly home visits of a subset of ECPs across treatment and control groups were digitally videorecorded; overall, a sampling of data was collected annually for each ECP. The *Getting Ready Coding Definition Guide* (adapted by the research team from the Home Visit Observation Form in McBride & Peterson [1997]) was used by trained coders to reliably record ECPs' fidelity in implementing a triadic and collaborative approach, along with parents' responsiveness to the intervention within home visits. A partial-interval recording for every 1-minute segment of the visit (range = 40–90 minutes) was used to obtain the rate of Getting Ready strategies used by the ECP, as well as the rate of interactions between the parent–child dyad. Additionally, ECPs' effectiveness in promoting parent engagement was rated every 10 minutes on a four-point Likert-type scale (1 = low; 4 = high). A full description of procedures used to assess intervention implementation fidelity is available in Knoche et al. (2010).

Observational home visit data indicated that the treatment group ECPs were observed using Getting Ready strategies in an average of 58.6% of intervals during home visits, as compared to use by ECPs in the control group in 44.2% of intervals ($t[25] = 2.34$; $p < .05$). ECPs' effectiveness at initiating parental interest and engagement was rated on average as 2.9 (out of 4) for the treatment group, indicating relatively high levels of quality in initiating parental interest and engagement with their children. ECPs in the control condition were rated significantly lower (1.9 out of 4; $t[19.6] = 4.87$; $p < .05$). In addition, parents in the treatment condition were observed interacting with their children on average for 40 minutes in a 60-minute home visit, significantly more than parents in the control condition who interacted with their children for approximately 26 minutes of an hour-long visit ($t[15.8] = 3.01$; $p < .05$; Knoche et al., 2010).

Finally, a documents analysis of parent communication documents (i.e., home visit reports, classroom newsletters) also yielded important indirect information on staff performance and implementation of the intervention model (Edwards, Hart, Rasmussen, Haw, & Sheridan, 2009). ECPs were trained and supported via the PD model to incorporate Getting Ready strategies in all interactions with families, including written communication. The review indicated strong evidence of treatment ECPs' spontaneous use of collaborative planning and problem solving with parents, more so than control ECPs. Specifically, generalization of ECPs' efforts to strengthen home–school collaboration, form relationships with parents, and spotlight and acknowledge child and parent competence was evidenced in ECPs' communication records with families.

Ongoing Core Component Evaluation

Following recommended practice (Fixsen et al., 2005), the core implementation components of training, coaching, and staff performance assessment were formatively evaluated throughout the efficacy trial to provide data that allowed continuous program improvement, including data to guide implementation practices in the short and long terms. The key evidence-based features of the Getting Ready intervention were not compromised; however, features of implementation that could vary without forsaking the intervention were improved to benefit all participants.

One source of data collected annually was the Consultant Evaluation Form (Erchul, 1987) completed by the ECPs. This provided data on the ECPs' level of satisfaction with their coach and an opportunity for the ECPs to make suggestions for modifications. These findings were incorporated into the training model, as appropriate and feasible, to support program improvement. Furthermore, regular focus group data were collected from ECPs regarding all aspects of the intervention. This provided key information on implementation practices and needed changes.

As previously mentioned, while organizational core components such as facilitative administration and systems interventions were relevant in this efficacy trial and highly related to implementation, these components were not systematically evaluated and are thus not discussed. However, both competency and organizational components are highly related and essential for effective program implementation.

Lessons Learned and Recommendations for Research and Practice

The initial implementation of the first efficacy trial of the Getting Ready project yielded lessons for others engaging in this type of intervention research. Through these lessons, our research team has generated recommendations for research and practice. The Getting Ready project shares many components with other early childhood interventions aimed at supporting school readiness; however, it varies on some key constructs that have implications for implementation research. Specifically, the individualized and dynamic nature of Getting Ready, in addition to its specific target on families, creates a unique environment for conducting implementation research as part of an initial efficacy trial. Furthermore, the context in which the Getting Ready study was conducted provided an opportunity for learning about research/practice partnerships.

Lesson 1

Our research team learned that individualized interventions pose unique challenges for implementation research. The variability inherent in individualized interventions might be considered "messy" in terms of implementation research, but it is the reality of many interventions in early childhood, particularly those focused on family engagement. Family-based, relationship-focused interventions that are targeting school readiness have characteristics that make them unique from typical classroom-based school readiness interventions. Specifically, the intervention tends to be more dynamic and responsive to individual family needs and somewhat less prescriptive in terms of steps and strategies. Though variation is a very real and essential part of many early childhood family-based interventions, particularly those that are relationship based, it does not negate the importance and relevance of implementation science. The core implementation components (Fixsen et al., 2005) are relevant to these relational and dynamic interventions in early childhood, and the challenge lies in determining appropriate measurement and analytic techniques to adequately capture the components. Thus, research is needed to support the development of tools that capture the dynamic nature of relational interventions. These tools can then be used to appropriately study implementation.

Lesson 2

The efficacy trial of Getting Ready was implemented in the context of fully operating early childhood agencies and programs serving infants, toddlers, preschoolers, and their families. While these agency/program contexts were helpful, and in fact essential, in providing an organizational structure and support system for implementing the Getting Ready intervention, the contexts became a key consideration in our implementation efforts. By conducting this efficacy trial within existing community agencies, we learned it is vital for the research and agency teams to be in agreement on expectations and desired results in order to achieve optimal outcomes for professionals, families, and children. Focus group data collected from Getting Ready ECPs indicated that the coordination of the research team with agency expectations and responsibilities alleviated stress and was most productive and supportive for ECPs (Brown et al., 2009). Though our study did not include measures of facilitative administration and systems interventions, we recommend others conducting this type of research incorporate these measures in future studies to operationalize ideal agency climate and context.

Lesson 3

As previously described, staff performance data in the form of observational assessments and documents analysis were collected from both treatment and control groups. While collecting data from the treatment group alone would have provided information on the implementation of Getting Ready practices, it would not help interpret the counterfactual. This is particularly salient for the Getting Ready strategies; the strategies themselves might be considered recommended practices in working with families and as such require no special curriculum or training. The likelihood of strategy use in the control group was fairly high, and observational data indicated that strategies were being used by control group participants across 44% of the home visit. Thus, it was critically important to measure strategy use across both the treatment and control groups for understanding intervention effects. We learned more about implementation by looking across conditions than within the treatment group alone. The comparison of practices was particularly informative when considering future implementation, such as scale-up efforts. Thus, we recommend collecting implementation data across experimental conditions.

Lesson 4

As previously described, the Getting Ready professional development model included in-service training and ongoing coaching as recommended (Joyce & Showers, 2002). This model included information delivery and exposure to the triadic/collaborative strategies, demonstrations of strategy use, and opportunities for practice. In introducing the strategies and providing PD, we encountered challenges with ECPs who considered the Getting Ready strategies to be part of their existing practice. Schoenwald and Hoagwood (2001) stated that when innovation is perceived as similar to existing practice, it is more likely to be adopted. The triadic/collaborative strategies are recommended practices in working with families; thus, many providers regularly incorporated some of the strategies in their practice (as evidenced by the observational data from the control group) and were therefore willing to incorporate and use them in their practice as they related to Getting Ready. However, intentional use of strategies based on situational need was the focus of the Getting Ready PD series. That is, through PD efforts, including training and coaching, we worked to move from a "let it happen" mentality to a "make it happen" orientation. This shift in orientation toward strategy use might benefit others who are working to implement interventions that are viewed by intervening agents as part of their existing practice.

Conclusions

The chapter has focused on the Getting Ready intervention, an ecological, relationship-based intervention developed to support school readiness in children up to age 5 years via parent engagement. In addition to describing the essential features of the Getting Ready intervention, we have highlighted how core competency implementation components are realized in a highly individualized and dynamic intervention with families and have provided lessons learned and recommendations for research and practice that will hopefully benefit others conducting and implementing similar programs.

The focus on implementation components provided recursive, iterative information to improve intervention delivery over the course of the study. Thus, it was beneficial to project development in the short term. Ultimately, by investigating implementation components at the initial implementation stage, we were also able to inform the project efforts in the long term. That is, our team was able to identify issues in the initial implementation stage that will contribute to later transportability and scale-up. Using the core implementation component framework at early stages in a research line is essential to knowing what will become important as evidence-based interventions are disseminated at scale.

References

Administration on Children and Families. (2010). *Head Start program performance standards and other regulations (45 CFR Parts 1301–1311).* Retrieved from http://www.acf.hhs.gov/programs/ohs/legislation/index.html

Bierman, K.L., Coie, J.D., Dodge, K.A., Greenberg, M.T., Lochman, J.E., McMahon, R.J., & Pinderhughes, E. (2002). The implementation of the fast track program: An example of a large-scale prevention science efficacy trial. *Journal of Abnormal Child Psychology, 30*(1), 1–17.

Bradley, R.H., Corwyn, R.F., Burchinal, M., McAdoo, H.P., & Coll, C.G. (2001). The home environments of children in the United States, Part II: Relations with behavioral development through age thirteen. *Child Development, 72,* 1868–1886.

Brown, J.R., Knoche, L.L., Edwards, C.P., & Sheridan, S.M. (2009). Professional development: A case study of early childhood professionals in the Getting Ready Project. *Early Education and Development, 20,* 482–506.

Burchinal, M.R., Campbell, F.A., Bryant, D.M., Wasik, B.H., & Ramey, C.T. (1997). Early intervention and mediating processes in cognitive performance of children of low-income African American families. *Child Development, 68*, 935–954.

Caspe, M., & Lopez, E.M. (2006). *Lessons from family-strengthening interventions: Learning from evidence-based practice.* Cambridge, MA: Harvard Family Research Project.

Chazan-Cohen, R., Raikes, H., Brooks-Gunn, J., Ayoub, C., Pan, B.A., Kisker, E.E., … Fuligni, A.S. (2009). Low-income children's school readiness: Parent contributions over the first five years. *Early Education and Development, 20*, 958–977.

Clark, K.E., & Ladd, G.W. (2000). Connectedness and autonomy support in parent–child relationships: Links to children's socioemotional orientation and peer relationships. *Developmental Psychology, 36*, 485–498.

Dane, A.V., & Schneider, B.H. (1998). Program integrity in primary and early secondary prevention: Are implementation effects out of control? *Clinical Psychology Review, 18*, 23–45.

Denham, S.A., Renwick, S.M., & Holt, R.W. (1991). Working and playing together: Prediction of preschool social-emotional competence from mother–child interaction. *Child Development, 62*, 242–249.

Downer, J., & Pianta, R. (2006). Academic and cognitive functioning in first grade: Associations with earlier home and child care predictors and with concurrent home and classroom experiences. *School Psychology Review, 35*, 11–30.

Dowrick, P.W. (1994). A review of self modeling and related interventions. *Applied and Preventive Psychology, 8*, 22–39.

Dunst, C., & Kassow, D. (2008). Caregiver sensitivity, contingent social responsiveness and secure infant attachment. *Journal of Early and Intensive Behavior Intervention, 5*, 40–56.

Dunst, C., Raab, M., Trivette, C., Parkey, C., Gatens, M., Wilson, L., … Hamby, D.W. (2007). Child and adult social–emotional benefits of responsive-contingent learning opportunities. *Journal of Early and Intensive Behavior Intervention, 4*, 379–391.

Dunst, C.J., Trivette, C.M., & Deal, A.G. (1988). *Enabling and empowering families: Principles and guidance for practice.* Cambridge, MA: Brookline Books.

Durlak, J.A., & DuPre, E.P. (2008). Implementation matters: A review of research on the influence of implementation on program outcomes and the factors affecting implementation. *American Journal of Community Psychology, 41*, 327–350.

Edwards, C.P., Hart, T., Rasmussen, K., Haw, Y.M., & Sheridan, S.M. (2009). Promoting parent partnership in Head Start: A qualitative case study of teacher documents from a school readiness intervention project. *Early Childhood Services, 3*, 301–322.

Edwards, C.P., Sheridan, S.M., & Knoche, L. (2010). Parent–child relationships in early learning. In E. Baker, P. Peterson, & B. McGaw (Eds.), *International encyclopedia of education* (Vol. 5, pp. 438–443). Oxford, England: Elsevier.

Egeland, B., Pianta, R., & O'Brien, M. (1993). Maternal intrusiveness in infancy and child maladaptation in early school years. *Development and Psychopathology, 5*, 359–370.

Epstein, J.L., & Sanders, M.G. (2002). Family, school, and community partnerships. In M.H. Bornstein (Ed.), *Handbook of parenting* (Vol. 5, pp. 407–437). Mahwah, NJ: Erlbaum.

Erchul, W.P. (1987). A relational communication analysis of control in school consultation. *Professional School Psychology, 2*, 113–124.

Feldman, R., & Masalha, S. (2010). Parent–child and triadic antecedents of children's social competence: Cultural specificity, shared process. *Developmental Psychology, 46*, 455–467.

Fixsen, D.L., Naoom, S.F., Blase, K.A., Friedman, R.M., & Wallace, F. (2005). *Implementation research: A synthesis of the literature* (FMHI Publication No. 231). Tampa, FL: University of South Florida, Louis de la Parte Florida Mental Health Institute, National Implementation Research Network.

Foster, M.A., Lambert, R., Abbott-Shinn, M., McCarty, F., & Franze, S. (2005). A model of home learning environment and social risk factors in relation to children's emergent literacy and social outcomes. *Early Childhood Research Quarterly, 20*, 13–36.

Grolnick, W.S., & Farkas, M. (2002). Parenting and the development of children's self-regulation. In M.H. Bornstein (Ed.), *Handbook of parenting* (Vol. 5, pp. 89–110). Mahwah, NJ: Erlbaum.

Grolnick, W.S., & Slowiaczek, M.L. (1994). Parents' involvement in children's schooling: A multidimensional conceptualization and motivational model. *Child Development, 65*, 237–252.

Hanft, B., Rush, D., & Shelden, M. (2004). *Coaching families and colleagues in early childhood.* Baltimore, MD: Paul H. Brookes Publishing Co.

Hill, N.E. (2001). Parenting and academic socialization as they relate to school readiness: The roles of ethnicity and family income. *Journal of Educational Psychology, 93,* 686–697.

Hirsh-Pasek, K., & Burchinal, M. (2006) Putting language learning in context: How change at home and in school affects language growth across time. *Merrill Palmer Quarterly, 52,* 449–485.

Hohmann, M., & Weikert, D. (2002). *Educating young children: Active learning practices for preschool and child care programs.* Ypsilanti, MI: High/Scope Press.

Hood, M., Conlon, E., & Andrews, G. (2008). Preschool home literacy practices and children's literacy development: A longitudinal analysis. *Journal of Educational Psychology, 100,* 252–271.

Hosford, R.E. (1980). Self-as-a-model: A cognitive, social-learning technique. *Counseling Psychology, 9,* 45–62.

Joyce, B., & Showers, B. (2002). *Student achievement through staff development* (3rd ed.). Alexandria, VA: Association for Supervision and Curriculum Development.

Kelley, S.A., Brownell, C.A., & Campbell, S.B. (2000). Child development: Mastery motivation and self-evaluative affect in toddlers: Longitudinal relations with maternal behavior. *Child Development, 71,* 1061–1071.

Kerns, K.A., Klepac, L., & Cole, A. (1996). Peer relationships and preadolescents' perception of security in the child–mother relationship. *Developmental Psychology, 32,* 457–466.

Knitzer, J., Steinberg, Z., & Fleisch, B. (1993). *At the schoolhouse door: An examination of programs and policies for children with behavioral and emotional problems.* New York, NY: Bank Street College of Education.

Knoche, L.L., Edwards, C.P., Sheridan, S.M., Kupzyk, K.A., Marvin, C.A., Cline, K.D., & Clarke, B.L. (2012). Getting Ready: Results of a randomized trial of a relationship-focused intervention on parent engagement in rural Early Head Start. *Infant Mental Health Journal, 33,* 439–458.

Knoche, L.L., Sheridan, S.M., Edwards, C.P., & Osborn, A.Q. (2010). Implementation of a relationship-based school readiness intervention: A multidimensional approach to fidelity measurement for early childhood. *Early Childhood Research Quarterly, 25,* 299–313.

Korfmacher, J., Green, B., Spellmann, M., & Thornburg, K.R. (2007). The helping relationship and program participation in early childhood home visiting. *Infant Mental Health Journal, 28,* 459–480.

Landry, S.H., Smith, K.E., Swank, P.R., Assel, M.A., & Vellet, N.S. (2001). Does early responsive parenting have a special importance for children's development or is consistency across early childhood necessary? *Developmental Psychology, 37,* 387–403.

Martinez, M. (1987). Dialogues among children and between children and their mothers. *Child Development, 58,* 1035–1043.

Masten, A., & Coatsworth, J. (1998). The development of competence in favorable and unfavorable environments: Lessons from research on successful children. *American Psychologist, 53,* 205–220.

McBride, S.L., & Peterson, C.A. (1997). Home-based early intervention with families of children with disabilities: Who is doing what? *Topics in Early Childhood Special Education, 17,* 209–233.

McCollum, J.A., & Yates, T.J. (1994). Dyad as focus, triad as means: A family-centered approach to supporting parent–child interactions. *Infants and Young Children, 6,* 54–63.

McNamara, K.A., Selig, J.P., & Hawley, P.H. (2010). A typological approach to the study of parenting: Associations between maternal parenting patterns and child behaviour and social reception. *Early Child Development and Care, 180,* 1185–1202.

Mendoza, J., Katz, L., Robertson, A., & Rothenberg, D. (2003). *Connecting with parents in the early years.* Champaign, IL: Early Childhood Parenting Collaborative, University of Illinois at Urbana-Champaign.

Mirenda, P., MacGregor, T., & Kely-Keough, S. (2002). Teaching communication skills or behavioral support in the context of family life. In J. Lucyshyn, G. Dunlap, & R. Albin (Eds.), *Families and positive behavioral supports: Addressing problem behavior in family contexts* (pp. 185–208). Baltimore, MD: Paul H. Brookes Publishing Co.

Morrison, F.J., Connor, C.M., & Bachman, H.J. (2006). The transition to school. In S.B. Newman & D.K. Dickinson (Eds.), *Handbook of early literacy research* (2nd ed., pp. 375–394). New York, NY: Guilford.

Mulvaney, M., McCartney, K., Bub, K.L., & Marshall, N.L. (2006). Determinants of dyadic scaffolding and cognitive outcomes in first graders. *Parenting, 6,* 297–320.

Neitzel, C., & Stright, A.D. (2003). Relations between mothers' scaffolding and children's academic self-regulation: Establishing a foundation of self-regulatory competence. *Journal of Family Psychology, 17,* 147–159.

NICHD Early Child Care Research Network. (2002). Early child care and children's development prior to school entry: Results from the NICHD Study of Early Child Care. *American Educational Research Journal, 39,* 133–164.

Pan, B., Rowe, M., Singer, J., & Snow, C. (2005). Maternal correlates of growth in toddler vocabulary production in low-income families. *Child Development, 76,* 763–782.

Panzano, P.C., Roth, D., Sweeney, H.A., Massatti, R., Carstens, C., Seffrin, B., & Bunt, E. (2007). The Innovation Diffusion and Adoption Research Project (IDARP): A process overview and a preview of qualitative data from interviews. In D. Roth & W.J. Lutz (Eds.), *New research in mental health* (Vol. 17, pp. 78–89). Columbus, OH: Ohio Department of Mental Health.

Parents as Teachers National Center. (2008). *Parents as teachers birth to three: Program planning and implementation guide* (Rev. ed.). St. Louis, MO: Author.

Parker, F.L., Boak, A.Y., Griffin, K.W., Ripple, C., & Peay, L. (1999). Parent–child relationship, home learning environment, and school readiness. *School Psychology Review, 28,* 413–425.

Pungello, L., Iruka, I., Dotterer, A.M., Mills-Koonce, R., & Reznick, S. (2009). The effects of income, race, and sensitive and harsh parenting on receptive and expressive language development in early childhood. *Developmental Psychology, 45,* 544–557.

Raikes, H., Alexander Pan, B., Luze, G., Tamis-LeMonda, C.S., Brooks-Gunn, J., & Constantine, J. (2006). Mother–child bookreading in low-income families: Correlates and outcomes during the first three years of life. *Child Development, 77,* 924–953.

Raikes, H., & Whitmer, J.M. (2006). *Beautiful beginnings: A developmental curriculum for infants and toddlers.* Baltimore, MD: Paul H. Brookes Publishing Co.

Rao, H., Betancourt, L.M., Giannetta, J.M., Brodsky, N.L., Korczykowski, M., Avants, B.B., … Farah, M.J. (2010). Early parental care is important for hippocampal maturation: Evidence from brain morphology in humans. *Neuroimage, 49,* 1144–1150.

Schoenwald, S.K., & Hoagwood, K. (2001). Effectiveness, transportability, and dissemination of interventions: What matters when? *Psychiatric Services, 52*(9), 1190–1197.

Sheridan, S.M., Knoche, L.L., Edwards, C.P., Bovaird, J.A., & Kupzyk, K.A. (2010). Parent engagement and school readiness: Effects of the Getting Ready intervention on preschool children's social-emotional competencies. *Early Education and Development, 21,* 125–156.

Sheridan, S.M., Knoche, L.L., Kupzyk, K.A., Edwards, C.P., & Marvin, C. (2011). A randomized trial examining the effects of parent engagement on early language and literacy: The Getting Ready intervention. *Journal of School Psychology, 49,* 361–383.

Sheridan, S.M., & Kratochwill, T. (2008). *Conjoint behavioral consultation: Promoting family–school connections and interventions.* New York, NY: Springer.

Sheridan, S.M., Kratochwill, T.R., & Bergan, J.R. (1996). *Conjoint behavioral consultation: A procedural manual.* New York, NY: Plenum.

Sheridan, S., Marvin, C., Knoche, L., & Edwards, C. (2008). Getting ready: Promoting school readiness through a relationship-based partnership model. *Early Childhood Intervention Services, 2,* 149–172.

Shonkoff, J.P., & Phillips, D. (2000). *From neurons to neighborhoods.* Washington, DC: National Academy Press.

Spouse, J. (2001). Bridging theory and practice in the supervisory relationship: A sociocultural perspective. *Journal of Advanced Nursing, 33*(4), 512–522.

Tamis-LeMonda, C.S., & Bornstein, M.H. (2002). Maternal responsiveness and early language acquisition. In R.V. Kail & H.W. Reese (Eds.), *Advances in child development and behavior* (pp. 89–127). San Diego, CA: Academic Press.

Trivette, C.M., Dunst, C.J., & Hamby, D.W. (2010). Influences of family-systems intervention practices on parent–child interactions and child development. *Topics in Early Childhood Special Education, 30,* 3–19.

Trivette, C., Dunst, C., Hamby, D., & Pace, J. (2007). *Evaluation of the Tune-In-and-Respond Tool Kit for promoting child cognitive and social-emotional development* (Winterberry Research Perspectives Vol. 1, No. 5). Asheville, NC: Winterberry Press.

Turnbull, A., Turnbull, R., Erwin, E., Soodak, L., & Shogren, K. (2011). *Families, professionals and exceptionality: Positive outcomes through partnership and trust.* Boston, MA: Pearson.

Weigel, D.J., Martin, S.S., & Bennett, K.K. (2006a). Contributions of the home literacy environment to preschool-aged children's emerging literacy and language skills. *Early Child Development and Care, 176*, 357–378.

Weigel, D.J., Martin, S.S., & Bennett, K.K. (2006b). Mothers' literacy beliefs: Connections with the home literacy environment and pre-school children's literacy development. *Journal of Early Childhood Literacy, 6*, 191–211.

CHAPTER 7

An Eye to Efficient and Effective Fidelity Measurement for Both Research and Practice

Chrishana M. Lloyd, Lauren H. Supplee, and Shira Kolnik Mattera

Fidelity is one of many components (including the contrast from usual practices, the context in which the program is being delivered, and who the intervention serves) that may be necessary for achieving program impacts. It is a multidimensional construct that includes adherence to, dose of, quality of, and participant engagement in an evidence-based practice (Dusenbury, Brannigan, Falco, & Hansen, 2003). The evaluation of fidelity captures the gap between the intended evidence-based practice and the actual implementation of the practice. It is specifically the gap between intended and actual practice that may prevent the promise of evidence-based programs from coming to fruition.

To date, measurement of fidelity has been limited, focused primarily on intervention adherence and occasionally on dose. Increasingly, however, research suggests that understanding and measuring across the *spectrum* of fidelity components is critical to program implementation (Fixsen, Naoom, Blase, Friedman, & Wallace, 2005). Capturing implementation processes via quality fidelity measurement and understanding how to use what has been learned to improve practice has the potential to strengthen both research and practice and can be useful for policy makers and funders who are increasingly making decisions about where to invest limited fiscal resources based on program effectiveness. One of the many challenges that evidence-based policy brings, though, is how to ensure that programs that have shown efficacy on a small scale within tightly controlled conditions will continue to produce effects when implemented more widely. Implementation science, located at the nexus between the science of evidence-based programs and the applied settings and populations intended to use and benefit from them, becomes a useful mechanism for understanding this and other intervention implementation issues related to fidelity.

As interventions go to scale, both researchers and practitioners need tools to help assess fidelity within research contexts and in applied settings. In fact, Schoenwald and colleagues (Schoenwald, 2011; Schoenwald et al., 2010) have made strong arguments that researchers and practitioners need to develop useful and practical tools that support intervention monitoring and quality implementation as a potential means to obtaining positive impacts.

Measuring fidelity, therefore, becomes important to researchers for ensuring an intervention is tested fairly and that the impacts are real—internal validity—as well as allowing one to understand the potential for similar impacts should the intervention be replicated—external validity (Moncher & Prinz, 1991). Moreover, Type III errors, in which studies fail to find impacts for a program because the intervention was not implemented as planned, may be reduced, increasing the likelihood that conclusions about the actual efficacy of the intervention theory are accurate (Dusenbury et al., 2003). In sum, measuring fidelity in a research context is important for ensuring the evidence-based program is occurring as intended, documenting how implementation unfolds, and understanding differentiation between the program of interest and usual practice (Gearing et al., 2011; Moncher & Prinz, 1991; Schoenwald et al., 2010).

Understanding how to achieve and monitor fidelity is equally important for practitioners as interventions move from being implemented in research settings to real-world contexts. In a meta-analysis of impacts across a range of social services interventions, Wilson and Lipsey (2001) found that intervention implementation quality was strongly associated with achieved effect size of the programs. This raises the question: How do practitioners support high-quality implementation? Gearing and colleagues (2011) conclude that monitoring of implementation is a core compo-nent of fidelity that allows for adjustments to training and intervention delivery to improve performance. Others have found that monitoring and assessment of fidelity provides critical information to program staff, such as trainers, coaches, and super-visors, about implementation efforts on the ground and can inform training and coaching efforts (Elliott & Mihalic, 2004; Fagan & Mihalic, 2003; Fixsen et al., 2005). These findings suggest that practitioners need not only to actively monitor fidelity but also to understand the levels of fidelity that need to be achieved to affect change.

This chapter directly addresses the aforementioned research and practice considerations, using an implementation science framework to explore fidelity in the Head Start CARES (Classroom-Based Approaches and Resources for Emotion and Social skill promotion) demonstration project. The chapter provides an over-view of the rationale and creation of standardized fidelity measures and tools in the Head Start CARES demonstration, offering key lessons learned about the process of developing fidelity measurement tools and reviewing how they were created to accomplish the goals and needs of researchers and practitioners within the context of scaling up and replicating previously existing interventions. It concludes by offering lessons for those interested in crafting fidelity measurement tools for both research and practice, making the final recommendation that fidel-ity measurement, though challenging, should move beyond intervention-specific, one-shot research trials, given the potential value and usefulness in both scientific and applied contexts.

Overview of the Head Start CARES Demonstration Project

Head Start CARES is a large-scale national research demonstration designed to test the effects of three social-emotional program enhancements in Head Start settings over the course of one academic year. MDRC, a nonprofit, nonpartisan, education and social policy research organization, coordinated the demonstration and provided technical assistance for implementation. The demonstration tested the enhancements at the field test stage, meaning it examined the scaling up of programs across multiple and diverse settings that had previously shown promise at a smaller scale.

Lead and assistant Head Start teachers were trained and coached together throughout the year in one of the three social-emotional enhancements:

1. The Incredible Years Teacher Training

2. Preschool PATHS (Promoting Alternative Thinking Strategies)

3. Tools of the Mind

The teachers' centers were randomly assigned to one of the three enhancements, with each center implementing one of the enhancements, or to a control condition, which continued as usual. The three enhancements that were part of the demonstration were chosen because 1) they had shown evidence of effectiveness in improving children's social-emotional development in previous efficacy trials conducted with low-income preschool children, 2) they conceptually fit within the structure and operation of Head Start grantees and classrooms, and 3) they had implementation support available, including training and technical assistance, written materials, and fidelity monitoring.

The Center on the Social Emotional Foundations for Early Learning defines social-emotional development as the developing capacity of a child, from birth through 5 years of age, to form close and secure adult and peer relationships; to experience, regulate, and express emotions in socially and culturally appropriate ways; and to explore the environment and learn—all in the context of family, community, and culture. The enhancements' theories of change emphasized distinct strategies for supporting children's social-emotional development. The Incredible Years Teacher Training enhancement focused on professional development of teachers to promote positive social development and discourage problem behaviors; Preschool PATHS focused on providing children the language and skills to positively engage with emotions and peer interactions; and Tools of the Mind used dramatic play and specific teaching practices to scaffold children to develop self-regulation. The three enhancements overlapped conceptually because of their focus on social-emotional outcomes, but there were clear distinctions in their theories of change, primarily around the focus and activities utilized to build and strengthen children's social-emotional skills.

In addition, as a component of each enhancement, teachers and administrators received instruction and technical assistance from enhancement developers and trainers on the enhancements, and Head Start programs hired coaches (who attended enhancement training with their assigned teachers) from the local community to support the teachers in their implementation of them. Technical assistance was also provided to sites, enhancement developers, trainers, and coaches (see Table 7.1).

Developing and Creating the Head Start CARES Fidelity Measures

In general, researchers who test evidence-based programs in trials create tools that are useful for the specific study, but they may be burdensome to implement

Table 7.1. Description of Head Start CARES key players

Function	Role in Head Start CARES	Employment and supervision
Coach	· Attended training sessions with teachers · Received ongoing content-related support from trainers and developers · Observed and met with teaching teams weekly to discuss implementation	· Employed by the grantee liaison · Supervised by the developer/trainer *and* grantee liaison/center director
Trainer	· Delivered training sessions to coaches and teachers on enhancement content · Visited classrooms to support coaches and teachers with implementation · Provided supervision and regular feedback on coach performance	· Employed and supervised by the enhancement developer
Grantee supervisor	· Recruited, hired, and supervised coaches · Monitored implementation throughout the year	· Employed and supervised by the grantee
Teacher[a]	· Attended training sessions alongside the coach · Received ongoing support from coaches and trainers throughout the year · Had responsibility for classroom implementation	· Employed and supervised by the grantee
MDRC research and technical assistance team	· MDRC launched and researched the Head Start CARES demonstration. MDRC project staff also provided ongoing technical assistance to grantees, enhancement developers, trainers, and coaches throughout the year.	

From Lloyd, C.M., & Modlin, E.L. (2012). *Coaching as a key component in teachers' professional development: Improving classroom practices in Head Start settings*. New York, NY: MDRC; adapted by permission.
[a]"Teacher" refers to both lead and assistant teachers.

outside of a research trial (Schoenwald et al., 2010). Given the increased interest in evidence-based practices and outcomes, the reality is that early childhood settings and other community-based agencies that receive external funding will likely have an increasing number of evidence-based programs in place over time. The challenge, then, is to create measurement tools that capture fidelity of implementation, that are multifaceted, that can be integrated into community-based programs, and that are ecologically valid (Schoenwald et al., 2010).

The creation of coherent and crosscutting fidelity measures in the Head Start CARES demonstration was influenced by the need to have data that were useful for the Head Start CARES research and technical assistance team and that could be integrated into the Head Start program and used by intervention staff. This meant that the project needed to document and receive data from *multiple reporters* across *different settings*.

Two primary groups of people reported on the fidelity of enhancement implementation: coaches and trainers. Coaches worked in classrooms weekly, observing teachers for an hour and meeting with them to debrief on their observations for 30 minutes. Trainers, who provided enhancement intervention support to coaches, visited the classrooms periodically as experts in the program, and they also trained teachers and coaches throughout the year on the enhancements. (See Office of Planning, Research & Evaluation [n.d.] for a more thorough review of the implementation measures used in the Head Start CARES demonstration.) In terms of settings, coaches and trainers worked in a range of sites and classrooms, including schools and community-based facilities.

The different enhancements, reporters, and settings necessitated development of measures that were common to the three enhancements but could still be used to identify unique features of each enhancement and setting that was thought to affect change. To accomplish this task, structured templates called "fidelity logs" were created by the research team in close partnership with the enhancement developers. These logs provided a space for coaches and trainers to report on enhancement implementation practices by highlighting two components of fidelity.

The logs focused on the practices of teachers and measured both adherence—how *much* or to what extent teachers implemented the program—and quality—how *well* teachers implemented it. For instance, logs reported on whether the teachers were using many of the identified enhancement's strategies and if "modifications or additions are consistent with" the enhancement's goals and objectives (Lloyd, 2009). Reports were then created out of the fidelity logs and used for collecting implementation data throughout the year and guiding the work of the MDRC research and technical assistance team (who worked with developers, trainers, and coaches) in improving the quality of implementation. In this way, fidelity was inherently tied to both research and ongoing practice.

The following section provides a detailed overview of the process of creating fidelity measures in the context of the Head Start CARES demonstration and reviews four key strategies and considerations:

1. The development of fidelity definitions, anchors, and measures that were internally valid to the individual program and externally valid across similar evidence-based programs

2. The creation and determination of meaningful thresholds for those instruments so that both researchers and practitioners knew whether implementation was going well or not

3. The collection of data from multiple sources to accurately document program implementation

4. The process of training on the measures to ensure that practitioners were able to use the data generated to monitor and respond to implementation challenges on the ground

General Measurement, Specific Measurement, and Anchors

Defining fidelity for both research and practice involved creating *universal* and *specific* measurement tools from which to monitor fidelity within and across enhancements. The logs were devised to ensure that information could be shared across enhancements (universal fidelity), with one section clearly differentiating the core enhancement components (specific fidelity). The measurement and monitoring of fidelity work in the Head Start CARES demonstration allowed for nuanced documentation of implementation at scale that took into account both *general* aspects of fidelity—those that were important to the delivery of all evidence-based programs—and *specific* components of fidelity that were important to the individual model used. To ensure that both tools provided clear, defined measurement, clearly articulated *anchors* were created for each item in the tools. These anchors allowed developers and the research/technical assistance team to work together to define each item, with clear demarcations between weak, average, and strong implementation for each item.

Universal Measurement   Components of fidelity that were *universal*—the same across all of the models—were identified to facilitate comparisons of the quality of implementation across enhancements and to provide a standardized metric for evaluating fidelity. Fidelity in this case was operationalized as implementing the program to such a degree that it was clear that teachers, children, and classrooms were steeped in their respective social-emotional enhancements. For example, one item asked whether observers could easily tell when they "enter this classroom and look around" that the identified enhancement was being used (Lloyd, 2009). Another asked whether "the children are actively engaged" in the enhancement all day long, rather than enhancement implementation being "just seen as a special event" (Lloyd, 2009).

These measures assumed a basic level of skill from the teacher that allowed for a new initiative to be implemented. For example, teachers needed to be able to understand the theory underpinning whichever enhancement they were implementing in order to be able to use and generalize it throughout the day. For the research/technical assistance team, understanding the prerequisite knowledge and the skills necessary for successful intervention implementation by teachers was critical for determining how to craft fidelity measures that captured intervention implementation practices accurately.

A Head Start CARES Demonstration Example   In the Head Start CARES log, the universal fidelity sections, "Modeling and Generalization" and "Fidelity of Teaching and Supporting Children," were each made up of five scaled items. Along with the items presented earlier about teacher practice, the items also addressed issues of child receipt of the enhancement, asking whether the children were responsive to the particular enhancement's strategies and if the strategies were effective in the teacher's classroom. The 10 questions asked in the universal fidelity section for a Tools of the Mind enhancement are listed next (Lloyd, 2009).

Enhancement-Specific Measurement   In order to support and improve the delivery of the individual enhancements, components of fidelity that were *specific* to each were also identified and measured. For example, the Preschool PATHS enhancement used lessons that had to be delivered weekly, while the Tools of the Mind enhancement asked teachers to aid children in completing plans for their playtime daily. These items were unique to the identified enhancement: Preschool PATHS was the only enhancement that used weekly large-group lessons to deliver enhancement content, and the Tools of the Mind enhancement was the only one to have children create play plans.

Modeling and Generalization of Tools of the Mind

1. It is clear when you enter this classroom and look around it is a Tools of the Mind classroom.

2. The teachers have taken extra steps to extend the Tools of the Mind concepts into other parts of the Head Start program by designing special activities or adapting standard activities to be consistent with Tools of the Mind themes.
3. The children are actively engaged in Tools of the Mind throughout the day. It is not just seen as a special event.
4. The teachers use Tools of the Mind as part of their strategies for managing conflicts, as part of classroom procedures, and to help build positive relationships between the children.
5. The teachers model and actively promote Tools of the Mind and praise the children when they use Tools of the Mind techniques.

Fidelity of Teaching and Supporting Children in Tools of the Mind

1. The teachers are prepared for Tools of the Mind activities and seem familiar with what to do.
2. The teachers use many of the Tools of the Mind strategies, and modifications or additions are consistent with Tools of the Mind goals and objectives.
3. Material is presented in an engaging manner. The teachers are positive, energetic, and enthusiastic about Tools of the Mind. There is flexibility in the presentation and the teachers appear comfortable with Tools of the Mind.
4. The teachers are patient and sensitive to the skill level of the children and adapt their style of presentation and pacing to match the children.
5. The children have fun during, and enjoy doing, Tools of the Mind activities. They are attentive and engaged during Tools of the Mind activities.

This more specific definition of fidelity provided a means to identify the presence of elements unique to and between the enhancements. That is, teachers not only had to generally implement the enhancements well, they also needed to adhere to a core set of program-unique skills and/or lessons that developers identified as being critical to their enhancements' effectiveness.

A Head Start CARES Demonstration Example In the Head Start CARES logs, a third section, "Fidelity of Programmatic Activities," asked coaches and trainers to rate the lead and assistant teachers on *how well* each was implementing the activities, strategies, or other programmatic activities for each enhancement. These differed by number and type for each enhancement, with Incredible Years having 13 items, Preschool PATHS 10, and Tools of the Mind 6. In this section, as well, coaches and trainers were asked to rate teachers on a five-point scale from 1 (*strongly disagree*) to 5 (*strongly agree*).

The specific fidelity sections were much more individualized, so items between enhancements did not match. For instance, the first item of the specific fidelity section asked about building relationships with students for Incredible Years, PATHS lessons for Preschool PATHS, and play planning and scaffolded writing for Tools of the Mind. However, the ratings for this section still followed a graduated pattern across enhancements. A rating of 1 meant that there was no evidence the teacher was using the strategy, or that its use was flawed. A rating of 5 meant that the teacher was using the strategy frequently, consistently, or in an exemplary fashion.

Creation of Anchors Along with the scaled items in each section, concrete examples of each rating, called "anchors," were created to help understand if the enhancements were being implemented as intended. The research and technical assistance team worked with developers to create detailed anchors for each item so that coaches and trainers could be trained to observe similar practices and rate them in a reliable and valid way.

Two primary tenets guided the scaling and anchoring work. First, the team wanted anchors that would accurately and meaningfully reflect the core components of the enhancements. This would allow for distinguishing between enhancements, but would also help the team to understand implementation practices, including faithful and nonfaithful implementation of the intervention. The anchors explicitly defined each rating so that the ratings could have the same meaning, regardless of who the reporter was or for which enhancement.

Second, the team wanted scales that would be sensitive to changes throughout the year, including variation in implementation and settings. Each item had a set of five anchors that accompanied its five-point scale. These anchors were created to match the conceptualization of fidelity outlined earlier. They were a mix of adherence (how much) and quality (how well) of implementation of the enhancement. The anchors were graduated, with a rating of 1 meaning that something happened never or with poor quality, while a rating of 5 meant that something happened very often or with exceptional quality. As teachers became more familiar with their assigned enhancement, the expectation was that change would occur in a positive direction on the rating of their implementation of the enhancement.

The anchors were a key component for allowing generalization across enhancements in the general fidelity of the logs. In some general fidelity items, the anchors looked the same across all three enhancements. In others, they differed in order to allow necessary enhancement-specific details to emerge. For example, in the general fidelity item "The teachers are prepared for [their identified enhancement] activities and seem familiar with what to do," anchors were the same for all enhancements (Lloyd, 2009):

- If the teachers are never prepared or familiar with [their enhancement] activities, *select "1 = strongly disagree."*
- If the teachers only rarely are prepared or familiar with [their enhancement] activities, *select "2."*
- If the teachers occasionally are prepared or familiar with [their enhancement] activities, but not consistently, *select "3."*
- If the teachers are usually prepared or familiar with [their enhancement] activities, *select "4."*
- If the teachers are exceptional in their preparation or familiarity with [their enhancement] activities, *select "5 = strongly agree."*

Therefore, although the details were different, the process of creating items and anchoring them to the definition of adherence and quality were the same.

In another general fidelity item, asking whether the teachers use their identified enhancement "as part of their strategies for managing conflicts, as part of classroom procedures, and to help build positive relationships between the children," the details of the anchors varied by enhancement. The anchors still followed a five-point scale, with "1" meaning that something almost never happened, "3" that it occasionally happened, and "5" that it happened an "exceptional" amount. But even though the anchors were the same, the verbal descriptions of the anchors differed by enhancement. The meaning of the item stayed the same, but the anchors allowed for individual definitions of what quality implementation of that enhancement component looked like. For instance, the anchors for a rating of 1 for each enhancement were as follows (Lloyd, 2009):

- [For Incredible Years] If teachers never use IY strategies for managing conflicts, as part of classroom procedures, or to help build positive relationships between the children, *select "1 = strongly disagree."*
- [For Preschool PATHS] If teachers never use PATHS routines..., materials (feeling faces or posters), or strategies (reflecting feelings, cuing turtle, supporting problem solving) for managing conflicts, as part of classroom procedures, or to help build positive relationships between the children, *select "1 = strongly disagree."*
- [For Tools of the Mind] If teachers never use Play Planning to work out disputes before they escalate, use mediators to help children take turns or focus on specific attributes, or use attention focusing activities to promote self-regulation during large groups or transitions, *select "1 = strongly disagree."*

Thresholds

As part of the process of creating the logs, thresholds for the ratings were developed, agreed upon, and clearly defined for each section of the logs in an effort to support the standards for acceptable levels of practice. The thresholds were integral to the conceptualization of fidelity in the Head Start CARES demonstration and were designed to take into account the complexity of real-world implementation and adaptation. For each of the log sections, the research and technical assistance team provided benchmarks for the ratings. The ratings became a point of reference against which the research and technical assistance team, developers, trainers, and coaches could monitor and assess the implementation of the enhancement and respond as necessary. This practice is different from the usual process of documentation of implementation because it set a standard level of implementation that all intervention implementers had to meet.

Coaches were the primary and most frequent raters of implementation quality within the Head Start CARES demonstration, so trainers, enhancement developers, and the research and technical assistance team worked closely with them to ensure they understood the principles of the intervention and the importance of providing reliable and valid data in advance of program implementation. Although the coaches would be working closely with teachers, it was clearly explained that documentation of fidelity was not about judging teachers or making them look good or bad, but was instead a necessary means of recording clearly and accurately what occurred during the year for both research and programmatic purposes.

In the Head Start CARES demonstration, items were considered implemented at an acceptable threshold and with fidelity if a score of 3 or above was given on a scale of 1 to 5. Throughout the year, the data were monitored on an ongoing basis, and scores below 3 were flagged. Definitions of what a "3" meant differed by question; in general, it signaled that an act had occurred, but that it had occurred only inconsistently or with moderate quality. The MDRC research and technical assistance team worked with enhancement developers, trainers, and sites not only to identify teachers or sites with below-threshold scores but also to brainstorm and implement steps to remedy the implementation challenges. The process of comparing fidelity of implementation practices based on what was happening in the classrooms occurred throughout the intervention year by researchers and practitioners alike.

Multiple Reporters and Intervention Documentation

Despite the various sources of data and the already complex conceptualization of fidelity, it was deemed important that multiple viewpoints of teacher fidelity be collected. As mentioned previously, the use of both coaches and trainers as reporters of teachers' performance in delivering the enhancements resulted in the measurement of fidelity from multiple perspectives across all three enhancements. Trainers were considered expert in their enhancement, but had fewer day-to-day interactions with teachers and classrooms, seeing them only during training and technical assistance visits. In comparison, coaches were not experts in the enhancements, but were in the classrooms weekly, working with teachers.

Coaches rated teachers' implementation of the enhancement through weekly logs documenting their classroom observations and contact with teachers (not discussed in this chapter) and monthly logs documenting fidelity of enhancement implementation in the classroom. Trainers' documentation of teachers' implementation of the enhancement occurred via a classroom visit log that assessed teachers' fidelity in the classrooms visited. Importantly, the coach monthly logs and trainer visit logs mirrored each other so that coaches and trainers reported on the same items. Each log consisted of approximately 15–25 scaled items that used a 1 (*strongly disagree*) to 5 (*strongly agree*) Likert scale to assess the critical facets of the implementation process and the core components of the enhancements. The perspectives of the two different reporters were thought to provide a more accurate assessment of teachers' implementation processes and how they compared to the enhancement models.

While not systematically assessed, the team also hypothesized that coaches and trainers would reach general consensus about ratings throughout the year, particularly as coaches became more knowledgeable about the enhancements. A preliminary review of the ratings indicated that trainers and coaches generally did agree on the extent to which a teacher was implementing an enhancement with fidelity. Trainers typically rated teachers a point lower on the five-point Likert scale than coaches did, but ratings between them followed the same pattern and were consistently in the same direction. For example, in one month, a coach might have rated a teacher a 3 on a particular question, while the trainer rated her a 2; in the following month, their ratings of that teacher might have been a 4 and a 3, respectively.

In short, the fidelity logs were designed to provide observational data—the gold standard for measurement of fidelity (Hamre et al., 2010)—and served as a comparative framework that afforded an objective, systematic, and structured way to provide feedback about program implementation, while facilitating understanding of implementation processes, trends, and outliers. Throughout the year, the research and technical assistance team and enhancement developers graphed and reviewed the ratings over time using the thresholds discussed above to evaluate and determine acceptable levels of fidelity of the enhancements.

Training

The experiences in Head Start CARES suggests that ratings derived from multiple raters—in this case, trainers and coaches—are useful for both researchers and practitioners in understanding fidelity. However, to ensure the reliability and usefulness of the data, it was important to train the various reporters on how to document and rate their observations.

The validity of the ratings depended in large part on the individuals completing them, their knowledge of the enhancement, and their reliability in reporting what they saw. To facilitate reliable ratings, coaches were trained to rate the core specific intervention components by developers and trainers in advance of program implementation. They also received training on the universal fidelity ratings by the research and technical assistance team.

The enhancement developers and trainers were encouraged to use the anchors as a tool for dialoguing with coaches throughout the year. Grounding the conversations with the anchors helped to ensure that coaches fully understood the principles of the interventions and provided a common framework and language for trainers and enhancement developers to discuss the ratings, ensuring that enhancement rater "drift" was less likely to occur.

Fidelity Documentation and Measurement Challenges

While there is a clear need in the field for a method to assess fidelity across different programs by different reporters, the rating scales used in the Head Start CARES demonstration raised some challenging but not insurmountable measurement issues that may inform future measurement efforts. In general, it was a long and complex process to create measures that tapped into universal enhancement implementation components while allowing for adaptations. Developers and researchers needed to clearly articulate their definitions of fidelity. This meant spending a significant amount of time negotiating each partner's perspective and incorporating it into a definition of fidelity that was agreed upon by all key stakeholders in advance of implementation.

Once fidelity was defined, individual items were needed both to encompass this general operationalization of fidelity and to create individualized anchors for each enhancement. For instance, although the item "It is clear when you enter this classroom and look around it is a [specific enhancement] classroom" (Lloyd, 2009) can be applied to any program, the anchors that specified what a PATHS classroom looked like were different from those that identified a Tools of the Mind classroom. Additionally, the five-point Likert scale anchors needed to denote the same incremental change between a rating of 1 and a rating of 2 for the scales to be comparable across enhancements. The ability to compare across enhancements is incredibly powerful, but requires considerable time and thoughtfulness about the measurement tool during development. In addition, creating the measures was, by necessity, an iterative process that used information during initial data collection to improve the measure over time.

As the tools were used throughout the intervention year, challenges emerged. The conceptualization of fidelity for the Head Start CARES demonstration included a mix of both adherence and quality. This occurred in numerous ways: Observers may have had different numbers of opportunities to observe an item happening (regardless of quality), and teachers may have actually used a strategy varying number of times. For instance, in some logs, the ratings were created in such a way that a score of 1 could be interpreted as indicating low or poor fidelity or that the reporter did not have a chance to observe that aspect of fidelity. In other logs, the ratings were defined such that a "1" could mean that a teacher used the strategy poorly or did not use the strategy at all.

The ability to separate adherence (i.e., did this component of implementation happen at all and to what extent?) from quality (i.e., when this component happened, was it done well?) taps into a larger question within the field of implementation research. Currently, the implementation measurement field is beginning to call for measurement that distinguishes between the multiple components of fidelity. The measurement process in the Head Start CARES demonstration took a first step toward teasing apart these components; however, further work is needed to clearly differentiate among these aspects of fidelity in a reliable and valid manner.

Considerations for the Early Childhood Field

Intervention research in the early childhood field is typically aimed at improving outcomes for children and families. By selecting and implementing programs that demonstrate evidence of effectiveness, the research and practice communities may better achieve their goal. However, implementation of evidence-based programs is complex. Both researchers and practitioners need tools to help support the monitoring of fidelity to support and strengthen program quality. The following section outlines key lessons learned from our efforts to document fidelity work in the Head Start CARES demonstration, providing suggestions for future research and practice efforts.

Lessons Learned for Research

The large-scale measurement and monitoring of fidelity in the Head Start CARES demonstration suggests some lessons that researchers can apply in future evidence-based intervention research scale-up efforts.

- *Development of fidelity measures requires collaboration and is a continuous process.* The Head Start CARES research and technical assistance team and enhancement developers agreed on appropriate measures of fidelity across interventions. Moreover, they planned for continued dialogue about the measures to ensure that they were capturing fidelity accurately. The creation of the measures and logs was an iterative process between the team and the developers, guided primarily by the experiences of the raters. The process included working with enhancement developers and practitioners to assess the face validity of both the universal and specific components of fidelity for the individual enhancement models. Over the course of the demonstration, the research and technical assistance team refined the instruments by changing the language to make the logs more reflective of actual implementation experiences, and enhancement developers continued to update and streamline their anchors for various items to make them more explicit and clear. By the end of the demonstration, the team felt confident the data collected through the logs would allow for analysis on fidelity across enhancements.

- *When measuring fidelity across multiple models, clarity around similar and different components of the models is necessary.* Being clear about which intervention components are similar and which are different for multiple interventions is critical for fidelity data to be useful. It is nearly impossible to compare fidelity *across models* within or across research trials unless similar items and measures are used from the essential components of fidelity identified for each model. It is recommended that researchers identify a comparable set of general fidelity components across all of the enhancements they are using to create equivalence across them for comparison. This requires understanding of the general theory of change for the evidence-based practices being instituted. For instance, in the Head Start CARES demonstration, one program required teachers to present lessons, another asked teachers to do specific play-planning activities with children, and the third had teachers use a specific strategy to respond to a behavior. These components were unique to each enhancement, but all focused on supporting the social and emotional development of children—a common core component.

- *Fidelity measurement captures multiple components of implementation, and capturing these distinctions is important.* Implementation researchers should diligently attempt to distinguish between the multiple components of fidelity to better understand research outcomes. For example, distinguishing adherence from quality in separate rating scales may help to present a clearer picture of intervention implementation by providing insight into important distinctions between varying levels of adherence and quality implementation.

- *Developing comparable anchors across models to create equivalence across reporters, so that all can report on the same item with a high level of reliability, is suggested.* Ensuring rating anchors are meaningful to each enhancement allows the raters to report ratings and eventually thresholds with validity across enhancements. Viewpoints may differ, and the ability to combine data from multiple reporters across enhancements and know that their scores have roughly the same meaning is powerful. Moreover, using general fidelity tools with well defined anchors provides a way to compare the level of teacher performance for delivering enhancements across reporters.

- *Psychometrically testing fidelity measures may provide a common framework for researchers and practitioners to think about fidelity in evidence-based programs.* Some of this work has already been started. For example, in the Preschool Curriculum Evaluation Research Initiative (Preschool Curriculum Evaluation Research Consortium, 2008), 14 different evidence-based programs were tested. Implementation in these studies was assessed through both a program-specific measure and a global measure. However, clearly laying out the process through which these types of measures were created and used will help inform the field by integrating knowledge. For example, in the Head Start REDI (Research-based, Developmentally Informed) trial, trainers assessed implementation across a number of different evidence-based *practices,* including Preschool PATHS, dialogic reading, and sound games (Bierman et al., 2008).

Lessons Learned for Practice

The tools discussed in this chapter not only are beneficial for research but also offer some distinct contributions to the practice field broadly. First, the fidelity tools were developed to allow for easy training of coaches and trainers to complete and report their observations in a consistent manner. Given the limited time and fiscal resources in many community-based programs, this feature is very appealing. Second, the tools allow for observations of practice, minimizing disruptions in and burdens on the classroom. Third, the tools discussed are crosscutting. Within the early childhood field, programs are increasingly implementing a mix of curricula, enhancements, and practices within one setting. Having the framework for a tool that minimizes data collection challenges and that can cross multiple evidence-based programs is important.

- *Well-designed and flexible fidelity tools can help guide decisions about implementation in practice by providing a gauge of thresholds of quality and adherence, as well as a platform for discussion and feedback with the teacher or practitioner.* In many implementation studies, documentation about the intervention generally ends after the initial training and data collection are completed; however, practitioners may want to sustain interventions after the training is over. Alternatively, more community-based settings are being directed to choose evidence-based practices or programs, independent of a study. Flexible fidelity tools may help support the scale-up and sustainability of an enhancement within and across early childhood settings by providing practitioners with concrete data to guide training and technical assistance efforts toward attaining and maintaining fidelity to the model. Supervisors, coaches, or other professional development staff can use the fidelity tool ratings to benchmark the minimum levels of quality and adherence necessary to achieve the desired outcomes.

- *Training practitioners on how to assess and report fidelity is feasible even if they do not have specialized backgrounds in implementation research.* In addition to the instruments themselves, the project created training processes and tools that guided the use of the fidelity instruments. Neither coaches nor trainers in the Head Start CARES demonstration had specialized training in data collection, reporting, or implementation science. The demonstration showed that it is possible to quickly and, more importantly, effectively train a significant number of program staff to successfully use fidelity monitoring instruments.

- *Fidelity instruments can help practitioners make decisions about the feasibility of potential adaptations.* When evidence-based programs are disseminated, the practitioners are often interested in adapting programs for their own contexts to better serve the needs of their populations or communities. Though adaptation should be done in conjunction with the intervention developer, well designed fidelity tools make explicit the core components of a program. Having this information easily available may assist in navigating the chasm between *intentional adaptation,* which might improve the likelihood of intervention success, and *unintentional program drift,* which has the potential to detract from the anticipated outcomes.

- *To best monitor implementation, programs interested in implementing a number of evidence-based interventions or practices may find it important to isolate components unique to each intervention versus components necessary to attain fidelity across all evidence-based interventions.* Measures that focus on specific strategies are very useful to ensure unique components of the intervention are being implemented. However, if measures focus only on isolated strategies, it becomes difficult to tell if the implementer is generally doing a good job of using strategies across interventions.

Future Directions

The Head Start CARES demonstration provided an opportunity to create a process for measuring social-emotional practices across multiple interventions, raters, and sites in the early childhood field. While the work in the demonstration was pioneering, there is still much that needs to be understood. The field must begin to pay attention to fidelity, including adherence, quality, dosage, and participant engagement. However, we should also not lose sight of the fact that other implementation processes are also integral to strong implementation, such as how implementation changes and unfolds throughout the year. The implementation science field needs to develop high-quality applied measurement tools to understand fidelity at the classroom level; the field should also examine 1) how factors such as fidelity are influenced by organizational culture and climate, 2) the relationship between the coach and teacher, and (3) the quality of professional development to fidelity in vivo.

Within the implementation process, it is clear that there are different stages of scientific inquiry into the evidence of effectiveness of an intervention, including piloting a new intervention, implementing it in a more controlled or clinical research setting, and moving to larger scale implementation. In each of these stages, it is essential that fidelity be measured thoughtfully, carefully, and clearly. However, the focus of that measurement might shift. In a pilot phase, fidelity measurement may be qualitative and more process oriented in order to inform future implementation and measurement efforts. In the research or efficacy phase, fidelity measurement may be more focused on deconstructing and understanding the various components of implementation (dosage, adherence, quality, general vs. specific) in a reliable and valid way. And when moving to a scale-up and replication phase, previously validated measures may need to be better contextualized with an eye toward appropriateness for the population using them, as well as how they mesh with other programs that are in place or might someday be added.

The fields of early childhood implementation research and practice would also greatly benefit from overarching measures that capture and operationalize fidelity to general early childhood recommended practices. For instance, what are the recommended practices regarding coaching or training that we can generalize across models? What models of coaching and training may be related to high fidelity? Can we create a definitive set of developmentally appropriate qualities or attributes that are necessary to achieve fidelity to any early childhood or professional development practice? To begin to develop a list of these attributes, measures are needed that clearly define and quantify dosage, adherence, and quality for each of the core components of effective implementation such as training and coaching. More research that begins to answer questions about how variability in these core components of implementation explains impacts of the intervention is also needed. By expanding research about *how* and *at what levels* various components of implementation influence impacts, the field can begin to create meaningful thresholds against which to determine fidelity.

In sum, early childhood implementation science is quickly growing, providing more clarification with each study about what best supports positive outcomes for children and families. This chapter has provided a glimpse into the detailed and nuanced processes initiated to move beyond a one-dimensional understanding of fidelity and fidelity measurement in Head Start CARES, a large-scale demonstration project. The process of documenting fidelity across multiple models, in multiple settings, and with multiple raters was challenging. The benefits, however, extend to and have relevance for both research and practice, making it clear that thoughtful, in-depth fidelity measurement is a worthy undertaking.

References

Bierman, K.L., Domitrovich, C.E., Nix, R.L., Gest, S.D., Welsh, J.A., Greenberg, M.T., ... Gill, S. (2008). Promoting academic and social-emotional school readiness: The Head Start REDI program. *Child Development, 79,* 1802–1817.

Dusenbury, L., Brannigan, R., Falco, M., & Hansen, W.B. (2003). A review of research on fidelity of implementation: Implications for drug abuse prevention in school settings. *Health Education Research, 18*(2), 237–256.

Elliott, D.S., & Mihalic, S. (2004). Issues in disseminating and replicating effective prevention programs. *Prevention Science, 5,* 47–53.

Fagan, A., & Mihalic, S. (2003). Strategies for enhancing the adoption of school-based prevention programs: Lessons learned from the Blueprints for Violence Prevention replications of the Life Skills Training Program. *Journal of Community Psychology, 31,* 235–253.

Fixsen, D.L., Naoom, S.F., Blase, K.A., Friedman, R.M., & Wallace, F. (2005). *Implementation research: A synthesis of the literature* (FMHI Publication No. 231). Tampa, FL: University of South Florida, Louis de la Parte Florida Mental Health Institute, National Implementation Research Network.

Gearing, R.E., El-Bassel, N., Ghesquiere, A., Baldwin, S., Gilles, J., & Ngeow E. (2011). Major ingredients of fidelity: A review and scientific guide to improving quality of intervention research implementation. *Clinical Psychology Review, 31,* 79–88.

Hamre, B.K., Justice, L.M., Pianta, R.C., Kilday, C., Sweeney, B., Downer, J.T., & Leach, A. (2010). Implementation fidelity of MyTeachingPartner literacy and language activities: Association with preschoolers' language and literacy growth. *Early Childhood Research Quarterly, 25,* 329–347.

Lloyd, C. (2009). *Head Start CARES Monthly Fidelity Form.* Washington, DC: Office of Planning, Research and Evaluation.

Lloyd, C.M., & Modlin, E.L. (2012). *Coaching as a key component in teachers' professional development: Improving classroom practices in Head Start settings.* New York, NY: MDRC.

Moncher, F.J., & Prinz, R.J. (1991). Treatment fidelity in outcome studies. *Clinical Psychology Review, 11,* 247–266.

Office of Planning, Research & Evaluation. (n.d.). *Head Start CARES (Head Start Classroom-based Approaches and Resources for Emotion and Social skill promotion), 2007–2013.* Retrieved from http://www.acf.hhs.gov/programs/opre/hs/cares/index.html

Preschool Curriculum Evaluation Research Consortium. (2008). *Effects of preschool curriculum programs on school readiness (NCER 2008–2009).* National Center for Education Research, Institute of Education Sciences, U.S. Department of Education. Washington, DC: U.S. Government Printing Office.

Schoenwald, S.K. (2011). It's a bird, it's a plane…it's fidelity measurement in the real world. *Clinical Psychology, 18,* 142–147.

Schoenwald, S.K., Garland, A.F., Chapman, J.E., Frazier, S.L., Sheidow, A.J., & Southam-Gerow, M.A. (2010). Toward effective and efficient measurement of implementation fidelity. *Administration and Policy in Mental Health and Mental Health Services Research, 38,* 32–43.

Wilson, D.B., & Lipsey, M.W. (2001). The role of method in treatment effectiveness research: Evidence from a meta-analysis. *Psychological Methods, 6*(4), 413–429.

CHAPTER 8

Applying Lessons Learned from Evaluations of Model Early Care and Education Programs to Preparation for Effective Implementation at Scale

Jason Downer

As Fixsen, Naoom, Blase, Friedman, and Wallace (2005) have pointed out, lists of evidence-based practices are proliferating in many fields, including early care and education (ECE), yet when it comes to moving from research to practice, there is a huge leap rather than a smooth transition. Large technical assistance networks that disseminate research-based strategies through print, online, and workshop-based methods often lack the skills or capacity to provide the necessary implementation supports to individual ECE practitioners or programs so that a particular evidence-based practice can be successful "on the ground" in situations that may vary significantly from the original conditions. At the same time, the developers and designers of these evidence-based practices tend to lack the skills, capacity, or interest in disseminating their work in a systematic way that is informed by recommended practices in implementation science.

As a partial solution, Schoenwald and Hoagwood (2001) propose that we redefine *evidence-based* so that it includes active consideration of practical factors (e.g., administrative support and buy-in, costs) during development stages and involves research on dissemination and sustainability as a final step in the validation process. In other words, it is crucial that researchers consider the transportability of their practices and interventions from initial development stages and then incorporate study design elements and measures during well-controlled efficacy trials that can inform more efficient and effective implementation during at-scale applications. ("Scale" usually refers to a program reaching the majority of the target audience. So, for instance, the implementation of a new professional development credential meant for infant/toddler caregivers would be said to have reached scale when about 60% of the infant/toddler specialists in a given area [e.g., ECE program, district, state] were pursuing that new credential. See Chapter 1 for further discussion of implementing at scale.)

It is clear from the three previous chapters, as well as a host of other recent work in the field of ECE, that conducting formative evaluation and examining intervention fidelity data during efficacy trials of promising interventions offers a host of lessons learned and therefore benefits to at-scale implementation. Attention to the core implementation components during these early stages of intervention development and testing holds great promise for reducing the research-to-practice gap. In particular, this chapter draws from the previous chapters in Section II and related work in the ECE field to underscore how important coaches are as *drivers* of implementation as well as the ways that intervention fidelity data in efficacy trials can be used to set the stage for successful implementation at scale.

Intervention Fidelity Versus Implementation Fidelity: Defining Terms

One of the main themes that runs through this chapter is the distinction between intervention fidelity (also referred to as program fidelity) and implementation fidelity, and a recommendation for better aligning the two earlier in the process of developing and testing interventions. To date, the term *fidelity* has been loosely applied to a broad set of factors that describe *how* an intervention or program is implemented. However, this has become conceptually confusing, as the term is applied similarly across the vastly different scenarios of initial research and development and the at-scale rollout of programs with an evidence-based track record. This chapter, therefore, brings explicit attention to the differences between these two concepts of fidelity and how the ECE field ought to be working toward considering both early in the development of interventions.

Most references to fidelity in ECE research fall under the category of intervention fidelity, including the studies covered in the previous three chapters. *Intervention fidelity* refers to the extent to which core program components are delivered as intended. There has been considerable work to break this catch-all definition into parts, such as dosage, quality, and so forth (Dane & Schneider, 1998; Sanetti & Kratochwill, 2009), and the focus is typically on describing what an intervention looks like on the ground and understanding why it does or does not work as planned. (See Chapter 4 for a further discussion of intervention fidelity.) In contrast, *implementation fidelity* is focused on the supports, also referred to as drivers, that are necessary to ensure that an intervention is implemented as intended. Fixsen et al. (2005) describe six integrated, complementary implementation supports, but in this chapter I will focus mostly on the coaching and evaluation components. In particular, I will discuss how intervention studies in ECE, such as the ones covered in Chapters 5–7, can pay attention to both intervention and implementation fidelity in ways that ease the eventual transition from establishing an evidence-based program to scaling it up during system-wide implementations.

Coaching and Consultation Supports

Coaching in ECE (used interchangeably throughout this chapter with the terms *consultation* and *mentoring*) is becoming an increasingly common component of interventions aimed at improving the contexts of at-risk children (e.g., family, classroom) and their school readiness, as evident in their consistent inclusion in special issues of peer-reviewed journals (e.g., *Elementary School Journal*), books (e.g., Howes, Hamre, & Pianta, 2012), and statewide quality rating and improvement systems (Isner et al., 2011). Though implemented in a variety of ways, both in person and remotely, coaching typically involves individualized professional development for an ECE provider from an experienced, knowledgeable professional. The following sections briefly summarize some of what we know and what else we need to know about coaching in ECE.

What We Know

A host of recent efficacy trials have included a coaching or consultation component to support early childhood educators (Bierman et al., 2008; Neuman & Wright, 2010; Powell, Diamond, Burchinal, & Koehler, 2010; Raver et al., 2008; Wasik & Hindman, 2011), and as Knoche points out in Chapter 6, this type of intensive, ongoing support is especially relevant for the highly complex and individualized interventions that have become more commonplace in the field. Across the board, these studies indicate that programs inclusive of coaching have a positive and sizable impact on teachers' instructional practice and interactions with children. For example, Raver et al. (2008) report positive effects of their Chicago School Readiness Project, a multicomponent intervention that included extensive mental health consultation, on teachers' creation of a positive classroom climate, responsiveness to children's needs, and proactive management of behavior (effect sizes = .52–.89). In addition, many coaching models also demonstrate positive, direct benefits for children, albeit to a lesser degree than effects on teacher practice in many cases. The work by Powell and colleagues (2010) noted in Chapter 5, for example, indicates that teachers receiving individualized coaching specific to promoting literacy and language development had children with better code-focused outcomes than teachers in a control group (effect sizes = .17–.29). In combination, these positive findings across multiple studies from different research teams suggest that interventions with early childhood educators that contain an individualized coaching component show promise in changing teacher practice and supporting improved child outcomes.

A major shortcoming of many studies on coaching with early childhood educators is the fact that coaching is just one of many components, along with curriculum, web resources, video exemplars, and others, which leaves it unclear as to whether the coaching makes a unique contribution to positive changes in teacher practice and child outcomes. This is where treatment-on-the-treated analyses play an important role in determining whether variability in the experience of coaching (as a component of the intervention model itself and, as such, part of intervention fidelity) is related to outcomes of interest.

These data were available as part of two recent evaluation trials of the professional development program MyTeachingPartner (MTP), which consists of web-based coaching, a video library of teaching exemplars, and access to language and literacy lesson plans. Mashburn, Downer, Hamre, Justice, and Pianta (2010) examined the extent to which variability in each of these intervention components made unique contributions to children's positive gains in language and literacy skills during the preschool year. They found that the number of hours teachers were

exposed to coaching during the year was positively related to children's development of receptive language skills (effect size = .30), above and beyond teachers' use
of the language and literacy activities or viewing of exemplar teaching videos.

More recently, Pianta, Hamre, and Hadden (2012) used intervention fidelity data from a 10-site randomized controlled trial of MTP to examine the dose–
response link between feedback that coaches provided teachers and improvements
in teachers' interactions with children in the classroom. Findings indicate that
when coaches give teachers feedback on their videotaped practice that focuses
on instructionally supportive interactions (e.g., modeling of language), teachers
provide more instructional supports during language and literacy activities (as
observed by independent coders blind to intervention condition).

Though limited in scope, these results from a multicomponent intervention
in early childhood provide some evidence that exposure to a coaching element in
particular may account for positive benefits to teachers and children in these classrooms. They also demonstrate the need for more interventions to track closely the
quality and quantity of exposure to coaching so that within-treatment analysis can
expand our understanding of how and to what extent coaching supports may play
a role in the effectiveness of multifaceted interventions with early childhood educators. This priority is evidenced by a 2012 Administration for Children and Families
(ACF) request for proposals that aims to "develop design options for a research
study that will provide strong evidence for the best and most efficient practices in
coaching within the context of Head Start professional development systems."

All together, this collection of findings does support the notion that coaching
can play a central role in ensuring high-quality implementation of a program and
is a strong, integral driver of implementation when taking programs to scale.

What We Need to Know

Despite the proliferation of an evidence base for coaching as a key component of
effective professional development for early childhood educators, this work has
generated a far greater number of questions with direct implications for taking an
evidence-based program to scale than it has answered. Two of the more common
sets of questions about coaching revolve around the concepts of how much and by
whom.

The first is basically a question of *dosage*—how much coaching is enough to
change teacher practice and impact children in their classroom?—and has significant implications for implementing a program at scale in terms of personnel costs.
Specific questions include: How many coaching contacts are needed in a year?
How long should each coaching contact be? Do teachers need more than 1 year of
coaching? Could multiyear coaching taper off in intensity during the second year?
What triggers an end to coaching? These and other practical questions center on
how to make the most efficient use of finite resources, while still retaining the positive effects of a program.

The second question is related to two of the six implementation drivers
outlined by Fixsen et al. (2005)—*staff selection* and *training*. Who should be doing
this coaching, and what kind of training is necessary to ensure coaches provide
high-quality, consistent support to teachers? As Isner et al. (2011) note from their
review of coaching studies, the vast majority of coaches have more experience

and education than the average early childhood educator. However, there is still considerable variability in the skills and experiences that coaches bring to these studies, and we know very little about what preexisting conditions lead to highly effective coaches. To a large degree, this is a problem of small sample size. Even in large studies of interventions with a coaching component, there is still only a small number of coaches, with caseloads of 15–20 teachers. Within this context, it is nearly impossible to learn much from data within a single study about what characteristics of coaches predict high fidelity to a coaching model or effectiveness at facilitating teacher change. In addition, though many professional development models for teachers now have coaching components, studies of these models often report little or no information about the experience and qualifications of staff who serve as coaches nor about the training necessary to ensure successful implementation of a particular program (Zaslow, Tout, Halle, Whittaker, & Lavelle, 2010).

When coaching is a critical component of the intervention itself, all six implementation drivers need to be brought to bear on the successful implementation of coaching as part of the intervention. Therefore, not only are staff selection and training of coaches important to assess (as noted above), but so are whether and how coaches themselves are provided ongoing supervision and support in fulfilling their roles, whether and how coaches are evaluated for their coaching, and what administrative supports (e.g., policies, procedures, processes) need to be in place to support effective coaching.

Although some attention has been paid to the staff selection and training of coaches (Zaslow et al., 2010), to date very little research has been conducted on the other four implementation drivers for successful implementation of coaching as a core intervention component. This dearth of information calls for more cross-study collaborations to use common sets of measures that 1) describe experiences and characteristics of coaches; 2) describe training, coaching, and assessment of coaches as well as the organizational policies and procedures that support effective coaching as part of an intervention model; and 3) capture generic intervention fidelity ratings that could be applied across projects. In this way, efforts during initial trials of promising interventions with early childhood educators could begin to pave the way for understanding which coach characteristics and other implementation drivers support effective coaching and thereby contribute to successful implementation of programs.

Now that the field is establishing that coaching is a promising component of effective professional development for early childhood educators, these kinds of practical issues come to the forefront as small, randomized controlled trials lead to interest in larger scale implementation of these programs. Researchers can play a crucial role in creating an evidence base for programs that work and can also begin to build measures into study designs that bring data to bear on the complex and practical elements of implementing these programs (as is evident in all three of the preceding chapters). In doing so, early studies of promising programs can set the stage for more efficient and successful implementation at scale.

Data-Driven Decision Making

As funding decreases and accountability increases, the use of data from formative evaluations of programs becomes essential not only to documenting impacts on targeted outcomes but also to informing continuous quality improvement efforts within and across years of implementation. In fact, ongoing program evaluation is a core component of implementation fidelity, which makes it important that this approach to using data is incorporated even at the initial phases of program development and testing. The following sections briefly summarize some of what we know and what we need to know about data-driven decision making in ECE interventions.

What We Know

Formative assessment and intervention fidelity data can be used to make informed, data-driven decisions about innovations or adaptations to an intervention that can increase its effectiveness and feasibility of use in certain contexts. Powell and colleagues in Chapter 5 provide a perfect example of this during the early stages of program research and development. Over a series of several trials, the combination of data on child outcomes and intervention fidelity revealed that the professional development intervention was likely having a focused effect on children's code-focused skills, rather than the anticipated broader effect inclusive of oral language skills, due to the fact that coaches were spending the majority of coaching sessions on code-focused teaching practices. When the subsequent version of the intervention added more emphasis on vocabulary instruction, there was a marked improvement in teachers' use of language-promoting practices (e.g., labeling statements). This careful progression of revisions to an intervention provides a blueprint for how researchers can use data to fully understand how the inner workings of a program lead to outcomes and therefore maximize its effectiveness when the time comes to implement at scale.

Beyond using data across multiple studies to inform large-scale revisions of programs as noted previously, intervention fidelity data can be used in real time during the implementation of a program to enhance adherence to the program model and support high-quality implementation. Each of the previous chapters in Part II noted how important it is to collect ongoing intervention fidelity logs that can be used to guide feedback to an agent of change—in many cases, a teacher or coach. The MTP professional development program provides another example of how coach supervisors can systematically collect intervention fidelity data and then use this in their support of coaches' work with teachers (Pianta et al., 2012).

In MTP, supervisors use a standardized rubric for assessing how a coach provides written feedback to teachers about their videotaped practice. This rubric includes items that reflect a coach's adherence to the core components of feedback, as well as items that capture the quality of feedback provided to teachers. Coaches are fully aware of this rubric from the beginning of their training and expect to receive feedback from their supervisor about areas of strength and challenge throughout the year. This data-driven approach to ensuring program adherence and quality has been so successful that, similar to work by Neuman and Wright (2010), efforts are under way to incorporate the rubric into an online interface that would share real-time data with both coaches and their supervisors. Perhaps the most important thing about these types of data-driven feedback loops within ECE interventions is that they are tested out during small-scale intervention trials, so that standardized rubrics and systems are in place to ensure the continued use of these procedures when programs are taken to scale.

What We Need to Know

Though researchers (and some scale-up efforts, such as the Parents as Teachers [2012] annual Web-based Affiliate Performance Report) are beginning to take advantage of technology to collect intervention fidelity data, there remain many questions about how the web can be used as a medium to make collection and active use of data efficient and feasible during at-scale implementations. For example, if data are being collected at a population level, would it be useful to build a system that shows an individual's fidelity data in comparison to the average fidelity data across the entire intervention? Are there any unanticipated negative effects of data sharing, either in comparative fashion or otherwise? Also, is it important for individuals to receive data as part of a personal feedback loop with a supervisor, or can individuals self-assess when provided a data report? These are all relatively unexplored issues that are relevant to implementation at a systems level (see Part IV, this volume) and require further study, ideally with a mixed-methods approach that provides recipients of data the opportunity to bring voice to their experiences.

In addition, using data to alter an intervention in midstream brings up questions about program adaptation and whether there are protocols in place to ensure that adaptations are made appropriately in alignment with core program goals and objectives (Blakely et al., 1987; Castro, Barrera, & Martinez, 2004). This is a particularly crucial issue given Hulleman and Cordray's (2009) study, which illustrates the large reduction in effectiveness of interventions when moving from an initial, small-scale lab setting to a large-scale field trial, as a function of reductions in adherence to the ideal program model.

Given the prevalence of coaching in professional development models for early childhood educators, there is a looming question about the extent to which coaches should use data to provide evaluative feedback about a teacher's practice. Powell and Diamond (Chapter 5) allude to this by noting that one prominent coaching process is evaluative, in which teachers receive direct feedback about their strengths and challenges. However, oftentimes, even when coaches are using a rubric to evaluate a teacher's performance (such as the Classroom Assessment Scoring System as part of the MTP professional development program; Pianta, Mashburn, Downer, Hamre, & Justice, 2008), teachers are provided verbal or written observational statements and feedback but no quantitative data. In the current K–12 policy context that prioritizes formal evaluation of teacher effectiveness, there is likely to be increasing pressure to provide teachers with precise data points that reflect their teaching strengths and challenges. Yet there is currently limited understanding in the field of how best to do this in ways that will lead to improvements in teaching and not leave teachers feeling underappreciated and overcriticized. There is clearly room for work by researchers to explore the use of providing data to teachers—in particular as a part of coaching efforts—to determine the best course of action.

Development of Fidelity Measures for Later Use in At-Scale Applications

A major theme across all the chapters in Section II is how well constructed, multimethod measures of both intervention and implementation fidelity have far-reaching implications. Measure development is the foundation to making data-driven decisions, and as Lloyd and colleagues (Chapter 7) note from their recent experiences across a variety of interventions, it works out best when intervention developers take the time to develop these measures in tandem with the intervention itself. The following sections briefly summarize some of what we know and what we need to know about developing fidelity measures for ECE interventions.

What We Know

Though complex and challenging, as described in detail by Lloyd and colleagues (Chapter 7), research studies can learn much more about which intervention practices work and under what conditions when fidelity measures are generic enough to be used across intervention and control groups. This approach is exemplified by the Preschool Curriculum Evaluation Research Consortium (2008), an initiative funded by the Institute for Education Science to conduct rigorous efficacy evaluations of preschool curricula. In that study, 12 different research teams applied the same global fidelity measure across *both* the intervention and control groups. Though each research team also had curriculum-specific fidelity measures, the inclusion of the generic measure allowed the consortium to make comparative statements about how well curricula were implemented, including conclusions that control and intervention curricula were both implemented with moderate fidelity.

With refinement of generic measures to be more extensive and detailed, these cross-condition comparisons hold great promise in differentiating which core components might best account for intervention effects. For example, imagine a scenario in which a researcher wants to contrast a dialogic reading intervention with "business as usual" in ECE classrooms. However, some of the key tenets of dialogic reading, such as asking open-ended questions and expanding what a child says about the book (Lonigan & Whitehurst, 1998), may already be common practices in some classrooms. Therefore, it would be important to measure the amount of open-ended questions and expansive statements that teachers make during comparable book readings in order to make sense of any effects (or lack thereof) on child outcomes as well as to isolate what element of dialogic reading may be the most active ingredient of the intervention.

It is equally important to understand the active ingredients of effective implementation. Continuing to follow the example introduced above, training of staff (in this case, teachers) to implement a dialogic reading intervention is likely to have multiple components, including didactic workshops, guided practice, supervision and feedback, and assessment of teachers' skill in conducting these readings in ECE classrooms. In addition, school administrators need to demonstrate support for the new dialogic reading intervention not only in attitude (i.e., "buy-in") but also in provision of resources (e.g., time for teachers to engage in the trainings, cost of the training and other curriculum materials) and the creation of administrative structures and procedures that support the intervention (e.g., investment in data systems to track teacher and child outcomes). Which of these core implementation components actually matters the most in developing staff skills or achieving the desired child outcomes is an empirical question worth addressing. Of course, implementation science would argue that the total package is necessary to ensure desired outcomes of the intervention. These empirical implementation questions can be explored by careful measurement of the quality and quantity of all six core implementation drivers.

It is clear in the literature that paying attention to both intervention and implementation fidelity measures that assess quality *and* quantity moves the field beyond a sole focus on adherence to a basic protocol and into the realm of understanding how and why an intervention works. As one example, a recent literature review (Downer & Yazejian, in press) indicates that published studies of ECE interventions are more likely to measure and report quantity of fidelity constructs, like number of workshops attended and amount of time spent during home visits, rather than measures of quality that reflect how *well* an intervention is implemented, such as a teacher's ability to engage children during a lesson on feelings words (intervention fidelity) or a center director's attitude and approach toward teachers who are implementing a social-emotional curriculum (implementation fidelity). This is unfortunate given the potential of quality measures to be particularly salient for understanding why an intervention does or does not work, not to mention their utility for providing specific, detailed feedback to teachers and coaches about their practice.

Quality measures of intervention fidelity tend to be more difficult to develop, as well as more expensive and logistically complicated to administer, which may explain in part their relative scarcity in the literature. Yet, given the utility of these types of measures to evaluation and continuous quality improvement efforts during at-scale implementations, it is essential that intervention developers and researchers follow Schoenwald and Hoagwood's (2001) vision and make it a priority to develop and test quality-of-implementation measures (including methods of training observers that are simple but effective) with an eye toward making them feasible in later at-scale applications.

What We Need to Know

To understand what activities to prioritize and protect during at-scale rollout of interventions, it is important to identify clearly specified core intervention components. However, many of the recently validated ECE interventions are comprehensive and complex, with limited evidence of which elements are necessary for positive program effects. For example, Head Start REDI (Research-based, Developmentally Informed) is an enrichment of at-risk children's typical Head Start program experience, including a set of research-based language and literacy activities, the PATHS (Promoting Alternative Thinking Strategies) social-emotional curriculum, and parent activities, as well as workshop training and ongoing coaching for teachers (Bierman et al., 2008). A recent study of Head Start REDI documented widespread, strong effects on both the quality of teachers' instructional practices and children's vocabulary, emergent literacy, emotional understanding, social problem solving, social behavior, and learning engagement.

Such findings are impressive and establish that enrichment of current ECE programs is a powerful way to improve the outcomes of at-risk children, yet the intervention is both time and resource intensive. The question becomes how to feasibly transport such an enrichment model to a system-wide scale-up, and to some degree this involves understanding which of the intervention components and implementation drivers are integral to ensuring positive outcomes. Is it simply exposure to the classroom activities, coaching support to the teachers, parent involvement aligned with classroom activities, or administration buy-in, or is it some synergistic combination of all of these that accounts for changes in teacher practice and children's learning and development?

Domitrovich, Gest, Jones, Gill, and DeRousie (2010) began to unpack this question by examining some Head Start REDI intervention fidelity measures in relation to changes in child outcomes, but they remain far from lining up all the core components and examining their relative impact on desired outcomes. This is a common issue in the ECE literature, as there now exist a growing set of interventions with documented impact on teachers, families, and children, but with considerable room for decomposing multiple components to dissect what exactly the active ingredients are. This amounts to the next frontier in intervention fidelity research with an eye toward transportability.

Though research and development efforts are paying greater attention to measuring intervention fidelity, the same cannot be said for assessing implementation fidelity during the early stages of developing and testing interventions. Earlier chapters of this book referenced "organizational support" as a key factor in determining the successful implementation of an intervention in ECE programs. Yet, very few studies incorporate measures of this construct in their data collection protocol, despite studies that have established administrative support as a key factor in ensuring the successful, effective implementation of a social-emotional curriculum in early elementary school (Kam, Greenberg, & Walls, 2003).

In fact, several other implementation drivers are undermeasured and understudied in early stages of intervention development, including practitioner training, staff selection, and what happens during teacher–coach or parent–home visitor contacts. Many ECE interventions involve some form of traditional training, like workshops, but measures of these experiences often stop at attendance or reports of satisfaction. Are there ways to observe how well these trainings are conducted and document whether core concepts are conveyed as intended? What about tracking participants' level of engagement during the trainings? How many hours of training are necessary to provide practitioners with enough of a solid foundation to implement a program? Staff selection was already referenced earlier in this chapter in relation to hiring coaches, but is worth reiterating. It is important to document minimum and/or ideal knowledge, skills, abilities, and experiences of staff—coaches, mentors, consultants, home visitors, and others—during development of interventions in order to help guide staff selection when transporting program to at-scale applications.

Finally, though it is clear from the three previous chapters that basic data on coach–teacher and coach–parent contacts are being assessed, these measures are largely self-reported by coaches. This continues to leave coaching session interactions as somewhat of a black box, despite their centrality to many interventions' theories of change. What type of mutual affect is evident during these sessions? Are the conversations one-sided or collaborative? How well does the coach convey ideas? Such qualitative elements of coaching are conceptually relevant to understanding what about coaching is effective, yet few objective approaches to measuring these aspects of coaching implementation have been undertaken (see Knoche, Sheridan, Edwards, & Osborn [2010] for one example of videotaping and coding early childhood professional visits to work with families at their home).

Next Steps for Aligning Initial ECE Program Development with Later At-Scale Applications

As is evident in each of the three previous chapters, intervention developers and researchers have an important role in setting the stage for more efficient and effective implementation of their work through careful attention to intervention fidelity data and at-scale implementation support drivers during initial development and testing. As Chapter 7 notes, if developers put more thought into these issues at the beginning, less work would be needed at the scale-up stage.

At the crux of this issue is the need for a shift in the way program developers and researchers approach early stages of intervention development and evaluation. Certainly, these interventions are being developed in a results-oriented policy context, but if intervention efforts place too much attention on outcomes and not enough on the process of getting there, even successful, effective interventions will be ill prepared for wider dissemination and implementation. In addition to using intervention fidelity data in the ways the previous chapters highlighted, there are a number of macro-level changes that are needed to ensure that the transportability of ECE interventions is brought to the forefront of developers' and researchers' minds.

First, as a field, we must redefine evidence-based practices to include paying attention to and researching issues that will contribute to successful dissemination to the practice world. And, as Schoenwald and Hoagwood (2001) and Fixsen et al. (2005) emphasize, this involves careful measurement and use of intervention fidelity data, as well as assessment of core implementation supports such as staff selection criteria and coaching supports; policies, procedures, and organizational structures to support the intervention; and the use of data to make informed decisions at the organizational level.

Second, funding mechanisms must be available to support the above-mentioned study of intervention and implementation fidelity, during intervention development and early trials as well as the actual at-scale implementations. The previously referenced ACF request for proposals that calls for a study design to isolate effective coaching components is an excellent example of this, as are the Institute for Education Sciences Goal 2 awards, which focus on intervention development and incorporate a heavy emphasis on creating intervention fidelity measures.

Third, scientist preparation programs ought to integrate implementation science into their training models for individuals who will be developing and researching early models of interventions. Intervention developers and researchers working in ECE represent a unique mosaic of interdisciplinary backgrounds, including education, developmental psychology, clinical psychology, school psychology, sociology, economics, and more. The connection between developmental science and education in particular has long been a strength of the field, yet few of the higher education training institutions in any of these disciplines provide opportunities for rising scholars to learn about implementation science. This is a substantial shortcoming in the training of individuals who will go on to form the research and development arm of the ECE field, given the ultimate goal of creating programs that are feasible and available for use at scale.

This is an exciting time to be involved in the ECE field. There is widespread recognition of the positive social, academic, and economic ramifications of providing high-quality early support to families and children who are underresourced (Heckman, 2006; Mashburn et al., 2008). The field has already developed a number of evidence-based programs that provide this high-quality support and result in marked improvements in teaching, parenting, and child outcomes (e.g., Landry, Swank, Smith, Assel, & Gunnewig, 2006; Sheridan, Knoche, Kupzyk, Edwards, & Marvin, 2011). However, to take the next step to ensuring that these types of model programs can be made available to the full range of at-risk children and families, a next generation of studies is needed that dives deeper into matters of intervention fidelity and implementation drivers, with transportability to system-wide applications being a targeted outcome on par with demonstrating positive child outcomes.

References

Administration for Children and Families (ACF). (2012, June). *Head Start professional development: Developing the evidence for best practices in coaching* (Request for Task Order Proposal Number 12-233-SOL-0040). Washington, DC: Author.

Bierman, K.L., Domitrovich, C.E., Nix, R.L., Gest, S.D., Welsh, J.A., … Gill, S. (2008). Promoting academic and social-emotional school readiness: The Head Start REDI program. *Child Development, 79*, 1802–1817.

Blakely, C.H., Mayer, J.P., Gottschalk, R.G., Schmitt, N., Davidson, W.S., Roitman, D.B., & Emshoff, J.G. (1987). The fidelity-adaptation debate: Implications for the implementation of public sector social programs. *American Journal of Community Psychology, 15*, 253–268.

Castro, F.G., Barrera, M., & Martinez, C.R. (2004). The cultural adaptation of prevention interventions: Resolving tensions between fidelity and fit. *Prevention Science, 5*, 41–45.

Dane, A.V., & Schneider, B.H. (1998). Program integrity in primary and early secondary prevention: Are implementation effects out of control? *Clinical Psychology Review, 18*, 23–45.

Domitrovich, C.E., Gest, S.D., Jones, D., Gill, S., & DeRousie, R.S. (2010). Implementation quality: Lessons learned in the context of the Head Start REDI trial. *Early Childhood Research Quarterly, 25*, 284–298.

Downer, J., & Yazejian, N. (in press). *Measuring the quality and quantity of implementation in early childhood interventions, OPRE Report 2013–12*. Washington, DC: Office of Planning, Research and Evaluation, Administration for Children and Families, U.S. Department of Health and Human Services.

Fixsen, D.L., Naoom, S.F., Blase, K.A., Friedman, R.M., & Wallace, F. (2005). *Implementation research: A synthesis of the literature* (FMHI Publication No. 231). Tampa, FL: University of South Florida, Louis de la Parte Florida Mental Health Institute, National Implementation Research Network.

Heckman, J. (2006). Skill formation and the economics of investing in disadvantaged children. *Review of Agricultural Economics, 29*, 446–493.

Howes, C., Hamre, B.K., & Pianta, R.C. (2012). *Effective early childhood professional development: Improving teacher practice and child outcomes*. Baltimore, MD: Paul H. Brookes Publishing Co.

Hulleman, C.S., & Cordray, D. (2009). Moving from the lab to the field: The role of fidelity and achieved relative intervention strength. *Journal of Research on Educational Effectiveness, 2*, 88–110.

Isner, T., Tout, K., Zaslow, M., Soli, M., Quinn, K., Rothenberg, L., & Burkhauser, M. (2011). *Coaching in early care and education programs and quality rating and improvement systems (QRIS): Identifying promising features*. Washington, DC: Child Trends.

Kam, C.M., Greenberg, M.T., & Walls, C.T. (2003). Examining the role of implementation quality in school-based prevention using the PATHS curriculum. *Prevention Science, 4*, 55–63.

Knoche, L.L., Sheridan, S.M., Edwards, C.P., & Osborn, A.Q. (2010). Implementation of a relationship-based school readiness intervention: A multidimensional approach to fidelity measurement for early childhood. *Early Childhood Research Quarterly, 25*, 299–313.

Landry, S.H., Swank, P.R., Smith, K.E., Assel, M.A., & Gunnewig, S.B. (2006). Enhancing early literacy skills for preschool children: Bringing a professional development model to scale. *Journal of Learning Disabilities, 39,* 306–324.

Lonigan, C.J., & Whitehurst, G.J. (1998). Relative efficacy of parent and teacher involvement in a shared-reading intervention for preschool children from low-income backgrounds. *Early Childhood Research Quarterly, 13,* 263–290.

Mashburn, A.J., Downer, J.T., Hamre, B.K., Justice, L.M., & Pianta, R.C. (2010). Consultation for teachers and children's language and literacy development during pre-kindergarten. *Applied Developmental Science, 14,* 179–196.

Mashburn, A.J., Pianta, R.C., Hamre, B.K., Downer, J.T., Barbarin, O., Bryant, D., … Howes, C. (2008). Measures of classroom quality in prekindergarten and children's development of academic, language, and social skills. *Child Development, 79,* 732–749.

Neuman, S.B., & Wright, T.S. (2010). Promoting language and literacy development for early childhood educators: A mixed-methods study of coursework and coaching. *Elementary School Journal, 111,* 63–86.

Parents as Teachers. (2012). Overview of the 2011–2012 affiliate performance report. Retrieved from http://www.parentsasteachers.org/images/stories/documents/2011-2012_APR_final.pdf

Pianta, R.C., DeCoster, J., Cabell, S., Burcinal, M., Hamre, B., Downer, J., … Howes, C. (2012). *Dose-response relations between preschool teachers' exposure to components of professional development and increases in quality of their interactions with children.* Manuscript submitted for publication.

Pianta, R.C., Hamre, B.K., & Hadden, D.S. (2012). Scaling up effective professional development. In C. Howes, B. Hamre, & R. Pianta (Eds.), *Effective early childhood professional development: Improving teacher practice and child outcomes.* Baltimore, MD: Paul H. Brookes Publishing Co.

Pianta, R.C., Mashburn, A.J., Downer, J.T., Hamre, B.K., & Justice, L. (2008). Effects of web-mediated PD resources on teacher–child interactions in pre-kindergarten classrooms. *Early Childhood Research Quarterly, 23,* 431–451.

Powell, D.R., Diamond, K.E., Burchinal, M.R., & Koehler, M.J. (2010). Effects of an early literacy professional development intervention on Head Start teachers and children. *Journal of Educational Psychology, 102,* 299–312.

Preschool Curriculum Evaluation Research Consortium. (2008). *Effects of preschool curriculum programs on school readiness (NCER 2008–2009).* National Center for Education Research, Institute of Education Sciences, U.S. Department of Education. Washington, DC: U.S. Government Printing Office.

Raver, C.C., Jones, A.S., Li-Grining, C.P., Metzger, M., Smallwood, K., & Sardin, L. (2008). Improving preschool classroom processes: Preliminary findings from a randomized trial implemented in Head Start settings. *Early Childhood Research Quarterly, 23,* 10–26.

Sanetti, L.M.H., & Kratochwill, T.R. (2009). Toward developing a science of treatment integrity: Introduction to the special series. *School Psychology Review, 38,* 445–459.

Schoenwald, S., and Hoagwood, K. (2001). Effectiveness, transportability, and dissemination of interventions: What matters when? *Psychiatric Services, 52,* 1190–1197.

Sheridan, S.M., Knoche, L.L., Kupzyk, K.A., Edwards, C.P., & Marvin, C. (2011). A randomized trial examining the effects of parent engagement on early language and literacy: The Getting Ready intervention. *Journal of School Psychology, 49,* 361–383.

Wasik, B.H., & Hindman, A.H. (2011). Improving vocabulary and pre-literacy skills of at-risk preschoolers through teacher professional development. *Journal of Educational Psychology, 103,* 455–469.

Zaslow, M., Tout, K., Halle, T., Whittaker, J., & Lavelle, B. (2010). *Toward the identification of features of effective professional development for early childhood educators: A review of the literature.* Washington, DC: U.S. Department of Education. Retrieved from http://www2.ed.gov/rschstat/eval/professional-development/literature-review.pdf

Aligning Stage-Appropriate Evaluation with the Stages of Implementation

Ongoing Monitoring and Scale-Up/Replication

Amy Blasberg

While Sections I and II of this volume examined implementation science frameworks, principles, and methodologies in the context of formative evaluations, Section III examines these topics in the context of scale-up and monitoring of larger-scale early care and education (ECE) interventions. Aligning the goals of research with the later stages of program implementation allows researchers to explore a different set of issues around measuring implementation, particularly with regard to the core implementation drivers, which may vary during different stages of implementation.

In Chapter 9, Julie Sarama and Douglas H. Clements discuss their work bringing Building Blocks, a school-based early math curriculum, to scale using their TRIAD scale-up model. The chapter begins with background information on the need for models of scale-up that can be applied universally to any intervention. Interventions are only beneficial for people who experience them, and as such, scaling up programs to saturate a particular area or fully reach a target population is of high importance. Scale-up is defined by the authors as being achieved when over 90% of the children in a given school district are experiencing a given intervention. They also highlight the complexities of achieving scale-up because it involves coordinated efforts across multiple stakeholders. The next section of the chapter addresses the specific theoretical framework behind the TRIAD model, highlighting its 10 guiding principles. A few of the tenets include "promot[ing] communication among key groups around a shared vision of the innovation" (p. 179), "provid[ing] professional development that is ongoing, intentional, reflective, [and] goal-oriented" (p. 180), and "ensur[ing] school leaders are a central force supporting the innovation" (p. 181). At the end of the chapter, the authors discuss lessons learned that highlight implications and challenges for implementation research in an ECE context.

Peggy Hill and David Olds, the authors of Chapter 10, share their experiences with scaling up the Nurse–Family Partnership (NFP), a home visiting program that focuses on improving family outcomes by facilitating regular meetings between parents and nurses during pregnancy and the first few years of a child's life. Prior to scaling up the program, several efficacy and effectiveness trials were conducted in regions throughout the United States with diverse populations. Once researchers ensured that the program model was demonstrating positive outcomes for children and families, the program was implemented in other areas around the country. As the NFP was being implemented to scale in many locations, the research team designed a set of implementation supports to ease program installation, including an extensive set of home visiting guidelines, an education program for new nurse home visitors, job descriptions for key personnel, and a data collection and reporting system. The chapter highlights the challenges and how each challenge was addressed. Key lessons learned and priorities for researchers, policy makers, and practitioners are discussed at the end of the chapter.

Chapter 11 is about Educare, an ECE intervention model that includes comprehensive wraparound services for high-risk children ages 0 to 5 and their families. The program is sustained in communities through robust public–private partnerships. Educare's main goal is to be an exemplar of high-quality service provision to low-income families within a geographic region in order to prevent or reduce the achievement gap. The Educare model is based on the 12 Head Start performance standards and either meets or exceeds each of these criteria, demonstrating what is possible in the ECE field when following evidence-based best practices.

Authors Noreen Yazejian, Donna Bryant, and Portia Kennel consider the role implementation science can play in achieving and maintaining model fidelity both within and across Educare's "learning network" of 12 geographically diverse sites during replication. For example, the Educare requirements for staffing, data utilization, and leadership support map directly onto the seven core implementation components identified by Fixsen, Naoom, Blase, Friedman, and Wallace (2005). Chapter 11 specifically explores the benefits and challenges of intentionally studying the replication of Educare through an implementation science framework. Lessons learned and next steps include identifying what aspects are central to the model and which could be adapted in a productive fashion, determining what community characteristics make a site an ideal location for Educare's replication, and conducting a randomized control trial of six Educare sites, which began in 2010.

Section III concludes with an integrative chapter by Carolyn Layzer that considers the connections among the three earlier chapters and their implications for researchers, policy makers, and practitioners.

References

Fixsen, D.L., Naoom, S.F., Blase, K.A., Friedman, R.M., & Wallace, F. (2005). *Implementation research: A synthesis of the literature* (FMHI Publication No. 231). Tampa: University of South Florida, Louis de la Parte Florida Mental Health Institute, National Implementation Research Network.

CHAPTER 9

Lessons Learned in the Implementation of the TRIAD Scale-Up Model

Teaching Early Mathematics with Trajectories and Technologies

Julie Sarama and Douglas H. Clements

Although the successes of research-based, visionary educational practices have been documented, equally recognized is the failure of these practices to be implemented at a scale that affects more than a trivial portion of children. Further, there may be no more challenging educational and theoretical issue than scaling up educational programs across a large number of diverse populations and contexts in the early childhood system in the United States, avoiding the dilution and pollution that usually plagues such efforts to achieve broad success (Clements & Sarama, 2011). In this chapter, we describe a model of scale-up at the school district level and its initial evaluation. Although our intent is that the model should apply to all subject matter domains and grade levels, any evaluation must involve a specific instantiation. Our evaluations have focused on early childhood mathematics. Therefore, we begin with background information on the need for models of scale-up, especially in early childhood education, as well as a consideration of the particular needs in mathematics education. Next, we introduce the theoretical framework, the model we developed, and the research corpus on which they were based. We then summarize the empirical evaluations we have conducted of this model. In the final section, we summarize what we have learned and describe implications and challenges for the field.

Background

Education needs generalizable models to scale up evidence-based practices and programs and longitudinal research evaluating the persistence of the effect of their implementations (Borman, 2007; Cuban & Usdan, 2003). Research-based educational practices that make practically and statistically significant differences in the development and learning of children have been documented (e.g., Clements & Sarama, 2011; Clements, Sarama, Spitler, Lange, & Wolfe, 2011; McGill-Franzen, 2010). Unfortunately, the "deep, systemic incapacity of U.S. schools, and the practitioners who work in them, to develop, incorporate, and extend new ideas about teaching and learning in anything but a small fraction of schools and classrooms" (Elmore, 1996a, p. 1) has also been documented (Berends, Kirby, Naftel, & McKelvey, 2001). How can we start to understand and *solve* this problem? Our story begins as we consider the careful planning that scale implementation involves. We then move to discuss the particular challenges.

At the simplest level, taking promising interventions to scale means implementing them successfully in many settings. To do so successfully, however, is to confront the complexity of such an enterprise. For example, with scale-up there is an increase not only in the number of students and teachers involved in the enterprise but also in both the number of categories of stakeholders and the number of different and often conflicting perspectives they hold. Therefore, we define scale-up as the instantiation of an educational intervention in varied settings with diverse populations, addressing the needs of multiple sociopolitical stakeholders, so as to achieve 1) satisfactory fidelity of implementation and, as a result, 2) the intervention's goals for over 90% of the children who could benefit from the intervention and ultimately 3) eventual transfer of the intervention to local ownership, sustainability, persistence of effects, and continuing diffusion. (This is based on a school-district adaptation and implementation; across wider areas and organizations, such as a state, a goal of 60% would be satisfactory.)

That definition alone could induce trepidation: It is a daunting task. Before we confront additional challenges, we will discuss some of this definition's components. First, consider the complexity of the perspectives, needs, and desires of the different categories of stakeholders within a school district—parents, various community groups, the professional teaching community, educational leadership in early childhood and in subject-matter content (often these are distinct groups), and higher level administrators such as school principals and superintendents (or child care directors), among others. To bring such diverse groups together to support an intervention is a challenging task indeed. Achieving an adequate fidelity of implementation of any intervention presents myriad challenges, such as sufficiency of materials and technology, professional development, in-class support, and so forth. Each of these challenges requires both financial and social capital. An example of social capital is the essential support of school leaders, which drives improvements in all others components of the system (Bryk, Sebring, Allensworth, Suppescu, & Easton, 2010).

Turning to another component of the definition, interventions are not useful if they do not live on after the initial thrust for the implementation. We categorize lasting effectiveness as *sustainability* or *persistence* with the potential for diffusion. Sustainability means the length of time an innovation continues to be implemented with fidelity. Persistence means continuation of the effects of an intervention on individual children's trajectories of learning. Diffusion is the process through which an intervention gets communicated over time among the members of a social system, that is, the process by which interventions get spread more widely beyond those initially exposed to it (Dearing, Maibach, & Buller, 2006). Diffusion may or may not be a direct goal, but can be important to other educators and students and to sustainability, because adoptions in other locales may help motivate continuing support within the intervention site.

As stated, a scale-up project has to do a lot to succeed. However, there are additional challenges for those in the field of early childhood and yet another set of challenges for those focused on mathematics education. Early childhood, especially before kindergarten, includes settings and organizational structures that vary far more than do those at any other age level (National Research Council, 2009). The workforce in those settings, their backgrounds, and their professional education are similarly diverse. Research suggests that the most critical feature of a high-quality educational environment is a knowledgeable and responsive adult; it also suggests that high-quality professional development is essential to innovation (Darling-Hammond, 1997; Ferguson, 1991; National Research Council, 2001, 2009; Sarama & DiBiase, 2004; Schoen, Cebulla, Finn, & Fi, 2003). Because of this, scaling up professional development has special challenges in early childhood contexts, including the diverse workforce, the equally diverse knowledge of teachers, and, for interventions such as ours, many teachers' resistance to or rejection of "academics." We must meet that challenge, however, because long-range benefits to children are greatest for interventions in that period (Clements & Sarama, 2009).

The learning of mathematics also presents special challenges. The importance of mathematics is well known, especially in a global economy with the vast majority of jobs requiring more sophisticated skills than in the past (Doig, McCrae, & Rowe, 2003). However, U.S. students do not perform well compared to students from many other nations, as early as kindergarten (Stigler, Lee, & Stevenson, 1990) and even the preschool years (Yuzawa, Bart, Kinne, Sukemune, & Kataoka, 1999). Such achievement gaps are most pronounced in U.S. children from low-resource communities (Siegler, 1993). This is especially worrisome because early knowledge strongly affects later success in mathematics (National Mathematics Advisory Panel, 2008).

Thus, we need to improve the basic academic mathematical concepts, skills, and motivation of low-achieving children early in their school career (Claessens, Duncan, & Engel, 2007). Although this can be achieved by providing high-quality experiences in early mathematics (Doig et al., 2003; Thomson, Rowe, Underwood, & Peck, 2005), few early childhood programs or settings do so (National Research Council, 2009).

In summary, scaling up high-quality mathematics education within early childhood settings holds particular challenges that range from the logistical (e.g., all-day professional development may take teachers away from emotionally dependent children) to the philosophical and motivational (why "push down" math onto young children?) to the practical (many teachers lack knowledge of the content of mathematics as well as its learning and teaching). A model of scale-up must address these challenges if it is to support a high-quality implementation.

The Implementation Key

Implementation of an intervention that has documented efficacy (i.e., has been shown in rigorous studies to be effective at least on a small scale) is the sine qua non of a successful scale-up. Without high-fidelity implementation, few positive results can be realized. One cannot even know if the intervention *could* have been effective or not. Lack of information about the fidelity of implementation is a key missing piece of the scale-up research puzzle (Borman, Hewes, Overman, & Brown, 2003). Indeed, just having certain characteristics such as a specific curriculum, professional development, or goals does not appear to matter—the *implementation* of these characteristics is what matters.

Appreciation of these research results is one reason educators are moving from "let it happen" to "help it happen" and, increasingly, to "make it happen" strategies of implementation (Greenhalgh, Robert, MacFarlane, Bate, & Kyriakidou, 2004, p. 593). That is, a let-it-happen view of natural emergence of the implementation has given way to helping the implementation with negotiated social supports that enable the implementation. More often, even stronger support is provided by scientific, planned systems that are managed and monitored. The following two sections describe 1) the theoretical framework we developed for our research and development work on implementation and wider scale-up and 2) the model we derived from it to make it happen.

Framework

The overarching theoretical framework for our research and the development of a scale-up model is an elaboration of the Network of Influences framework (Sarama, Clements, & Henry, 1998), describing our theory of the relationships and influences that must be attended to achieve successful scale-up. Most are important for any intervention; however, in small interventions, components can often be compensatory or even ignored. In scale-up efforts, we posit that many are critical.

We consider successful implementation of an intervention at scale to involve multiple coordinated efforts to introduce, implement, and maintain the integrity of the vision and practices of an innovation through increasingly numerous and complex socially mediated filters. The depiction of the Network of Influences framework in Figure 9.1 illustrates the hypothesized influences of context and implementation variables on outcomes such as teacher knowledge, child achievement, and sustainability. The "Follow Though" model (U), at bottom right in the figure, most relevant to this study, is simply a microcosm of the framework.

In Figure 9.1, *contextual variables*, in dotted ovals, include contexts that are situations not determined by the model, such as school (A–D), teacher (E), and child (F–H) factors. As an example of these variables in the framework, child socioeconomic status (SES; G) impacts children's initial knowledge (H), which influences their achievement (R)—an outcome variable indicated by the solid rectangle. *Implementation variables* are depicted in solid ovals. These are features that the project can encourage and support, but cannot control absolutely. For example, heavy arrows from professional development (J) to teacher knowledge (N) to implementation fidelity (O) to child achievement (R) indicate the strong effects in that path. Support from coaches (L) also has a strong effect on teachers' knowledge and practice, while other factors (J, K, M) are influential, but only to a moderate degree (small effects are not depicted).

The following subsections describe our elaborations of the Network of Influences framework, including the major stakeholders (e.g., administrators, teachers, children and their families) and their relationships and interactions.

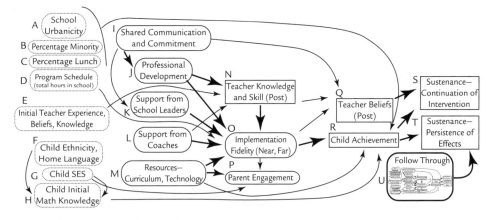

Figure 9.1. Revised Network of Influences theoretical framework. The "Follow Though" model at the bottom right, most relevant to this study, is simply a microcosm of the framework. Contextual variables in dotted ovals include the school (A–D), teacher (E), and child (F–H) factors. For example, child socioeconomic status (SES) (G) affects children's initial mathematics knowledge (H), which influences children's achievement (R)—an outcome variable indicated by the solid rectangle. Implementation variables in solid ovals are features that the project can encourage and support but cannot control absolutely. For example, heavy arrows from professional development (J), to teacher knowledge (N), to implementation fidelity (O), to child achievement (R), indicate the strong effects in that path. Support from coaches (L) also has a strong effect on implementation fidelity, whereas other factors (J, K, M) are influential but only to a moderate degree (not all small effects are depicted). (From Sarama, J., Clements, D.H., Wolfe, C.B., & Spitler, M.E. [2012]. Longitudinal evaluation of a scale-up model for teaching mathematics with trajectories and technologies. *Journal of Research on Educational Effectiveness*, 5[2], 105–135; reprinted by permission of Taylor & Francis Ltd, http://www.tandf.co.uk/journals.)

Educational Interactions A successful model for scale-up in education must move beyond simply adopting a new curriculum or teaching model—a common but unsuccessful intervention. Instead, it must scale up all the supports necessary to positively affect the "interactions among teachers and children around educational material" (Ball & Cohen, 1999, p. 3). This strategy creates extensive opportunities for teachers to focus on subject matter, goals, and children's thinking and learning, which improves teachers' knowledge of subject matter, teaching, and learning and increases child learning and development (Ball & Cohen, 1999; Cohen, 1996, p. 98; Schoen et al., 2003; Sowder, 2007).

Administrators and Other School Leaders Principal leadership (Figure 9.1, K) is strongly related to levels of implementation and effectiveness (Berends et al., 2001; Bodilly, 1998; Bryk et al., 2010; Fullan, 1992; Heck, Weiss, Boyd, & Howard, 2002; Kaser, Bourexis, Loucks-Horsley, & Raizen, 1999; Klingner, Ahwee, Pilonieta, & Menendez, 2003). Effective administrators provide the time for teachers to experiment, discuss, and, in general, construct their own meanings of the innovation. They communicate continuing commitment (Figure 9.1, I), not just in verbal form but also in other ways, such as resource allocation (Bodilly, 1998).

School-level leaders, such as supervisors or coordinators, in a particular subject matter or grade level (e.g., early childhood) serve as essential bridges between administrators and teachers (Cobb, McClain, de Silva, & Dean, 2003). District-level leaders and their decisions also affect implementation (Bodilly, 1998; Klingner et al., 2003; Snipes, Doolittle, & Herlihy, 2002; Spillane, 2000). Communication between principals and all other groups is particularly essential. Principals forgetting the study and their involvement in it and similar communication lapses can be a huge challenge, and it increases with the size of the school district (Foorman, Santi, & Berger, 2007).

Communication   Positive communication, collaboration, and agreement among all groups are essential (Figure 9.1, I; Bryk et al., 2010; Elmore, 1996a; Huberman, 1992; Kaser et al., 1999; Klingner et al., 2003; Sarama et al., 1998). Our own previous research revealed multiple missed opportunities for facilitation of innovations due to the divergent beliefs of social groups, even about ostensibly observable "facts" (Sarama et al., 1998). As one example, the principal of a building answered affirmatively to the question "Is adequate technology available to the teachers?" The teachers said there was not. The principal pointed to the computer laboratory and a schedule giving each teacher access, with "borrowing" time from each other allowed. The teachers countered that 1) many educational technology applications (including the one we were studying) were better situated in the classroom, not a distant computer laboratory; 2) the schedule for the laboratory often did not correspond with their schedule; and 3) borrowing time did not work, because the teachers who did not use the laboratory refused to give up their time and thus tacitly admit that they did not use computers, which the principal wanted them to do.

Teachers and Professional Development   Research suggests that the most critical feature of an educational environment is a knowledgeable and responsive adult and that effective professional development is essential to innovation (Figure 9.1, J, N; Darling-Hammond, 1997; Ferguson, 1991; National Research Council, 2001; Sarama & DiBiase, 2004; Schoen et al., 2003; Sowder, 2007). Scaling up such professional development has special challenges and opportunities in the early childhood setting, as noted previously. Other intervention specifics can affect the strengths of effects, as well. For example, we specify only a weak effect of *initial* teacher expertise (Figure 9.1, E) because of the low level of mathematics content and pedagogical content knowledge of most prekindergarten teachers, regardless of background (Copley, 2004; Sarama, 2002; Sarama & DiBiase, 2004); this would vary for other goals. Changes in beliefs follow changes in practice (Figure 9.1, N, Q; Showers, Joyce, & Bennett, 1987); moreover, we believe that changes in beliefs help *sustain* teacher practices (Figure 9.1, Q, S).

Research suggests strategies that help meet those challenges (Klingner et al., 2003; National Research Council, 2001; Sarama, 2002). Use of theory, demonstrations, practice, and feedback, especially from coaches, quadruples the positive effects of information-only training (thus, the model shows strong effects from J and L to N and O in Figure 9.1; see also Foorman et al., 2007; Pellegrino, 2007; Showers et al., 1987). Effective professional development eschews "one-shot" interventions, begins with a specific strategy or curriculum (Figure 9.1, M), and weaves together content, pedagogy, and knowledge of child development and family relationships (Schoen et al., 2003; Sowder, 2007).

To anticipate, this is one reason that research-based learning trajectories are at the core of our theoretical framework. Learning trajectories are "descriptions of children's thinking and learning...and a related, conjectured route through a set of instructional tasks" (Clements & Sarama, 2004, p. 83). Thus, learning trajectories have three components: 1) a goal (that is, an aspect of a subject-matter domain children should learn), 2) a developmental progression or learning path along which children move through levels of thinking, and 3) instruction that helps them move along that path. As previously stated, our scale-up model is intended to be general across subject matter and grades. Fortunately, learning trajectories have been or are being developed for many developmental areas (e.g., CCSSO/NGA, 2010; International Reading Association and National Association for the Education of Young Children, 2000; National Research Council, 2007).

Children and Their Families Interventions are more effective if they involve parents (Figure 9.1, P), especially by providing activities to do with their children (Bryk et al., 2010; Halpern, 2004; Ramey & Ramey, 1998). As with prekindergarten teachers, parents often have a limited view of the breadth of subject-matter content appropriate for young children (Sarama, 2002). Low-income parents (Figure 9.1, G), compared to middle-income parents, believe that education is the responsibility of the preschool and that children cannot learn aspects of content that research indicates they *can* learn (Starkey et al., 1999). Communications that change these beliefs are important components of our scale-up model, to which we turn.

Description of the TRIAD Model for Scale-Up: Research-Based Guidelines

Our scale-up model is called TRIAD (Technology-enhanced, Research-based, Instruction, Assessment, and professional Development). The model's acronym suggests that successful scale-up must address the triad of essential components of any educational intervention and that the model is based on research and enhanced by the use of technology. However, TRIAD is a general model for scaling up varied educational interventions, based on the Network of Influences framework and research on successful efforts to take such interventions to scale.

Recall our definition of a successful scale-up is instantiation of an intervention in varied settings with diverse populations, addressing the needs of multiple sociopolitical stakeholders, so as to achieve 1) satisfactory fidelity of implementation and, as a result, 2) the intervention's goals for the maximum number of children (>90% in a district) and ultimately, 3) eventual transfer of the intervention to local ownership, sustainability, persistence of effects, and continuing diffusion. In our description of the TRIAD model, we note that some processes are common to successful implementations at any scale, such as work in a single school or classroom (see Guidelines 4 and 5 below); however, although they are helpful in most contexts, the vast majority of the processes are uniquely required for successful scale-up (e.g., we have conducted many research and development projects, such as the efficacy study cited below, that did not substantially involve the other processes or guidelines).

The following summarizes the 10 research-based guidelines in the TRIAD model, connecting it to the original Network of Influences theoretical framework. Implementing these guidelines is the responsibility of an implementation team.

1. *Involve and promote communication among key groups around a shared vision of the innovation* (Hall & Hord, 2001). Emphasize connections between the project's goals, national and state standards, and greater societal need. Promote clarity of these goals and of all participants' responsibilities. School and project staff must share goals and a vision of the intervention (Bryk et al., 2010; Cobb et al., 2003). This institutionalizes the intervention, for example, in the case of ongoing socialization and training of new teachers (Elmore, 1996a; Fullan, 2000; Huberman, 1992; Kaser et al., 1999; Klingner et al., 2003; Sarama et al., 1998).

2. *Promote equity* through equitable recruitment and selection of participants, allocation of resources, and use of curriculum and instructional strategies that have demonstrated success with underrepresented populations (Kaser et al., 1999).

3. *Plan for the long term.* Recognizing that scale-up is not just an increase in number but also of complexity, provide continuous, adaptive support over an extended period of time. Plan an incremental implementation and use dynamic, multilevel, feedback, and self-correction strategies (Bryk et al., 2010; Coburn, 2003; Fullan, 1992; Guskey, 2000). Communicate clearly that change is not an event but a process (Hall & Hord, 2001).

4. *Focus on instructional change that promotes depth of children's thinking, placing learning trajectories at the core* of the teacher–child–curriculum triad to ensure that curriculum, materials, instructional strategies, and assessments are aligned with 1) national and state standards and a vision of high-quality education, 2) each other, and 3) recommended practices, as determined by research, including formative assessment (Ball & Cohen, 1999; Bodilly, 1998; Bryk et al., 2010; Fullan, 2000; Kaser et al., 1999; National Mathematics Advisory Panel, 2008; Raudenbush, 2008; Sowder, 2007). This guideline is important for implementation with fidelity at any scale, although alignment is increasingly important at larger scales.

5. *Provide professional development that is ongoing, intentional, reflective, goal oriented, focused on content knowledge and children's thinking, grounded in particular curriculum materials, and situated in the classroom and the school.* A focus on content includes accurate and adequate subject-matter knowledge both for teachers and for children. A focus on children's thinking emphasizes the learning trajectories' developmental progressions and their pedagogical application in formative assessment. Grounding in particular curriculum materials should include all three aspects of learning trajectories, especially their connections. This also provides a common language for teachers in working with each other and other groups (Bryk et al., 2010).

    "Situated in the classroom" does not imply that all training occurs within classrooms. However, off-site intensive training remains focused on and connected to classroom practice and is completed by classroom-based enactment with coaching. In addition, this professional development should encourage sharing, risk taking, and learning from and with peers. Aim at preparing to teach a specific curriculum and develop teachers' knowledge and beliefs that the curriculum is appropriate and its goals are valued and attainable. Situate work in the classroom, formatively evaluating teachers' fidelity of implementation and providing feedback and support from coaches in real time (Bodilly, 1998; Borman et al., 2003; Bryk et al., 2010; Cohen, 1996; Elmore, 1996a; Guskey, 2000; Hall & Hord, 2001; Kaser et al., 1999; Klingner et al., 2003; Pellegrino, 2007; Schoen et al., 2003; Showers et al., 1987; Sowder, 2007; Zaslow, Tout, Halle, Vick, & Lavelle, 2010).

    As with the previous guideline, this one is important for implementation with fidelity at any scale. However, the planning, structures, common language, formative evaluation, and school-level context are increasingly important as the implementation moves to larger scales.

6. *Build expectations and camaraderie to support a consensus around adaptation.* Promote buy-in in multiple ways, such as dealing with all participants as partners and distributing resources to support the project. Establish and maintain cohort groups. Facilitate teachers visiting successful implementation sites. Build local leadership by involving principals and encouraging teachers to become teacher leaders (Berends et al., 2001; Borman et al., 2003; Elmore, 1996a; Fullan, 2000; Glennan, Bodilly, Galegher, & Kerr, 2004; Hall & Hord, 2001).

7. *Ensure school leaders are a central force supporting the innovation and provide teachers with continuous feedback that children are learning what they are taught and that this learning is valued.* Leaders, especially principals, must show that the innovation is a high priority, through statements, resources, and continued commitment to permanency of the effort. An "innovation champion" leads the effort within each organization (Bodilly, 1998; Bryk et al., 2010; Glennan et al., 2004; Hall & Hord, 2001; Rogers, 2003, p. 434; Sarama et al., 1998).

8. *Give teachers and schools latitude for adaptation, but maintain integrity.* Emphasize the similarities of the curriculum with sound practice and what teachers already are doing. Help teachers distinguish productive adaptations from lethal mutation (Brown & Campione, 1996). Also, do not allow dilution due to uncoordinated innovations (Fullan, 2000; Huberman, 1992; Sarama et al., 1998; Snipes et al., 2002).

9. *Provide incentives for all participants, including intrinsic and extrinsic motivators linked to project work,* such as external expectations—from standards to validation from administrators. Show how the innovation is advantageous to and compatible with teachers' experiences and needs (Berends et al., 2001; Borman et al., 2003; Cohen, 1996; Darling-Hammond, 1996; Elmore, 1996b; Rogers, 2003).

10. *Maintain frequent and repeated communication, assessment ("checking up"), and follow-through efforts at all levels within each school district, emphasizing the purpose, expectations, and visions of the project, and involve key groups in continual improvement through cycles of data collection and problem solving* (Fullan, 1992; Hall & Hord, 2001; Huberman, 1992; Kaser et al., 1999; Snipes et al., 2002). Throughout, connections with parents and community groups are especially important to meet immediate and long-range (sustainability) goals.

Empirical Evaluation

A series of studies has been conducted to evaluate instantiations of the TRIAD model and its components (Clements & Sarama, 2008a, 2008b; Clements, Sarama, Spitler, Lange, et al., 2011; Clements, Sarama, Wolfe, & Spitler, in press; Sarama & Clements, 2009; Sarama, Clements, Starkey, Klein, & Wakeley, 2008). The main studies are summarized below.

Two experiences with the *Building Blocks* curriculum (Clements & Sarama, 2007/2013) convinced us that we needed a model of scale-up. Early efficacy studies without the supports described previously resulted in large effect sizes (1–2 standard deviations), but this was in a small number of classrooms (Clements & Sarama, 2007). Invited to another state to present the curriculum, follow-up visits revealed spotty implementation, at best, despite our enthusiastic presentations.

After developing the TRIAD model, we conducted an initial evaluation in 25 prekindergarten classrooms serving children at risk for later school failure (about half Head Start and half public preschool programs). We assigned volunteer teachers to either a TRIAD or a control group (Sarama et al., 2008). We attempted to implement most components of the TRIAD model (some, such as planning for the long term, were not possible in this limited scale-up). For example, we began by meeting with administrators and teachers to encourage them to have a shared understanding of the goals of the intervention. We provided incentives in the form of rationales for the intervention and the provision of curriculum materials and especially professional development. Adequate fidelity (e.g., an average of *agree* on a four-point Likert scale from *strongly disagree* to *strongly agree* for all fidelity measures) led to strong gains in mathematics achievement (effect size = .62).

Our largest implementation and evaluation to date involved 1,375 preschoolers in 106 classrooms serving low-resource communities in two states. This implementation was also the most valid and therefore generalizable because the administration of both school systems agreed to the implementation across their districts. Therefore, we could both randomly *select* and randomly *assign* schools. Further, teachers were not volunteers—a common limitation in many such studies. We attempted a complete implementation of the TRIAD-based intervention in these two school districts. This led to similar results, including adequate fidelity and outcomes for children (effect size = .72). Further, the TRIAD group outperformed children in the control group on a measure of oral language, suggesting general educational benefits (Sarama, Lange, Clements, & Wolfe, 2012).

Finally, we have investigated sustainability. Preliminary analyses are positive; for example, fidelity at multiple levels (intervention and implementation) has increased in the 4 years since the end of support from the funded research project. In the following section, we concretize the TRIAD model by describing the guidelines that were instantiated in this last study.

Implementation of the TRIAD Scale-Up Model: An Illustration

Our definition of scale-up and our TRIAD model suggest an incremental implementation of the intervention, including introduction, adoption, initial implementation, improved implementation, and structural accommodations, institutionalization, and diffusion. In this study, the introduction was through negotiations with administrators, although some members of each school district had cooperated on some aspect of the formation and early piloting of the materials.

1. *Involve and promote communication among key groups around a shared vision of the innovation.* In our work, the team that "makes it happen" is organized and led by the researchers. We expect different teams to instantiate the model within districts or other organizations. The implementation team began by meeting with administrators and teachers to encourage them to have a shared understanding of the goals of the intervention. Presentations, brochures, and a video of previous implementations provided both the rationale for the

intervention and the particulars of it to broad audiences of administrators, coordinators, supervisors, teachers, and parents. We highlighted alignment to national, state, and district goals and showed how the intervention met those goals with specific examples.

2. *Promote equity.* We showed how past evaluations of the intervention helped close achievement gaps. We explained the phased adoption (each teacher receives all the benefits, with the schedule determined fairly with public random selection). We discussed allocation of resources with principals and upper administration.

3. *Plan for the long term.* We worked with administrators to plan the incremental implementation (i.e., phased adoption) and to garner support for our use of formative assessment for the intervention (e.g., more coaching is provided immediately for those teachers who request it or show any signs of struggling). We obtained agreement to allow "release time" for not only teachers but also teacher assistants, coordinators, and supervisors to attend the professional development sessions and classrooms to generate long-term commitment to sustaining the intervention past the end of the funded support.

4. *Focus on instructional change that promotes depth of children's thinking, placing learning trajectories at the core.* Meetings of every type were illustrated with examples of children's thinking and learning and of the teacher–child–curriculum interactions that promote development along learning trajectories. The learning trajectories became useful "boundary objects" that helped facilitate coordination and communication among those in varied educational roles. Similarly, they served to align standards, curriculum, and assessment.

5. *Provide professional development that is ongoing, intentional, reflective, goal oriented, focused on content knowledge and children's thinking, grounded in particular curriculum materials, and situated in the classroom and the school.* The first year was a "gentle introduction" to the curriculum with no pressure from assessments, because our previous experience and others' research suggested that teachers often need at least a year of experience before completely and effectively implementing a curriculum (Berends et al., 2001; Clements & Sarama, 2009; Cobb et al., 2003). Thus, teachers participated in 8 full days of professional development during the school day, beginning with 2 consecutive days and about 1 day per month for the rest of the year.

Introductory discussions emphasized the "developmental appropriateness" of the intervention's mathematics education and its importance to the teachers and children, especially in promoting equity. This work focused on the learning trajectories for each mathematical topic, usually as woven into the *Building Blocks* curriculum.

Training addressed each of the three components of the learning trajectories. To understand the goals, teachers learned core mathematics concepts and procedures for each topic. For example, they studied the system of verbal counting based on cycling through 10 digits and the concept of place value (based on content similar to that presented in National Research Council [2009]). To understand the developmental progressions of levels of thinking, teachers studied multiple video segments illustrating each level and discussed the mental "actions on objects" that constitute the defining cognitive components of each level. To understand the instructional tasks, teachers studied the tasks, and they viewed, analyzed, and discussed video of the enactments of these tasks in classrooms.

A central tool to study and connect all three components was the web-based software application Building Blocks Learning Trajectories (BBLT), which provides scalable access to the learning trajectories via descriptions, videos, and commentaries. Two sequential aspects of the learning trajectories—the developmental progressions of children's thinking and connected instruction—are linked to the others. Teachers used the "Test Yourself" feature of the BBLT to evaluate their abilities to diagnose children's level of counting (by identifying the level evinced by children in randomly selected videos). They also used the BBLT's links to view research-based instructional strategies to promote children's progress to the next level.

Teachers worked in small groups to plan how activities from their curriculum might promote, or be modified to promote, learning for the relevant levels. The coaches and project staff joined the teachers in the professional development activities, as well as several days of training on coaching, most of which focused on the unique aspects of mentoring/coaching early mathematics education. Coaches worked with teachers during the year to avoid dilution of the intervention, to promote productive adaptations, and especially to provide teachers with continual feedback and support.

In Year 2, teachers and mentors participated in an additional 5 days of professional development spread throughout the year. They continued to study the learning trajectories, including discussions of how they conducted various curricular activities the previous year. As part of this work, teachers brought case studies of particular situations that occurred in their classrooms to the group to facilitate these discussions; thus, this work included elements of lesson study.

6. *Build expectations and camaraderie to support a consensus around adaptation.* Beyond what has already been described, the curriculum-based assessments also built local leadership by involving each districts' early childhood and mathematics specialists in all our planning meetings and professional development sessions to plan for sustainability. We encouraged them to rely on teachers in our sessions as teacher leaders to support wider implementation after the conclusion of the data collection.

7. *Ensure school leaders are a central force supporting the innovation and provide teachers with continuous feedback that children are learning what they are taught and that this learning is valued.* Similarly, we involved principals in as many meetings and classroom visits as their schedule allowed (only a handful ever attended professional development sessions, although they were invited). We created a "walk-through" version of the classroom fidelity instrument for supervisors and principals. This form helped make the implementation more concrete and visible and helped the administrators assist teachers in developing their skills more effectively. The form also served as a way to communicate our goals to both teachers and administrators.

8. *Give teachers and schools latitude for adaptation, but maintain integrity.* For example, help teachers learn to change surface features (e.g., changing the pictures on a game board to fit a class "theme") without altering the core components of the instruction (Winter & Szulanski, 2001). These are productive adaptations (Brown & Campione, 1996). In contrast, a lethal mutation might simplify the rules of a board game to avoid the need for children to interact with the mathematics.

9. *Provide incentives for all participants, including intrinsic and extrinsic motivators linked to project work.* We provided incentives in the form of rationales for the intervention and the provision of curriculum materials and especially professional development.

10. *Maintain frequent and repeated communication, assessment ("checking up"), and follow-through efforts.* We met with supervisors (both of early childhood education and of mathematics education) and principals on a regular basis. Our staff monitored signs for any source—teachers, coordinators, administrators, and parents—to address any problems or blockages before they became serious.

In summary, evidence supports the effectiveness of this instantiation of the TRIAD model. We are presently working on complex statistical analyses that identify which components of the model were most important. The next section addresses such questions qualitatively. (Institutionalization and diffusion are occurring at the time of this writing; we discuss this briefly and will address this issue in more detail in future reports.)

Lessons Learned

TRIAD was implemented well and had positive effects. What else have we learned?

- *Efforts will be more effective if they are based on scientifically validated early childhood interventions.* Early childhood educators frequently champion the individual teacher's interpretation of and even creation of the educational program. In contrast, this body of work suggests that implementation of systematic, scientifically based practice is more effective than private, idiosyncratic practice (Raudenbush, 2009). This is not to say that teachers should deliver "scripted" curriculum; indeed, such an approach contradicts TRIAD's use of hypothetical learning trajectories in the service of formative assessment and its insistence on adaptation to local conditions (Guideline 8). Rather, focusing on the shared scientific base is a more effective and efficient way to improve education for children. Furthermore, such scientifically grounded shared practice is, somewhat paradoxically, *more* likely to generate creative contributions. Teachers will constitute modifications of effective practice that are already shared, and thus understood and more easily adopted, and that in turn will be accessible to discussion and further scientific investigation. We found it crucial to help teachers differentiate between productive adaptations and lethal mutations (Brown & Campione, 1996) to the intervention. In a similar vein, the introduction of uncoordinated interventions had to be continually monitored for the effects they may have on the intervention. This leads to the next lesson.

- *It is critical that all teachers receive professional development.* Our data suggest that certain factors are sine qua non for an effective scale-up effort. Our evaluations (including mediators of effects, not discussed here due to space constraints) indicate that effectiveness depends on the development of teachers' skills and knowledge (i.e., Guideline 5). A total of 50 to 70 hours of professional development—we provide about 75 hours—is consistent with previous research documenting what is necessary to achieve measurable effectiveness (Yoon, Duncan, Lee, Scarloss, & Shapley, 2007). Situating the materials not just in the classroom but also at each school is important for related but additional reasons. Because it establishes a cultural practice and provides peer support, school-based implementation supports both fidelity and sustainability of a new curriculum (Zaslow et al., 2010) and reaches more than 90% of students in the school (not just one classroom, hoping for "spillover"). Several findings indicate that learning trajectories played a critical role in both teachers' and children's learning (Guideline 4). Finally, respect of teachers by project staff and the resultant acceptance of in-class support from coaches and technology support staff appeared to be as or more important than whole-group professional development sessions. Note that this was especially striking in another later project in which we used coaches employed by the school district. They were not able to schedule meetings regularly and our initial impressions are that they were not as effective. If valid, this has serious ramifications for scaling up coaching-intensive models.

- *Consistent communication with and among all key groups promotes implementation and sustainability.* Project activities would not have been achieved without consistent communication and continued collaboration (Guidelines 1, 7, and 10). We found it necessary to repeatedly provide higher level administrators with updates and reminders of the projects' goals and activities. Similarly, every change in administration had to be monitored and new people introduced to the project and its successes quickly. The early introduction of the project was facilitated by prior awareness of the researchers' work and a strong commitment to achieving the project goals. A challenge is to institutionalize such continuous commitments within each district. Presentations of the evaluations and corresponding discussions of how to maintain the implementation infrastructure within the organization appeared to have positive effects on sustainability. Also significant was the implementation team's consistent efforts to involve midlevel staff, such as supervisors and coordinators, in professional development sessions, classroom visits, and separate meetings. Such involvement created essential advocates for the intervention within the organizations.

- *Fidelity tools are important for research, but also for implementation fidelity.* We quickly saw the need for additional formats for the classroom observation tools. For example, we created an "iFidelity" form for use by coaches and teachers. It simply changed the grammatical structure to say, for example, "*I* began by engaging and focusing children's mathematical thinking" (Clements & Sarama, 2000/2012). More importantly, everyone understood that *no one but the teacher and coach* would see the completed forms. They were for self-directed professional development. Tools such as these and the similar "walk-through" version for supervisors and principals should aid institutionalization of future monitoring of fidelity of implementation at the local site and help ensure that practices are sustained.

- *Maintaining the model for new teachers is challenging.* Having districts maintain the model for new teachers has been a serious challenge. Even districts that collaborated on generating the research that showed the effectiveness of the model and the necessity of it asked us to provide a two-hour workshop to replace the 12 days of professional development.

  We are tracking diffusion within districts, but especially to surrounding districts (Dearing et al., 2006). The availability of teacher trainers and independent coaches was especially crucial at one site, as they were asked by administrators of nearby school districts who had heard about the implementation to build new implementation teams within their districts. Having in-house leaders (e.g., early childhood and mathematics supervisors or coordinators) organize and lead such teams not only is logistically important but also promotes positive spread and shift in ownership (Glennan et al., 2004).

- *Leaders of the implementation team must understand the components and collaborate with others.* Each rigorous evaluation project so far has been led by the developers, and this is a challenge for future research. Fortunately, the just-mentioned diffusion to surrounding districts provides at least anecdotal evidence that this is possible. That is, we know that it appears necessary to have leaders from outside or inside the district who have knowledge of, and a serious commitment to, the implementation. However, in the case of the diffusion we have observed, it was not necessary for these leaders to be *experts* in the scale-up model, curriculum, professional development, and other components. As long as they understood the components and collaborated with others who were experts (such as those who have served as coaches in a previous implementation, in our instance), the implementation was complete and successful. Again, these hypotheses based on informal observations need to be evaluated.

Final Words

The goal of the TRIAD project was to create a theoretically and empirically grounded model of scale-up and to increase knowledge of scaling-up by conducting research that investigates the effectiveness of an instantiation of that model. Evaluations indicate that the TRIAD model shows promise in scaling up at least one educational intervention across a large number of diverse populations and contexts in the early childhood system, avoiding the dilution and pollution that often frustrates interventionists. This supports not only the TRIAD model but also the more general hypothesis that intentional, theoretically and empirically based models can support initial interventions, scale-up, and sustainability.

Still, many challenges remain. First, our research design could not identify which components of the TRIAD model and its instantiation are critical components. Such research would be theoretically and practically useful.

Second, our research supports a major guideline of the TRIAD model, the use of learning trajectories, contributing to the growing research corpus that supports the educational usefulness of learning trajectories, including evaluations of curricula built on them (Clements & Sarama, 2007, 2008a; Sarama et al., 2008), elementary curricula based on related trajectories such as Math Expressions (Agodini & Harris, 2010), studies of successful teaching (Wood & Frid, 2005), and professional development projects (Bright, Bowman, & Vacc, 1997; Clarke et al., 2002; Wright, Martland, Stafford, & Stanger, 2002). This supports the use of such structures in standards, such as the recently released Common Core State Standards (CCSSO/NGA, 2010). Again, however, the specific contribution of the learning trajectories per se needs to be disentangled and identified.

Third, our intent has always been that the TRIAD model should generalize to other subject-matter domains and other age and grade levels. TRIAD's 10 research-based guidelines are consistent with, but more detailed than, generalizations from the empirical corpus (Pellegrino, 2007). However, the model has not been implemented outside of the early childhood age range or in other subject-matter domains. Evaluations of such varied implementations are needed. For example, for certain subject-matter areas such as science and aspects of literacy, learning trajectories appear to be viable and useful. It may be that for other areas of language, or for literature or the social sciences, some but not all of the TRIAD guidelines constitute "core components." Addressing these challenges will make further contributions to the education sciences.

References

Agodini, R., & Harris, B. (2010). An experimental evaluation of four early elementary school math curricula. *Journal of Research on Educational Effectiveness, 3*, 199–253.

Ball, D.L., & Cohen, D.K. (1999). *Instruction, capacity, and improvement.* Philadelphia, PA: Consortium for Policy Research in Education, University of Pennsylvania.

Berends, M., Kirby, S.N., Naftel, S., & McKelvey, C. (2001). *Implementation and performance in New American Schools: Three years into scale-up.* Santa Monica, CA: Rand Education.

Bodilly, S.J. (1998). *Lessons from New American Schools' scale-up phase.* Santa Monica, CA: Rand Education.

Borman, G.D. (2007). Designing field trials of educational interventions. In B. Schneider & S.-K. McDonald (Eds.), *Scale-up in education* (Vol. 2, pp. 41–67). Lanham, MD: Rowman & Littlefield.

Borman, G.D., Hewes, G.M., Overman, L.T., & Brown, S. (2003). Comprehensive school reform and achievement: A meta-analysis. *Review of Educational Research, 73*, 125–230.

Bright, G.W., Bowman, A.H., & Vacc, N.N. (1997). Teachers' frameworks for understanding children's mathematical thinking. In E. Pehkonen (Ed.), *Proceedings of the 21st Conference of the International Group for the Psychology of Mathematics Education* (Vol. 2, pp. 105–112). Lahti, Finland: University of Helsinki.

Brown, A.L., & Campione, J.C. (1996). Psychological theory and the design of innovative learning environments: On procedures, principles, and systems. In R. Glaser (Ed.), *Innovations in learning: New environments for education* (pp. 289–325). Mahwah, NJ: Erlbaum.

Bryk, A.S., Sebring, P.B., Allensworth, E., Suppescu, S., & Easton, J.Q. (2010). *Organizing schools for improvement: Lessons from Chicago.* Chicago, IL: University of Chicago Press.

CCSSO/NGA. (2010). *Common core state standards for mathematics* (Vol. 2010). Washington, DC: Council of Chief State School Officers and the National Governors Association Center for Best Practices.

Claessens, A., Duncan, G.J., & Engel, M. (2007). *Kindergarten skills and fifth-grade achievement: Evidence from the ECLS-K.* Evanston, IL: Northwestern University.

Clarke, D.M., Cheeseman, J., Gervasoni, A., Gronn, D., Horne, M., McDonough, A., ... Rowley, G. (2002, February). *Early Numeracy Research Project final report.* Melbourne, Australia: Department of Education, Employment and Training, the Catholic Education Office, and the Association of Independent Schools Victoria.

Clements, D.H., & Sarama, J. (2000/2012). *Building Blocks fidelity of implementation.* Buffalo, NY, & Denver, CO: University of Buffalo, State University of New York, & University of Denver.

Clements, D.H., & Sarama, J. (2004). Learning trajectories in mathematics education. *Mathematical Thinking and Learning, 6*, 81–89.

Clements, D.H., & Sarama, J. (2007). Effects of a preschool mathematics curriculum: Summative research on the Building Blocks project. *Journal for Research in Mathematics Education, 38*, 136–163.

Clements, D.H., & Sarama, J. (2007/2013). *Building Blocks, volumes 1 and 2*. Columbus, OH: McGraw-Hill Education.

Clements, D.H., & Sarama, J. (2008a). Experimental evaluation of the effects of a research-based preschool mathematics curriculum. *American Educational Research Journal, 45*, 443–494.

Clements, D.H., & Sarama, J. (2008b, March). *Scaling-up interventions: The case of mathematics.* Paper presented at the American Educational Research Association, New York, NY.

Clements, D.H., & Sarama, J. (2009). *Learning and teaching early math: The learning trajectories approach.* New York, NY: Routledge.

Clements, D.H., & Sarama, J. (2011). Early childhood mathematics intervention. *Science, 333*(6045), 968–970.

Clements, D.H., Sarama, J., Spitler, M.E., Lange, A.A., & Wolfe, C.B. (2011). Mathematics learned by young children in an intervention based on learning trajectories: A large-scale cluster randomized trial. *Journal for Research in Mathematics Education, 42*(2), 127–166.

Clements, D.H., Sarama, J., Wolfe, C.B., & Spitler, M.E. (in press). Longitudinal evaluation of a scale-up model for teaching mathematics with trajectories and technologies: Persistence of effects in the third year. *American Educational Research Journal.*

Cobb, P., McClain, K., de Silva, T., & Dean, C. (2003). Situating teachers' instructional practices in the institutional setting of the school and district. *Educational Researcher, 32*(6), 13–24.

Coburn, C.E. (2003). Rethinking scale: Moving beyond numbers to deep and lasting change. *Educational Researcher, 32*(6), 3–12.

Cohen, D.K. (1996). Rewarding teachers for student performance. In S.H. Fuhrman & J.A. O'Day (Eds.), *Rewards and reforms: Creating educational incentives that work* (pp. 61–112). San Francisco, CA: Jossey-Bass.

Copley, J.V. (2004). The early childhood collaborative: A professional development model to communicate and implement the standards. In D.H. Clements, J. Sarama, & A.-M. DiBiase (Eds.), *Engaging young children in mathematics: Standards for early childhood mathematics education* (pp. 401–414). Mahwah, NJ: Erlbaum.

Cuban, L., & Usdan, M. (Eds.). (2003). *Powerful reforms with shallow roots: Improving America's urban schools.* New York, NY: Teachers College.

Darling-Hammond, L. (1996). Restructuring schools for high performance. In S.H. Fuhrman & J.A. O'Day (Eds.), *Rewards and reform: Creating educational incentives that work* (pp. 144–192). San Francisco, CA: Jossey-Bass.

Darling-Hammond, L. (1997). *The right to learn: A blueprint for creating schools that work.* San Francisco, CA: Jossey-Bass.

Dearing, J.W., Maibach, E., & Buller, D.B. (2006). A convergent diffusion and social marketing approach for disseminating proven approaches to physical activity promotion. *American Journal of Preventative Medicine, 10*(4), 1–12.

Doig, B., McCrae, B., & Rowe, K. (2003). *A good start to numeracy: Effective numeracy strategies from research and practice in early childhood.* Canberra, Australia: Australian Council for Educational Research.

Elmore, R.F. (1996a). Getting to scale with good educational practices. *Harvard Educational Review, 66*, 1–25.

Elmore, R.F. (1996b). Getting to scale with good educational practices. In S.H. Fuhrman & J.A. O'Day (Eds.), *Rewards and reform: Creating educational incentives that work* (pp. 294–329). San Francisco, CA: Jossey-Bass.

Ferguson, R.F. (1991). Paying for publication education: New evidence on how and why money matters. *Harvard Journal on Legislation, 28*(2), 465–498.

Foorman, B.R., Santi, K.L., & Berger, L. (2007). Scaling assessment-driven instruction using the Internet and handheld computers. In B. Schneider & S.-K. McDonald (Eds.), *Scale-up in education* (Vol. 2, pp. 69–89). Lanham, MD: Rowman & Littlefield.

Fullan, M.G. (1992). *Successful school improvement.* Philadelphia, PA: Open University Press.

Fullan, M.G. (2000). The return of large-scale reform. *Journal of Educational Change, 1,* 5–28.

Glennan, T.K., Jr., Bodilly, S.J., Galegher, J.R., & Kerr, K.A. (Eds.). (2004). *Expanding the reach of education reforms: Perspectives from leaders in the scale-up of educational interventions.* Santa Monica, CA: Rand.

Greenhalgh, T., Robert, G., MacFarlane, F., Bate, P., & Kyriakidou, O. (2004). Diffusion of innovations in service organizations: Systematic review and recommendations. *Milbank Quarterly, 82*(4), 581–629.

Guskey, T.R. (Ed.). (2000). *Evaluating professional development.* Thousand Oaks, CA: Corwin Press.

Hall, G.E., & Hord, S.M. (2001). *Implementing change: Patterns, principles, and potholes.* Boston, MA: Allyn and Bacon.

Halpern, R. (2004). Parent support and education: Past history, future prospects. *Applied Research in Child Development, 6,* 1; 4–11.

Heck, D.J., Weiss, I.R., Boyd, S., & Howard, M. (2002, April). *Lessons learned about planning and implementing statewide systemic initiatives in mathematics and science education.* Presentation at the annual meeting of the American Educational Research Association, New Orleans, LA. Retrieved from http://www.horizon-research.com/presentations/2002/ssi_aera2002.pdf

Huberman, M. (1992). Critical introduction. In M.G. Fullan (Ed.), *Successful school improvement* (pp. 1–20). Philadelphia, PA: Open University Press.

International Reading Association and National Association for the Education of Young Children. (2000). Joint position statement on learning to read and write: Developmentally appropriate practices for young children. Reprinted in S. Neuman, C. Copple, & S. Bredekamp (Eds.), *Learning to read and write: Developmentally appropriate practices for young children.* Washington, DC: National Association for the Education of Young Children.

Kaser, J.S., Bourexis, P.S., Loucks-Horsley, S., & Raizen, S.A. (1999). *Enhancing program quality in science and mathematics.* Thousand Oaks, CA: Corwin Press.

Klingner, J.K., Ahwee, S., Pilonieta, P., & Menendez, R. (2003). Barriers and facilitators in scaling up research-based practices. *Exceptional Children, 69,* 411–429.

McGill-Franzen, A. (2010). The National Early Literacy Panel Report: Summary, commentary, and reflections on policies and practices to improve children's early literacy. *Educational Researcher, 39*(4), 275–278.

National Mathematics Advisory Panel. (2008). *Foundations for success: The final report of the National Mathematics Advisory Panel.* Washington, DC: U.S. Department of Education, Office of Planning, Evaluation, and Policy Development.

National Research Council. (2001). *Eager to learn: Educating our preschoolers.* Washington, DC: National Academy Press.

National Research Council. (2007). *Taking science to school: Learning and teaching science in grades K–8.* Washington, DC: National Academies Press.

National Research Council. (2009). *Mathematics learning in early childhood: Paths toward excellence and equity.* Washington, DC: National Academies Press.

Pellegrino, J.W. (2007). From early reading to high school mathematics: Matching case studies of four educational innovations against principles for effective scale-up. In B. Schneider & S.-K. McDonald (Eds.), *Scale-up in education* (Vol. 2, pp. 131–139). Lanham, MD: Rowman & Littlefield.

Ramey, C.T., & Ramey, S.L. (1998). Early intervention and early experience. *American Psychologist, 53,* 109–120.

Raudenbush, S.W. (2008). Advancing educational policy by advancing research on instruction. *American Educational Research Journal, 45,* 206–230.

Raudenbush, S.W. (2009). The *Brown* legacy and the O'Connor challenge: Transforming schools in the images of children's potential. *Educational Researcher, 38*(3), 169–180.

Rogers, E.M. (2003). *Diffusion of innovations* (5th ed.). New York: Free Press.

Sarama, J. (2002). Listening to teachers: Planning for professional development. *Teaching Children Mathematics, 9,* 36–39.

Sarama, J., & Clements, D.H. (2009, April). *Scaling up successful interventions: Multidisciplinary perspectives.* Paper presented at the American Educational Research Association, San Diego, CA.

Sarama, J., Clements, D.H., & Henry, J.J. (1998). Network of influences in an implementation of a mathematics curriculum innovation. *International Journal of Computers for Mathematical Learning, 3*, 113–148.

Sarama, J., Clements, D.H., Starkey, P., Klein, A., & Wakeley, A. (2008). Scaling up the implementation of a pre-kindergarten mathematics curriculum: Teaching for understanding with trajectories and technologies. *Journal of Research on Educational Effectiveness, 1*, 89–119.

Sarama, J., Clements, D.H., Wolfe, C.B., & Spitler, M.E. (2012). Longitudinal evaluation of a scale-up model for teaching mathematics with trajectories and technologies. *Journal of Research on Educational Effectiveness, 5*(2), 105–135.

Sarama, J., & DiBiase, A.-M. (2004). The professional development challenge in preschool mathematics. In D.H. Clements, J. Sarama, & A.-M. DiBiase (Eds.), *Engaging young children in mathematics: Standards for early childhood mathematics education* (pp. 415–446). Mahwah, NJ: Erlbaum.

Sarama, J., Lange, A., Clements, D.H., & Wolfe, C.B. (2012). The impacts of an early mathematics curriculum on emerging literacy and language. *Early Childhood Research Quarterly, 27*, 489–502.

Schoen, H.L., Cebulla, K.J., Finn, K.F., & Fi, C. (2003). Teacher variables that relate to student achievement when using a standards-based curriculum. *Journal for Research in Mathematics Education, 34*(3), 228–259.

Showers, B., Joyce, B., & Bennett, B. (1987). Synthesis of research on staff development: A framework for future study and a state-of-the-art analysis. *Educational Leadership, 45*(3), 77–87.

Siegler, R.S. (1993). Adaptive and non-adaptive characteristics of low income children's strategy use. In L.A. Penner, G.M. Batsche, H.M. Knoff, & D.L. Nelson (Eds.), *Contributions of psychology to science and mathematics education* (pp. 341–366). Washington, DC: American Psychological Association.

Snipes, J., Doolittle, F., & Herlihy, C. (2002). *Foundations for success: Case studies of how urban school systems improve student achievement.* Washington, DC: Council of the Great City Schools.

Sowder, J.T. (2007). The mathematical education and development of teachers. In F.K. Lester, Jr. (Ed.), *Second handbook of research on mathematics teaching and learning* (Vol. 1, pp. 157–223). New York, NY: Information Age.

Spillane, J. (2000). Cognition and policy implementation: District policy-makers and the reform of mathematics education. *Cognition and Instruction, 18*, 141–179.

Starkey, P., Klein, A., Chang, I., Qi, D., Lijuan, P., & Yang, Z. (1999, April). *Environmental supports for young children's mathematical development in China and the United States.* Paper presented at the Society for Research in Child Development, Albuquerque, NM.

Stigler, J.W., Lee, S.-Y., & Stevenson, H.W. (1990). *Mathematical knowledge of Japanese, Chinese, and American elementary school children.* Reston, VA: National Council of Teaching of Mathematics.

Thomson, S., Rowe, K., Underwood, C., & Peck, R. (2005). *Numeracy in the early years: Project Good Start.* Camberwell, Victoria, Australia: Australian Council for Educational Research.

Winter, S.G., & Szulanski, G. (2001). Replication as strategy. *Organization Science, 12*, 730–743.

Wood, K., & Frid, S. (2005). Early childhood numeracy in a multiage setting. *Mathematics Education Research Journal, 16*(3), 80–99.

Wright, R.J., Martland, J., Stafford, A.K., & Stanger, G. (2002). *Teaching number: Advancing children's skills and strategies.* London, England: Paul Chapman/Sage.

Yoon, K.S., Duncan, T., Lee, S.W.-Y., Scarloss, B., & Shapley, K.L. (2007). *Reviewing the evidence on how teacher professional development affects student achievement* (Issues & Answers Report, REL 2007-No. 033). Washington, DC: U.S. Department of Education, Institute of Education Sciences, National Center for Education Evaluation and Regional Assistance, Regional Educational Laboratory Southwest.

Yuzawa, M., Bart, W.M., Kinne, L.J., Sukemune, S., & Kataoka, M. (1999). The effects of "origami" practice on size comparison strategy among young Japanese and American children. *Journal of Research in Childhood Education, 13*(2), 133–143.

Zaslow, M., Tout, K., Halle, T.G., Vick, J., & Lavelle, B. (2010). *Towards the identification of features of effective professional development for early childhood educators: A review of the literature.* Washington, DC: U.S. Department of Education. Retrieved from http://www2.ed.gov/rschstat/eval/professional-development/literature-review.pdf

Improving Implementation of the Nurse–Family Partnership in the Process of Going to Scale

Peggy Hill and David Olds

This chapter describes the scientific process and business requirements of moving from development of an effective innovation to implementation of that innovation at a significant scale with high quality, thus producing improved health and early childhood development at a scale that matters. This complex process is not entirely linear, but is methodical, intentional, and iterative, informed by both experiential and empirical data. It is fostered by a constant awareness of the likelihood—given the history of failed attempts to take research-based programs successfully to scale—that initial assumptions will be wrong or inadequately informed by current contextual realities and that rapid course corrections will be critical.

One must have data on a robust set of indicators tied closely to core elements of the model to provide feedback along the way, letting program staff know whether they are achieving good implementation or not. Even with this objective feedback, taking a program to scale is a bit of an art form. At some point, even models that are implemented with fidelity may show signs of slippage from the desired level of predicted outcomes. When that happens, the program's underlying theory of change and core intervention principles become a compass for discerning when closer adherence to the original model will produce better outcomes, or if something must be adapted to the new context in order for practitioners to achieve the best outcomes possible. Success depends on this ability to achieve fidelity to the core principles and critical features of the well tested model and to adapt intelligently.

The process of using research-based programs to impact health and social outcomes at scale begins with rigorous research to develop an effective innovation that warrants public investment. We have taken the position that only when a practice, program, process, or policy has been demonstrated to have the capability to improve health and well-being is the effort warranted to take it to greater scale. Once one knows that positive impacts are possible, the process of taking an innovation to scale can begin—with an entirely new set of attendant challenges. The following challenges are associated with helping people completely unfamiliar with the evidence-based innovation to conduct it skillfully and achieve sustained effectiveness:

1. Creating an initial set of implementation supports for installation in new settings, including the capacity to monitor and steadily address implementation challenges in partnership with local leaders and practitioners

2. Developing consultation methods to guide new practitioners and their organizations toward sustained high-quality implementation, with the expectation and resources necessary for those consultants with expertise in conducting the model program to remain involved and in relationship with local implementing agencies for the time necessary to establish sustainability

3. Building commitment at multiple levels in an implementing agency to rely on data to monitor program quality and outcomes and to use those data for continuous quality improvement

4. Building purveyor, intermediary agency, and often government capacity to deliver both direct services and implementation supports at scale

5. Conducting ongoing adaptation and improvement of the evidence-based innovation itself and its supports for implementation

Developing a Preventive Intervention that Warrants Implementation at Scale

For more than 3 decades, David Olds and his research colleagues at Cornell University, the University of Rochester, and the University of Colorado developed, tested, and refined a program of prenatal and infancy home visiting by nurses known as the Nurse–Family Partnership (NFP). Their work is founded on four principles: 1) develop and define the program well before testing it; 2) test it thoroughly before offering it for public investment, making sure it is not only efficacious but can also produce results of public health and social importance reliably in settings that will be typical when replicated at greater scale; 3) develop the resources and consultative supports necessary to enable others to replicate the program carefully; and 4) improve it continuously. This approach has contributed to the NFP's recognition as meeting the Coalition for Evidence-Based Policy's "Top Tier" of evidence (Coalition for Evidence-Based Policy, 2010), as the program with the strongest evidence that it prevents child abuse and neglect (MacMillan et al., 2009), and as a program that produces significant economic return on investment (Aos, Lieb, Mayfield, Miller, & Pennucci, 2004).

Olds's team carefully developed the NFP before testing it and offering it for public investment. The formulation of the intervention itself was guided by epidemiology, theories of attachment and behavioral change, and an ecological model of influences on human development. NFP nurses have three major goals: 1) improving pregnancy outcomes by helping women focus on prenatal health (including reducing smoking and obtaining prompt treatment for obstetric complications), 2) strengthening children's subsequent health and development by helping parents provide competent care of their infants and toddlers, and 3) increasing parents' economic self-sufficiency by helping them develop a vision for their future and make decisions about staying in school, finding work, and planning future pregnancies that are consistent with their aspirations. Because the intervention is home based and requires a great deal of autonomous clinical practice judgment, the NFP selects registered nurses as home visitors, with a strong preference for those with baccalaureate preparation and relevant experience with low-income populations, cultural diversity, and community health, maternal and child health, or public health practice.

Local agencies implement the program with 18 well-defined model elements, and nurse home visitors follow detailed visit-by-visit guidelines that they adapt to parents' needs and interests. Using strategies that capitalize on parents' intrinsic motivation to protect themselves and their children, nurses join with parents to improve their prenatal health, care of their children, and economic self-sufficiency. They engage parents in establishing a schedule of visits every 1 to 2 weeks, beginning as early in pregnancy as possible and continuing through the child's second birthday. During those visits, nurses engage the mothers and other family members in activities and dialogue expressly designed to foster learning, skill development, and behavioral change related to the program's three major goals.

The NFP focuses on low-income women bearing their first child for three reasons. First, maternal and child health problems and educational disparities are greater among poor families living in concentrated social disadvantage. Second, women bearing first children (first children account for about 40% of the births in the United States) have a natural sense of vulnerability. This vulnerability increases their willingness to engage in this program, in part because it is delivered by nurses who can address with authority their concerns about pregnancy, labor, delivery, and care of fragile newborns. And third, the program is designed to achieve many of its most long-lasting effects by helping parents clarify their aspirations for themselves and their children. These effects result in parents choosing to delay future pregnancies until they are positioned to assume responsibility for another child, with benefits likely carrying over to subsequent children. Today, the program is estimated to cost $5,000 per year per participant over approximately a 2.4-year period.

The first trial, in Elmira, New York, was conducted through a local nonprofit organization in collaboration with the local health department, obstetricians, and pediatricians. Olds and the nurses hired for the program developed the detailed outline that covered content and clinical methods for various stages of the program, grounding that work in theories of attachment, human ecology, and self-efficacy. Given that the program itself was overseen by Dr. Olds, who worked with local nurses to develop and implement it, it was closer to an *efficacy* trial—that is, a study in which the conditions for implementation of the intervention are particularly favorable because factors like organizational context are highly supportive and staff members are highly motivated.

The second trial was conducted through the Memphis–Shelby County (Tennessee) Health Department. By that time, Harriet Kitzman, a nurse coinvestigator, had used the original program outline to transform the materials for the prenatal and infancy phases into detailed visit-by-visit guidelines. Given that the trial registered nearly the entire population of low-income women who met the eligibility criteria and were bearing first children, and that the program was conducted in a local health department without intensive investigator involvement, this study came closer to an *effectiveness* trial—a trial conducted under real-life conditions where, for example, organizational factors and staffing are representative of typical settings.

The third trial examined the relative impact of the NFP when delivered by nurses, compared to paraprofessional home visitors selected because they shared many of the social characteristics of the families they served. The program served the entire Denver metropolitan area. Nurses Pilar Baca and Ruth O'Brien, who were involved in conducting the Denver trial, added visit-by-visit guidelines for the toddler phase of the study. The Denver trial fell in between the Elmira and Memphis trials in its placement on the efficacy–effectiveness continuum, given that the nurses worked with the multiplicity of health care providers in the Denver area in delivering the program.

Over each of the trials, the specific content of the program was updated to reflect the most recent standards of practice in maternal and child health. The methods of supporting behavioral change with self-efficacy theory and parents' care of their children using attachment-theory–based interventions were also upgraded.

Olds held off on offering the program for public investment until 1996. The reasons for that caution included 1) his commitment to first determine if the positive results would replicate with different populations, living in different contexts; and 2) his desire to be sure the program would produce enduring impacts. Olds also knew that the process of replicating the research trials in new locations would form an initial base of experience in assisting new teams of nurses in new community settings to deliver the program properly.

By 1996, however, it was clear that the Elmira program was producing long-term positive effects on the rates of state-verified cases of child abuse and neglect through children age 15 (a 48% reduction) and that it was altering the life-course trajectories of these low-income mothers, bringing reductions in the rates of subsequent pregnancies, mothers' use of welfare, and involvement with the criminal justice system (Olds et al., 1997). The program also was producing effects on the histories of arrests among children born to mothers who were unmarried and from low-income families at registration (Olds et al., 1998).

In the Memphis trial, the program was producing replicated positive impacts on childhood injuries, rates of closely spaced subsequent births, and the early language development of children born to mothers with limited psychological resources (Kitzman et al., 1997). While the results of the Denver trial were not yet in (but would eventually replicate the effects found in earlier trials with nurses), the program guidelines had been developed in sufficient detail that Olds and his team decided to wade into the process of community-based replication of the NFP (Olds, Hill, & O'Brien, 2003).

Preparing to Support Installation in Community Settings

Once the NFP model was thoroughly defined, tested, and shown to be effective for the populations most likely to be enrolled at scale, the shift from conducting research to supporting implementation of the program in new communities began in earnest. As is typical in many university settings, resources for taking research into practice were slim, with few institutional incentives. Nevertheless, Olds enjoyed the significant benefit of administrative support from within both the

School of Medicine and the School of Nursing where he was on faculty, and he was given the freedom to seek funding for this next phase of work.

Olds's team knew that in moving the program to community settings, it would be crucial to create an implementation system that would help the program develop deep roots in local communities and would include an information system that would allow assessments of performance, based upon implementation and outcome benchmarks from the trials. The Denver-based research team designed a skeletal set of implementation supports that included the following:

1. A more comprehensive and detailed set of home visit guidelines matched to each developmental phase of the model (prenatal visits, infancy, toddlerhood)

2. A planning process that included orientation to the model and its requirements for the leaders in organizations wanting to host the program and guidance to establish adequate and sustainable financing

3. A rudimentary program start-up guide, including a detailed program budget and narrative that specified exactly what new program administrators had to procure to run the program properly

4. An education program for new nurse home visitors and their supervisors to learn the unique practice skills inherent to the relationship-based, strengths-focused intervention

5. Job descriptions for key positions

6. A data collection and reporting system that would enable evaluation of how well key features of the model were being implemented and whether or not early indicators of anticipated program effects were positive. The system incorporated descriptive data on the population enrolled to make sure it was consistent with the aim to enroll those most likely to benefit (primiparous women living in poverty); elements of program implementation such as visit frequency, duration, and content; critical aspects of program management such as the frequency of reflective supervision; and selected indicators of desired outcomes that could be observed during the course of the intervention such as women's use of tobacco and alcohol during pregnancy, birthweight, measures of maternal depression, and results of child development screenings.

From the initial pilot sites where the program was replicated in community settings nationally, some big lessons were quickly learned through attentive trial and error, with helpful input and feedback from local partners. The first several years were committed to near constant refinement and revision of those initial resources and processes. During these formative years, state and local partners urged the leadership of the program replication effort to address more of the practical aspects of start-up (e.g., space requirements, purchasing supplies and equipment, charting practices, recommended practices for interviewing candidates for key positions, techniques for getting a good referral system in place) and not just issues related to learning to apply the theoretical framework of the preventive intervention with families. Reports from the implementation data system identified more pervasive challenges with implementation that could then be addressed by systematically strengthening implementation supports.

From this early experience, a clearer and more thorough view of what must happen to successfully move the NFP to greater scale nationally was developed. One of the most important shifts in perspective came with the realization that organizational structure and culture, policy, and financing could deeply influence the way nurses practiced with families. The focus of most of the early implementation support was on developing and providing the guidance and resources new nurse home visitors would need to learn to practice the NFP with families. Appreciation of the ecology of a successful NFP program soon grew to parallel the program leaders' knowledge of the ecology of human development.

Variables like the expectations of a nurse supervisor's upper-level administrators for staff coverage of other agency responsibilities, union rules governing the workday, a human resources system's rules for hiring, the reputation of an implementing agency in the larger community, and the rules that come with a program's funding streams all became familiar targets for assessment of contextual factors that could either promote or severely undermine program implementation and outcomes. In addition, program leaders learned that while an implementing agency might successfully perform on most or all indicators of fidelity to the structural aspects of the program model (reaching the correct population, enrolling women at the right gestational age in pregnancy, visit frequency and duration, etc.), outcomes could suffer if the way nurses actually interacted with families did not conform with the underlying philosophy of the model and its deeply respectful, client-centered approach to supporting behavioral change.

It became clear just how crucial it was for the program to align its goals, behavioral objectives, and methods for bringing about behavioral change (see Figure 10.1). This awareness led to additional recommendations for team and supervisory processes (such as reflective supervision and case conferencing) to mirror and reinforce those processes nurses are asked to use in working with their clients. In addition, guidance to implementing agency administrators was refined to outline procedures and recommended structures within organizations and communities to support effective delivery of the program. This guidance included making sure that organizational leaders at all functional levels fully embraced the NFP and supported the nurses' work in practical ways and that leaders and organizations outside the implementing agency understood and endorsed allocation of community resources to make the program work well. The national leadership also improved its approach to educating NFP nurses in the core practices of the model and enhanced its web-based information system so that it produced useful, real-time reports on program implementation and outcome benchmarks to be used as a foundation for continuous quality improvement.

With these resources in place, program leaders gained greater confidence that the actual services delivered would be in alignment with the goals and objectives of the program and strengths-based methods for achieving them. With actual services in greater alignment with the underlying model, the program can be expected to produce improvements in maternal and child health that correspond to those achieved in the trials. Variations in communities, organizations, visitors, and families are likely to affect implementation and outcomes, but attentiveness to these influences on the program and its effects become important sources of information to improve the NFP and its implementation over time.

Conceptual framework for NFP home visiting program

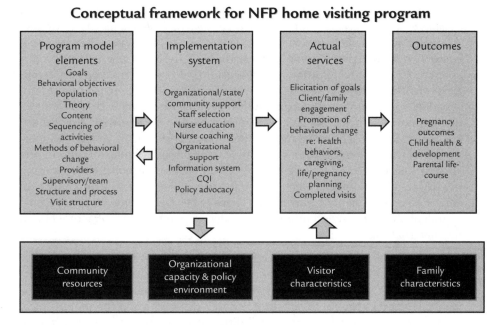

Figure 10.1. Determinants of successful program implementation.

The program quality data system and its use by both staff at the NFP National Service Office (NSO, the national nonprofit created in 2003 to support national program implementation) and local program supervisors remain critical components of an integrated and compensatory system of implementation supports. Using reports based on data gathered from every supervisor and every nurse home visitor on every home visit enables regionally based NFP nurse consultants to recognize and address implementation challenges in their consultation with nursing team supervisors.

Feedback from the field based on data system reports also shapes the service improvement priorities of the NSO. When patterns of concern are observed in the data from many different implementing agencies, changes can be planned in the guidance provided to new agencies, the education required for all new NFP home visitors and supervisors, and the focus of ongoing consultation with supervisors and higher level administrators in established local programs.

A few examples of patterns NFP was able to address as a result of using the data for quality improvement are described below.

- *Identified challenge: Enrolling women later in pregnancy than was ideal for intervention to have time to produce health improvement.* Recognizing that too many local agencies were challenged to get women referred early in their pregnancies and to follow through quickly on those referrals led NSO staff to strengthen preimplementation community and organizational readiness assessment and referral system development. It also led to enhanced coaching of new NFP supervisors to help them and their nurse home visitors more comfortably communicate the program's value to potential referral sources earlier in their tenure.

- *Identified challenge: Nurse home visitors spending excessive visit time on health-related domains of family functioning and not enough on maternal role and life course development.* NFP implementers realized that, depending on the type of nursing new home visitors did prior to their hire into the NFP, the comprehensive approach of the program model to promoting health and well-being could be very familiar or quite new. Nurses new to the more comprehensive approach might have a tendency to revert to a focus on physical health as the domain of family functioning in which the nurse felt most comfortable and experienced. This pattern led NSO staff to coach supervisors to reference reports during reflective supervision showing how much time each nurse spent on each domain of functioning and to consider nurses' experience and educational background when shaping professional development plans. It also led to a greater focus during NFP core education on experiential learning exercises to help new home visitors become confident using the intervention tools related to parent–infant attachment and the maternal role.

- *Identified challenge: Supervisors not conducting weekly one-on-one reflective supervision or timely case consultation sessions.* This led NSO staff to strengthen orientation to the model for administrators so they understood what made the frequency and nature of supervision in NFP different from the more typical administrative supervisory responsibilities to which they were accustomed. Too often, supervisors indicated they wanted to provide weekly reflective supervision time, but their higher level administrators saw that time commitment as a luxury and a source of inefficiency. The NSO also added specificity to recruitment guidance for the role of NFP nurse supervisor and intensified training on reflective supervision for new supervisors. Perhaps the most significant investment in meeting this critical challenge was strongly encouraging new implementing agencies to assign supervisors to NFP full-time rather than part-time, even if they were not immediately able to hire a full team of eight nurse home visitors (the maximum a full-time NFP supervisor can support).

Achieving Sustained Effectiveness

During periods of time when innovative programs are expanding rapidly, the temptation is strong to focus all purveyor resources on community planning and new implementing agency start-up. While installation of a new program and its first few years of operation are an important time for "getting it right" and laying the foundation for longer-term strong performance, the job of assuring that a program produces sustained outcomes for participants isn't done when the first cohort of staff becomes competent and confident with the practice. There are some local nursing teams who continually improve with time; they tend to have strong and committed agency leadership, a community that knows about and values the program, sustainable funding, and nursing staff who are constantly motivated to learn and improve. However, there are also fairly common developmental challenges to high-quality implementation that tend to appear only after those first vulnerable and perhaps most closely watched years are over. In our experience, those emergent challenges fall into five broad categories:

1. Difficulties handling worker turnover

2. Shifts in the nature of the population served

3. Changes in the organization hosting the program

4. Changes in program financing or the emergence of related political pressures

5. Gradual and sometimes subtle compromises in the conduct of the program that can affect the experience of program participants and the program's effectiveness

Most of these challenges are not readily identified through monitoring of program quality data, though changes in the data may indicate that one or more are affecting program performance. This is why an attitude of curiosity and open-minded inquiry must be part of the continuous improvement process and of ongoing consultation with agency leaders.

Nurse Home Visitor Turnover

Evidence from the NFP's information system has indicated that client dropout is associated with the client's nurse leaving. The relationship disruption was difficult for clients to handle, and the effort to establish a relationship with a new nurse was an obstacle to continued participation. Implementing agencies that became successful handling these relationship transitions would sometimes introduce clients to multiple members of the nursing team over time, so that even when another nurse might need to step in, she or he was already known to the family. Joint visits by the departing nurse and a nurse new to the client during a period of time in advance of the initial home visitor's departure were also successful. Another useful technique was to allow clients to "step out" for a time and reenter the program later in response to invitations to continue participation.

Shifts in the Nature of the Population Served

A number of factors can produce shifts in who actually enrolls in the NFP at the local level. Immigration patterns, shifts in the zip codes or neighborhoods that particular funders want prioritized, or changes in the availability of other programs may result in referral agents directing even higher risk pregnant women into the NFP. Program administrators and supervisors have to remain aware and responsive to these changes to support nurse home visitors as they adapt to serving new cultural or linguistic groups or higher levels of acuity in the medical or social needs of the women and families they serve. Any failure of the organization hosting the NFP to provide adequate resources for adjusting well can result in higher levels of burnout among home visitors or challenges with client retention.

Changes in the Organization Hosting the Program

Major shifts in the mission of a host organization or changes at the highest levels of leadership can dramatically affect program delivery and sustainability. Both types of change can either help or hinder, but if an organization's new mission or a new leader's priorities are inconsistent with the focus or requirements of an evidence-based innovation, then sustainability may be threatened. Preparing midlevel administrators to "manage up" through positive, sensitive communication with a new leader and applying supportive pressure from the wider community can counteract these risks, but the changes should be anticipated as far in advance as possible to deploy appropriate strategies, which can range from smart internal communications to wholesale relocation of a program to a more appropriate host agency in the community.

Changes in Program Financing or the Policy Environment

One of the most common sources of change in the context of program operation is a shift in funding from start-up support to long-term funding that will sustain the program over time. If several years go by while multiyear grants or county line items support the program consistently, it is easy for program managers and administrators to neglect the political and outreach work necessary to cultivate new funding opportunities and groom political support. Election years pass, and the promises made by those on the campaign trail may fade with competing priorities. New county officials or state legislators take office, and new advocates must be identified to keep public funding secure for any program.

When frontline staff become insecure about program funding, they are more likely to leave or to practice under conditions of lower morale that affect their relationships with families. Further, under duress an agency may accept funding from a source with requirements that are poorly aligned with the model's core elements or that distract home visitors from what should be their main focus. Examples include pressure to serve more families than the model's caseload limits allow or to produce results with families that are of interest to a funder but are not among the program's main goals. Upon inquiry, a consultant may begin to hear comments from supervisors or home visitors about additional data collection required by a funder that is irrelevant to clients' interests or needs or about pressure from agency administrators to "make it work" even though the fit between the funding and the program model is poor.

Compromise

Nurse home visitors and their supervisors are human. They get tired, and they may seek efficiencies in the way they do their work that save time but sacrifice comprehensiveness. They may neglect learning certain features of the program model because of their confidence in practices learned earlier in their careers that seem more expedient. They may sacrifice reflective supervision time in the face of time-management challenges while building full caseloads for the first time. Supervisors may be tempted not to pursue difficult-to-reach families who are most likely to benefit from the program when there is a waiting list of mothers who want to enroll. With each of these compromises, program effectiveness can be lost.

The need to provide refresher courses on fundamental aspects of the intervention, incentives and recognition for particularly good work, reminders to home visitors that the hardest-to-serve families are generally those who benefit most in the long run, and time as a team to learn together and continue growing are all examples of methods team leaders need to use to keep their staff focused, supported, energized, and excelling. Administrators may need to be reminded that investing in the mental health and sustained performance of frontline staff may well be the most important investment they can make in keeping their program producing the outcomes that their funders are paying for.

Even the strongest systems for implementing evidence-based innovations need to make deep adjustments from time to time in order to remain effective. Inevitably, some pattern will emerge that small-scale adaptation is insufficient to address. In these cases, the solutions may require new programs of research or more involved policy advocacy to address deeper, systemic barriers to effectiveness. For the NFP, two of those emerging issues were 1) widespread challenges with retaining clients in the program for its entire duration and 2) the moderating effect of domestic violence on the program's reduction of child abuse and neglect.

As a result of these observations, we have undertaken a program of research focused on understanding the characteristics of participants, nurses, and sites associated with participant retention and have used this information to develop and test innovations in the program model that show considerable promise in increasing retention and rates of completed home visits. Starting with a mixed-methods study of participant retention, followed by a 15-site quasi-experimental study of an intervention designed to increase retention and then a large-scale 26-site cluster randomized controlled trial, we have transformed the way nurses are guided in the delivery of the program. The core of this innovation emphasizes the importance of adapting the NFP to the expressed needs of the clients. While adaptation has been a key ingredient in the program model since its beginning, the tested innovation provided greater operationalization of the adaptation process.

We also are in the midst of testing an innovation in the program model to help nurses more effectively address intimate partner violence (IPV) when they encounter it during their visits. This intervention has gone through a series of studies, including a qualitative study of the experience of IPV by NFP families, NFP nurses' experience serving families with IPV, and community stakeholders' experience with IPV; a formative pilot study of an intervention informed by the qualitative study; and a cluster randomized controlled trial.

Creating a Learning Organization to Support Implementation at Scale

In the late 1990s, funding from the U.S. Department of Justice's Weed and Seed Initiative and commitments from several states and local communities that were early adopters of the NFP led to a dramatic spike in demand for program implementation support services. These services were still being provided by research staff led by David Olds at the Prevention Research Center for Family and Child Health, and their ability to meet demand was limited. Unwilling to compromise on either the center's research agenda or the quality of support for community-based program implementation, Dr. Olds and his colleagues sought dedicated funding from several major foundations to establish greater capacity for the work of taking NFP to scale nationally. The Robert Wood Johnson Foundation, the Doris Duke Charitable Foundation, and the Colorado Trust were all instrumental in making funding commitments to the University of Colorado to support making the NFP more widely available.

In 2002, the NFP leadership partnered with the Edna McConnell Clark Foundation to develop a business plan and build capacity to support implementation of the NFP at greater scale. The aim of the business plan was to assure fiscal sustainability of the organization leading national program expansion and assuring quality. The plan suggested that at sufficient scale, fees charged for implementation support services to ensure good program outcomes would be sufficient to finance the organization's services for the long term. Such fees would amount to less than 3% of each implementing agency's total budget, yet would allow the national organization leading NFP's expansion to become almost entirely self-sufficient.

The result of this business plan was creation in 2003 of the NFP National Service Office, an independent nonprofit organization that could take the program to significantly greater national scale. The NSO was affiliated with the university through a memorandum of understanding that gave it a perpetual, royalty-free, exclusive license to use the university's NFP intellectual property to replicate the program nationally. The university retained control over the parameters of the program model. A national board of directors was formed (which did not include the program's founder, Dr. Olds) and most of the staff involved with NFP implementation activities moved to the NSO's employment.

As an organization, the NSO was designed to be disciplined and focused on using data to monitor and improve local program quality; flexible and responsive to the needs of state and local implementation partners; and sufficiently agile to quickly identify and adapt to new challenges. Among the most important new capabilities established in the organization were communications, government relations, and policy advocacy to work in states and at the federal level to create sustainable financing for local community NFP programs that would be well aligned with the core model elements and therefore capable of financing attainment of desired outcomes.

In 2006, the NFP built a financial model that incorporated the costs of executing a growth strategy and providing implementation support. The model indicated that approximately 10 years and $52 million would be required to support the NSO to the scale that would enable self-sufficiency. With significant help from the Edna McConnell Clark Foundation, the NFP launched a $50 million growth capital campaign in 2007, completing it in 14 months, with six other national foundations joining the Edna McConnell Clark Foundation: the Robert Wood Johnson Foundation (which had supported Olds's research for many years), Kellogg Foundation, Kresge Foundation, Bill and Melinda Gates Foundation, Picower Family Foundation, and Robertson Foundation.

What It Takes to Succeed: Resources and Commitments at Multiple Levels

One of the strongest lessons learned from the first 15 years of putting implementation science to work in practice is that a complex set of systems has to align well to produce and sustain program effectiveness. The start is a well-articulated program or practice with strong evidence of effectiveness. From there, someone must design and be able to provide an integrated and compensatory system of essential implementation supports to others who will become the next "generation" of program operational leaders.

Following those two critical investments of intellectual and financial capital, there is a series of alignments in the world of practice that have to be in place or be put in place. If misalignment among these systems occurs, a certain degree of torque is placed on practice, for which compensatory efforts may or may not be sufficient once the source is identified and understood.

First, there must be a good match between the *community* of people to be served and the evidence-based program itself. Leaders within the preexisting *service system* to which an evidence-based program relates should agree that introduction of the program is important and valuable, and they must be willing to adjust their own practices and behavior in whatever way will foster necessary integration. Leaders at multiple levels in the *host organization* must value what the program will bring, understand its implementation requirements, recognize and address changes in usual organizational behavior that will be necessary for the program to be introduced and survive, and commit to providing the resources and personnel necessary to implement and sustain the program with fidelity.

Last, the *policies that govern workforce behavior and program financing* must align with and adequately support the underlying principles, practices, and implementation requirements of an evidence-based program with incentives that encourage excellent practice and a focus on outcomes. Anyone who underestimates the power of these policy forces needs to be cautioned that the implementation of recommended practices can become difficult, and sometimes impossible, in the face of conflicts between the directives of money and institutional power and the directives of an evidence-based program's requirements. Conversely, when well aligned, these institutional and fiscal incentives can dramatically reinforce and motivate all that needs to be done to assure reliable positive outcomes from investments in the program.

This is often more challenging than one might anticipate, given that most public systems are focused far more on system outputs than outcomes. The result of that conflict, between what is valued by evidence-based programs and their advocates versus the inherent structural influences of most public systems, is pressure to deliver something to more people by less well prepared personnel over a shorter period of time than may be necessary to make a difference. There is often further pressure on workers to do all this in a highly regulated manner according to generic standards that are readily monitored but not necessarily important or sensitive to the requirements of a particular model or context. We are very excited to be partnering at both the local and state levels with an increasing number of public agencies whose leadership is conscious of these risks and is finding ways to use those same systems to promote both good practice and good practice environments.

The challenge of demonstrating scientifically validated impact on desired outcomes at the local level without investments in multiple randomized controlled trials was not easily addressed given the resources available to most community agencies. Initially, it was fairly easy to make the case that high-quality program implementation would most likely result in outcomes comparable to those demonstrated in the original research trials. But as the amount of public funding deployed to bring the NFP to greater scale in a city or state increased, so did the pressure to demonstrate local results.

Fortunately, one of the assets of the NFP's system of supports for implementation was consistent data gathering on relevant indicators of program outcomes that could be observed in the time period when participants were enrolled in the program. When programs were serving a large enough number of participants, those data could be analyzed and compared to outcome standards established in the research trials and from local norms for similar populations. This would allow local program managers to at least make good estimates of how well mothers and children participating in the NFP were doing on targeted outcomes compared to families served in the research trials or to families of similar demographic backgrounds from the same state or locality who were not enrolled in the program.

This use of what is essentially quality improvement data in reporting on outcomes has its limitations. Population group norms on particular outcomes are not always available, at least not from populations that are truly comparable to those participating in the NFP. Without random assignment to participating and nonparticipating groups, there is little ability to rule out biases. For example, if a client drops out of a local program early, she cannot be "tracked" and asked to complete assessments at later stages of development, because she is not participating in a research study funded to provide such follow-up. The number of clients reporting data on these later outcomes may be too small to allow valid interpretation. For reasons like these, it is difficult to draw conclusions about the program's impact in all the ways expected.

One excellent solution to this dilemma was developed by the state of Pennsylvania. With a relatively small amount of additional funding, Dr. David Rubin and his team at the Children's Hospital of Philadelphia designed a study to identify a closely matched comparison group based on administrative data and birth records to determine if NFP participants had better outcomes than did non-NFP participants. The results were generally very encouraging for important outcomes such as reduction of cigarette smoking during pregnancy and postponement of subsequent births. The study also identified important differences in the performance of different agencies across the state, and it provided extremely helpful data to guide program improvement.

In Oklahoma, a corresponding propensity-matching study was conducted to examine the possible impact of the program on preterm delivery and infant mortality, with apparently positive effects of the NFP. While these studies do not have the same scientific validity as randomized controlled trials, they have provided some evidence from community replication sites that the program appears to be maintaining its capacity to benefit pregnant women and children in the target population.

Lessons Learned that Suggest Next Steps for Research, Policy, and Practice

The effort to successfully take research-based programs and practices to large scale is relatively new, at least in education, social services, and community-based interventions. It is also complex work involving behavioral change among individuals, organizations, and systems. There is still much to be learned. The following outlines some of our thoughts about future areas for exploration.

First, research priorities should include further development of already-proven models to either enhance their effectiveness or test adaptations that appear both important and likely to work. Much more research needs to be done to determine what types of implementation supports contribute the most to strong program implementation at the level of the client, practitioner, and local organization and what institutionalizes key supports to sustain high-quality programming. Moreover, research that documents the ways in which policy and financing support or interfere with strong program implementation and the adaptability that is necessary to achieve good outcomes at scale would be extraordinarily helpful, as public funding is inevitably necessary to achieve significant scale.

Second, policy work that identifies new ways for government to ensure accountable use of funds, program quality, and important outcomes that do not default to traditional regulatory methods would begin to resolve conflicts between evidence-based programs and bureaucratic organizations. This policy work should include experiments with new incentives to integrate the work of nongovernmental purveyor organizations alongside government agencies in ways that take advantage of the strengths of each.

Third, the practice of implementing evidence-based programs would be advanced if new professionals learned some core skills and thought processes as part of the curriculum across disciplines in higher education. This should result in a growing number of young professionals and emerging leaders with the ability to reflect on their own practice, use data for improvement, and understand the basics of implementation science and the management practices and policies that support it. Whether a student is in a learning track focused on clinical practice, administration, or policy, he or she should be taught that acquiring expertise and managing for excellence is a process, not an event, and should learn to value and use the tools that support those processes.

References

Aos, S., Lieb, R., Mayfield, J., Miller, M., & Pennucci, A. (2004). *Benefits and costs of prevention and early intervention programs for youth.* Olympia, WA: Washington State Institute for Public Policy.

Coalition for Evidence-Based Policy. (2010). *Social programs that work.* Retrieved from http://evidencebasedprograms.org/wordpress

Kitzman, H., Olds, D., Henderson, C., Hanks, C., Cole, R., Tatelbaum, R., … Barnard, K. (1997). Randomized trial of prenatal and infancy home visitation by nurses on pregnancy outcomes, childhood injuries, and repeated childbearing. *Journal of the American Medical Association, 278,* 644–652.

MacMillan, H.L., Wathen, N., Barlow, J., Fergusson, D.M., Leventhal, J.M., & Taussig, H.N. (2009). What works? Interventions to prevent child maltreatment and associated impairment. *Lancet, 373,* 250–266.

Olds, D.L., Eckenrode, J., Henderson, C.R., Jr., Kitzman, H., Powers, J., Cole, R., … Luckey, D. (1997). Long-term effects of home visitation on maternal life course and child abuse and neglect: 15-year follow-up of a randomized trial. *Journal of the American Medical Association, 278,* 637-643.

Olds, D., Henderson, C.R., Jr., Cole, R., Eckenrode, J., Kitzman, H., Luckey, D., … Sidora, K. (1998). Long-term effects of nurse home visitation on children's criminal and antisocial behavior: 15-year follow-up of a randomized controlled trial. *Journal of the American Medical Association, 280*(14), 1238–1244.

Olds, D.L., Hill, P.L., O'Brien, R., Racine, D., & Moritz, P. (2003). Taking preventive intervention to scale: The nurse–family partnership. *Cognitive and Behavioral Science, 10*(4), 278–290.

CHAPTER 11

Implementation and Replication of the Educare Model of Early Childhood Education

Noreen Yazejian, Donna Bryant, and Portia Kennel

Educare is a comprehensive early education program for high-risk children, birth to age 5, and their parents. Educare is designed to prevent or substantially reduce the achievement gap and help launch children and families on a trajectory for school readiness and later success in school and life. Twelve structural and process components of high-quality early childhood education (ECE) are central to the Educare approach. The educational model was developed by the Ounce of Prevention Fund (hereafter referred to as the Ounce) and first implemented in 2000 in a school in an impoverished southside Chicago neighborhood.

In the first years of operation, the Buffett Early Childhood Fund (BECF) began collaborating with the Ounce to take the model to other communities across the country: The Omaha Educare school opened in 2003, Milwaukee in 2005, and Tulsa in 2006. This formed the beginning of the Bounce Learning Network, which is now known as the Educare Learning Network (ELN). By 2011, the ELN comprised 13 operational Educare schools and another 13 in various stages of construction or development. The ELN is part of a broader early childhood mission funded by the BECF and other foundations, including the Irving B. Harris Foundation, the George Kaiser Family Foundation, the Bill & Melinda Gates Foundation, and the W.K. Kellogg Foundation.

The ELN is characterized by four related P's: Local public–private *partnerships* create and support an Educare school—the *place*—following the Educare model— the *program*—which serves as a *platform* for broader policy and systems change. The intention of the ELN is not to replicate Educare schools in hundreds of communities, but to build a geographically diverse network of high-quality programs following evidence-based recommended practices. The ELN goal is to use these programs and their public–private partnerships as levers to increase quality for all early learning programs, serving as examples of what is possible in the early education field. Therefore, a slow and deliberate growth of the network of schools was expected and has been maintained, while the policy-related activities have increased as well.

This chapter focuses on the Educare schools and considers the role of implementation research in achieving and monitoring fidelity to the Educare program model, both within a site and across sites in the ever growing network. First, we describe the Educare model and its core components and how the schools begin and are supported in implementation. Second, we introduce the Educare implementation evaluation, a study designed to provide data to inform the continuous program improvement efforts at the individual school level. Next, we describe the phase and level of implementation across the Educare sites. After that, we discuss issues that Educare and its implementation study have encountered as the network of Educare schools has expanded. We conclude with some lessons we have learned that might enhance Educare's application of implementation science principles and perhaps serve as guidance for other programs, researchers, or policy makers.

Description of Educare

Early Head Start/Head Start Foundation

Educare represents the blending of two proven approaches to intervening in the lives of children living in poverty. First, relying on what is known from Early Head Start (EHS) research, Educare starts early and includes a strong family empowerment component. Second, relying on what is known from the seminal research on model child-focused interventions (i.e., Infant Health and Development Program, Perry Preschool, Abecedarian, and Chicago Child-Parent Centers), Educare uses intentional practices to support children's language, cognitive, and social-emotional development.

Educare schools have a shared mission, vision, and purpose that result in full-day, full-year, high-quality early education for low-income, high-risk children through age 5. The program model focuses on fortifying the key foundations for children's long-term school success: improving intellectual development, language and early literacy skills, and social-emotional development. Educare's foundation begins with the current EHS and Head Start (HS) performance standards, but goes beyond them by following 12 core features based on recommended practices and research literature. The 12 Educare core components either exceed the EHS/HS performance standards or explicitly define them to ensure a high level of implementation and focus on strategies that theory and research predict will produce the most positive outcomes for low-income, high-risk children and families.

Educare's Core Components

Educare was developed by practitioners who believed that only a comprehensive package of high-quality components of ECE and parent support could effectively close the achievement gap for at-risk young children by kindergarten entrance. The Educare model comprises 12 core practices that each program is expected to implement through full-day, year-round programming: 1) start early, emphasizing prenatal services; 2) maintain small class size and high staff–child ratios; 3) provide continuity of care; 4) maintain high staff qualifications and intensive professional development; use 5) reflective supervision and 6) an interdisciplinary service model; have a strong focus on 7) language and literacy development,

8) social-emotional development, 9) numeracy and problem solving, and 10) the arts; 11) provide on-site family support with a strong parent engagement component; and 12) use data collection and analysis to drive quality and ensure student success. Educare emphasizes that it is this *comprehensive package* of components that produces results and not any one component. We elaborate further on these 12 components below.

Start Early   Educare programs emphasize early enrollment, enable families to enroll children as young as 6 weeks old, and are required to apportion 50% of classroom space for infant/toddler rooms.

Deliver High-Quality Early Education   Educare's teacher education and adult–child ratios exceed recommendations. Its professional development is intensive, ongoing, and data based, and children experience continuity of care.

- Programs must maintain class sizes and ratios of 8:3 for infants and toddlers and 17:3 for preschoolers.

- All lead teachers are required to have BA degrees in ECE or equivalent and at least 2 years of early childhood classroom experience. Educare master teachers are required to have MA degrees in ECE or related fields and at least 5 years of early childhood classroom or supervisory experience.

- Programs must provide continuity of care by assigning each child a primary caregiver and having babies remain with the same teaching team from program entry until transition to the preschool/Head Start classrooms.

- Professional development must be frequent, including master teachers engaging in reflective supervision; structuring regular opportunities for teacher collaboration; and providing coaching with teachers (4 hours per week per classroom) that involves planning, observing/modeling, and engaging in reflection and providing supervision and feedback focused on the content that Educare emphasizes, including the following:

  1. Sensitive and responsive teaching to support social-emotional development: biannual child assessments and reflective supervision/coaching from master teachers focused on relationships

  2. Instructionally meaningful and intentional teaching to support oral language, vocabulary, and concept development, as well as early literacy and numeracy/problem-solving skills: coaching and supervision from master teachers and data feedback from child assessments and classroom observations collected by a local evaluator to support teachers with systematically developing and individualizing the curriculum and interactions/instruction

  3. Integration of the arts into daily activities: designation of an arts coordinator and involvement of families and community artists

- All staff receive training in reflective practice and supervision, appropriate to their position (supervisors pass a specially designed course). Low supervisor–supervisee ratios are maintained, and individual and group reflective supervision meetings are required monthly. The focus is on quality programming.

Provide High-Quality Family Support   Going beyond EHS/HS requirements and mirroring the ratio, staff qualifications, and continuity requirements of Educare's high-quality classroom programming, Educare family support staff have lower caseloads (1:30 vs. 1:45), all family support staff must have a bachelor's degree, and families remain with the same family support staff while in Educare. Family support services focus on promoting and supporting parent–child relationships, involvement in their child's education, and improving parents' ability to advocate for their child.

Provide Services That Are Integrated and Interdisciplinary   Educare programs are required to be interdisciplinary in their approach to understanding and serving each child and family. Teaching, family support, and leadership staff conduct regular case reviews of each child, with a goal of three meetings a year with appropriate staff involved.

Conduct Local Evaluation   Educare requires the employment of a local evaluation partner who participates as a member of the school's Research–Program Partnership to propel continuous improvement efforts and data-use practices. The local evaluator collects child, parent, staff, and classroom data and supports use of the data by program staff in efforts to improve practices and individualize services for children and families. The goal is for local evaluators to share new data regularly with master teachers, family support supervisors, and direct service staff and for program leadership to use the data for program improvement and development. Individual site and cross-site data are used to plan ELN system-wide professional development.

Partnerships and Leadership

Many individuals and systems are involved in the successful implementation of Educare. Leaders at the Ounce developed the model, currently operate the Chicago school, and along with the BECF are the purveyors of the model. Many other local philanthropies support their efforts, as well as individual Educare schools. Each site consists of program leaders and staff who must operate a program that meets the standards of each of their funders (EHS, HS, public pre-K, etc.) and those of Educare. As good programs do, Educare schools collaborate within their local and state early childhood communities, too. The Frank Porter Graham Child Development Institute (FPG) at the University of North Carolina at Chapel Hill (UNC-CH) acts as the national evaluator, receiving and combining each site's data into a cross-site Educare database. These various partners work together to establish structures and processes to facilitate implementation.

As the purveyors, staff at the Ounce provide implementation assistance (IA) to the Educare schools throughout the process of implementation. As described by Fixsen, Naoom, Blase, Friedman, and Wallace (2005), program implementation progresses through stages, from exploration of a new intervention through adoption, installation, initial implementation, full operation, innovation, and finally sustainability. As a network, Educare can be classified as generally looping in the full-operation, innovation, and sustainability stages, and the national evaluation of Educare is matched to these stages; evaluators currently do not gather data at earlier stages. However, the development of an individual Educare school can take up to 3 years from the time a community begins considering whether to pursue developing an Educare school to the day the doors are open to children and families.

During the cultivation and partnership-building phase, which matches Fixsen's exploration stage, leaders at the Ounce and BECF provide information about the requirements of the model and learn about the strengths and challenges of the local partners. The goals of this stage are to determine whether community needs and resources match the Educare program and to start building relationships among the partners. At the end of this stage, a decision is made to proceed or not.

During the readiness and planning stage, which corresponds to Fixsen's adoption stage, the Ounce and BECF teams help the local partners work out the details of how the new school will be operated and sustained; agreements are formalized, and the leaders begin positioning the new Educare project as a platform for change at the local and state levels.

At the ramping-up stage ("program installation" in Fixsen's terms), the Ounce's IA team begins working with a site to assist with selection and hiring of staff, program design and management, obtaining a local evaluator, and establishing administrative procedures. The Ounce has developed a variety of implementation aids, such as trainings and orientations to the model with corresponding PowerPoint presentations, budget analysis tools, policy manuals, printed external communications materials, and implementation assistance manuals.

The technical assistance work of the purveyor teams during these initial stages of implementation, before the opening of the school, marks the beginnings of building the leadership and staffing infrastructures that will support effective implementation of the Educare model.

After opening (Fixsen's initial implementation), the Ounce IA team assists implementation through individualized consultation with a site, conducting or facilitating group and individual training and other learning events to increase staff's skills and knowledge, linking the new site staff into the ELN professional learning community (e.g., topic-specific conference calls, web-based materials), and holding twice yearly training meetings that selected staff members attend. The Ounce IA team emphasizes content and bases activities of their IA work on both the locally collected and cross-site data noted above, thus modeling the data-based approach that undergirds effective implementation of the Educare model. In these ways, the purveyors at the Ounce continue to support implementation by strengthening leadership, staff, and organizational structures.

Strategic collaborative funding is essential to an Educare program's ability to provide high-quality education services. Core funding comes from federal EHS and HS, supplemented with state and local education funding (e.g., public pre-K), child care funding (e.g., subsidies and scholarships), and philanthropy. Several sites have specific program enhancement initiatives funded either publicly or privately. The model is, ultimately, a public–private partnership. The Abecedarian and Perry Preschool educational programs are sometimes considered too "ivory tower" to be replicable, and indeed they were not reproduced. However, Educare has found a formula that *is* replicable, based primarily on public dollars that are available in almost all communities, with a strategic infusion of relatively small amounts of private money and a large dose of collaborative leadership.

Educare and Implementation Science Components

The 12 Educare core components, along with the principles embodied by the part-nership and leadership strategies described above, consist of both *implementation components* and *intervention components* as described by Fixsen et al. (2005). The core implementation components establish Educare's capacity to develop, improve, and sustain the skills of early childhood educators and create hospitable organizational and systems environments for the Educare model to thrive. Essentially, these core implementation components represent the infrastructure elements required for successful replication of the Educare model.

The Educare components regarding staffing and data utilization, as well as the leadership supports provided by the Ounce, map directly onto Fixsen et al.'s (2005) seven core implementation components. Specifically, Fixsen's selection, preservice training, consultation and coaching, and staff evaluation components are embodied by Educare's requirements around staff qualifications, provision of professional development and coaching, and use of reflective supervision. The Educare core component of requiring local evaluation and the Research–Program Partnership corresponds to Fixsen's decision-support data systems component. Finally, the component that Fixsen et al. describe as "facilitative and administra-tive supports" has an Educare counterpart in its interdisciplinary practices and the partnership and leadership strategies described in the previous section. In particular, the collaborative funding and technical assistance provided by the Ounce's IA team facilitate the implementation of the program. Together, these core implementation components support the full and effective operation of the Educare model.

The remaining Educare components are intervention components that spec-ify the elements necessary for achieving the desired child and family outcomes for Educare participants. These components include the provision of full-day, full-year services; starting services early and emphasizing prenatal care; having small class sizes and appropriate ratios of both children to teachers and fami-lies to family support workers; providing continuity of care by having children stay with the same primary teacher over time and having families stay with the same family support worker over time; providing a classroom curriculum that integrates the arts and addresses social-emotional development, language and literacy, and numeracy and problem solving; and offering on-site family support services and parent engagement that address the parent–child relationship, involvement in their child's education and learning, and educational advocacy for their child. These components facilitate classroom and family support processes and practices that lead to improved child and family outcomes, specifically chil-dren who have language, cognitive, and social-emotional skills that prepare them to take advantage of the learning opportunities in school and parents who are knowledgeable, engaged, and strong advocates and thus prepared to support their children in school.

Using an implementation science framework and language, Figure 11.1 presents a modified version of the Educare theory of change. The core components, processes, and outcomes are divided between those that support implementation (top of the model) and those that are necessary for achieving participant outcomes (core intervention components and processes).

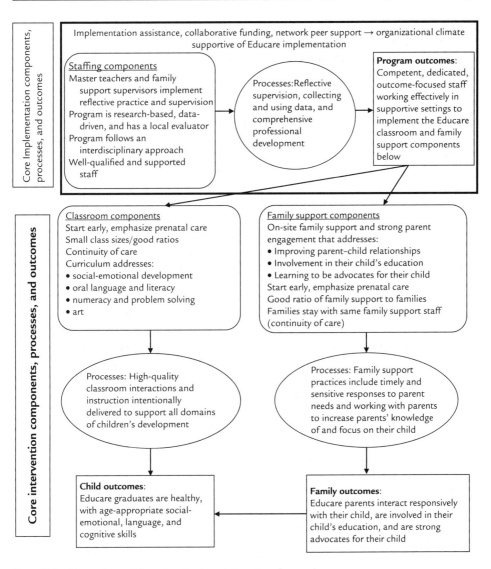

Figure 11.1. Educare theory of change in an implementation science framework.

Measuring Educare's Implementation

Since 2005, the work of the local evaluation partners has been guided and coordinated by a team at FPG. Local philanthropies fund the local research costs, and the BECF and the George Kaiser Family Foundation have funded the Educare Implementation Study leadership, data coordination, analyses, and reporting. The Implementation Study has internal and external audiences. For the internal audience, data are used for continuous program improvement, tailored help from the Ounce IA team, and investigation of site-specific questions. For the external audience, data are used to document the core features, to showcase the characteristics of high-quality programs, and to contribute to the early childhood literature on effective early education.

The first Implementation Study task was to arrive at consensus on the specific measures that would be considered "core" measures to be collected cross-site for assessing classroom quality and child and family outcomes. Because the five operational sites had made their own measurement decisions and had collected data for 1–5 years, collegial compromising among local evaluators and program leadership was required. We arrived at the basic birth-to-5 data collection plan (Educare and Frank Porter Graham Child Development Institute, 2012).

Subsequent tasks included training local evaluators and data collectors on measures that were new to them, obtaining annual reliability assessments on observation and child assessment measures, obtaining Policy Council approvals where needed, establishing data transfer systems that met local and UNC-CH Institutional Review Board requirements, and creating data review and feedback mechanisms for sharing the cross-site implementation and outcome data within and outside the network. Some of these issues will be addressed in more detail later in this chapter.

All sites and all Educare staff participate in the evaluation, and the majority of children and families agree to participate and are assessed. Annual staff questionnaires document experience, education, attitudes, and practices. Teaching staff rate children's social-emotional development at least twice a year, and their classrooms are observed annually by local evaluators to measure both structural and interactional quality. The measures used were the Infant/Toddler Environment Rating Scale–Revised (ITERS-R) and Classroom Assessment Scoring System (CLASS) Toddler (La Paro, Hamre, & Pianta, 2012) for infant/toddler classrooms and the Early Childhood Environment Rating Scale–Revised (ECERS-R) and CLASS for preschool classrooms. Family support staff interview the child's parent or primary caregiver each fall and when children exit Educare for kindergarten.

The data gathered from these procedures allow documentation of the majority of Educare's core features. For example, across sites, more than 90% of teachers and family support staff meet the educational requirements, and those few who do not are following an approved educational plan. The mean quality scores are high across sites, as well. For example, in 2010, the ITERS-R mean of 47 classrooms was 5.7 and the ECERS-R mean of 59 classrooms was 5.8. Even the difficult CLASS Instructional Support domain score was higher than in most other studies ($N = 48$, mean = 3.5). In terms of child outcomes among children whose home language was English, across 3 program years (2007–2010), the 2-year-old Bayley language scores averaged 94.3 ($N = 161$), the 3-year-old Peabody Picture Vocabulary Test–4 (PPVT) averaged 92.1 ($N = 312$), and the 5-year-old PPVT scores averaged 94.8 ($N = 473$)—scores that are much higher than typically would be expected for children living in poverty, even those enrolled in EHS and HS. (These Educare child outcomes have all been adjusted for several child and family characteristics that have been shown to be related to child outcomes.)

The local evaluators collect and support the use of the data by programs in their efforts to maintain high levels of quality programming and fidelity to the Educare model. FPG summarizes these data for the ELN so that it can respond with appropriate site-level implementation assistance and cross-site training at biannual meetings, and so that Educare leaders can showcase for policy makers the value of high-quality educational programs for children and families living in poverty.

Another measure of implementation fidelity is the Educare Program Implementation Checklist, an annual self-assessment completed by each site's leadership team. It reflects the core components of Educare and the activities that should be occurring if these components are being followed. This provides a comparison with data obtained independently through the classroom observations and staff and parent questionnaires. Checklist data can be more of a reflection of the program design, and the comparison with Implementation Study data helps the implementation advisor initiate conversations about any gaps between design and practice. For example, classroom observation data can be compared with checklist items on class sizes, ratios, teaching practices, language environment, social-emotional emphasis, and overall quality. Data from staff questionnaires provide information about the extent of reflective practices and supervision as they are actually experienced. Parent interview data demonstrate evidence of the extent of family support and development of strong parent engagement. Implementation advisors at the Ounce facilitate this self-assessment process and base a good deal of their technical assistance to sites on Program Implementation Checklist data.

Summarizing Educare's ability to document implementation fidelity within and across sites, we think the different types of data noted above provide good to excellent measures of eight of the Educare core features. We continue to search for or develop objective measures that would do justice to the four remaining core features: providing integrated interdisciplinary services, providing high-quality family support, using reflective practices in supervision, and using research and data to guide program implementation and improvement.

Phase and Level of Implementation

The Institute of Education Sciences developed categories (and corresponding funding levels) of educational research based on the expected progress of an intervention from pilot project to scale-up. Basic translational research is considered to be in the Exploratory category. Developing and studying a new intervention or improving an existing one is in the category of Development and Innovation. The third category, Efficacy and Replication, includes experimental or quasi-experimental research that evaluates the efficacy of supported interventions. The fourth category, Scale-up Evaluations, includes evaluating the impact of interventions that are implemented without special support from developers or research teams.

The Educare model as a whole can be described as being in the replication phase, although because it was not initially designed to be replicated or scaled up, it has not evolved in the typical way. Programs that are replicated often begin with a more extensive set of efficacy findings and protocol manuals before replication than did Educare. For example, the Nurse–Family Partnership (NFP) home visiting intervention discussed in Chapter 10 had been through the rigor of a randomized control trial before it was replicated (and eventually was tested through two more random studies). Also, before replication, NFP had developed a detailed protocol and accompanying manual for the nurse home visitors.

How did Educare arrive so quickly at the Efficacy and Replication phase, having not intended to do so? The components of the model had been supported by extensive previous research, so one factor may have been that the leaders of new programs still in the planning stages found a nice fit between their own vision for their new program and Educare's existing programs. It was also helpful that the child outcome results from the first site and, shortly thereafter, the second site were positive: Children were scoring near national averages, much higher than similar children in other studies who did not receive early education and even higher than children in the Head Start Family and Child Experiences (FACES) studies. Another factor that made new sites want to join the ELN was the opportunity to join with like-minded colleagues to both deliver a quality program and participate in the broader Four P's policy work that the ELN accomplishes. The chance to receive various types of training from the Ounce's implementation team and to collaborate within a network of philanthropies no doubt played a part, too. A qualitative study of the cultivation and start-up process would probably yield even more factors that continue to motivate new sites to join the network.

In terms of the level of implementation that Educare occupies, it crosses boundaries—an early education program that occurs at the child, classroom, program, network, and system levels. As part of the Educare program model, data are gathered to individualize instruction for children (child level), to provide feedback at the classroom level for improvement, and to provide program-level information for answering site-specific questions and to provide implementation assistance. At the network level, the ELN uses data to determine how well programs are implementing the components of the model and to examine outcomes of children and families participating in schools across the sites. And as part of Educare's broader mission, data are used to inform the field and provide a platform for policy change (system level).

One can imagine this multilevel system as a multilayered, cascading logic model (Blase, 2009) in which the outcomes at one level serve as the intervention components at another level. For a simple example, consider that at the program level professional development and coaching (intervention) is designed to improve classroom quality (outcome), while at the next level, classroom quality—the outcome at the level above—is now the intervention, designed to improve child outcomes.

While the Educare intervention occurs at these multiple levels and implementation data are gathered to some extent at each level, the multisite implementation evaluation of Educare occurs primarily at the network level. As a model being implemented at 13 (and counting) sites, Educare is being evaluated to determine how well programs are implementing the components of the model and to answer questions about the degree of child outcomes that can be achieved. Fruitful areas for new research would be the process of matching technical assistance to the Educare schools' needs, how programs respond to and use technical assistance (measuring an aspect of participant responsiveness; see Berkel, Mauricio, Schoenfelder, & Sandler, 2011), and the activities engaged in by Educare teams that seem to be influential in effecting change in local or state systems.

Issues Encountered

The Implementation Study has encountered many issues that are faced by most multisite evaluation projects, whether or not they are in replication mode. Using data for program improvement at the individual site level and using data for over-all Educare Network improvement and to inform replication requires 1) selection of and agreement on measures that answer questions about fidelity to the model, quality of practices, and program outcomes; 2) trusting the data (training, reliability, data checking); and 3) quick turnaround and use of data. In this section, we will describe how the ELN has chosen and modified the assessment protocol, how we establish confidence that sites are reliable and comparable collectors of data, and how the data are used, interpreted, and presented.

Selection of Measures

As noted earlier, the Implementation Study assessment protocol is a product of compromise at four levels. First, the initial Educare sites were each collecting various classroom and child measures for program improvement when the network was formed. Through discussion and sharing of data, the early sites compromised on a standard battery and later sites have had to accept and agree to collect the measures in this core battery. Programs are free to collect other measures that are not part of the Implementation Study protocol, and many do. For example, Educare schools that are part of their community's public prekindergarten program typically have additional data requirements.

The second level of compromise was between program and evaluator staff. Evaluators needed to be sensitive to program staff concerns about overtesting young children and overtaxing teaching and family support staff. Both types of staff collect data that are not part of the Implementation Study protocol—teachers collect curriculum-specific data (e.g., measures in the *Creative Curriculum* system) and family support staff complete needs assessments and other forms that are part of EHS and HS requirements.

Third, data are used for multiple purposes in Educare, including to individualize services for children and families, for program improvement, to examine fidelity to the model, and as a lever for cultivation and policy. These multiple data uses and purposes dictate a selection of measures that can to the greatest extent possible meet multiple objectives to reduce data collection burdens and possible redundancies in measures. At times, this has led to tensions among the different data purposes. For example, local evaluators continue to gather and use extensive staff questionnaires to document implementation components such as staff qualifications and professional development, organizational climates, and reflective and interdisciplinary practices, as well as characteristics and beliefs of staff that have been shown in other research to be related to implementation of high-quality programs (e.g., depression, job stress, motivation, views on child rearing). Initially, these data were used for program improvement, to measure fidelity to the model components related to staffing, and, by comparison with other national studies using similar measures, as a lever for cultivation and policy. Later, additional questions were added to document more fully the supervision and Research–Program Partnership aspects of the model, resulting in a quite lengthy questionnaire. We therefore decided, in order to reduce staff burden, to drop some parts of the questionnaire—those that have been less useful in documenting the model and those that may have once been useful in targeting implementation assistance but are not necessary each year. Collaboratively weighing the different uses of data should help us be more efficient.

Finally, while the goal of the Implementation Study data collection protocol was to be comprehensive, it had to realistically be manageable. Most Educare sites have an annual evaluation budget of less than $200,000 and are responsible not only for collecting the data but also for quickly summarizing data and returning it to program staff for use in individualizing children's educational programming and classroom quality improvement.

Modifying the measurement battery is occasionally necessary, and the process for modifications has been equally collaborative. An example is the network's inclusion of the CLASS observation in preschool classrooms. Because the classroom observation measures were less useful for program improvement at the teacher–child interaction level, and because Head Start required all programs to use the CLASS, the network decided to add it to the protocol. Now that the CLASS Toddler is available, it too will be collected in Educare. Adding measures sometimes requires dropping other measures, which has also happened.

Gathering Data Issues

Each Educare school has a local evaluator who gathers data as part of the model and then feeds those data into the cross-site Implementation Study, so data integrity must be assured through cross-site training and reliability procedures. These cross-site efforts also ensure that the data are truly comparable. FPG arranges training sessions on new measures adopted by the network and provides orientation and training to new sites through conference calls, site visits, and meetings as part of biannual network gatherings. In addition, we ensure reliability on classroom observation measures, certify child assessment data collectors, and perform quality assurance checks on samples of the data gathered at each site.

Our goal for the data collected for the Implementation Study is that it be as trustworthy as in any research study. The main challenge to this is that neither the local evaluators nor any data collectors are "blind," that is, they know that all children and families are part of the Educare program. The local evaluator is typically a university faculty researcher and is responsible for hiring the data collectors (usually graduate students or research assistants), coordinating the data collection, and summarizing data for the teachers, family support staff, and program leaders. In the course of frequent visits to the schools, these evaluation team members may get to know the teaching and family support staff and children and might be inclined to see the best in them when assessing children or observing classrooms. For this reason, FPG or the local evaluator trains each new staff member on basic research procedures and ensures that they have the proper study manuals.

Each year, FPG observes and grades videos of each data collector assessing children with the various measures and provides feedback on technique. To maintain the reliability of the observational tools, FPG evaluators also observe three or four classrooms every year together with the local data collectors at each site, and on these visits, they check a 10% random sample of paper records to compare with the computerized data submitted. Statistically, the evaluators look for outliers, compare site data year to year and with other sites, and look for explanations of unusual changes; for example, the mean Bracken scores fell one year, but the obvious cause was the recent switch to the new, renormed Bracken.

We would use the procedures noted above for any research study as a matter of course, but the difference in the Educare Implementation Study is that it is a voluntary collaboration. Just as the Educare schools participate in the network voluntarily, likewise, the research teams at the sites participate in the Implementation Study voluntarily. This requires a high level of cooperation and collegiality among the researchers. These procedures are critically important given the decentralized nature of the study, with independent research teams located from Maine to Miami to Seattle.

Use of the Data

Educare is a research-based program, as evidenced by its adoption of several structural features of high-quality ECE (e.g., small class sizes, high ratios, continuity of care) and its aspiration to deliver high-quality classroom and family services through, for example, a strong focus on language and literacy. These features had been found to be, and continue to be, positively related to children's outcomes in numerous ECE research studies. However, to those of us who work within Educare programs, one of their most striking features is the commitment to collect and intentionally use data gathered on children, families, and classrooms to inform routine decision making and program improvement over time. This core feature has been hard to document.

At a simple level, one can count the number of Research–Program Partnership meetings and memos between the evaluators and master teachers, teachers, and family support staff—artifacts that document that some data sharing is taking place. However, the key ingredients of these meetings are elusive, and measuring how, and how well, the data are then used for individualizing services or program improvement has been a challenge. The evaluators at FPG have gathered information from the sites on how data are shared and have observed a few feedback sessions, but we have yet to design a measure to fully capture this critical component.

One example of how sites use data for improvement is the sharing of classroom observation quality scores. Typically, the local evaluator meets with the master teacher and teaching team (including assistants) following an observation to discuss the observation and the scores; this meeting may occur as soon as the same afternoon of the observation or as late as several weeks afterward. At some sites, this meeting includes the development of action plans to address lower scoring items/subscales, while at other sites this planning occurs at a separate meeting that may or may not include the local evaluator. We do not know whether these differences in timing or process are related to effective use of the data, and we struggle to devise ways to examine this empirically.

Another example of data use is the sharing of parent interview data to highlight areas of family need. When FPG shared cross-site data to the network on food insecurity, individual sites saw that their scores were higher than other sites' or higher than they had expected. This knowledge led to strengthening links to local food banks and, at two sites, the establishment of a food distribution point at the Educare school. Data the following year suggested that these efforts were successful in reducing families' food insecurity.

Data are also used at other levels in the model, and documenting these uses of data is complex. Anecdotally, we know that the cross-site data are shared with new partnerships that are considering building Educare schools and that these data are very useful in the cultivation process. We do not, however, have detailed knowledge about this data-sharing process. Evaluators also share data with the IA team at the site and cross-site levels and know that this has led to tailoring of implementation assistance, but we do not currently have systematic data collection to document the process. For example, one site previously had lower fidelity scores on continuity of care, one of the core components. This site was practicing continuity of care, but using a different model than other sites. The IA team worked with the site, resulting in a change in procedures, and subsequent data showed greater continuity. We know of other examples of effective data use and hope in the future to be able to develop more systematic ways to document these processes on an ongoing basis.

Issues Related to Interpretation of Results

Having noted the regular sharing of data that takes place at the local Educare site level, we now consider some issues regarding the cross-site results. First, a positive aspect of merging data across sites is that collectively the sample sizes of children, parents, teachers, and family support staff become large enough to conduct interesting data analyses that would not be possible at just one site. For example, studies of families at different risk levels and children with different home languages are possible with the multisite database. Educare's age-of-entry results—findings that were first obtained with only 2 years of cross-site data from the first five schools and have been replicated with the addition of new schools (Yazejian & Bryant, 2012)—make a strong case for enrollment as early as possible. A single site may never have been able to conduct such analyses.

This relatively large (and growing) data set has not yet helped our efforts to study potential links between fidelity of implementation and child or family outcomes. We believe the reason for this is that the quality of the programs is fairly high with low variability in structural and process measures of ECE quality. This lack of variability makes it difficult to show patterns of results, including associations between quality and outcomes, that might be expected based on studies of larger, more diverse samples.

As others have found (see Durlak & DuPre [2008] for a review), the lack of variability in implementation levels (fidelity) at the program level also makes it difficult to show relationships between level of implementation of the core components and outcomes. When FPG has conducted analyses to predict child outcomes from the measurable core components, no single component stands out. This is probably because Educare programs are of quite high quality and implement to high levels of fidelity, so we see very little variation among their component scores. It is also possible that the difficult-to-measure components (e.g., reflective supervision, being data driven) are the very ones that result in higher child outcomes than many other early education programs.

Data and Presentation Review Process

The Educare procedures for sharing results publicly are different than most other replication studies. Each site collects and uses its own data as it wishes and without review by others in the network, but the cross-site Implementation Study data belong to all members of the ELN. Thus, a process was needed for determining when the data were ready for use and how to access them. As FPG completes summaries of each year's data and of each particular type of analyses (e.g., dosage or risk factor analyses), we prepare figures and tables of key data and text to describe the particular analyses and our interpretation. Essentially, FPG creates a PowerPoint presentation that anyone in the network might use. These slides are reviewed by a Data Review Committee comprised of several executive directors and local evaluators, Ounce staff, and the funders. Clarifications usually result, and then the data are made available to all ELN leaders on a secure web site. Members of the network who wish to use these data for a public presentation (excluding presentations to local Educare boards) are asked to submit their complete presentation for review by the same committee. This process has worked for us to date, and we hope that the "story" of Educare that is told at various meetings and conferences around the country is the same.

Advantages and Disadvantages of Applying an Implementation Science Perspective to Evaluating Educare

Measurement Issues

The implementation science literature has helped us refine the measures to better understand the core components. The literature related to core implementation components has helped the evaluators and model purveyors ensure that Educare components are aligned with components known to be important for successful implementation, particularly the driver model described by Fixsen et al. (2005).

The literature has also led evaluators to dig deeper into measurement of competence, and not simply compliance, in examining implementation. The Implementation Study documents competence and compliance better for the classroom component of Educare than for the family support component. For example, in classrooms, we both document structural factors such as group size, ratio, and staff education (compliance) and obtain observations of interactions between teachers and children, warmth and sensitivity, organization and use of time, and instructional style (competence). In the family services domain, we document the education and experience of family support staff and the ratio of family support staff/families (compliance) and are working now with family support staff to incorporate new indices that will document the effectiveness of their interactions with and support of families.

Replication and Adaptation Issues

The recent focus on implementation science had helped the Educare model purveyors realize the need to clearly define and specify the Educare components, specify the limits of variability that are acceptable, and develop the roles of Educare leaders in an effort to ensure sustainability within the model. As the network grows and more variability is encountered from site to site, the Educare leadership continues to consider what level of variability is acceptable within the model and when to intervene with IA when model drift occurs. Educare leaders acknowledge that adaptations are not necessarily evidence of lack of fidelity, and in fact, Educare is more open to some adaptations than other early educational models. Curriculum use is one example.

Although most programs use *Creative Curriculum* (Dodge, Colker, & Heroman, 2002), and EHS and HS require the use of a curriculum, no particular ECE curriculum is required by Educare. In fact, as long as overall quality of teaching and learning in the classrooms stays high (as measured by ITERS-R, ECERS-R, and CLASS), Educare embraces experimentation. For example, many sites have adopted special and supplementary curricula (e.g., *LearningGames* with parents [Sparling & Lewis, 2007] and early literacy or math supplements), and six sites have been trained in Brazelton's Touchpoints approach and practices for parent engagement. The measures used in the Implementation Study are not sensitive enough to these types of intervention differences, nor is the Implementation Study designed in such a way to determine whether the addition of a particular practice is helpful. A controlled comparison study would be needed to examine the effects of such variations. However, the Implementation Study addresses program adaptations by monitoring the core processes and outcomes (see Figure 11.1). If a program adopts new procedures and practices, these are not seen as model drift (or helpful adaptations) unless there are changes in core processes or outcomes. For example, if a new mathematics initiative were to be implemented in one site and the classroom observation data (e.g., CLASS Instructional Support scores) showed improvements and/ or child outcome scores on math assessments increased, then training and technical assistance related to the math initiative might be offered to other schools in the ELN. While these types of modifications challenge the evaluators, they are signs that the entire network is truly a learning organization that values and uses data for continuous program improvement.

Lessons Learned and Next Steps

As the network of Educare schools grows, ELN leaders will find the theory and terminology of implementation science increasingly useful as the reality of variability within the network increases with each new site. What is a useful adaptation and what is central to the model? Educare evaluators hope to be even more valuable to network leaders by finding new and better ways to document the more process-oriented aspects of Educare practices. Another potential focus of network leaders concerns the process of replication. Educare has been successfully replicated 12 times and even more schools are being developed, but we do not yet know the particular conditions in a community that make their initial interest blossom into a fully realized Educare program, nor do we have good information about exactly what it takes from the purveyors, funders, and IA team to help a site get up and running most successfully. Answers to these questions would be interesting and useful to network leaders.

Applying implementation science principles in evaluating Educare has helped the evaluators see the holes in the current evaluation plan. We are aware that we are not measuring all levels of implementation, and for the levels we are measuring, we are not measuring them at the same depth. At the program level, we have detailed information about child outcomes and classroom quality, but less about the family support process. We have quantitative information about staff training, but would like more information on the quality of training. It also would be useful to document the IA process more fully. As described above, we want to improve measurement of the core component of data utilization, one of the features that makes Educare unique and a possible explanation for its effectiveness.

A random study of Educare is also a new research activity. Although randomized clinical trials typically precede replication, Educare began its first one in 2010, a decade after the first Educare opened its doors in Chicago. The Implementation Study was not designed to test whether Educare is effective, and although the age-of-entry findings are promising, we do not know whether there are differences in the children and families who enroll early that explain these variations in outcomes at kindergarten entry.

The randomized clinical trial was launched in the summer of 2010 at five Educare sites with almost 240 infants and toddlers randomly assigned to either Educare or the community control group. We will follow these children through age 3 and hope to secure additional funding to follow them into school. The study will allow us to answer the basic effectiveness question and possibly other questions related to risk levels, dosage, and children's language background.

References

Berkel, C., Mauricio, A.M., Schoenfelder, E., & Sandler, I.N. (2011). Putting the pieces together: An integrated model of program implementation. *Prevention Science, 12*, 23–33.

Blase, K. (2009, May). *Evaluating organizational and systems change: An implementation perspective.* Paper presented at the National Child Welfare Evaluation Summit, Washington, DC. Retrieved from http://www.jbassoc.com/reports/documents/panels/panels/panel%203/panel3crowel.pdf

Dodge, D.T., Colker, L.J., & Heroman, C. (2002). *The creative curriculum for preschoolers, 4th edition.* Washington, DC: Teaching Strategies.

Durlak, J.A., & DuPre, E.P. (2008). Implementation matters: A review of research on the influence of implementation on program outcomes and the factors affecting implementation. *American Journal of Community Psychology, 41*, 327–350.

Educare and Frank Porter Graham Child Development Institute. (2012, July). *Educare Learning Network Implementation Study data collection measures.* Retrieved from http://eln.fpg.unc.edu/sites/eln.fpg.unc.edu/files/eis-measures-table.pdf

Fixsen, D.L., Naoom, S.F., Blase, K.A., Friedman, R.M., & Wallace, F. (2005). *Implementation research: A synthesis of the literature* (FMHI Publication No. 231). Tampa, FL: University of South Florida, Louis de la Parte Florida Mental Health Institute, National Implementation Research Network.

Harms, T., Clifford, R., & Cryer, D. (2005). *Early Childhood Environment Rating Scale* (revised). New York, NY: Teachers College Press.

Harms, T., Cryer, D., & Clifford, R. (2006). *Infant/Toddler Environment Rating Scale* (revised). New York, NY: Teachers College Press.

La Paro, K.M., Hamre, B.K., & Pianta, R.C. (2012) *Classroom Assessment Scoring System (CLASS) Toddler.* Baltimore, MD: Paul H. Brookes Publishing Co.

Sparling, J., & Lewis, I. (2007). *The creative curriculum learning games: Birth-12 months.* Washington, DC: Teaching Strategies.

Yazejian, N., & Bryant, D.M. (2012). *Promising early returns: Educare implementation study data, August 2012.* Chapel Hill, NC: FPG Child Development Institute, UNC-CH. Retrieved from http://eln.fpg.unc.edu/sites/eln.fpg.unc.edu/files/FPG-Demonstrating-Results-August-2012-Final.pdf

Using Implementation Science to Support Replication, Scale-Up, and Ongoing Monitoring

Carolyn Layzer

The authors of the three foregoing chapters in this section all describe interventions that have already moved through the stages of exploration, installation, and initial implementation and are established enough that they can be replicated—some even without formal replication studies—with some guidance from the developers. All three are also being implemented on a large scale—at multiple sites, distant from the developers, with many providers using the program—but none of the three is yet at the stage where it can be used "out of a box" without guidance. In fact, given the level of care and attention each set of authors describes, it is unlikely that they will ever be implemented with fidelity without guidance.

All three of the developers in this section of the book describe the carefully thought-out plans for coaching and fidelity, the support furnished to providers and practitioners in the process of handing over program implementation, and even ongoing monitoring and technical support. They have developed systems to enable providers and practitioners to take over the role of monitoring and supporting ongoing implementation. But once the developer relinquishes his or her role in guiding and monitoring implementation, practitioners of the intervention are more likely to begin making adaptations that could substantially change the intervention in ways that are potentially connected to the program's theoretical model. One enormous challenge for implementers as they install the model in multiple locations or contexts (replication) or attempt to reach a greater proportion of the target population (scale-up) is how to innovate or make adaptations that are neutral to outcomes or that enhance rather than undermine the effectiveness of the intervention.

In this chapter, I consider the approaches that the authors of the previous three chapters have taken to achieve the objective of *intervention fidelity* (sometimes referred to as *program fidelity*) as well as ensuring *implementation fidelity* at these more mature phases in the life of an intervention. (Here I follow Downer's distinctions [see Chapter 8] between intervention fidelity—the extent to which core program components are delivered as intended—and implementation fidelity—the extent to which core implementation "drivers" are installed within a system so that programs can reach their intended outcomes. See also Chapter 4.) At replication and scale-up, alignment of stage-appropriate evaluation with stages of implementation is no less important, but the relative importance of particular features (model components and implementation drivers) shifts.

Why Align Stage-Appropriate Evaluation with Stages of Implementation?

There are many possible reasons for aligning stage-appropriate evaluation with the intervention's stage of implementation, including hypothesizing causal associations, providing insight for formative purposes, supporting continuous quality improvement, and uncovering strategies that can be shared for supporting sustainability of the intervention. In Chapters 9–11, the authors describe how they have used implementation and outcome data to inform program development and revision, to support ongoing implementation, and to provide information about the program's efficacy. Central to these efforts are the various measurement tools and systems for data collection and dissemination the authors describe.

At initial to full implementation, and particularly when replication studies (also referred to as effectiveness trials) are involved, aligned evaluation provides some assurance that what intervention practitioners do is "it" (i.e., actually the intervention, enactment of the program model) so that outcomes will reflect the best shot at replicating results originally obtained by developers. This is one of the reasons for alignment discussed by Sarama and Clements in Chapter 9. The authors describe developing measurement tools at both the program-to-practitioner level (fidelity tools, online professional development tools) and practitioner-to-participant level (assessment measures, child learning trajectory tools). The authors present these as conceptual—their examples are drawn from actual work with a particular curriculum, but the theoretical framework and approach could be used with any classroom-based intervention.

Hill and Olds (Chapter 10) present several examples of how the Nurse–Family Partnership (NFP) has been able to identify challenges and share solutions throughout the network by using a program quality data system to continuously monitor program implementation from the pilot phase all the way through to replication and scale-up. Drawing on program evaluation findings to develop a conceptual framework for the NFP Home Visiting Program is an example of how data use enabled the NFP to better understand the intervention components and their interactions, to see parallels between goals and objectives at different levels (program model, community, provider/agency, visitor, and family), and to hone the guidance the NFP provides at the various levels.

Yazejian, Bryant, and Kennel (Chapter 11) describe the Educare Learning Network (ELN) as serving the function of both providing formative information for providers and their organizations and providing monitoring information for the whole network—again as a form of assurance that "it," the Educare model, is actually being implemented. Although *Creative Curriculum* is the most commonly used curriculum in Educare sites, the model does not rely on a particular curriculum but rather emphasizes process and characteristics, with tools measuring instructional approaches and the environment as outcomes at the implementation level (in addition to the Educare Program Implementation Checklist) and participant outcomes (such as direct child assessment scores and behavioral reports).

A Conceptual Framework for Implementation Analysis

The elements of implementation in play during replication can be thought of in a framework initially developed to analyze implementation in a large replication study. Its purpose is to help show key implementation components and the hypothesized links between them, as illustrated in Figure 12.1. The framework builds on the work of implementation researchers who identified the key components and hypothesized mediators (Berkel, Mauricio, Schoenfelder, & Sandler, 2011; Dane & Scheider, 1998; Durlak & DuPre, 2008; Dusenbury, Brannigan, Falco, & Hansen, 2003).

Along the horizontal axis of the schematic are rough approximations of the implementation stages at which each element is more prominent, although there is not a point at which any of the key implementation drivers ceases to be important. On the left-hand side of the figure are elements that fall in the early stages of implementation—from exploration through installation—and have to do with readiness and preparation at the system level, which we believe are crucial to the ability of systems (agencies, providers) to implement an intervention as intended by the developer.

We have identified five aspects of readiness and preparation, three of which have been identified by Metz, Blase, and Bowie (2007) as drivers of successful implementation: 1) the capacity of the system and partners in the endeavor to deliver the program; 2) staff selection and preparation; 3) the specificity or "manualization" of the intervention or program; 4) the specificity of the implementation

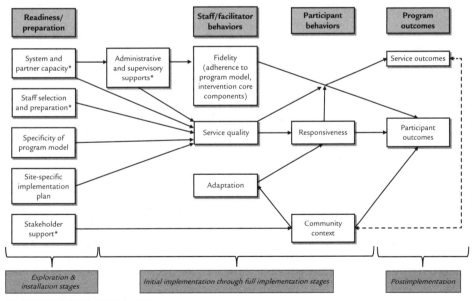

*implementation "drivers" (Metz et al., 2007)

Figure 12.1. A conceptual framework for implementation analysis. (*Source:* Layzer & Layzer, 2011.)

plan; and 5) stakeholder support. The staff selection and preparation aspect encompasses "competency drivers" such as staff recruitment and selection as well as preservice or in-service training. Program and partner capacity includes systems-level partnerships. While these drivers are urgently critical at exploration and installation, ongoing staff development, decision-support data systems, and other competency and organization drivers continue to be important, but they must be established before intervention implementation can begin. (See Chapter 2 for examples of these components in greater detail.)

Chapters 9–11 describe evidence-based programs that were well specified and in such demand that developers were more or less compelled to extend the reach of the services. For someone who has invested a great deal of thought and years of work in developing a program, allowing it to move away from one's direct control must be difficult; each component was selected for a reason and seems important. Below, I examine this dilemma and strategies the authors in these three chapters used to address it.

Diffusion Versus Adherence

Spreading an intervention—to additional sites (replication) or to a larger proportion of target population served (scale-up)—is often pitted against adherence to intervention fidelity. That is, implementation of model components as designed by the developer is viewed as competing with the aim of implementing the model in different contexts or reaching more participants. This is a false dichotomy, but it highlights the fact that effective implementation brings ongoing challenges. Adaptation that hews to the principles on which the model rests can increase the program's effectiveness, while changes to the program that violate the model's theory of action can be counterproductive even if the changes are made with the best intentions.

In a recent *New Yorker* article (Seabrook, 2011), the author describes how particular types of apples carefully developed to have particular characteristics gradually lose those characteristics as growers distant from the original developers produce them under different conditions. The distant growers believe that they are providing adequate conditions, but some of the conditions are different, and as a result, the apples lose their distinctive characteristics—for example, becoming less crunchy, less sweet, or less tangy. This is an example of how replication or widespread scale-up without appropriate attention paid to critical elements of implementation fidelity can lead to unintended consequences. Similar to the case of the apples, a school might adopt a math curriculum that uses computer software as one of its components and decide instead to use different software that doesn't link to the particular curriculum but nevertheless is designed to teach math to young children. The school administrator, and maybe even the teachers, might view this as reasonable, doing all of the other curriculum activities but substituting for this one. Or they might even leave out the computer component altogether ("not enough time" is the usual reason given for this). The effect of removing or substituting is to dilute the original curriculum.

At some point, either because of geographic separation (replications at sites distant from the developer) or because of the sheer number of participants (scale-up) such that the close involvement of the developer would be impractical or unfeasible, program models are implemented without the direct participation of the model developer (or at least, with a lower degree of participation than during the process of development and refinement). At this point, attention to the stages of implementation and which implementation drivers are especially important at each stage becomes crucial. Below I consider how the authors in Part III used implementation science to strengthen the implementation of their respective program models in replication and scale-up.

Ensuring Adherence without Dilution in Replication and Scale-Up

A *program model* is the operationalization of a model's theory of action—the set of underlying assumptions about how to move participants from their original state to a different state. A developer uses a theoretical model to construct a program model whose components are intended to produce the desired outcomes through enactment of a theory of action. Using empirical evidence to design an intervention is a challenging and complex process that, as described by the authors in this part, takes a considerable amount of time and effort. For this reason, the developers have a strong investment in trying to ensure that replications adhere as closely as possible to the enhanced evidence-based program model. That is, they are intent on achieving intervention fidelity. In addition, they each demonstrate a commitment to achieving implementation fidelity, which is adherence to the core drivers—staff selection, training and coaching, using data systems to monitor intervention fidelity, and sustaining infrastructure support. Each of the contributors gave powerful examples of the strategies they have employed.

Sarama and Clements's TRIAD model (Chapter 9), which is their operationalization of an implementation framework, is applied to an early mathematics curriculum in the examples they have described (although, in theory, it could be applied to any curriculum implementation in a school or early learning setting). They developed a detailed manual that includes dynamic online support through which teachers can use examples from their own classroom to obtain clarification, strategies, or instructional techniques; this serves a dual function of supporting ongoing professional development (staff training) and assisting staff in maintaining intervention fidelity. Sarama and Clements have developed aligned classroom observation and fidelity tools that participants and supervisors or coaches can complete on their own, along with aligned child outcome measures that also have online support (through which teachers can obtain information about children's cognitive development as well as instructional activities to move children to the next level of understanding). These systems support ongoing staff training, attention to intervention fidelity, and quality of service delivery and provide a means of documenting outcomes (both service outcomes and child participant outcomes).

After conducting rigorous efficacy trials, Sarama and Clements have scaled up the intervention, and they are currently documenting the results of diffusion, finding what happens to the intervention when it is long out of the hands of the developer. Teachers have access to information online, but how they use the information is at the teachers' own discretion, or the discretion of the administrators. What proportion of teachers take advantage of this support, under what conditions (e.g., contextual conditions including administrative support, teacher characteristics such as preparation and disposition), and to what effect? These are questions of interest to the authors that become pressing once the intervention has reached the scale-up phase of its life.

Educare's theory of change model (Chapter 11) maps the Educare components via implementation processes to desired program outcomes. This enables providers to document the presence or absence of processes (for needs assessment to inform technical assistance) as well as to document quality (for continuous program improvement, accountability, or marketing to child care consumers). By stipulating expected outcomes at each level, Educare provides a template for providers to measure how well they're doing—whatever the purpose of the measurement. Implementation measures include a program implementation checklist (a sine qua non for replication), a staff questionnaire, and observation protocols. Participant outcome measures include both direct assessments and interviews of parents or primary home caregivers, recognizing that support for home caregivers is a crucial part of provision of adequate support for children's development.

Because Educare has systematized the data collection through its national network, there is a greater likelihood that implementation monitoring and support could continue into broader scale-up, as providers would be able to both share information about their sites and have access to information about the program, about implementation at other sites, about challenges encountered and strategies employed to overcome them, and about innovations that are compatible with the model's theoretical framework.

The Nurse–Family Partnership (Chapter 10) has a model with 18 elements and provides detailed visit guidelines that operationalize the elements in a low-inference approach—that is, an approach that requires little subjective judgment and is clearly spelled out, leaving little room for practitioners to guess what might be in line with the developers' intentions. Hill and Olds argue that this is essential for scale-up, where the NFP itself might have to be less involved in monitoring and supporting implementation. In the current stage of model replication, the NFP provides ongoing support for providers at initial and full implementation through the use of coaching and reflective feedback. As sites move to independent operation and sustaining the intervention beyond replication, it will be important to know more about whether local implementation teams supporting local replication take on the coaching and reflective feedback and how the process and outcomes change. Even with NFP guidelines, site-level decisions about implementation (one example of which Hill and Olds described in their chapter, in which a supervisor would reduce the frequency of coaching and reflective feedback because of staff workload or budget constraints) may hold sway irrespective of consequences for effectiveness of the implementation.

What do all of these authors' chapters have in common? All view the establishment of a support network—be it a national network or a professional community within a school or district—to be crucial to the success of their enterprise. All three chapters provide clear steps for intervention practitioners and system staff to follow, and all conduct ongoing monitoring, including measurement and feedback to intervention practitioners and participants. All three have developed and used program-level cross-site evaluation (for program improvement and revision). And all three likely have substantial information that can be used for further dissemination and potentially to influence the development of early care and education policy.

Evaluating Effectiveness:
Replications, Scale-Up, and Ongoing Monitoring

The authors of Chapters 9–11 all discussed implementation at two different levels: the system/agency/institution level, which we could call the system level, and the practitioner/caregiver/teacher level, which we could call the practitioner level. Each has slightly different accompanying considerations, and each has different measurement tools, but all three chapters place a great deal of importance on system-level implementation—since without that support, there is little hope of the intervention enduring long enough to reach full implementation, ensure sustainability, and permit effective innovation.

Hill and Olds (Chapter 10) and Yazejian et al. (Chapter 11) describe using their measures of fidelity of implementation in a powerful way to amass data about what is going on at both the system level and the provider level. They also collect and maintain data on outcomes at the participant level (in these examples, outcomes of the young children participating in the interventions), which may later enable them at least to analyze correlations between program elements and outcomes. While not described in their chapter in this volume (Chapter 9), Sarama and Clements are also using implementation data from multiple randomized control trials to examine mediators of the TRIAD model when replicating the model across multiple sites (Sarama, Clements, Wolfe, & Spitler, 2012). In the next section, I will discuss some of the strategies and tools described by the authors that enable them to effectively evaluate implementation in these phases of the intervention's life.

Evaluating Implementation in Replications

As Yazejian et al. (Chapter 11) describe, it can take up to 3 years of planning and consideration—what they term the "cultivation and partnership-building," "readiness and planning," and "ramping-up" phases—for Educare schools to reach the point at which they are ready to open their doors. During this time, the leaders at their partner agencies work closely with the school to conduct needs assessments and locate resources, work out details of operation, and plan for sustainability, and finally the Ounce's Implementation Assistance (IA) team assists with staff selection, hiring, obtaining a local evaluator, and establishing procedures for site-level operation. IA team support continues with staff preparation efforts to ensure that the provider is well prepared for the program's launch.

Similarly, the NFP's detailed home visit guidelines, planning process, start-up guide, and education program ensure that as little as possible is left to the community setting provider to infer, and that providers have clear, comprehensible information about what is required and what is expected of providers in implementing the home visiting program (Chapter 10). Sarama and Clements's Network of Influences (Chapter 9) represents their understanding of the importance of players outside the classroom in supporting successful ongoing implementation. They invite school administrators to participate in every step of the process (although many do not take advantage of these opportunities).

All three previous chapters in Section III tout the importance of the administrators and supervisors, those who support the frontline staff who in turn deliver the program. Some of the effective ways in which they describe these administrators and supervisors as fostering positive staff behaviors include: 1) including frontline staff in decision-making and problem-solving processes, 2) providing clear rules and performance standards, 3) providing high-quality in-service training and/or consultation/coaching that is responsive to staff needs, 4) monitoring fidelity and performance, 5) providing regular feedback to improve performance, and 6) working effectively with external systems to ensure continuing needed support for the program or intervention. Coaching, mentoring, and supervision as well as internal management support are also among the drivers of successful implementation identified by Metz et al. (2007). All three of the preceding chapters illustrate many of these features and reinforce how central they are to effective implementation, especially once the intervention is mature, at replication and scale-up.

Perhaps nowhere is administrative and supervisory support better illustrated than in the NFP's reflective supervision model, involving training of supervisors, guidelines regarding supervisors' maximum effective workload, and weekly reflective supervision time. If implemented correctly, this kind of system should provide technical and social support for the nurse home visitor while also giving supervisors detailed knowledge of the work being done by their supervisees.

Similarly, in both the Educare and TRIAD models, teachers participate in preservice training but then also receive consultation and coaching visits throughout the year. Data collected by coaches using the fidelity checklist in the TRIAD model are used in conjunction with those collected by the teachers rating their own practice to form the basis of consultation and coaching sessions. In both models, outcome data include information on teacher practices and classroom environments that can be used to highlight areas of need for teacher professional development.

Is Intervention Fidelity Less Important at Replication and Scale-Up?

As shown in Figure 12.1 above, staff/facilitator behaviors (also referred to as practitioner behaviors) and participant behaviors (which in early care and education are children's behaviors or parents' behaviors) contain key features of the later stages of implementation—from initial implementation through sustaining practice and full implementation. There has been an increasing amount of emphasis on monitoring fidelity of implementation across the stages of implementation, and without a doubt, it is important for staff to adhere to the core program elements, at least those that are central to the model's own theoretical framework. However, researchers recognize that the *quality* of the service provided is at least as important as *what* is provided—it is necessary but not sufficient to deliver the services in the prescribed environment.

An example of this would be leading a small group activity in grouping objects by attributes (an intervention subcomponent) but conducting it as a closed-ended activity rather than eliciting children's reasoning in solving the problem (a quality aspect of the subcomponent). Superficially, participants are enacting the same behaviors (the teacher sets up the game, the children solve the problem), but it doesn't adhere to the developer's theory of action underlying the activity because the point of the activity was to engage children in questioning and thinking about the problem, not just to arrive at an endpoint.

While all three chapters describe implementation fidelity measurement tools, all three interventions face the challenge of a need for better measurement tools to capture information about quality and of participant responsiveness, or take-up. All three chapters discuss the importance of the quality of services provided, but evidence that would be needed to support the development of measures of this aspect is not readily available.

As noted above, adaptation is also a terribly important element to consider, as not all adaptation adversely affects outcomes. At the full implementation stage, practitioners' understanding of the theory underlying the program model may be sufficient to allow them to devise novel and innovative solutions to challenges they encounter. Innovation (i.e., adaptation that is in line with the program model's theoretical framework or theory of action) can be desirable, whereas drift (i.e., adaptation without adherence to the "active ingredients" of the model) is generally undesirable, particularly if the latter type of adaptations conflicts with or undermines the model's theory of action. Documenting and analyzing the adaptations in a given setting is important if one is evaluating the effectiveness of that instance of implementation.

Hill and Olds (Chapter 10) described one adverse adaptation of the NFP model: supervisors not conducting weekly one-on-one reflective supervision sessions because they viewed it as a lower priority activity compared with their other responsibilities. A possible innovative adaptation that would not conflict with the model (but was not described in the chapter) would be providing home visits in Spanish or tailoring consultations to be more culturally sensitive even if the model was neither developed nor tested in large numbers of Spanish-speaking homes or didn't take into account particular cultural values. Hill and Olds describe adaptations that they made along the way in the course of developing the current version of the NFP model, but once the model is adopted beyond their immediate control, other adaptations could come into play.

The Educare and TRIAD approaches to documenting and analyzing participant behaviors (Chapters 11 and 9, respectively) include use of the Classroom Assessment Scoring System (CLASS) observation measure in Educare classrooms and the use of a mathematics-content-oriented observational tool for classroom observation and close observation in the form of ongoing assessment of children on the part of teachers in TRIAD. These behaviors are among the most challenging to observe and document systematically in a low-inference manner that provides useful information beyond the classroom. The CLASS, because it is now so widely used and includes several dimensions that focus on participant behaviors rather than just teacher/caregiver behaviors, provides a possible tool for insight into how participants are responding to the services provided. This information is probably most useful in two ways: 1) for informing teacher practice in the context of everyday operation and 2) for helping to explain outcomes in the context of replication.

Issues and Lessons Learned

All three preceding chapters highlighted the fact that providing the level of specificity and the types of implementation supports necessary to replicate their program models was a long, involved process that required a great deal of thought, data-supported reflection and analysis, and testing of adaptations. The replications themselves then provided further data—both qualitative and quantitative—that laid the groundwork for implementation on a large scale. The TRIAD model provides a framework for thinking about the kinds of supports necessary for effective implementation of a curriculum in a school or early learning setting, including the interesting realization that implementation team leaders, especially school or center administrators, do not need to be experts in the curriculum content area, but they must at least "[understand] the components and [collaborate] with others who [are] experts (such as those who have served as coaches in a previous implementation)" (Chapter 9, p. 187). For diffusion without fatal dilution, this could be a realistic approach to scaling up an intervention.

It is also interesting that all three chapters describe dedicated commitment to enhancement of the well-being of the participants with less sentimental attachment to particular components. As Sarama and Clements point out, "Our research design could not identify which components of the TRIAD model and its instantiation are critical components" (Chapter 9, p. 187). Educare and the NFP face the same challenge. Identifying the most effective components (or critical "active ingredients") would require either a series of planned variation experiments, which would be hard to accomplish, or a massive amount of data, which the ELN or the NFP would be on their way to having if they were not supporting adherence to model components as closely.

The paradox here is that in order to identify a critical component at this stage, it is necessary to remove it—either from a very large number of cases or at random—which feels irresponsible if the elements have been carefully selected based on other empirical evidence. The NFP approach strongly urges participants to use weekly one-on-one reflective supervision sessions, but they do not have actual evidence (nor am I suggesting they should try to obtain it) that these sessions could not be just as effective if held regularly on a biweekly schedule or after every sixth workday, for example. The weekly session is the developer's best guess at a frequency that is effective. The field of early care and education is filled with these kinds of program elements that are not based on empirical evidence but nevertheless make a lot of sense and so become indispensable. This is another challenge for implementation science: When elements of the evidence-based program are not based on empirical evidence, are adaptations that affect only those elements allowable?

Conclusions

The chapters in Section III really call attention to the need for the field to capitalize on work done to date to spread promising models effectively, and they show how using implementation science has enabled developers, systems, and practitioners to work systematically toward steady program improvement, increasingly clear specification of both intervention fidelity and implementation fidelity, and broader dissemination of the lessons they have learned along the way. These three chapters also make a strong case for leveraging implementation science to push for development of measures in difficult-to-measure areas that are known to be key implementation components, such as quality of service and participant responsiveness.

One of the central challenges at both the system and practitioner levels is matching evaluation to implementation stage by focusing on components that are most powerful and salient at the various stages. The three preceding chapters show how this can be done artfully, using the tools of implementation science, albeit with a great deal of work. Implementation science can help us achieve a crunchy, tangy apple, but it won't be easy.

References

Berkel, C., Mauricio, A., Schoenfelder, E., & Sandler, I. (2011). Putting the pieces together: An integrated model of program implementation. *Prevention Science, 12*, 23–33.

Dane, A., & Schneider, B. (1998). Program integrity in primary and early secondary prevention: Are implementation effects out of control? *Clinical Psychology Review, 18*, 23–45.

Dodge, D.T., & Colker, L.J. (1992). *The creative curriculum for early childhood (The Creative Curriculum®)*. Bethesda, MD: Teaching Strategies.

Durlak, J., & DuPre, E. (2008). Implementation matters: A review of research on the influence of implementation on program outcomes and the factors affecting implementation. *American Journal of Community Psychology, 41*, 327–350.

Dusenbury, L., Brannigan, R., Falco, M., & W. Hansen. (2003). A review of research on fidelity of implementation: Implications for drug abuse prevention in school settings. *Health Education Research, 18*, 237–256.

Layzer, J., & Layzer, C. (2011). *A conceptual framework for implementation analysis.* Initially developed with funding from the U.S. Department of Health and Human Services, as part of the Feasibility and Design contract for the Teen Pregnancy Prevention Replication Study, under contract number HHSP23320095624WC, Task Order HHSP2333010T. Belmont, MA: Belmont Research Associates/Abt Associates.

Metz, A.J.R., Blase, K., & Bowie, L. (2007). *Implementing evidence-based practices: Six "drivers" of success* (Research-to-Results Brief #2007-29). Washington, DC: Child Trends. Retrieved from http://www.childtrends.org/files/child_trends-2007_10_01_RB_6successdrivers.pdf

Sarama, J., Clements, D.H., Wolfe, C.B., & Spitler, M.E. (2012). Longitudinal evaluation of a scale-up model for teaching mathematics with trajectories and technologies. *Journal of Research on Educational Effectiveness, 5*, 105–135.

Seabrook, J. (2011, November 21). Crunch: Building a better apple. *New Yorker,* 54–64.

Implementation
Science at the Systems Level

Tamara Halle

Applying an implementation science framework to examining early care and education (ECE) systems (as opposed to individual programs) is at an early stage of development. As such, the two chapters in this final part of the book represent a relatively new frontier for the early childhood field. The chapters by Kathryn Tout, Allison Metz, and Leah Bartley (Chapter 13) and Diane Paulsell, Kathryn Tout, and Kelly Maxwell (Chapter 14) provide several important considerations for early childhood researchers, program developers, and funders who aim to understand how to better investigate and support the effective functioning of ECE systems. Each of the two chapters explores the use of an implementation lens to highlight the challenges and opportunities surrounding the implementation and evaluation of ECE system-wide initiatives.

In their chapter, Tout, Metz, and Bartley address how to apply an implementation science lens to professional development (PD) systems within ECE as well as school-age care. They begin by describing existing state PD systems and the challenges of delivering integrated services across sectors and across diverse practitioners. They contrast this "system as is" with an ideally integrated state PD system—the "system to be"—and offer a set of goals to guide system change efforts. The authors discuss these goals using a framework proffered by Coffman (2007) that identifies five targets for improving systems initiatives: the political and policy *context* in which the system functions, *components* of the system, *connections* across system components, *infrastructure* (i.e., system supports), and *scale* (i.e., system accessibility and reach). The authors highlight the many challenges that are presented for achieving a fully integrated PD system; one example is the difficulty in aligning PD standards across sectors and funding streams.

The latter half of Chapter 13 incorporates implementation strategies to facilitate PD systems change by targeting the same five areas of systems improvement identified by Coffman (2007): context, components, connections, infrastructure, and scale. Specific examples are offered for bringing about change within several of the target areas. The authors emphasize how strategies may differ based on the stage of implementation for each target of PD systems change. For example, a strategy targeting accessibility of professional development ("scale") may differ depending on whether a state is in a stage of initial implementation or full implementation.

Special emphasis is given to the role of implementation teams for crafting and navigating PD systems improvement initiatives at the state level. The authors point out the importance of establishing implementation teams at each level of the PD system (e.g., local, state, national) and ensuring strong communication and working relationships across these levels. The reality of systems functioning in the "real world" is that each component of the system may be at a different stage of implementation, so implementation teams must first plan and then intervene accordingly to bring about the fully integrated and well-functioning system they hope to achieve. These teams must learn to use rapid-cycle feedback loops to share information within and across levels of the system on how things are functioning in real time and make strategic adjustments along the way for each of the multiple target areas of a system, keeping the intention of highly integrated and well-functioning PD systems as their ultimate long-term goal.

Implementation teams may be convened to support short-term implementation goals, or they may continue to function over time to support sustained changes in practices and system components. Establishing implementation teams and using continuous data feedback loops are not easy tasks, and the authors do not promise it will be easy, but the concrete examples they offer provide some reassurance to practitioners as well as evaluators that taking a systematic approach that is stage-based and informed by the engagement of implementation teams can be beneficial.

Paulsell, Tout, and Maxwell in Chapter 14 consider how implementation science frameworks can inform the development and evaluation of quality rating and improvement systems (QRIS). QRIS are multifaceted, system-wide ECE initiatives that include five key components: 1) quality standards, 2) program monitoring and assignment of ratings, 3) quality improvement initiatives for ECE staff across sectors, 4) financial incentives, and 5) consumer information. The first part of the chapter provides a thorough consideration of each of these key components of a QRIS and the current state of the research on QRIS. The authors point out a critical dilemma: the evidence to support the efficacy of implementing any of these five key components of QRIS is currently limited, yet states are nonetheless actively engaged in establishing these systems in their states. QRIS may be seen at the current time as an "evidence-informed" ECE initiative rather than an "evidence-based" one.

To move the field to more rigorous levels of evidence for system-wide quality initiatives such as QRIS, strong systems frameworks and evaluation frameworks need to be employed more consistently. Chapter 14 shows how the implementation science frames of "core implementation components" and "stages of implementation" can be used to think about the functioning of QRIS, but they also employ systems theory (e.g., Hargreaves, 2010) to understand how to operationalize the effectiveness of QRIS at the systems level. The authors provide examples of the use of tools honed within implementation science (such as cascading logic models) to demonstrate how the use of such frameworks can inform rigorous evaluation of QRIS. They suggest that the use of implementation strategies (such as establishing implementation teams) can lead to evidence-based, high-quality, and fully implemented QRIS, similar to what the authors of Chapter 13 call the "system to be."

Chapter 14 ends with a discussion of implications and future directions for state child care administrators and other practitioners, evaluators, and policy makers.

These two chapters in Section IV provide a promising starting point for the exploration of the science of implementation as it extends to and encompasses systems issues within the field of early care and education. We will explore further implications for research, policy, and practice in Chapter 15.

References

Coffman, J. (2007). *A framework for evaluating systems initiatives.* N.p.: Build Initiative. Retrieved from http://www.buildinitiative.org/files/BuildInitiativefullreport.pdf

Hargreaves, M.B. (2010). *Evaluating systems change: A planning guide.* Princeton, NJ: Mathematica Policy Research.

CHAPTER 13

Considering Statewide Professional Development Systems

Kathryn Tout, Allison Metz, and Leah Bartley

Early care and education (ECE) and school-age care (SAC) practitioners are the heart of high-quality programs for young children. The knowledge and skills of practitioners and their ability to engage children and families in positive relationships that enhance child development are a critical component of an effective ECE-SAC system. Statewide professional development (PD) systems are responsible for supporting practitioners through an integrated web of services and resources that include education and training opportunities, technical assistance, and financial assistance. Ideally, these supports would be available to and delivered across practitioners who provide direct services to children and families in different sectors, in different types of settings, and with children spanning the age spectrum. PD systems support would also be available to trainers, faculty in higher education, technical assistance providers, and agency staff at the state level or in organizations working on behalf of those providing direct services. Expectations for practitioners would be aligned with expectations for children's development, and PD systems would ensure that services are based on an assessment of individual practitioners' strengths and needs.

In reality, statewide PD systems do not function in this integrated manner (LeMoine, 2008). The type, availability, and quality of PD opportunities vary greatly, depending on the sector and settings in which practitioners work. These variations reflect different entry requirements, regulatory structures, funding streams, and PD service providers that are distinct for practitioners in programs across ECE-SAC, including school-based prekindergarten programs, community-based child care centers, Head Start, early intervention programs, licensed family child care homes, and before- and afterschool care. This inconsistent service delivery and quality in PD systems has negative implications for ECE-SAC practitioners and the children and families they serve.

Despite these gaps and challenges, statewide PD systems are expected to play a central role in supporting the workforce as part of quality improvement initiatives such as quality rating and improvement systems (QRIS) and other initiatives aimed at facilitating young children's positive outcomes. Given these high expectations and recent federal investments emphasizing PD systems as a core feature of an ECE-SAC system (e.g., the Race to the Top–Early Learning Challenge grants), it is an ideal time to strategize about the steps needed to strengthen the components and overall functioning of PD systems.

Working toward the goal of effective, integrated statewide PD systems for ECE-SAC practitioners, this chapter presents two frameworks to support both a *vision* for PD systems and *action* to achieve and maintain effective system functioning. The vision is outlined using a *systems initiative framework* that specifies five targets of systems initiatives (context, components, connections, infrastructure, and scale) and the mechanisms by which activities to address each component can result in meaningful outcomes for system beneficiaries (Coffman, 2007). The guide to action applies a *staged implementation framework* to the systems initiatives targets and describes how the application of implementation science principles to the development of integrated PD systems can promote system effectiveness (achieving better outcomes) and efficiency (consolidating services and leveraging limited resources). A central premise of the chapter is that the strength and sustainability of the ECE-SAC workforce is a goal worthy of setting and pursuing along with the ultimate goal of supporting young children's development. A vision and action for an integrated PD system need to include both children and practitioners as beneficiaries of system activities.

The following section begins with an overview of Julia Coffman's (2007) systems initiatives targets and uses them to guide a description of the status of existing statewide PD systems (the "system as is"). The discussion then turns to a vision for an ideal PD system (the "system to be") and the goals and outcomes that a PD systems initiative would set and achieve for children and practitioners. This is followed by a section describing how an implementation framework can facilitate the development of the system to be. The chapter concludes with recommendations for concrete action steps to support and strengthen statewide PD systems.

Status of Professional Development Systems and Research: The System As Is

Existing national models for PD systems outline infrastructure, policy principles, and goals and have been used by states to assist with the development and organization of PD system activities. Three models that have been influential in state efforts are as follows:

1. The Child Care and Development Fund (CCDF) plan components promoted by the Office of Child Care and the National Center on Child Care Professional Development Systems and Workforce Initiatives which closely reflect the components described previously by the former National Child Care Information Center (NCCIC; 2007)

2. The National Association for the Education of Young Children (NAEYC) Policy Blueprint (LeMoine, 2008)

3. The National Professional Development Center on Inclusion (NPDCI; 2008, 2010; Buysse, Winton, & Rous, 2009)

Though there are differences in focus and content of these models, they emphasize a set of common PD systems features that must be attended to in systems-building efforts, including finance and governance, supportive policies and work environments, defined core knowledge and competencies, evidence-based practice, quality assurance, access to PD opportunities, and data and evaluation. Our intent in this chapter is not to provide a full description and comparison of each of these models and features. Instead, it is to focus on improvement of PD systems by describing specific steps and structures to achieve system integration.

We use two definitions from the existing models to establish common language for the chapter. First, we use the NPDCI definition of *professional development*, which states that "professional development is facilitated teaching and learning experiences that are transactional and designed to support the acquisition of professional knowledge, skills, and dispositions as well as the application of this knowledge in practice" (National Professional Development Center on Inclusion, 2008, p. 3). Second, we use language from NAEYC's Early Childhood Workforce Systems Initiative to define an *integrated PD system* as one that serves professionals working in direct and nondirect services roles across sectors, decreases duplication of effort, and increases accountability and sustainability (LeMoine, 2008).

We use Coffman's systems initiatives targets to guide our description. In this framework, Coffman (2007, p. 5) outlines five areas that may be targeted by systems improvement efforts:

1. A focus on *context* includes efforts to build political will and produce policy and funding changes.

2. A focus on *components* includes efforts to improve programs and services within the system.

3. A focus on *connections* includes efforts to build linkages across system components.

4. A focus on *infrastructure* includes efforts to develop system supports.

5. A focus on *scale* includes efforts to build a broad and inclusive system.

Coffman notes that most systems initiatives do not focus on all five targets simultaneously. Initiatives might focus on only one or two target areas. They may also weight efforts to improve certain targets more than others. In this chapter, we use the targets to structure our discussion of vision and action for a PD systems improvement initiative.

Table 13.1 outlines each target and briefly notes the gaps and challenges in existing PD systems. Each of these is described in more detail below. It is important to note that the purpose of including this framework is to offer a rubric for considering different efforts, not to suggest strict boundaries or definitions. For example, some content described in the following sections might rightfully be described as a "connection" or as "infrastructure." The intent is to provide handles to support discussion, not to be rigid in our conceptualization of these elements.

Current Context

Context refers to the political and social environment of a system (Coffman, 2007). In PD systems, the current context—that is, the existing regulatory environment and work conditions—is a central challenge to achieving effective PD systems.

Table 13.1. Outline of a vision for improving early care and education and school-age care professional development systems using Coffman's (2007) systems initiatives framework

	Context	Components	Connections	Infrastructure	Scale
Goal	Increase public support for early care and education (ECE) and school-age practitioners and political will to enact policy changes leading to compensation parity and higher baseline requirements.	Increase options and the quality of workforce preparation, support, and leadership programs.	Increase integration of workforce preparation and support programs across the early childhood sectors.	Create a sustainable, aligned set of system standards, incentives, quality assurance structures, and processes for tracking progress toward system goals.	Increase accessibility of workforce preparation and support programs and opportunities.
System as is	Minimal licensing requirements for the workforce in most states. Low compensation and benefits. Limited opportunities to advance. Lack of system focus on practitioner outcomes as worthy goals.	Inconsistent quality of preparation programs in institutes of higher education. Greater focus on knowledge building than on demonstration of skills. Insufficient focus in preparation programs on current realities of families, including cultural and linguistic diversity and children with special needs. Insufficient focus on leadership in early childhood programs.	Early childhood sectors (child care, Head Start, prekindergarten, special education) function in silos with separate funding and requirements.	Separate professional standards and expectations for quality programming exist by sector. Monitoring systems are separate by sector. Data and evaluation efforts are conducted within sector. Funding for infrastructure is limited.	Workforce does not have equal access to supports and opportunities. Logistical and financial obstacles are barriers.
Challenges to professional development (PD) system initiatives	Many ECE practitioners are in private businesses and may resist new requirements. Increased regulations would create hardships for the current workforce.	Students entering ECE preparation programs may need additional support before they can take coursework. A significant proportion of workforce preparation and support programs are not credit bearing.	Early childhood sectors serve distinct populations with specific needs; one size can't fit all.	Efforts to integrate may be resisted if they dilute a focus on groups with particular needs. Monitoring and quality assurance are costly and require adherence to rigorous measurement protocols.	Funding for statewide scale-up will need to be increased from current levels.
Opportunities to address PD system target	Raised awareness about the importance of a skilled and supported workforce could increase public investment. PD initiatives and supports could attract a skilled workforce and offer more sustainable careers.	Increased quality of workforce preparation and support programs will lead to increased quality of practices with children and families. Increased focus on leadership will help build more supportive ECE programs.	Leveraging and sharing limited resources across sectors will improve quality, reach, and efficiency of the system.	Improved infrastructure to incentivize the workforce and track progress toward higher quality will promote targeting of resources toward highest needs.	Increased reach and depth of supports for the workforce will expand high-quality practices to more children and families.

Regulations for education and training of ECE-SAC practitioners vary by setting and are generally minimal (according to data summarized in U.S. Government Accountability Office [GAO], 2012). Family-based providers have the fewest requirements. States typically have no entry-level educational licensing requirement for family-based providers and require 9 to 16 hours of annual training. Common requirements for lead center-based teachers are less than a high school diploma (16 states) or a high school diploma (16 states); fewer states require some college (9 states), a state certificate or credentials (5 states), a Child Development Associate credential or associate degree (3 states), or a bachelor's degree (2 states) (National Association of Child Care Resource and Referral Agencies [NACCRRA], 2011). Ongoing training requirements for lead teachers are typically 11 to 15 hours annually. In contrast, the most common educational requirement for teachers in state prekindergarten programs is a bachelor's degree with 15 hours of annual training (GAO, 2012).

Mirroring the regulations, the educational qualifications of the ECE workforce vary significantly by sector and specific occupation. Overall, nearly three quarters of the workforce (72%) has less than an associate degree (GAO, 2012). Program directors (making up 5% of the workforce) and preschool teachers (a quarter of the workforce) are the most likely to have a bachelor's degree (46% and 32%, respectively). Nearly half of center-based workers and family child care providers have a high school diploma as their highest educational level. The majority of the 333,000 ECE workers with a bachelor's degree do not have a degree in early childhood education (GAO, 2012).

The environments in which ECE-SAC practitioners work are characterized by low compensation, limited benefits, and few opportunities or incentives to advance. (Efforts to compare compensation and other characteristics of the ECE-SAC workforce are limited by the availability of data sources that make critical distinctions—for example, whether preschool teachers work in child care centers or in schools and whether work is full- or part-time.) Data from the American Community Survey indicate that there were 1.8 million workers in ECE settings (including before- and afterschool care programs) in 2009 (Institute of Medicine [IOM] and National Research Council [NRC], 2012; GAO, 2012). Just under two thirds of full-time ECE workers (61%) earned less than $22,000 per year, which is less than the 2009 federal poverty guidelines for a family of four, $22,050 (GAO, 2012). The 2009 data also demonstrated a limited range of annual incomes between the highest ($22,500) and lowest ($20,000) paid workers in ECE (not including program directors), which provides little reward for advancement in the field and negatively impacts the recruitment and retention of qualified practitioners. There are also discrepancies in compensation by occupation and setting. For example, in 2010, "child care workers" had annual earnings of $20,800, compared to $32,292 for preschool and kindergarten teachers and $14,000 for family child care providers (IOM & NRC, 2012).

Few practitioners are able to access benefits such as health insurance, paid vacation and sick leave, and retirement savings. For example, 31% of child care workers and 75% of preschool teachers have access to health insurance, compared to 84% of all workers across occupations. Similarly, only 30% of child care workers and 47% of preschool teachers have access to retirement benefits, compared to 69% of workers in general (IOM & NRC, 2012). Access to these benefits is higher for workers in schools than in other facilities. Turnover among center-based child care staff is estimated at 30% annually, with 18% exiting the ECE field altogether (IOM & NRC, 2012; Whitebook & Sakai, 2003).

In addition to the challenges of minimal educational qualifications, low compensation, and limited access to benefits, efforts to support the ECE-SAC workforce face an additional barrier of elevating goals for practitioners to the level of goals for children. In PD systems as they exist, improving the quality of early childhood programs and the quality and conditions of the workforce is articulated primarily as intermediate steps to reaching desired goals for improving children's outcomes.

Current Components

Components refers to the quality of the programs and services that are provided within a system. In the PD system as is, the components are highly variable and difficult to characterize adequately with existing data. Professional development for ECE-SAC practitioners is delivered through a variety of institutions of higher education and community organizations (such as resource and referral agencies and professional associations) and a diverse set of faculty and professional trainers working independently and for community programs. It includes experiences that range from preservice, credit-bearing courses and supervised practicums delivered in community colleges or universities to one-hour trainings on cardiopulmonary resuscitation delivered in a local library by a health consultant and on-site coaching delivered to support the use of a new curriculum in a child care center. In this section, we highlight four key challenges of the components that exist in the system as is.

First, within institutions of higher education, the content of early childhood preparation programs is of concern. In a recent overview of evidence examining degrees in early childhood, Whitebook and Ryan (2011) note that many early childhood preparation programs in schools of education are geared more toward preparing teachers for early elementary grades than for preschool, while coursework in other departments such as child development or family and consumer sciences typically does not focus on teacher preparation. ECE preparation programs also struggle to integrate concepts of developmentally appropriate practice with pedagogy that also focuses on children's academic skills and school readiness (Whitebook, Gomby, Bellm, Sakai, & Kipnis, 2009a). Whitebook and Ryan (2011) further note that competencies for early childhood educators developed in a particular state may not be considered in the curricula or certification programs in institutes of higher education in that state. To date, states vary greatly in the extent to which their early educator competencies are being integrated into preservice programs.

Second, PD programs—whether preparatory programs in institutes of higher education or programs in community-based organizations providing in-service training—are inconsistent in the extent to which they offer opportunities for supervised fieldwork or for demonstrating application of new knowledge to their practice (IOM & NRC, 2012; Whitebook & Ryan, 2011). Though existing research is not precise enough to specify an exact formula for delivering professional development, reviews of the evidence are clear that PD is most effective when specific, research-based knowledge is intentionally and tightly linked to opportunities for reflective practice (Weber & Trauten, 2008; Whitebook, Gomby, Bellm, Sakai, & Kipnis, 2009b; Zaslow, Tout, Halle, Vick Whittaker, & Lavelle, 2010). These opportunities may be included during preservice education as well as when a practitioner is employed in the field and working to adopt new practices. Yet currently, student teaching placements for early childhood teachers are uncommon, and while coaching and mentoring opportunities have increased, they are still inaccessible to the majority of practitioners in the workforce (Whitebook et al., 2009b; Whitebook & Ryan, 2011).

Third, existing ECE preservice and PD opportunities do not focus adequately on issues related to diversity, poverty, and children who are dual language learners (Ray, Bowman, & Robbins, 2006; Whitebook et al., 2009a). In one study of bachelor's degree programs for early childhood practitioners, only 7% of sampled programs indicated that they expect the students in their programs to gain experience teaching in settings with children of diverse races, cultures, languages, and abilities before they graduate (Ray et al., 2006). Studies of ECE preparatory programs also indicate that existing faculty do not reflect the diversity of either the students or the children who will be served by the students, and many of them may not have recent experience in the field, particularly teaching diverse children (Whitebook & Ryan, 2011). Some faculty also lack grounding in research and theory, which limits their ability to help students be good consumers of research in their implementation of evidence-based practices (Hyson, Tomlinson, & Morris, 2009).

Fourth and finally, existing preservice and PD programs lack a focus on developing leadership strategies for early childhood practitioners. In a survey conducted by Hyson and colleagues (2009), less than half of the faculty respondents indicated that effective leadership is a priority for enhancing their students' effectiveness. With rapidly shifting policy and program initiatives in the ECE field, the lack of attention paid to developing leadership and professionalization of the field is a gap in the current system.

Current Connections

Connections in a system are the linkages between components (Coffman, 2007). A defining feature of existing PD systems is the lack of connections and alignment across components—a gap that is highlighted in each of the models noted above (LeMoine, 2008; NCCIC, 2007; NPDCI, 2011) and by members of the Committee on Early Childhood Care and Education Workforce convened by the Board on Children, Youth, and Families (IOM & NRC, 2012).

In descriptions of professional development for ECE-SAC practitioners, the term *silo* is often used to describe how activities are organized by sector and by the primary funding stream for that sector. These funding streams include the CCDF, early childhood special education, early intervention, Head Start/Early Head Start, and prekindergarten programs in school districts, among others. In addition to different funding streams, these programs are also characterized by distinct purposes and professional standards. The practitioners employed in each sector are distinct (as described above), and the populations of children served in each sector are unique. Career pathways for ECE-SAC practitioners are not linked or aligned across sectors, and activities in one sector or pursued for one function may not be recognized in another sector (LeMoine, 2008). Duplication of services is common in the system as is.

Despite these strong barriers, states have begun the process of launching integration efforts to link professional development across sectors. These efforts include, for example, planning for integrated data systems, early learning councils that provide cross-sector PD oversight, and QRIS that work to provide common or aligned elements across sectors. These opportunities are described in further detail later in this chapter.

Current Infrastructure

Infrastructure refers to the supports in a system (Coffman, 2007). In current PD systems, infrastructure elements exist but are often not coordinated across sectors. Thus, limited resources are spread thin with redundant services and efforts. Duplicative efforts also are confusing or challenging for practitioners to navigate. Here we describe four infrastructure elements that are problematic in PD systems.

The first element is professional standards and expectations for high-quality practice. These standards provide a foundation for PD activities because they guide the goals and define desired outcomes for practitioners. In existing PD systems, multiple voluntary standards are available at the national and state levels that are distinct by sponsor and sector (IOM & NRC, 2012). This is problematic because the multiple recommendations for standards may not be aligned with each other and may or may not reflect the most current research base on effective practices for working with diverse children (IOM & NRC, 2012). Standards may be developed at the federal level (those for Head Start and Early Head Start, for example) or by the state (typically called "core knowledge and competencies for practitioners"). In some cases, program standards or quality indicators are also included as part of a state QRIS, or they may be available from national organizations that provide program accreditation or other certification options for programs or practitioners (such as NAEYC and the Division of Early Childhood of the Council for Exceptional Children).

A second and related infrastructure issue is the existence in the system of multiple monitoring and quality assurance strategies that are organized primarily by sector. Head Start monitoring, for example, is a structured process at the national level that includes a comprehensive annual review of grantees and their compliance with Head Start performance standards. Depending on the size of the grantee, on-site monitoring visits may take a week or more to complete and include document review, interviews, and structured observations. Monitoring for child care licensing, in contrast, varies dramatically between states. Regulations regarding which facilities and programs need to be licensed are different from state to state, and states conduct on-site inspections at different rates (with 20 states requiring no more than one on-site inspection per year) (NACCRRA, 2011). QRIS monitoring processes typically cover fewer standards and indicators than state licensing or Head Start, and ratings are valid for a year or two, depending on the QRIS (Tout et al., 2010). The Office of Special Education Programs conducts monitoring visits annually to determine compliance with federal regulations for programs serving children with disabilities. Thus, some early childhood programs and practitioners are overseen by multiple monitoring systems with standards that may or may not be aligned with each other, while other programs may not be covered by even basic licensing regulations.

A third issue in existing PD systems is a lack of coordinated data and evaluation to document the status of the workforce as a whole and the effectiveness of efforts to improve the workforce. While advances have been made in the data infrastructure for PD systems, there are still different systems used by different sectors. For example, registries for practitioners, containing information on practitioner qualifications, training, and employment history, are in use in more than 30 states (National Registry Alliance, 2012). Registries may also house information about approved training and trainers in a PD system. Most registries are voluntary, however, which results in coverage that is not uniform within or between sectors. In addition, states usually have registries for licensed teachers in the K–12 system, so preschool teachers employed by schools may have more than one registry in which they can enroll. Data collection at a federal level of workers and of business establishments is conducted annually by the Census Bureau (the American Community Survey and the Current Population Survey) and the Department of Labor's Bureau of Labor Statistics (the Occupational Employment Survey), but none of these surveys covers or distinguishes the full range of settings and ECE-SAC practitioners (GAO, 2012). Evaluation efforts in PD systems are limited by the funding stream (which is typically sector specific and thus dictates sector-specific priorities for evaluation questions) as well as the amount of funding (which usually is not adequate to cover efforts across multiple sectors or programs).

Finally, funding levels present significant infrastructure challenges across PD systems and limit the availability of PD opportunities of sufficient intensity and with incentives to promote participation.

Current Scale

Scale refers to the depth and breadth of a system (Coffman, 2007). In existing PD systems, issues related to scale are best conceptualized as access issues that cover not only the availability of appropriate PD opportunities for practitioners but also the significant logistical and financial obstacles that practitioners encounter in accessing PD (Whitebook & Ryan, 2011). For example, access to PD is limited in rural and remote areas. Though opportunities for distance learning are becoming more prevalent, many practitioners still encounter challenges operating their own computers or finding high-speed Internet connections that can support their use of distance-learning strategies. Additionally, many ECE-SAC practitioners seeking PD are full-time employees who are diverse in their cultures and languages (Whitebook & Ryan, 2011). PD offerings do not often take into account the needs of the targeted population and the accommodations and incentives that may be needed to promote participation (IOM & NRC, 2012).

PD systems have made definite strides toward increasing access for practitioners using a variety of tools, though these are still available primarily by sector. For example, cohort programs are being tested to understand how the existence of a peer group and other support may assist students in completing a bachelor's degree program (e.g., Kipnis, Whitebook, Almaraz, Sakai, & Austin, 2012). Career advising is available in some states to facilitate access to appropriate PD (LeMoine, 2008). Scholarships (such as the Teacher Education and Compensation Helps – T.E.A.C.H. – Early Childhood Project) and retention programs are available to offset the cost of seeking an ECE degree and of staying in the workplace once the degree has been received. While these strides in bringing PD systems to scale are important to acknowledge, they are not yet at a point where they serve more than a small proportion of the workforce.

Summary of Strengths and Challenges in the System As Is

Before turning to a vision of an effective and integrated PD system, we should summarize the key strengths and challenges in current PD systems, as these are important contextual factors to consider in developing an action plan for implementation.

One strength to highlight in current PD systems is the recognition that integration and improvement are critical goals to set. Though many of these integration efforts are still in nascent stages, the fact that states acknowledge the need to build a system across sectors and across funding streams is an important starting point for action.

A second strength to embrace in system improvement initiatives is the diversity and dedication of the existing workforce. We have noted numerous concerns related to the educational qualifications and PD profiles of ECE-SAC practitioners. Yet, it is also important to highlight the strengths of a multicultural and multilingual workforce that is needed to serve an increasingly diverse population of children, as well as the dedication of practitioners who are willing to work in an industry with low compensation and status.

Though we have noted the prevalence of silos across sectors and the inefficiencies and inequities that result when a system is not integrated, the "specialization" of PD services activities in existing PD systems is a strength that should be included in an integrated system. For example, family child care practitioners work in environments that are unlike the sectors and settings of other practitioners. They care for children of different ages and interact with families in ways that are distinct from what teachers in center-based settings do. In some cases, family child care practitioners may be related to the children in their care. They are responsible for developing daily activities with children as well as administrative policies for their business. PD activities that are tailored specifically for practitioners who serve unique populations or who have different educational qualifications and levels of experience are a critical component of an integrated system.

The challenges in existing PD systems are prevalent and include 1) workplaces with low compensation and limited benefits, 2) components that do not meet expectations for quality and accessibility, 3) a lack of cross-sector connections among components, 4) duplication of services, and 5) multiple standards for practice that are not aligned and are confusing for practitioners to navigate. The diversity of the workforce—noted as a strength above—is also a challenge because many ECE practitioners live and work in rural and/or home-based settings that are harder to reach with traditional PD activities and services. Many work full-time and have difficulty participating in PD opportunities that require significant allocations of time and financial resources.

Perhaps the most pressing challenge facing PD systems is the weight of the charge to increase the effectiveness of teaching and practice so that each child's learning and development is supported (NPDCI, 2011). This ultimate goal will be difficult to achieve without the recognition that goals for practitioners and the workforce—and the system that supports them—must first be articulated and prioritized at a policy level. Placing the full burden of improving children's learning and development on the existing workforce without acknowledging the range of political and system supports that are still needed will result in failure to achieve the desired results of PD efforts.

Reflecting on a System to Be: The Vision for an Integrated, Effective Professional Development System

With an understanding of the system as is, we turn now to a vision for an integrated, effective PD system, again using the five components of systems initiatives as a structure. For each component, we briefly outline a system goal that can serve as the focus of a systems initiative and describe critical challenges that will need to be addressed in actions to support the component (see Table 13.1 for an overview). Details about the "how" are provided later.

Context in an Integrated Professional Development System

Goal: Increase public support for ECE and SAC practitioners and political will to enact policy changes leading to compensation parity and higher baseline requirements. Changes in the policy context are essential for strengthening the foundation of PD systems. Raising the bar of licensing regulations is a difficult but important step in this process to ensure that children's basic health and safety are protected and to increase the professionalization of the ECE-SAC workforce. Recruiting to the field new educators who meet higher qualifications and are rewarded for their work through increased compensation and benefits is a second step in building public trust and investment in the workforce. The Center for the Study of Child Care Employment (2012) recommends that a national campaign be launched that would convey the benefits of a highly skilled ECE-SAC workforce and could be used to garner public support and recruit new entrants to the field.

There are numerous challenges to achieving these context changes that need to be addressed using implementation strategies that are described later in the chapter. In particular, resistance to new regulations is expected to come from current ECE-SAC business owners who would incur costs of meeting and maintaining higher licensing requirements and from parents who would bear increased costs in the form of higher tuition or child care fees. Supports both for practitioners to meet the new requirements and access PD and for parents to defray the cost of higher requirements are key elements of improving the PD system context.

Components in an Integrated Professional Development System

Goal: Increase options and the quality of workforce preparation, support, and leadership programs. The knowledge and skills of the workforce must be supported by strong education and training options that are aligned with professional standards for practice. Options for preservice preparation and for ongoing support of the workforce can be bolstered by 1) integrating new research-based content into existing education and training, 2) offering diverse options for accessing PD (including creating a stronger emphasis on preparing the workforce to work with an increasingly diverse group of children and families), 3) requiring and supporting application and demonstration of skills in real-world settings, and 4) promoting leadership development across all levels of the workforce.

Efforts to improve the quality of existing preservice and ongoing education and training (including technical assistance) will be challenged by capacity issues in higher education and in community-based organizations offering PD. Revising course content and requirements is time intensive, and many institutions of higher education have lost faculty and staff in recent years. In addition, revisions to existing PD systems must be sensitive to the needs of a diverse workforce that benefits from varying entry points to the system, including remote learning options. Practitioners will need support to navigate courses and training opportunities with more stringent entry and exit requirements.

Connections in an Integrated Professional Development System

Goal: Increase integration of workforce preparation and support programs across the ECE and SAC sectors. In addition to strengthening the content and requirements of existing PD opportunities, it is essential to provide integration of PD opportunities across ECE-SAC sectors. As noted, integration does not imply that all practitioners in the workforce have the same requirements or experiences. It does imply, however, that requirements and opportunities across sectors are made transparent so that practitioners can easily move within and between them. The benefit of integration is that practitioners have clear pathways outlining the qualifications needed for various positions in the field.

The challenge of systems initiatives focused on connections in a PD system emerges in the potential that integration efforts are viewed as a "one size fits all" solution. Indeed, successful efforts to build connections will embrace the strength of the current system in providing opportunities to meet practitioners where they are. A well-connected system can acknowledge the diversity of the workforce within and across sectors and offer pathways for accessing a coherent and relevant set of individualized supports and resources to improve their knowledge, skills, and practices with children and families.

Infrastructure in an Integrated Professional Development System

Goal: Create a sustainable, aligned set of system standards, incentives, quality assurance structures, and processes for tracking progress toward system goals. When developing the connections across sectors described above, it will be necessary to retool the infrastructure elements in the PD system to fit and support an integrated system. This retooling must recognize the building blocks that are in place already and engage in a process to align and integrate resources. For example, a PD registry for early childhood practitioners likely exists in parallel with a system that tracks credentials and qualifications of staff employed in K–12 settings. Rather than merging these two data systems, integration may involve developing processes to share and access data across them.

Challenges arise in the creation of integrated opportunities if there is a perception that requirements have been diluted or weakened to accommodate a broader workforce. There is also a need to prevent a de facto tiered system that conveys different quality profiles based on the workforce requirements or standards associated with different sectors. A QRIS could play an important role in creating a quality framework across sectors that identifies levels of quality based on aligned standards. Building integrated monitoring and quality assurance processes that can support a cross-sector QRIS will require innovative models and funding structures.

Scale in an Integrated Professional Development System

Goal: Increase accessibility to workforce preparation and support programs and opportunities. The final component to acknowledge in an integrated PD system is scale, which refers to the depth and breadth of the system. Improvements in system scale would focus on ensuring that practitioners across sectors and physical separation can access PD activities that are of high quality and that contribute to improved knowledge and skills. These efforts will involve increasing the capacity of the system as well as increasing supports for practitioners (e.g., scholarships, distance learning opportunities) to access system offerings.

The challenge to efforts to improve scale is largely, though not solely, financial. Additional financial resources are needed to increase the capacity of the system and to provide practitioners with scholarships, computer access, release time, and other supports needed to allow engagement in PD opportunities.

Summary of the System to Be

An integrated, effective PD system for ECE-SAC practitioners is built around supporting goals for children, but it also acknowledges and values goals for workforce outcomes such as compensation parity, stability, and effective teaching. Policies and governance are in place to support an integrated system. Practitioners can move between sectors and can find multiple entry points to PD activities that will build their knowledge, skills, and practice and prepare them to work with an increasingly diverse population of children. Articulation agreements are in place to support movement between institutes of higher education and recognition of coursework or training completed in different institutions. The latest research and evaluation findings inform the development of coursework, practicum, and technical assistance. System-wide data are collected to inform progress toward collective goals for the workforce, for program quality, and for children's development.

How Can Implementation Science Facilitate the Integrated Professional Development System to Be?

The vision for an integrated and effective PD system is ambitious and complex, and action to address each of the system targets described above requires intentional planning, development of coordinated goals, and resources to support change. In this section, we discuss how an implementation science framework could support the system to be, and we present a stage-based framework (Blase & Fixsen, 2011) that outlines core activities and structural elements that must be addressed at each stage of implementation to facilitate sustainable systems change. At the end of the chapter, we provide a guide for action to achieving systems change through the use of implementation teams and linking communication protocols and by aligning activities with stage of implementation.

As noted in Chapter 2 (see also Metz & Bartley, 2012), implementation science describes the necessary conditions to support the effective delivery of a well defined program approach or systems change effort so that systems change can be sustained and expected goals can actually be achieved. Applying Coffman's (2007) systems initiative framework to a vision of an integrated PD system helps to fully operationalize the system, clarify the goals of systems initiatives, and identify targets for action so that implementation principles can be used to effectively and sustainably implement PD systems change, with the ultimate goal of improving outcomes for the workforce and for children.

Stage-Based Framework for Professional Development Systems Change

As noted in this volume (Chapters 1 and 2), implementation happens in four discernible stages, with the intentional development of key elements and activities taking place at specific stages. These stages are as follows:

1. Exploration

2. Installation

3. Initial implementation

4. Full implementation

Sustainability activities are embedded within each stage.

Implementing a well constructed, well defined, well researched program, approach, or system change involves the completion of specific stage-based activities and the installation of implementation supports during particular stages. The entire process from initial exploratory stages to full implementation can be expected to take 2 to 4 years (e.g. Bierman et al., 2002; Fixsen, Blase, Timbers, & Wolf, 2001; Panzano & Roth, 2006; Prochaska & DiClemente, 1982; Solberg, Hroscikoski, Sperl-Hillen, O'Conner, & Crabtree, 2004). Application of implementation science to ECE-SAC PD systems initiatives should operate under the premise that stage-related work is necessary for successful service and system change and that different targets of the system may be addressed in different time frames. A stage-based approach provides differentiated guidance for navigating the steps that are needed across complex systems change initiatives.

The first stage is exploration. The overall goal of exploration is to assess whether and in what ways the target of PD systems change is desirable and feasible and to make a decision to move forward or not with a selected systems change effort aimed at achieving the system to be. In this first stage of implementation, states must assess the goodness of fit between particular systems change strategies and the needs of ECE providers and the children and families they serve. Core activities of this stage include the following:

1. The formation of an implementation team that will serve as the accountable structure for assessing the fit and feasibility of potential strategies to achieve the system to be and making a decision to move forward to the next stage of implementation

2. The analysis of data to determine need and the prevalence of needs

3. The development of communication plans

4. The development of plans to assess readiness and garner buy-in from key stakeholders

5. Recommendations to move forward or not with particular initiatives

The second stage is installation. This often overlooked stage of implementation is the time to install the necessary structural and instrumental changes that will be needed to support high-fidelity implementation of the PD system to be. Core activities during this stage include the following:

1. Installation of structural and functional changes needed to initiate change in the PD system as is

2. Development of staff selection protocols for those staff who will be implementing changes to align with system goals

3. Identification of training and coaching resources across organizations and sectors for staff who are implementing new procedures or initiatives associated with a fully integrated PD system

4. Assessment and development of data systems to capture fidelity and outcome data of the integrated PD system

5. Development of new policies, procedures, or processes at different levels of the system to support the effective integration of the PD system

6. Establishment of communication links between practice and policy levels to identify barriers and facilitators for effective and sustainable implementation of the integrated PD system

The third stage is initial implementation. During this stage, the new systems change strategy is put in place and efforts are focused on learning from mistakes, making data-driven improvements, and continuing to achieve buy-in from key stakeholders. Core activities during this stage include the following:

1. Ongoing communication to inform stakeholders of key launch dates and other activities

2. The institution of policy–practice feedback loops

3. The institution of coaching processes and staff performance assessments

4. Evaluation of data from decision-support data systems

5. Documentation of barriers

This stage is characterized by continuous improvement and rapid-cycle problem solving at all levels of the system.

The fourth stage is full implementation, in which PD systems change strategies are integrated into organizational and systems environments, and new structures and activities are functioning effectively to achieve desired outcomes. Core activities include the following:

1. Ongoing monitoring of implementation supports (e.g., training, coaching, leadership, data systems)

2. The ongoing use of functional and sustainable policy–practice feedback loops to feed information up and down the system rapidly so that accountable teams or individuals can make decisions to improve ongoing implementation efforts

To assist with the application of the stage-based implementation framework to PD systems change activities, Table 13.2 provides an illustration of how stage-based activities could be considered when using change strategies to address scale and improve access to PD across a state or other geographical region. Note that this is an example of strategies to address one target of PD systems change; other corresponding strategies would need to be implemented across the other targets of PD systems change to achieve the full range of goals articulated for the system.

The importance of a stage-based approach in a PD systems change initiative is evident when considering that some system targets are foundational to developing an integrated PD system while other targets are appropriate to launch only after foundational elements are in place. For example, the infrastructure element of standards is foundational to other elements. Standards for practitioners provide direction on the development of curriculum content for preservice and ongoing PD. A focus on improving statewide access to PD, in contrast, is dependent upon having well-developed and aligned content. In addition, many of the elements of the system to be are being addressed by select statewide initiatives. For these activities that are already in process but need more resources or more alignment with other efforts to be effective, it is critical to determine the status of planning and implementation. A state that has been implementing an ECE-SAC coaching initiative for 3 years but wants to change it to be more research-based may not need to spend as much time in the exploration stage, but it may need more time in the installation stage to identify resources and supports and to develop a data system.

Conducting stage-appropriate work has several policy and practice implications. First, it is not feasible to skip a stage of implementation and expect sustainable, high-quality outcomes, though states that are enhancing or improving existing efforts may not need as long an exploration stage as they would with an entirely new initiative. Second, judgments about "effectiveness" should not be made prematurely; stage-based implementation provides guidance to implementers about the time frame during which success or effectiveness should be judged. Third, activities need to match the stage of implementation. It is likely that different components of complex initiatives such as integrated PD systems will be at different stages of implementation. Leaders of PD systems change efforts need to ask themselves, "Where are we now with *this* component?" For example, an initiative focused on scale and increasing access to PD may be launched after efforts to establish PD systems infrastructure has been successfully launched. Finally, stages will need to be revisited. As new practitioners, new communities, new partners, new government officials, and new families come on board, revisiting stages may be necessary.

Table 13.2.   Example of stage-based framework for implementation of change strategies to improve access to professional development

Stage 1: Exploration

Assess and document the need for expanded access, explore the readiness for change among practitioners not accessing the professional development (PD) system, examine how access issues differ across target populations and range of early care and education (ECE) and school-age care (SAC) settings, assess the feasibility of implementation of various strategies, and look at the training and technical assistance needs and resources to accomplish this systems change. Core activities include the following:

· Form implementation team.
· Develop communication plan to describe exploration process (e.g., activities, participants, timeline, benefits, risks) to key stakeholder groups across sectors.
· Analyze data and information to determine need and prevalence of the need for expanded access.
· Select targeted areas to address the need (sectors of ECE setting).
· Review and identify PD systems change strategies/initiatives that would improve access to PD that match target area and need.
· Review and discuss feasibility of implementing different initiatives (e.g., distance learning, shared resources across resource and referral agencies, higher education, school districts and other agencies providing PD).
· Select PD strategies for continued exploration based on results of feasibility analysis.
· Develop methods to promote exploration and assess buy-in for range of impacted stakeholders.
· Analyze information and results from exploration activities.
· Implementation team makes recommendations to appropriate system level (e.g., state administration).

Stage 2: Installation

Assure the availability of resources to initiate the PD systems change strategy/initiative selected during exploration (e.g., distance-learning initiative) such as staffing, organizational supports, technology, and new operating policies and procedures. Core activities include the following:

· Identify and make structural and functional changes needed at practitioner, regional, and state levels to implement PD strategy.
· Develop selection protocols for staff who will train, monitor, and evaluate PD strategy.
· Identify training resources for those implementing and those affected by new PD strategy.
· Develop coaching and support plans for those implementing new PD strategy.
· Evaluate readiness and sustainability of data systems at practitioner level.
· Evaluate readiness and sustainability of data systems to capture implementation and outcomes associated with new PD strategies.
· Evaluate readiness and sustainability of fidelity assessments for PD strategy (e.g., monitoring or distance-learning course offerings).
· Analyze and problem-solve around selection, training, and coaching of those implementing new PD strategy.
· Establish communication links to report barriers and facilitators during next stage.

Stage 3: Initial Implementation

Organization and systems initiate the new way of work related to selected PD strategy, learn from mistakes, and continue to achieve buy-in from key stakeholder groups involved in implementation efforts. This stage is characterized by continuous improvement and rapid-cycle problem solving at all levels of the system. Core activities include the following:

· Develop communication plan(s) to inform stakeholders of launch dates and activities and to convey support for new PD strategy.
· Develop communication protocols for identifying barriers and adaptive challenges and problem solving at each level of system.

(continued)

Table 13.2.   (*continued*)

- Leadership develops support plans to promote persistence of use of new PD strategies.
- Ensure coaching systems are in place for those implementing new PD strategy.
- Ensure data systems are in place for evaluating fidelity of new PD strategy.
- Document barriers to initial implementation.
- Recommend improvements to implementation infrastructure to support sustainable, aligned, effective implementation of new PD strategy.

Stage 4: Full Implementation

Assure new PD strategies are integrated into organizational and systems environments and are functioning effectively to achieve desired outcomes. Staff who implement these strategies are skillful in their activities, and new processes and procedures have become routine and the new PD strategy is fully integrated statewide. Core activities include the following:

- Ensure monitoring and support systems are in place for selection, training, and coaching of staff implementing PD strategy.
- Ensure data systems are in place and fidelity is monitored.
- Ensure feedback processes from practitioners to, for example, higher education, school districts, training organizations, and resource and referral agencies that are supporting implementation of new PD strategies are in place and functional.
- Ensure feedback processes from organizations in the field to state administrators are in place and functional.
- State uses data to make decisions about new PD strategies.
- Use improvement processes to address issues through the analysis of data, development of plans, monitoring of plan execution, and assessment of results.

From Blase, K.A., & Fixsen, D.L. (2011). *Stage-based measures of implementation components.* Chapel Hill, NC: National Implementation Research Network. Retrieved from http://nirn.fpg.unc.edu/learn-implementation/implementation-stages; adapted by permission.

A Guide to Action for Achieving an Integrated, Effective Professional Development System

An implementation science framework can inform and support the vision of an integrated PD system and provide a structure for concrete action steps necessary to engage in a systems change initiative. In this section, we provide recommendations for action to achieve the PD system to be. These are practical ideas that focus on the activities and actors in the system and that recognize the complexities of cross-sector integration.

Step 1: Form Implementation Teams

Conducting the stage-based activities needed for PD systems change requires organized expert assistance in the form of an implementation team that can provide an accountable structure to move PD systems change efforts through the stages of implementation. An ECE-SAC PD system implementation team should consist of members representing the many participants and recipients: multiple state agencies with responsibility for PD for early childhood practitioners across sectors, institutions of higher education (representing preservice and continuous education programs), professional associations for practitioners across sectors, trainers, technical assistance providers, professional registries, and evaluators, among others.

Generally, it is important for implementation team members to have the following competencies (not necessarily at the time of selection, but their ability to achieve competency should be considered and supported to help the team develop and is relevant to the initiative):

- Understand the selected PD systems change strategy and systems transformation methods. Members need to have an understanding of what they are changing in the system as is and what they are doing to support the system to be. Ultimately, they should have an understanding of the outcomes desired and what their role will be in their achieving the goals of the system.

- Be a skillful user of implementation methods for PD strategies. Members need to know recommended practices and strategies related to implementation and systems change.

- Be thoroughly engaged in continuous quality improvement cycles in all aspects of their activities. Members should have an understanding and ability to apply processes for improvement and use data for decision making.

When these competencies don't exist on a team, expert support needs to be engaged to promote the competencies that are lacking. This expert support might come in the form of consultants, program developers, model purveyors, or intermediary organizations. For example, PD system leaders in state agencies may engage the expertise of technical assistance providers in universities, national organizations, or federal technical assistance initiatives (such as the National Center on Child Care Professional Development Systems and Workforce Initiatives supported by the Office of Child Care and the Office of Head Start in the Administration for Children and Families, U.S. Department of Health and Human Services).

Given the size and scope of the PD systems initiatives, it will likely be necessary to develop a linked teaming structure. A linked teaming structure consists of implementation teams at different levels of the PD system to ensure that implementation effectively supports policy and practice change in the system. Figure 13.1 depicts the linked teaming structures necessary to put into place coordinated and meaningful connections between every level of the PD system.

It is not enough just to have these designated persons in place; their activities must also be relevant, coordinated, and connected. At each of the system levels, every team is a representative, active, working group that provides an accountable structure for the work, aids with communication and coordination, has the appropriate power to make decisions or take action, and sustains the responsibility of the work through an organized group of people. Each team has an internal memorandum of understanding that describes how it functions, communicates, makes decisions, and moves forward with its mission and objectives.

Developing connected teams that have clear responsibilities at every level of the system will provide the necessary support to improve ECE-SAC PD systems. Implementation teams can be convened to include representatives who are responsible for policy, administration, or direct provision of PD services.

The use of implementation teams has been effective in other realms. For example, Higgins, Weiner, and Young (2012) studied implementation teams (defined as "a team charged with designing and implementing an organization-wide change strategy"; p. 16) in the U.S. public school system and found that an implementation

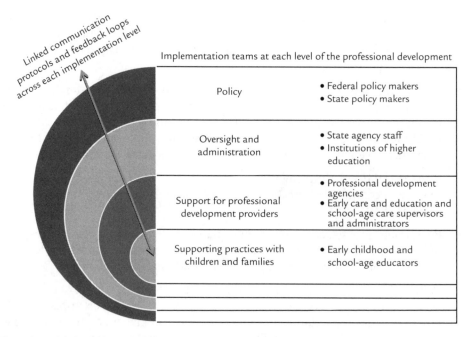

Figure 13.1.   Linked teaming structures. (From Metz, A., & Bartley, L. [2012]. How to use implementation science to improve outcomes for children. *Zero to Three, 32*(4), 11–18; reprinted by permission.)

team's defined role and the role of its members were critical to its success, along with positional diversity at each level of the school system.

Step 2: Develop Linking Communications Protocols

To ensure that teams are working in alignment to promote systems change that positively affects practice change, linking communication protocols need to be developed. These protocols provide a feedback process for creating a hospitable policy, funding, and operational environment for PD systems change efforts. This bidirectional communication should be formalized and practiced regularly. Teams at each level of the system are responsible for soliciting this information from the teams at other levels of the system to which they are connected and taking action based on the needs or challenges identified.

The specific purposes of linking communication protocols are as follows:

- Communicate progress and celebrate success throughout the system.

- Report systemic barriers that are preventing or hindering implementation and 1) should be resolved by one of the groups or 2) need to be moved "up the line" to the group that can best address the barrier.

- Report on actions taken related to past issues.

- Revisit past decisions and agreements periodically to ensure that solutions are still functional.

In promoting system alignment, the implementation team may be developing a "chain" of protocols from the practice level to the state level or may be developing protocols between and among partners in a collaborative group. Depending on a number of factors (e.g., how new the relationships are, how cohesive the groups are, how much a common purpose is shared), it may take one or several meetings to work out the first draft of the protocols. After the protocols have been tried out a couple of times, the process should be evaluated for satisfaction and functionality and then adjusted.

Issues that may be particularly salient for communications protocols for PD system implementation teams include reports on challenges or successes with work occurring across sectors, monitoring of practitioner buy-in to new initiatives, and development of data systems.

Step 3: Formulate Key Questions to Address During Each Stage of Implementation

Implementation teams will need to consider key questions that need to be addressed for the area of systems change they have chosen to focus on for implementation. These questions will differ depending on the stage of implementation and will align closely with the core activities for each implementation stage described in Table 13.2.

During exploration, implementation teams move toward recommendations for new PD systems strategies to address the goals for system context, components, connections, infrastructure, and scale (such as those outlined in Table 13.1). Questions asked during this stage include those about need, capacity, and readiness of the system to implement new practices. Given the diversity of the ECE-SAC workforce, it is critical that this stage include a focus on understanding the implications of new initiatives for practitioners in the different sectors and how the unique context of sectors will impede or promote the effectiveness of PD systems change initiatives.

In the installation stage, the implementation team asks questions about changes that are necessary in policies, procedures, staffing, technology, and roles of different actors in the PD system to install new practices. For example, a state may conduct an inventory of all available training that specifically targets diversity as a key activity in developing integrated training related to cultural diversity. Questions are also asked about the training and data systems that are needed to support staff and others who are installing new practices or initiatives. These considerations are especially important because initiatives to support ECE-SAC professional development may have staff who serve practitioners across sectors and organizations with different levels of internal supports (e.g., higher education versus resource and referral agencies).

During initial implementation, the implementation team asks about the barriers that are being encountered and the leadership that is needed to support the launch of new initiatives. Data may be reviewed from registries, QRIS, and other integrated data systems to inform the team about implementation of new practices. For example, data from the QRIS will provide insights into the effectiveness of initiatives to support access to professional development that will promote quality improvement in the QRIS. Implementation teams can use the QRIS data to understand patterns in initial scoring on quality indicators as well as patterns of movement up or down the QRIS levels.

In full implementation, the team asks how to improve and sustain the integrated PD system. It asks about the competencies of staff who are implementing the practices and initiatives and use data from the system to drive decision making.

Step 4: Institute Continuous Improvement Cycles

New practices and approaches do not fare well in existing organizational structures and systems. Without constant and consistent attention to the change effort, the current early childhood PD system will exert pressure on new, effective approaches to PD systems change to shape them to fit the existing system, and in the process, the effectiveness of the new approach will be diminished. For this not to happen, the existing system must change to support the new practices, approaches, and strategies. New structures, new positions, and new job functions will be needed at multiple levels. For example, if an ECE-SAC PD system is implementing a new coaching initiative to support the application of knowledge to practice, new structures may be needed for the development of competencies for coaches and an approval system to ensure that qualifications are met. Often these new structures, positions, and job functions can be created using current resources and funding to repurpose the positions and job functions to meet the needs of the new way of doing things, but not layered onto current structures and job descriptions. For example, when implementing a new coaching initiative, it will be critical to ensure that staff who are repurposed as coaches have adequate training, qualifications, and ongoing supervision and support.

In addition, people, organizations, and systems cannot change everything at once. Many of the types of changes being considered in the ECE-SAC PD system (e.g., context, connections, components, infrastructure, scale) are complex and involve multiple actors and organizations that make it impossible to change simultaneously. These types of change processes can be particularly challenging because the people, organizations, and systems are not able to stop and retool; changes to the system must be made while the work continues. For these reasons, it is important to develop a culture of learning that sees each new attempt to improve the ECE-SAC PD system as a valuable endeavor that leads to new learning, whether or not the outcome is completely successful.

A common framework for achieving this learning culture is the "plan, do, study, act" (PDSA) cycle (DeFoe & Barnard, 2005; Deming, 1986; Shewhart, 1924).

- *Plan:* Decide on the specific objective and the processes to achieve this objective.

- *Do:* Implement the processes as intended.

- *Study:* Monitor the processes, assess whether they were implemented as intended, and analyze the outcomes achieved.

- *Act:* Make adjustments and apply what was learned during the process.

- *Cycle:* Do it over and over again until the intended benefits are realized.

There are different uses of the improvement cycle method that would benefit the effective and sustainable implementation of ECE-SAC PD systems change to achieve an integrated PD system. Below we describe two potential methods.

Rapid-Cycle Problem Solving   Implementation teams can serve as rapid-cycle problem-solving teams to address a challenging problem or to guide ongoing improvement efforts through the analysis of fidelity and outcome data and the development and implementation of long-term solutions. When conducting rapid-cycle problem solving, implementation team members will be focused on their role of analyzing and solving the problem, using a PDSA process. Once this problem has been solved, the group will meet again when another problem arises or when ongoing fidelity assessments have been scheduled.

Returning to the example of a statewide coaching initiative, rapid-cycle problem-solving teams may be deployed to provide periodic checks of fidelity to the selected coaching model. If it is determined that coaching is not being implemented as intended, recommendations can be made for training or onsite supports provided to the coaches. The team may also determine that take-up of coaching differs across sectors and make a decision to invest in new infrastructure for marketing and promoting the PD system in different sectors.

Policy–Practice Feedback Loops   Often PDSA cycles are carried out on a practice level; however, the practice–policy feedback loop is a variation of the PDSA cycle that is carried out on a larger scale in the more complex early childhood PD systems environment. A challenge in the early childhood context is that policy is not always developed with sufficient understanding of the reality of practice, and many times there are no formal mechanisms to have practice inform the policy. Instead, there are usually layers of individuals between those implementing the practice and the policy makers. Whether intentional or not, these layers often buffer the policy makers from hearing about or experiencing the unintended problems created by the policy or from understanding other variables that may be preventing implementation from occurring as intended. The policy–practice and practice–policy feedback loops can help ensure that barriers to effective practice are brought to the attention of policy makers and assist in the development of "policy-enabled practices" and "practice-informed policies."

Conclusions

This chapter proposes both a vision and a structure to support action in the development of an integrated PD system for ECE-SAC practitioners. It builds on and extends existing conceptualizations of PD systems by adding a detailed focus on action and recommendations for how to realize the vision of an integrated PD system. We use a systems initiatives framework (Coffman, 2007) and tools based on implementation science to outline this action- and change-oriented perspective.

As initiatives are coordinated and launched in ECE-SAC PD systems, it will be essential to conduct both formative and summative evaluations that can capture the challenges and successes in this complex and difficult work of systems change. Coffman (2007) outlines the evaluation strategies that can be used with each target in a systems initiative.

There is an urgent need for an evidence base on successful initiatives to transform PD systems. In particular, data are needed to document effective practices across the targets of the PD system and the multiple levels at which new initiatives are implemented—from federal and state agencies through higher education and community training organizations to coaches working with individual practitioners who are, in turn, working daily with children. The issues described in the PD system as is will be resolved not only by focusing on individual practitioners but also by recognizing that achieving the system to be requires changes that are implemented across all levels and targets of the system.

References

Bierman, K.L., Coie, J.D., Dodge, K.A., Greenberg, M.T., Lochman, J.E., & McMahon, R.J. (2002). The implementation of the fast track program: An example of a large-scale prevention science efficacy trial. *Journal of Abnormal Child Psychology, 30,* 1–17.

Blase, K.A., & Fixsen, D.L. (2011). *Stage-based measures of implementation components.* Chapel Hill, NC: National Implementation Research Network. Retrieved from http://nirn.fpg.unc.edu/learn-implementation/implementation-stages

Buysse, V., Winton, P.J., & Rous, B. (2009). Reaching consensus on a definition of professional development for the early childhood field. *Topics in Early Childhood Special Education, 28,* 235–243.

Center for the Study of Child Care Employment. (2012). *Rewarding work environments.* Retrieved from http://www.irle.berkeley.edu/cscce/priorities/rewarding-environment

Coffman, J. (2007). *A framework for evaluating systems initiatives.* N.p.: Build Initiative. Retrieved from http://www.buildinitiative.org/files/BuildInitiativefullreport.pdf

DeFoe, J.A., & Barnard, W. (2005). *Juran Institute's six sigma breakthrough and beyond: Quality performance breakthrough methods.* New York, NY: McGraw-Hill Professional.

Deming, W.E. (1986). *Out of crisis.* Cambridge, MA: MIT Press.

Fixsen, D.L., Blase, K.A., Timbers, G.D., & Wolf, M.M. (2001). In search of program implementation: 792 replications of the Teaching-Family Model. In G.A. Bernfeld, D.P. Farrington, & A.W. Leschied (Eds.), *Offender rehabilitation in practice: Implementing and evaluating effective programs* (pp. 149–166). London, England: Wiley.

Higgins, M.C., Weiner, J., & Young, L. (2012). Implementation teams: A new lever for organizational change. *Journal of Organizational Behavior, 33*(3), 366–388.

Hyson, M., Tomlinson, H.B., & Morris, C. (2009). Quality improvement in early childhood teacher education: Faculty perspectives and recommendations for the future. *Early Childhood Research & Practice, 11*(1). Retrieved from http://ecrp.uiuc.edu/v11n1/hyson.html

Institute of Medicine (IOM) and National Research Council (NRC). (2012). *The early childhood care and education workforce: Challenges and opportunities.* Washington, DC: National Academies Press.

Kipnis, F., Whitebook, M., Almaraz, M., Sakai, L., & Austin, L.J.E. (2012). *Learning together: A study of six B.A. completion cohort programs in early care and education, year 4.* Berkeley, CA: Center for the Study of Child Care Employment, University of California.

LeMoine, S. (2008). *Workforce designs: A policy blueprint for state early childhood professional development systems.* Washington, DC: NAEYC.

Metz, A., & Bartley, L. (2012). How to use implementation science to improve outcomes for children. *Zero to Three, 32*(4), 11–18. Retrieved from http://www.zerotothree.org/about-us/areas-of-expertise/reflective-practice-program-development/metz-revised.pdf

National Association of Child Care Resource and Referral Agencies (NACCRRA). (2011). *We can do better: NACCRRA's ranking of state child care center regulation and oversight.* Arlington, VA: Author. Retrieved from http://www.naccrra.org/sites/default/files/default_site_pages/2011/wcdb_sum_chpts1-5.pdf

National Child Care Information and Technical Assistance Center (NCCIC). (2007). *Early childhood professional development systems toolkit.* Retrieved from http://nccic.acf.hhs.gov/pubs/goodstart/index.html

National Professional Development Center on Inclusion (NPDCI). (2008). *What do we mean by professional development in the early childhood field?* Chapel Hill, NC: FPG Child Development Institute, University of North Carolina.

National Professional Development Center on Inclusion (NPDCI). (2010). *Building integrated professional development systems in early childhood: Recommendations for states.* Chapel Hill, NC: FPG Child Development Institute, University of North Carolina.

National Professional Development Center on Inclusion (NPDCI). (2011). *The big picture planning guide: Building cross-sector professional development systems in early childhood* (3rd ed.). Chapel Hill, NC: FPG Child Development Institute, University of North Carolina.

National Registry Alliance. (2012). *Registry map.* Retrieved from http://registryalliance.org/about-the-alliance/registry-map

Panzano, P.C., & Roth, D. (2006). The decision to adopt evidence and other innovative mental health practices: Risky business? *Psychiatric Services, 57,* 1153–1161.

Prochaska, J.O., & DiClemente, C.C. (1982). Transtheoretical therapy: Toward a more integrative model of change. *Psychotherapy, 19,* 276–287.

Ray, A., Bowman, B., & Robbins, J. (2006). *Preparing early childhood teachers to successfully educate all children: The contribution of four-year undergraduate teacher preparation programs.* Report to the Foundation for Child Development. Chicago, IL: Erikson Institute.

Shewhart, W.A. (1924). Some applications of statistical methods to the analysis of physical and engineering data. *Bell Technical Journal, 3,* 43–87.

Solberg, L.I., Hroscikoski, M.C., Sperl-Hillen, J.M., O'Conner, P.J., & Crabtree, B.F. (2004). Key issues in transforming health care organizations for quality: The case of advanced access. *Joint Commission Journal on Quality and Safety, 30,* 14–24.

Tout, K., Starr, R., Soli, M., Moodie, S., Kirby, G., & Boller, K. (2010). *Compendium of quality rating systems and evaluations.* Washington, DC: Office of Planning, Research and Evaluation, Administration for Children and Families, U.S. Department of Health and Human Services.

U.S. Government Accountability Office (GAO). (2012). *Early child care and education: HHS and Education are taking steps to improve workforce data and enhance worker quality* (GAO-12-248). Washington, DC: Author.

Weber, R., & Trauten, M. (2008). *Effective investments in the child care and early education profession.* Corvallis, OR: Oregon State University Family Policy Program.

Whitebook, M., Gomby, D., Bellm, D., Sakai, L., & Kipnis, F. (2009a). *Effective teacher preparation in early care and education: Toward a comprehensive research agenda.* Part II of *Preparing teachers of young children: The current state of knowledge, and a blueprint for the future.* Berkeley, CA: Center for the Study of Child Care Employment, University of California.

Whitebook, M., Gomby, D., Bellm, D., Sakai, L., & Kipnis, F. (2009b). *Teacher preparation and professional development in grades K–12 and in early care and education: Differences and similarities, and implications for research.* Part I of *Preparing teachers of young children: The current state of knowledge, and a blueprint for the future.* Berkeley, CA: Center for the Study of Child Care Employment, University of California.

Whitebook, M., & Ryan, S. (2011). *Degrees in context: Asking the right questions about preparing skilled and effective teachers of young children.* Preschool Policy Brief, No. 22. Berkeley, CA: National Institute for Early Education Research.

Whitebook, M., & Sakai, L. (2003). Turnover begets turnover: An examination of job and occupational instability among child care center staff. *Early Childhood Research Quarterly, 18,* 273–293.

Zaslow, M., Tout, K., Halle, T., Vick Whittaker, J., & Lavelle, B. (2010). *Toward the identification of features of effective professional development for early childhood educators: Literature review.* Washington, DC: Policy and Program Studies Service, Office of Planning, Evaluation, and Policy Development, U.S. Department of Education.

CHAPTER 14

Evaluating Implementation of Quality Rating and Improvement Systems

Diane Paulsell, Kathryn Tout, and Kelly Maxwell

Quality rating and improvement systems (QRIS) are multifaceted initiatives that aim to improve the quality of early care and education (ECE) and young children's developmental outcomes. QRIS have emerged from state and local ECE systems and are at various stages of implementation in more than 25 states and local communities. Although there is no single model, QRIS typically include five components:

1. Quality standards

2. A process for monitoring or assigning ratings based on quality standards

3. A process for supporting providers in quality improvement

4. Financial incentives

5. Dissemination of ratings to parents and other consumers (Mitchell, 2005; Tout, Starr, Soli, et al., 2010)

While there is a large body of research demonstrating the positive impact of high-quality ECE on children's developmental outcomes, QRIS do not have a strong evidence base at this early stage of development to support the implementation of each of the five components. For example, the research base does not provide clear guidance on the type and amount of financial incentives that promote participation, the duration and intensity of quality improvement supports that facilitate movement from lower to higher QRIS tiers or levels, or the design and structure of quality indicators and levels that most efficiently address the key aspects of quality critical to children's later school success. Nevertheless, most states are in the process of developing, piloting, or implementing a QRIS either statewide or in selected communities—using the best available research. These systems contain the five components, but vary greatly in how the components operate in practice.

QRIS is a prime example of bold action among state policy makers to develop a multifaceted strategy to drive quality improvement and child outcomes. Policy makers were ready for this audacious move before specific practical findings about implementation of QRIS components were available. These state actions are driving QRIS research and evaluation—not the other way around. The intention of this chapter is to strengthen QRIS efforts by applying research and theory regarding the science of implementing evidence-based practice.

Tools drawn from implementation science and systems thinking can be useful for strengthening QRIS designs and monitoring and fine-tuning implementation. This chapter begins with a brief history of the emergence of QRIS and a description of key features of current systems (the "system as is"). The next sections apply core implementation components, stages of implementation, and systems concepts to an examination of QRIS. We then provide a vision for an evidence-based, high-quality, and fully implemented QRIS (the "system to be") and highlight ways in which concepts from implementation science and systems theory could be incorporated to achieve this vision. The chapter ends with a discussion of implications and future directions for state child care administrators and other practitioners, evaluators, and policy makers.

Emergence and Current Status of Quality Rating and Improvement Systems

To set the stage for the rest of the chapter, this section provides a brief history of the emergence of QRIS from state and local ECE systems. The process of developing QRIS in states and communities usually involves obtaining input from multiple stakeholders, often within tight time frames and financial constraints. We will also describe the five components of QRIS and provide an overview of the research literature on QRIS validation, implementation, and outcomes. A comprehensive description of QRIS design and implementation in five "pioneer" states will provide foundational information about strategies and processes used in QRIS (Zellman & Perlman, 2008). For additional information, detailed descriptions of features and cross-QRIS comparative analysis can be found in the *Compendium of Quality Rating Systems and Evaluations* (Tout, Starr, Soli, et al., 2010).

Emergence of Quality Rating and Improvement Systems

QRIS emerged in the late 1990s, ostensibly as a two-pronged strategy to improve children's outcomes (see the logic model by Zellman, Perlman, Le, and Setodji [2008]). One part of the strategy focuses on quality improvement and provision of supports to help child care providers improve and sustain high quality over time to enhance children's development. A second part of the strategy focuses on marketing quality information to parents in an effort to influence their decision making and ensure that parents are selecting high-quality care for their young children. Together, these two parts of the strategy are intended to result in an increased supply of high-quality providers in the market (in part, theoretically, because lower quality providers leave the market) as well as increases in parent recognition of quality settings and knowledge to demand and select high-quality settings for their children (Zellman et al., 2008).

To date, strong empirical evidence documenting these hypothesized outcomes—parent demand and increases in the overall supply of high-quality

ECE—is minimal. A review of QRIS administrative activities indicates that 12 of 19 QRIS providing budget information on marketing activities have no funding earmarked for QRIS marketing to parents (Tout, Starr, Soli, et al., 2010). Activities to support quality improvement among QRIS-rated providers are more prevalent, with the majority of QRIS offering on-site assistance to providers across quality levels (Smith, Schneider, & Kreader, 2010). Yet, Smith and colleagues (2010) also found that on-site assistance is not always used by providers. For example, most QRIS reported that less than 25% of lower rated providers received on-site quality improvement assistance. Although some states with QRIS have documented increased quality over time, the research designs used do not permit causal statements about the effects of QRIS on quality improvement (Tout & Maxwell, 2010). Thus, evidence suggests that activities identified as critical in a QRIS logic model are not always implemented with consistency or with adequate investment to support desired outcomes of improving quality and increasing parent demand for high-quality care.

QRIS have a number of strengths to support their potential success. Evidence collected across states and stakeholders demonstrates that QRIS are credited with raising awareness of the importance of quality improvement in ECE systems (Tout, Starr, Isner, et al., 2010; Zellman & Perlman, 2008). Though buy-in is not universal, QRIS have broad appeal to a variety of stakeholders for their potential to support both parents and ECE providers in promoting and increasing the quality of early childhood settings. Additionally, many QRIS have used pilots successfully as a strategy for testing and refining their processes before launching the system statewide. Fifteen of the twenty-six QRIS profiled in Tout, Starr, Soli, et al. (2010) began with a pilot in selected geographical areas or by implementing a portion of ratings (e.g., ratings for center-based providers only). Zellman and Perlman (2008) note that a pilot process that allows for iterative revisions before a system is brought to scale is important for promoting positive relations with stakeholders.

Other features of QRIS implementation create challenges for optimal functioning. For example, QRIS are often launched under very tight schedules and with considerable pressure from stakeholders to achieve outcomes rapidly (Swenson-Klatt & Tout, 2011; Zellman & Perlman, 2008). Achieving goals for recruitment, enrollment, and provision of quality improvement supports often requires that multiple agencies establish programs and services quickly, thus increasing the likelihood that some aspects of implementation will be left unattended. In addition, resources are spread across multiple activities and may not be adequate to support the intensity or scope of services needed to achieve anticipated goals.

Quality Rating and Improvement System Components

QRIS typically include up to five key components: 1) quality standards; 2) a process for monitoring or assigning ratings based on quality standards; 3) a process for supporting providers in quality improvement; 4) financial incentives; and 5) dissemination of ratings to parents and other consumers.

Quality Standards Quality standards in a QRIS describe the aspects of quality that the QRIS is trying to promote. The standards define the features of quality that will be rated, and indicators are developed to measure the standards. In Tout,

Starr, Soli, et al. (2010), 13 different categories of quality standards were identified through a review of QRIS: 1) licensing compliance; 2) ratio and group size; 3) health and safety; 4) curriculum; 5) environment; 6) child assessment; 7) director, teacher, and family child care provider (staff) qualifications; 8) family partnerships; 9) administration and management; 10) accreditation; 11) provisions for children with special needs; 12) community involvement; and 13) cultural and linguistic diversity. Certain categories of standards such as licensing compliance, staff qualifications, and the environment are included in most or all of the 26 QRIS examined. Other categories of standards such as provisions for children with special needs and cultural and linguistic diversity are included in fewer systems. While inclusion of certain categories of standards looks similar across QRIS, the indicators measured for each standard can vary widely.

QRIS typically rely on committees and expert consultants to determine the particular standards to be included in the system. There is an emphasis on selecting a concise but important set of standards; QRIS are intentionally not as comprehensive as other program standards. Some QRIS utilize a research review and review of standards for professional practice (e.g., accreditation standards) as part of their decision-making process to determine which standards are critical to include and the extent to which particular standards are related to quality. The state and local context and personal experiences of stakeholders also influence the decision about which standards are included in the QRIS.

Although the ultimate goal of most QRIS is to support children's development and school success, not all standards have strong research links to child outcomes. Standards in a QRIS may, in part, be based on the best available research evidence but are also based on the values, beliefs, and principles of the QRIS developers. This flexibility to individualize standards to "fit" the context can be beneficial by encouraging buy-in to the system and tailoring the focus of the QRIS to those aspects of quality deemed most important by research and stakeholders. Still, in the current systems, the standards—which form the foundation of the QRIS rating—may vary in the degree of alignment in reaching the overall goal of improved outcomes for young children.

Assigning Ratings   Each participating provider in a QRIS is rated on the various standards and indicators and assigned a quality level. In North Carolina, for example, a provider can receive a 1- to 5-star rating. Ratings may be based on evidence gathered through review of existing provider documents (e.g., lesson plans, provider handbook) and verified credentials (e.g., teacher transcripts housed in a Professional Development Registry) as well as observations of classroom quality (the environment standard) by independent assessors. Assessors may be employees of a state agency or independent contractors. They may assess providers as their full-time job or as part of a range of job responsibilities; they may also vary in their knowledge of and experience with early childhood programs. Most states have a prescribed protocol for training assessors who conduct the observations and determining inter-rater reliability periodically, with clear standards for expected levels of performance. The extent to which similar training and inter-rater reliability protocols are used for staff who review documents and make decisions or assign points based on the evidence reviewed is unclear.

Quality Improvement The quality improvement component of QRIS typically includes a set of strategies that align with an individualized quality improvement plan for participating providers and account for the provider's stage of participation (from not yet rated to newly rated to having received multiple ratings; Isner et al., 2011; Smith et al., 2010). The strategies may involve training that is required in the QRIS or that is needed to achieve particular QRIS indicators. The content of this training varies across QRIS but may address topics such as assessment of the environment (or specifically, training on use of the Environment Rating Scales), practices to promote language and literacy, specific curriculum, social and emotional development, business practices, and safety (Tout, Starr, Soli, et al., 2010).

The quality improvement also usually involves some form of on-site technical assistance. This technical assistance may be referred to by different names—coaching, consultation, mentoring—and is designed to address a variety of issues ranging from navigation of the QRIS (e.g., assistance with preparing documentation, explanation of the rating system) to classroom layout and support in implementing particular curricula (Tout, Starr, Soli, et al., 2010). The bulk of the QRIS that reported on on-site technical assistance in Tout, Starr, Soli, et al. (2010) stated that the duration of assistance varied based on the needs of the provider.

While providers in QRIS have reported satisfaction with the quality improvement services they have received (see, for example, findings from Indiana, Kentucky, and Minnesota in Elicker et al., in press; Tout et al., 2012; and Tout, Starr, Isner, et al., 2010, respectively), recent research findings highlight the importance of continuing to gather evidence on the content, scope, and effectiveness of different approaches. Smith and colleagues (2010) note that QRIS quality improvement strategies are not yet fully incorporating features that have been demonstrated in effective models. For instance, on-site visits and the use of modeling of practices with young children occur infrequently, and the majority of QRIS administrators reported that there is no formal guide for the providers of on-site technical assistance, which may cause unintentional variability in the services that are provided.

The degree of alignment between provider standards and technical assistance is also important to consider. QRIS may invest in approaches that emphasize improving scores on the Environment Rating Scales, but these scores represent only a portion of the overall provider rating. Additionally, depending on the construction of the QRIS rating, significant improvements in Environment Rating Scale scores may not translate into a higher overall rating (Boller et al., 2010). Understanding more about the resources needed for implementation of effective quality improvement approaches in QRIS is a significant challenge for future work.

Financial Incentives Financial incentives to support or reward quality improvement include tiered reimbursement, quality awards, scholarships, wage enhancements, and retention bonuses (Tout, Starr, Soli, et al., 2010). *Tiered reimbursement* provides a higher subsidy payment rate to providers that meet higher tiers in the QRIS and potentially facilitates access to high-quality providers by covering a greater proportion of the cost to parents (providers are eligible to receive a higher subsidy rate as long as that rate does not exceed the rate they charge to families who do not receive subsidies). The tiered rates are typically set at a percentage above the rate or at a flat rate that is differentiated by star level and geographic location. *Quality awards* provide bonus payments (either one-time or on an annual basis) to providers that are linked to the quality level they receive. In Pennsylvania and Kentucky, the bonus is also tied to the population density of children served who receive a child care subsidy. Typically, there are few stipulations in how providers can or should utilize these additional funds, though some states, like Ohio, provide guidance about allowable uses for at least a portion of the funds (Step Up to Quality, 2010). *Scholarships, wage enhancements,* and *retention bonuses* are focused at the level of individual practitioners and staff, supporting their continued education and reducing turnover.

Other financial incentives may be used to help families access and afford higher quality. These could include direct scholarships or subsidies and provisions around the use of these funds that promote continuity in high quality (such as extended eligibility or relaxed recertification policies; Adams & Compton, 2011; Gaylor, Spikes, Hebbeler, & Williamson, 2009; Gaylor, Spikes, Williamson, & Ferguson, 2010, 2011). Little research has been done to provide evidence for the effectiveness of any particular financial strategy or combination of strategies in improving the quality of providers. Current QRIS data systems may capture some data regarding financial incentives (e.g., amount of funding received), but likely do not capture enough data to help QRIS administrators understand the role of financial incentives in supporting particular quality improvements.

Marketing and Consumer Education   The QRIS logic model often specifies the role of parents in choosing higher quality care for their children—with the assumptions that 1) the quality rating makes it easier for parents to identify higher quality settings and 2) quality is a critical factor in parental choice of child care arrangements. Thus, marketing the QRIS and provider ratings becomes an important part of efforts to improve the quality of care of the entire system. No research has been done, though, regarding the effectiveness of particular marketing strategies to affect parental choice of child care arrangements.

Administrators also must market the QRIS to providers. Almost all of the state QRIS are voluntary, so administrators need to recruit providers to participate. Some QRIS evaluations have gathered preliminary data about provider engagement in QRIS and why providers do or do not choose to participate in a QRIS. In Miami-Dade County, for example, a sample of directors who did not initially participate in the QRIS reported that they were either planning to participate or needed additional information before deciding (Iruka, Yazejian, Hughes, Robertson, & Maxwell, 2010). In the first year of the pilot QRIS in Minnesota, stakeholders raised concerns about the ability to engage family child care providers and providers who are culturally and linguistically diverse (Tout, Starr, & Cleveland, 2008).

Additional research is needed to better understand what would best motivate and support providers to join a voluntary QRIS. Efforts to understand providers' readiness to engage in QRIS could inform the outreach approaches that are used. Different strategies will be appropriate for different readiness levels. None of the evaluations have examined the effectiveness of particular strategies for recruiting providers. Thus, QRIS administrators must make their best guesses regarding allocation of funds and strategy selection to recruit providers.

Overview of the Quality Rating and Improvement System Research Literature

The literature on QRIS is small but growing. The research questions addressed by the extant literature within individual state QRIS focus primarily on characteristics, perceptions, and satisfaction of programs in the QRIS; patterns of scoring and improvement on the QRIS rating scale; description of strategies for providing quality improvement; parents' knowledge of the QRIS; validation of the quality standards; and linkages between ratings and children's development. The findings from these studies have been used to inform revisions to QRIS components within individual systems. For example, findings showing that scores on the Early Childhood Environment Rating Scale are not significantly different between each level of the QRIS have led to discussions in Indiana and Minnesota on how to better differentiate the quality levels in the system (Elicker et al, in press; Tout et al., 2012). However, because of the considerable variability between QRIS, it is difficult to use research from individual systems to build a definitive evidence base. The examples from Indiana and Minnesota provide information about what is not working ideally, but no clear answers for what would work better.

Cross-QRIS analyses provide an important complement to the within-QRIS studies. These cross-QRIS studies have addressed early system development (Zellman & Perlman, 2008); density of participation, structural features of the rating, and associations with distribution of rating levels (Tout, Starr, Soli, et al., 2010); comparability of quality standards and rating levels (Caronongan, Kirby, Malone, & Boller, 2011); quality improvement strategies and processes (Isner et al., 2011; Smith et al., 2010); elements of system integration (Kirby, Boller, & Zaveri, 2011); and prediction of observed quality levels from QRIS components using a common metric (Malone, Kirby, Caronongan, Tout, & Boller, 2011).

Cross-QRIS analyses may build the QRIS evidence base faster than individual studies, because they require the creation of structures or analytic frameworks that foster comparison. For example, Malone and colleagues (2011) created a common QRIS metric for examining quality rating components across three QRIS. This strategy allowed the researchers to compare basic descriptive information across QRIS (e.g., what percentage of providers meets the commonly defined criteria for curriculum?) as well as to conduct more complex analyses (such as identifying predictors of observed quality levels across the three systems). Ultimately, both individual state and cross-state QRIS analyses will be essential to building the QRIS evidence base.

Application of Implementation Science to Quality Rating and Improvement Systems

Implementation science typically refers to the study of translation, replication, and scale-up of evidence-based interventions or practices into "real world" settings. Although QRIS is not a single intervention and does not yet have a strong evidence base for the effectiveness of the five components, tools from implementation science can inform the design and implementation of QRIS and build knowledge about approaches to high-quality implementation. Building knowledge about how to effectively implement the five components can serve as an important step toward building the QRIS evidence base and supporting high-quality, rigorous evaluations to test effectiveness.

Core Implementation Components

The implementation science literature points to core implementation components or "drivers" that are necessary for effective and sustained implementation:

1. *Staff selection:* Decisions about which agencies and staff should implement the intervention

2. *Preservice and in-service training:* All training needed to deliver the intervention with fidelity

3. *Coaching:* Observation, feedback, and support for staff implementing the intervention

4. *Performance assessment:* Regular assessment and feedback to staff about how well the intervention is being implemented

5. *Decision support data systems:* Systems for collecting and reporting data needed to monitor implementation and outcomes and make decisions related to the intervention

6. *Facilitative administration:* Administrative leadership that aligns policies, procedures, and structures to support implementation of the intervention

7. *Systems interventions:* Interventions with external systems to ensure that needed resources are available to implement the intervention (Fixsen, Blase, Naoom, & Wallace, 2009)

Examining QRIS implementation in light of these core implementation drivers can help state administrators and other planners and implementers develop comprehensive implementation plans and identify areas in need of strengthening and fine-tuning once implementation gets under way. Ideally, QRIS planners and stakeholders would examine each of the implementation drivers for each QRIS component (as if they were a separate intervention) as well as the QRIS as a whole. Examples of how each of the core implementation components applies to the QRIS components are provided below.

The Competency Drivers   Selection, preservice and in-service training, coaching, and performance assessment—sometimes referred to as the *competency drivers* of implementation—can be useful for examining the quality rating component of QRIS. Of 26 QRIS examined in a recent study, 23 employ observational measures of quality as a component of the rating process (Tout, Starr, Soli, et al., 2010). Most QRIS use the Environment Rating Scales developed by Harms, Clifford, Cryer, and colleagues at the University of North Carolina (Harms, Clifford, & Cryer, 2005; Harms, Cryer, & Clifford, 2006, 2007; Harms, Jacobs, & Romano, 1995), but other scales such as the Classroom Assessment and Scoring System (Pianta, La Paro, & Hamre, 2008) are used as well. The use of observational measures to assign ratings requires QRIS to hire staff with the skills necessary for conducting the observations and to provide specific kinds of training, support, and monitoring for these staff.

In deciding whether to use an observational measure as a component of the rating process and selecting a specific measure, QRIS planners must consider the selection driver to identify the specific qualifications staff need to conduct the observations. Which qualifications can be taught in training, and which should be part of staff selection criteria because they are difficult to teach? For example, observers must be able to adhere to a specific observation protocol and assign ratings on individual items in alignment with a training or "gold standard" observer. The ability and willingness to adhere to a specific protocol, rather than relying on professional judgment, may be difficult to teach in training and thus may be an important criterion for selection. Next, are candidates with the needed qualifications available in the workforce? If the observation work will be assigned to an existing agency, do staff employed by the agency have the right qualifications?

Observation measures used in QRIS require specific training by measure developers or other trainers who have been certified as gold-standard observers by the developers. Observers must successfully complete preservice training before they begin conducting observations, usually defined as achieving a specific level of reliability or agreement with the trainer's ratings. Most QRIS require observers to demonstrate 85% agreement with the gold-standard observer (Tout, Starr, Soli, et al., 2010). Observers may also need periodic refresher training over time. Applying the training driver, QRIS planners must consider how many observers need to be trained, who will conduct the training, how long it will take for trainees to achieve reliability, how to identify care settings in which practice observations can be conducted, and how much the training will cost.

The performance assessment driver is also important for the quality rating component of QRIS. After observers establish initial reliability, they must continue conducting the observations reliably over time to provide consistent quality ratings of the care settings they observe. Most QRIS check reliability during every 6th to 12th time an observer conducts an observation, by comparing the observer's ratings with those of a gold-standard rater (Tout, Starr, Soli, et al., 2010). QRIS planners need to consider how often reliability will be reassessed, who will serve as the gold-standard observer for the reliability checks, and the steps to be taken for observers who do not maintain reliability, such as additional reliability observations, additional training, coaching, and/or suspension of observation visits until reliability is reestablished.

Decision Support Data Systems The quality rating component of QRIS also demonstrates the use of decision support data systems for high-quality implementation. To calculate quality ratings and use them effectively, implementers need a data system in which to enter individual provider scores for each component of the rating system, calculate overall ratings, check the quality of the data, and track changes in ratings over time. Calculating ratings may involve compiling data from quality observations, licensing, provider self-reports, and other sources.

Often, data systems facilitate the use of quality ratings for the financial incentive component. The majority of QRIS use financial incentives to encourage and reward participation and support quality by providing tiered reimbursement through the child care subsidy system, in which providers with higher ratings receive higher levels of reimbursement for each subsidized child in care (Tout, Starr, Soli, et al., 2010). Some QRIS provide quality awards based on the size of the facility or, in some cases, the proportion of subsidized children in care. Data systems are critical to the accuracy and efficiency of this component, as data from multiple sources are needed to calculate and disperse incentives. Quality rating data must be merged with data from the child care subsidy system about the number of subsidized children in care and reimbursement rates. Revised reimbursement rates must be calculated and applied to each child care provider.

Facilitative Administrative Support   Facilitative administrative support (in which leaders seek to align policies, procedures, and structures with the needs of implementers) is also critical to successful implementation of QRIS. For the quality rating component, leaders at the state level must facilitate training and reliability checks for raters and ensure that the timing of those activities is coordinated with the rating schedule. Within agencies that employ rating staff, administrators must ensure that raters have sufficient time for conducting observations and other rating activities in addition to their other duties and receive sufficient ongoing support to do so. Raters may also need support from administrators to schedule observation visits with providers. More broadly, state administrators and other key stakeholders must ensure that processes and structures are in place to support an efficient and accurate rating process, support child care providers in quality improvement, and communicate ratings to parents and the public. Agencies and individuals involved in each of the five QRIS components must be focused on the goal of improving child care quality as measured by a specific set of standards, which requires administrators to clearly communicate those standards and support their use. Because QRIS typically involve multiple public and private agencies working together to implement multiple components, facilitative administration may take on a systems dimension as well (see below).

Systems Interventions   Even within a single component, the systems intervention driver (approaches to working with external systems to ensure needed resources are available) may be needed to implement QRIS effectively. To conduct quality ratings, for example, implementers must establish partnerships with developers of observation measures or other gold-standard observers to arrange for training and put into place a system to check reliability. Similarly, implementing the quality improvement component of QRIS requires action at multiple systems levels, as illustrated in Table 14.1. This "cascading logic model" displays the actions needed at each level of the system (from the federal government to the ECE provider) and how these actions build on each other to achieve the ultimate goal of the quality improvement component: supporting positive child outcomes through the provision of high-quality ECE (Blase, 2008; Metz & Bartley, 2012).

To provide these high-quality settings, providers need effective quality improvement services, which in turn requires the funding and support of quality improvement assistance providers. State systems must be in place to provide this funding and support to quality improvement providers, guided by a state policy vision and systems to monitor implementation and outcomes. Finally, state systems are supported by federal guidance and support for creating state quality improvement systems.

Stages of Implementation

The literature also indicates that implementation is a 2- to 4-year process that occurs in six stages:

Table 14.1. System interventions for delivering effective quality improvement services in a Quality Rating and Improvement System

Population	Intervention strategy	Desired intervention outcomes
Children ages birth to 13	Provide high-quality early care and education	Positive child outcomes
Early care and education and after-school care program staff	Provide effective quality improvement (QI) services	High-quality early care and education
Agencies that provide QI services to early care and education and after-school programs	Provide qualified agencies with funds to deliver high-quality QI, training and other resources needed to implement effective interventions, and ongoing supports to sustain high-quality implementation	Provision of high-quality, effective QI services
State and regional agencies responsible for provision of QI to early care and education and after-school settings	Develop state systems to fund and support QI providers, select QI interventions to implement, and link QI providers with that need QI	Provide qualified agencies with funds to deliver high-quality QI, training and other resources needed to implement effective interventions, and ongoing supports to sustain high-quality implementation
State policy makers, funders, and other key stakeholders	Create a shared vision for provision of QI services in the state that is aligned with needs and adequately funded; develop systems to monitor implementation and outcomes of QI interventions and provide technical assistance and supports	Develop state systems to fund and support QI providers, select QI interventions to implement, and link QI providers with that need QI
Federal agency leaders on child care policy	Communicate federal vision and requirements for provision of QI services through federal funding streams, including required components, desired outcomes, expectations for monitoring and reporting, and technical assistance and supports	Create a shared vision for provision of QI services in the state that is aligned with needs and adequately funded; develop systems to monitor implementation and outcomes of QI interventions and provide technical assistance and supports

Source: Blase (2008).

1. *Exploration:* Assessment of the potential match between an intervention and community needs and decision making about whether to move forward with adopting an intervention

2. *Installation:* All tasks that must be accomplished before implementation can begin

3. *Initial implementation:* The initial phase of implementing a new intervention for the first time

4. *Full implementation:* Implementation at a steady state

5. *Innovation:* Consideration of adaptations that may improve implementation in a particular community without changing core features of an intervention

6. *Sustainability:* Efforts to ensure continued and stable implementation of the intervention (Fixsen, Naoom, Blase, Friedman, & Wallace, 2005)

While these stages typically do not occur in a linear fashion and/or in isolation of each other, it is useful to think about each one separately, along with the activities that should be carried out at each stage.

In the case of QRIS, stages may not occur simultaneously for each QRIS component. For example, to get started on building a QRIS, a state may develop quality standards and begin initial implementation of a rating system. A year later, the state may begin initial implementation of quality improvement services for participating providers and begin the exploration phase for a financial incentive program to be implemented through the child care subsidy system. Table 14.2 provides an illustrative set of questions that QRIS developers and implementers should consider at each implementation stage, for each QRIS component.

Application of Systems Theory to Quality Rating and Improvement Systems

A "system" can be defined as a set of interacting and interdependent parts, connected by a network of relationships; together, these parts form a whole that is greater than the sum of its parts (Hargreaves, 2010). Systems interventions, such as QRIS, aim to change system-wide behavior patterns by making changes to the system's underlying structures, dynamics, and conditions (Coffman, 2007; Eoyang, 2007; Hargreaves, 2010). Although the previous section examined each of the QRIS components separately, in reality they are not implemented in isolation. The components influence and interact with each other. For example, quality ratings affect the level of financial incentives providers receive, and quality improvement supports may, in turn, affect providers' quality ratings. Moreover, QRIS typically involve multiple public and private agencies and stakeholders (e.g., parents, providers, local and state agencies responsible for child care licensing, quality improvement providers). These diverse stakeholders operate at different levels (community, regional, state, federal) and across overlapping systems (e.g., child care subsidy systems, professional development systems, child care resource and referral systems).

In this context, alignment of priorities and timelines, efficient flows of information, and effective communication throughout the system are essential to successful implementation and ongoing operation of QRIS. However, evaluating systems initiatives in all their complexity is daunting—systems are complicated, constantly evolving, and challenging to measure (Coffman, 2007). Nevertheless, just as tools from implementation science can be useful for monitoring and assessing QRIS implementation, tools from systems theory can provide another useful lens through which to assess and refine QRIS. Systems theory encompasses a growing body of literature on theoretical models and their application to evaluating a range of systems interventions (Coffman, 2007; Hargreaves, 2010; Hargreaves & Paulsell, 2009; Schaack, Tarrant, Boller, & Tout, 2012).

This chapter draws on the literature about complex adaptive systems (Eoyang, 2007; Hargreaves, 2010; Holland, 1995) and focuses on three important attributes of

Table 14.2. Illustrative questions for each stage of implementation, by QRIS component

Stage of implementation	QRIS components				
	Quality standards	Quality ratings	Quality improvement (QI)	Financial incentives	Consumer education
Exploration	What are the state's goals for quality improvement? Which dimensions of quality are important to stakeholders? How much support exists for developing or adopting specific quality standards? What research evidence is available about the links between child outcomes and quality standards of interest?	Can existing data sources be used to assign ratings? Is an observational measure of quality needed? If so, which measure should be used? Are qualified staff available to carry out the rating process? Do staff need to be hired? How open are care providers to being rated?	Which dimensions of quality are most in need of improvement? Are QI interventions with evidence of effectiveness available in those areas? Who will provide QI services? How will QI be funded? Which providers will be eligible to receive which QI services? How receptive are providers to participating in QI interventions?	What quality improvements need to be incentivized? What incentive mechanisms will be used? Are subsidy system staff receptive to providing financial incentives? Are data systems available to support a financial incentive program? What magnitude of financial incentives is feasible? What is the evidence on effectiveness for incentives?	What sources of information do parents use to find child care? Are child care resource and referral agencies receptive to providing information about a QRIS and care provider ratings to consumers? What strategies can be used to provide consumer education? What is the evidence of effectiveness on consumer education? How much will consumer education cost?
Installation	What is the process for developing the standards? Who will be involved? What strategies will be used to educate providers, parents, and other stakeholders about the content of the standards, and how they will be used? Is more work needed to operationalize the standards, including defining terms and decision rules for assigning ratings?	Do data systems need to be created or refined to produce the ratings? Who will assign ratings? How will the standards and indicators be measured? Who will conduct observations if needed, and on what schedule? Who will train raters and observers, and how many staff need to be trained? Is pilot testing needed? Is a plan in place to monitor the rating process?	Which interventions have been selected? Who will deliver them? Is funding in place? Do staff need training to deliver the interventions? Are needed data systems in place? Have eligibility criteria been developed? Have promotional materials been developed to inform providers about the QI services? Is a plan in place for monitoring fidelity?	Have subsidy staff been trained on how to implement the financial incentive program? Are data systems in place to support the financial incentive program? Have promotional materials been developed to inform providers and parents about the incentives and how providers can obtain them? Is a plan in place for monitoring implementation?	Have marketing materials been developed and pilot-tested with parents and other consumers? Has a dissemination plan been developed for marketing materials? Have staff involved in consumer education been trained on delivering key messages?

(continued)

Table 14.2. (continued)

Stage of implementation	QRIS components				
	Quality standards	Quality ratings	Quality improvement (QI)	Financial incentives	Consumer education
Initial implementation	How well do providers and other stakeholders understand the standards? Is additional education needed? What feedback have providers and other stakeholders provided on the standards? Are there areas of disagreement that need to be addressed?	Are raters able to assign ratings and conduct observations reliably? How much effort is the rating process taking? Is it more or less than expected? How are providers reacting to the rating process? Do adjustments need to be made to address any concerns? What lessons from initial implementation can be used to fine tune the process? How valid are the ratings? Do they adequately differentiate levels of quality as expected?	What is the uptake of QI services? Is additional outreach to providers needed? Are eligibility criteria appropriate? How well do QI services offered match the needs of eligible providers? Are staff delivering the interventions with fidelity? Is additional training and support needed? What are the early outcomes of QI services? Are changes in observed quality occurring as expected? What lessons from initial implementation can be used to fine-tune QI?	Are staff implementing financial incentives as intended? Are data systems adequate to support the financial incentive program, or are changes needed? What is the uptake of financial incentives? Are providers aware of them? What are the early outcomes of financial incentives? Are they producing expected changes in provider behavior? What lessons from initial implementation can be used to fine-tune the financial incentives?	What is the uptake of marketing materials? Are marketing materials being broadly disseminated? Through what channels? Are consumers interested in the QRIS and ratings? Do consumers understand key messages, especially the quality ratings? Is there any evidence that consumers are selecting care based on the ratings?
Full implementation	Is there consensus on the quality standards among key stakeholders? Is a system for periodic review and updating of the standards needed?	Has a validation study been conducted to confirm that the ratings are working as expected? Are systems in place for ongoing training and reliability checks for ratings and observers, if used?	Are sufficient services available to meet the demand for QI? Is a system for periodic review of QI services needed to ensure that services offered match the needs of providers? Is a system in place to monitor fidelity?	Is a system in place for periodic review of incentive structure and amounts to determine if changes are needed? Is a system in place for monitoring fidelity of implementation?	Is a system in place for periodic review and updating of marketing messages and materials? What is the impact of consumer education? Are there plans to evaluate the effect of consumer education on parents' child care choices?

	Quality Standards	Quality Ratings	QI Services	Financial Incentives	Consumer Education
		Are systems in place for reviewing and updating ratings periodically? Are sufficient numbers of providers participating in the rating process?	What is the impact of QI services on observed quality and quality ratings? Are there plans to evaluate the services' effectiveness in improving quality?	What is the impact of financial incentives on observed quality and quality ratings? Are there plans to evaluate the effect of financial incentives in improving quality?	Are changes needed to marketing messages, materials, and outlets to reach particular groups of consumers?
Innovation	What refinements should be made to improve the quality standards? Does recent research suggest any needed revisions to the standards?	Do validation study results indicate the need for changes in quality ratings? Are there improvements that can be made to the rating process to reduce the burden on providers? To increase provider participation?	Do evaluation results indicate needed changes to delivery of QI services or the mix of services offered? Are cultural or other adaptations to existing QI services needed to better address needs of providers?	Do evaluation results indicate needed changes to financial incentive structure or amounts? Are any changes needed to reduce burden on providers and/or increase participation?	
Sustainability	Are systems in place to continually educate policy makers and stakeholders about the importance of the quality standards to supporting positive child outcomes? Are quality standards well accepted in the state?	Is a well-established system in place for ongoing training and monitoring of raters and for training new raters over time? Are funding streams in place for the rating process? Are quality ratings viewed as established practice in the state?	Are systems in place to continually educate stakeholders about the importance of providing ongoing QI services? Are systems for funding, delivering, and monitoring QI service delivery well established? Are QI services viewed as established practice in the state?	Is the system for calculating and providing financial incentives well established? Are policy makers and key stakeholders educated about the benefits of the financial incentive structure? Are financial incentives viewed as established practice in the state?	Are well-established systems in place for ongoing consumer education? Is provision of quality rating information to parents and other consumers searching for child care viewed as accepted practice in the state?

systems—boundaries, relationships, and perspectives—that can provide a useful framework for assessing implementation of QRIS at all stages, from exploration to sustainability. These attributes define the individuals and institutions that are part of the system, how they interact and share information, and their diverse points of view. An examination of system attributes at regular intervals may be useful for examining the dynamics of how the five QRIS components are functioning in relation to each other and troubleshooting implementation challenges or barriers that arise.

System Boundaries

System boundaries are defined as demarcations of the individuals, organizations, social systems, levels of government, and other entities that are inside and outside the system and separate activities within a system (Hargreaves & Paulsell, 2009; Midgley, 2007). For our purposes, which entities are inside and outside the QRIS and each of its components? One approach to determining the boundaries of a system is to identify an issue or problem of interest (e.g., the quality of ECE) and ask who is addressing this issue, has influence on the issue, or is influenced by it (Checkland & Poulter, 2006; Foster-Fishman, Nowell, & Yang, 2007). In a QRIS, a range of state and local public and private agencies, quality improvement and technical assistance providers, child care provider associations, individual providers, child care resource and referral agencies, parents, and others is involved.

In addition to boundaries for the QRIS as a whole, it may be useful to examine the boundaries for each QRIS component and at different systems levels. For example, the quality improvement component includes quality improvement intervention funders, agencies delivering the interventions to providers, home-based caregivers, child care center directors, prekindergarten program and Head Start center administrators, and classroom staff. It may also include community colleges and other institutions of higher education that offer degree programs in ECE and Child Development Associate (CDA) credentialing programs.

Boundaries may also vary by system level; for instance, there are different sets of QRIS stakeholders at the state, regional, and community levels. Mapping the boundaries of a QRIS and each component by system level may be useful for monitoring implementation and ensuring that all relevant stakeholders are engaged at each stage. During the exploration stage, for example, it may be useful to map the boundaries of a likely QRIS to ensure that all stakeholders are consulted about the content of quality standards. Which agencies and individuals are likely to participate in each component, and how receptive are they? During the installation phase, who needs to be consulted about how the QRIS may affect their daily operations? For example, which agencies need to be consulted about implementing a financial incentive program? How would data systems need to be adapted? Would attendance reporting and payment systems need to change? At the innovation stage, are there cultural adaptations to components of the QRIS that should be considered? Do the system boundaries need to be expanded to include new groups or individuals with the cultural expertise required to develop these adaptations?

Relationships within a System

Relationships are the connections and exchanges that occur within the system, such as flows of information, referrals, collaborative arrangements, and funding and other resources (Olson & Eoyang, 2001; Parsons, 2007). In a QRIS, relationships and exchanges of information are critical both within and across components. All stakeholders must receive accurate information about the quality standards, which serve as the basis for all other components. To assign ratings, information must be obtained from multiple sources such as licensers, quality observers, providers, and possibly professional development systems. The consumer education component requires development of relationships with, and feedback from, parents and other consumers. The quality improvement component requires relationships between funders of quality improvement interventions, agencies that deliver quality improvement interventions, and providers who receive the services.

Once system boundaries are mapped, assessing key relationships both within and across components can help QRIS planners and implementers ensure that collaboration is occurring and information and funding are flowing as needed for each component to function as planned. At the exploration phase, relationships are critical for building support for a QRIS and consensus about the quality standards. During initial implementation, positive relationships must be established between providers and observers who rate care settings. Licensers and quality improvement service providers must communicate to ensure they are providing consistent direction and advice to providers. Information about quality ratings must flow to the child care subsidy system so that tiered reimbursement rates can be calculated. In the sustainability phase, systems for information sharing must be maintained and adapted as technology changes. Key stakeholders must continually communicate with a changing set of state and local government officials and policy makers about the importance of the QRIS to achieving positive child outcomes. Information from evaluation and performance measurement systems must be available to provide evidence about the value of the QRIS, and key messages must be coordinated among stakeholders.

Perspectives within a System

Perspectives are the points of view, purposes, and goals of stakeholders within a system (Hargreaves & Paulsell, 2009; Parsons, 2007). Stakeholders in a system often have different perspectives and pursue different goals. For example, they may have different points of view about the quality of care, reasons why an insufficient proportion of settings have achieved high quality, and how to improve it (e.g., by increasing resources through higher subsidy payments, by providing scholarships for provider education, by providing on-site coaching). At times, the perspective of a particular group may be overlooked or may not be voiced, especially if it differs from the majority point of view. For example, home-based child care providers may define quality differently from center-based providers. Frontline staff delivering quality improvement services may have a different perspective than managers or funders about which interventions should be used.

As with boundaries and relationships, mapping the perspectives of stakeholders within a system is important at each stage of implementation. For example, if perspectives of providers are not taken into account in the development of quality standards during the installation phase, many may decline to participate when initial implementation gets under way. If providers do not feel that quality improvement interventions are meeting their needs or are being delivered in convenient and accessible formats, they may not take up the services. For the consumer education component, parents' perspectives about quality and their awareness and understanding of the rating standards should be assessed and used to refine consumer education messages.

Perspectives may be more difficult to assess than boundaries and relationships, as some stakeholders may be reluctant to share their points of view or may not have a clear forum for doing so. QRIS planners and implementers might consider periodic surveys or focus groups to solicit the perspectives of key groups of stakeholders such as different types of providers, parents, and quality improvement service providers. Specific topics may include the quality standards, quality rating process, alignment of quality improvement services with provider needs, structure of financial incentives, and impact of consumer education messages.

Summary

Concepts from systems theory can be useful for helping QRIS planners and implementers to monitor, troubleshoot, and fine-tune QRIS, especially in regard to interaction across components. Key questions to consider are as follows:

- Who is involved in the QRIS, within each component and at each system level?

- How well is information being shared within and across components and levels, and are needed feedback loops in place?

- What are the perspectives of QRIS stakeholders across components and system levels, and how do these align with QRIS goals and operations?

Achieving an Evidence-Based, High-Quality, and Fully Implemented Quality Rating and Improvement System

To make significant progress toward implementation of effective QRIS, it is necessary to articulate a vision of what an ideal QRIS looks like and what it achieves. This section outlines a prospective QRIS, focusing on each of the five QRIS components and how they would function to achieve outcomes for children and families, practitioners, providers, and markets.

Standards

In an ideal QRIS, standards would be developed based on evidence from research about what aspects of practice are critical to support children's development, either directly or indirectly. One challenge with putting forth a model for how standards could be incorporated in QRIS is preserving the beneficial aspects of current strategies that allow for standards to be tailored to state and local contexts and needs. A nationally prescribed set of quality standards and indicators may be useful in providing a core set of standards on which states could build, tailoring them to their own state and local contexts or needs. Ideally, QRIS would include standards that fit the context but also have an evidence base demonstrating that they promote high-quality, developmentally appropriate practices that support children's learning and development. Key stakeholders within the boundaries of the QRIS would be involved in the adoption of these standards.

QRIS evaluations offer an important opportunity to conduct needed studies of quality standards that will build the research base. As knowledge about ECE settings and practices becomes more sophisticated, it will likely be possible to identify quality standards that support children's development in indirect and direct ways and to recommend strategies for including those standards in a QRIS. An ideal QRIS would include a mechanism that allows for regular review and revision of the standards.

Ratings

In an ideal QRIS, the process of assigning ratings would be based on proven strategies for obtaining documentation of quality indicators and, if used, for collecting observations from providers. Intentional selection of staff, training, coaching, and ongoing monitoring would be used to support staff in their roles. Expectations and procedures would be outlined clearly in a written manual for staff. Inter-rater reliability standards would be set at the most rigorous levels that are feasible to achieve, and a regular process would be established for assessing reliability with a trained anchor. A process would be in place to examine the validity of the rating process and to use the validation analyses as the basis for revising or improving aspects of the process. These validation analyses could examine the extent to which the established QRIS levels differentiate quality and relate to children's development.

Quality Improvement

The process of providing quality improvement services in an ideal QRIS involves assessing providers' needs (areas of practice that are in need of improvement), agreeing on a shared measurable goal, and matching appropriate services and resources to those needs. For example, the quality improvement staff would assess a provider's openness and readiness to change. Providers that are reluctant or unwilling to consider adoption of new practices would not be expected to reach high goals for quality in the first rating cycle, and resources would be allocated to improvements that are within reach for a provider. Coaching and/or consultation would be provided to support providers in the application of new practices, and ongoing support would be provided to ensure that the coaches are effectively supporting change in provider staff. In concert with the quality standards component, individualized technical assistance would be aimed at improving those quality standards and elements of practice that are proven to support children's school readiness. All of the quality improvement strategies would be well defined (e.g., written manuals available) and have some evidence of their effectiveness in improving quality. Strong relationships among local, regional, and state quality improvement experts as well as facilitative administration leadership would ensure that a coordinated, cohesive set of activities is effectively implemented to raise quality as defined by the QRIS standards.

Financial Incentives

In the ideal QRIS, financial incentives would function both to promote QRIS participation among providers and to support progress in meeting quality standards. Incentives would also be offered to parents to help them access and afford high-quality programs. QRIS would offer only those financial incentives—and at a particular amount—that have evidence demonstrating a relationship to quality improvement on one or more standards in the QRIS or to helping promote parent choice of high quality. Providers would have clear expectations about how the financial incentives could and should be spent to support particular aspects of quality improvement. Likewise, guidelines would be available to parents to help them tie the financial incentive to higher quality arrangements. Research would provide evidence on the effectiveness of particular strategies with different types of providers (lower quality vs. higher quality, centers vs. homes) and in supporting access to quality among parents. The QRIS data system would capture the detailed data needed to help leaders continue to "tweak" key features of the financial incentives (e.g., amount, timing) linked to quality improvement.

Marketing and Consumer Education

Finally, an ideal QRIS includes marketing and consumer education strategies that are proven to attract new providers as well as new consumers or system users. QRIS would set participation targets for providers serving high-priority populations, and outreach strategies would help QRIS meet those targets. Similarly, targets would be set for system use by consumers. Procedures would be in place to track meaningful use of the system, and data would be used to refine the process.

Summary

An ideal QRIS is not a static system in which structures and processes are set and unchanging. Rather, an ideal QRIS assumes that knowledge will continue to be gathered to build the evidence base about recommended practices and strategies for supporting all participants in the system. Evaluation and performance management are critical tools for QRIS to support examination of implementation and outcomes and to make system changes that promote continuous improvement.

Future Directions for Quality Rating and Improvement System Stakeholders

As noted at the beginning of this chapter, implementation science usually refers to the science of scaling up and replicating evidence-based practices. Although the QRIS is more than a single practice and does not have a well developed evidence base to support specific features of its implementation, this chapter has provided examples of how implementation science (core implementation components and stages of implementation) and systems theory (boundaries, relationships, and perspectives) can be used as tools for supporting QRIS design and implementation. The chapter has also contrasted the current status of QRIS implementation with a vision for an optimally functioning QRIS. The key question for QRIS developers, planners, and implementers is: What steps can we take to transform existing QRIS into optimally functioning systems in the context of limited budgets, staff time, and other resources? This section provides a suggested road map for using the tools presented in this chapter to improve QRIS.

Step 1: Create an Implementation Team

One strategy for increasing focus on QRIS implementation is to identify a team of stakeholders in the QRIS who are interested in engaging in an ongoing process of examining implementation, suggesting system improvements, and evaluating how well the changes are working. Selecting the right set of stakeholders to be part of this team is important. Members should be engaged in the system, motivated to make improvements, and willing to learn about implementation science. If individuals from other sectors (e.g., public health, home visiting programs) have expertise or experience in implementation science, then it might be useful to reach out to them for advice or to consider creating or joining a broader state-level systems implementation learning community.

Tools from systems theory may also be helpful for forming an optimal team. For example, it may be useful to consider the QRIS boundaries. Does the team need to include stakeholders from all QRIS components, or will it focus on a single component? Should the team include stakeholders from all levels of the system (e.g., state agencies, community organizations, providers)? Does the team include stakeholders with diverse perspectives and points of view?

Step 2: Set Priorities and Goals

Not everything can be done at once. After an implementation team is established, it should set priorities and goals. For example, a team might begin by identifying the stage of implementation of each component and what is needed to move selected components to the next stage (see Table 14.2). Another approach would be to examine the financial resources, training and support, and data systems available to support each QRIS component and consider whether they are adequate to support installation of the core implementation components identified earlier. For example, in the quality ratings component, this would include the resources, training, and data systems needed to select raters, train them on conducting ratings, coach them during the training process, assess their inter-rater reliability, compute and document ratings in a data system, support the rating process administratively, and make them available to support other QRIS components (e.g., financial incentives, quality improvement).

Depending on the status of an individual QRIS, other priorities might include increasing alignment across QRIS components, improving information flows within and across components, examining and possibly realigning resources dedicated to each component, strengthening performance assessments, or supporting the competencies of staff implementing particular components. In the area of alignment, for instance, are the quality improvement interventions being implemented aligned with quality standards and targeted to standards on which providers receive lower ratings? Are financial incentives targeted to improve low-rated areas, and do requirements for using the incentives reinforce this objective? Regarding information flows, do quality improvement providers have access to providers' quality ratings to facilitate targeting of services? In the area of resources, does the consumer education component have sufficient resources to implement marketing strategies that target populations of interest? To strengthen performance assessments, is there a detailed description of the various quality improvement strategies and performance expectations for coaches? Finally, do quality improvement providers have sufficient training, coaching, and supervision to implement evidence-based quality interventions?

Step 3: Develop and Implement a Work Plan and Timeline

Once priorities and goals are set, the implementation team should develop a work plan and timeline for achieving the goals. The work plan should include identification of needed information and steps to be taken to collect it, a plan for evaluating the information, a process for recommending changes or other actions based on the team's assessment, and a process for evaluating any actions taken. For example, an implementation team might determine that quality improvement activities for family child care are not aligned with results of quality ratings, because while most quality improvement services are focused on the caregiving environment, quality ratings are low in the area of provider–child interactions and language. To improve alignment, the team will gather information about quality improvement interventions for family child care providers that target interactions and language, identify which quality improvement providers can best deliver the intervention, and develop a plan for training, coaching, and assessing the performance of providers on the new intervention. The team will also monitor quality ratings of providers who receive the new intervention to assess how well it is working.

Step 4: Educate Stakeholders

A QRIS implementation team should also consider strategies for educating stakeholders about the implementation process, including core implementation components necessary for successful implementation, stages of implementation, and the amount of time needed to achieve full implementation. This may help policy makers align their expectations for how quickly a QRIS can achieve desired outcomes and the resources needed to implement each component well. It may also help stakeholders involved in the system to understand the steps required to implement the system and the changes in practice, data systems, and allocation of resources that may be needed to align activities across QRIS components.

Future Directions for Quality Rating and Improvement System Researchers

As QRIS continue to scale up across the country, research evidence is crucial to inform design and implementation. More research on QRIS is needed to inform stakeholders about the evidence of effectiveness of QRIS and individual components, as well as about promising implementation strategies for creating high-quality, sustainable systems. To make full use of the tools available from implementation science, researchers should place emphasis on identifying effective approaches for QRIS components. Which quality improvement interventions produce the largest gains in quality? What kinds of financial incentive structures improve quality? What magnitude of incentives is needed? Does technical assistance in how to spend the incentives make a difference? Which marketing strategies are effective in promoting selection of higher quality settings by parents?

As research to identify effective strategies is conducted, researchers should also attend to carefully documenting implementation and identifying the processes, strategies, and tools needed for successful replication of those strategies. When effective strategies are identified, additional implementation research must be conducted to facilitate replication in a variety of state and local contexts. This includes, for example, manualizing implementation processes and then testing those manuals in different contexts; developing valid and reliable measures of fidelity; documenting data system requirements; developing staff selection criteria, training curricula and procedures, approaches to coaching, and supervision procedures; and other tools to support replication.

To keep pace with the rapid scale-up of QRIS and inform the field about the most promising approaches, researchers must work alongside planners and implementers to identify and test promising innovations, replicate them in diverse settings, and document effective implementation strategies. Tools from implementation science can be used to promote high-quality implementation of QRIS in real-world settings, facilitate tests of their effectiveness, and support scale-up and dissemination of proven strategies.

References

Adams, G., & Compton, J.F. (2011). *Client-friendly strategies: What can CCDF learn from other systems?* Washington, DC: The Urban Institute. Retrieved from http://www.urban.org/UploadedPDF/412526-client-friendly-strategies.pdf

Blase, K. (2008). *Cascading logic model.* Chapel Hill, NC: National Implementation Research Network.

Boller, K., Del Grosso, P., Blair, R., Jolly, Y., Fortson, K., Paulsell, D., ... Kovac, M. (2010). *The Seeds to Success modified field test: Findings from the impact and implementation studies.* Princeton, NJ: Mathematica Policy Research.

Caronongan, P., Kirby, G., Malone, L., & Boller, K. (2011). *Defining and measuring quality: An in-depth study of five child care quality rating and improvement systems* (OPRE Report #2011-29). Washington, DC: U.S. Department of Health and Human Services.

Checkland, P.B., & Poulter, J. (2006). *Learning for action: A short definitive account of soft systems methodology and its use for practitioners, teachers, and students.* Chichester, England: Wiley.

Coffman, J. (2007). *A framework for evaluating systems initiatives.* Retrieved from http://www.buildinitiative.org/content/evaluation-systems-change

Elicker, J., Langill, C., Ruprecht, K.M., Lewsader, J., Anderson, T., & Brizzi, M. (in press). Paths to QUALITY: Collaborative evaluation of a new child care quality rating and improvement system. *Early Education and Development.*

Eoyang, G. (2007). Human systems dynamics: Complexity-based approach to a complex evaluation. In B. Williams & I. Imam (Eds.), *Systems concepts in evaluation: An expert anthology* (pp. 123–140). Point Reyes Station, CA: American Evaluation Association.

Fixsen, D.L., Blase, K.A., Naoom, S.F., & Wallace, F. (2009). Core implementation components. *Research on Social Work Practice, 19,* 531–540.

Fixsen, D.L., Naoom, S.F., Blase, K.A., Friedman, R.M., & Wallace, F. (2005). *Implementation research: A synthesis of the literature* (FMHI Publication No. 231). Tampa, FL: University of South Florida, Louis de la Parte Florida Mental Health Institute, National Implementation Research Network.

Foster-Fishman, P., Nowell, B., & Yang, H. (2007). Putting the system back into systems change: A framework for understanding and changing organizational and community systems. *American Journal of Community Psychology, 39,* 197–215.

Gaylor, E., Spiker, D., Hebbeler, C., & Williamson, C. (2009). *Saint Paul Early Childhood Scholarship evaluation: Annual report.* Menlo Park, CA: SRI International.

Gaylor, E., Spiker, D., Williamson, C., & Ferguson, K. (2010). *Saint Paul Early Childhood Scholarship evaluation: Annual report year 2.* Menlo Park, CA: SRI International.

Gaylor, E., Spiker, D., Williamson, C., & Ferguson, K. (2011). *Saint Paul Early Childhood Scholarship evaluation: Final evaluation report—2008–2011.* Menlo Park, CA: SRI International.

Hargreaves, M.B. (2010). *Evaluating systems change: A planning guide.* Princeton, NJ: Mathematica Policy Research.

Hargreaves, M.B., & Paulsell, D. (2009). *Evaluating systems change efforts to support evidence-based home visiting: Concepts and methods.* Washington, DC: Children's Bureau, Administration for Children and Families, U.S. Department of Health and Human Services.

Harms, T., Clifford, R.M., & Cryer, D. (2005). *Early Childhood Environment Rating Scale* (Rev. ed.). New York, NY: Teachers College Press.

Harms, T., Cryer, D., & Clifford, R.M. (2006). *Infant/Toddler Environment Rating Scale* (Rev. ed.). New York, NY: Teachers College Press.

Harms, T., Cryer, D., & Clifford, R.M. (2007). *Family Child Care Environment Rating Scale* (Rev. ed.). New York, NY: Teachers College Press.

Harms, T., Jacobs, E.V., & Romano, D. (1995). *The School-Age Care Environment Rating Scale.* New York, NY: Teachers College Press.

Holland, J.H. (1995). *Hidden order: How adaptation builds complexity.* Reading, MA: Helix Books, 1995.

Isner, T., Tout, K., Zaslow, M., Soli, M., Quinn, K., Rothenberg, L., & Burkhauser, M. (2011). *Coaching in early care and education programs and quality rating and improvement systems (QRIS): Identifying promising features.* Washington, DC: Child Trends.

Iruka, I.U., Yazijian, N., Hughes, C., Robertson, N., & Maxwell, K. (2010). *Report of year 2 Quality Counts survey findings.* Chapel Hill, NC: FPG Child Development Institute, University of North Carolina.

Kirby, G., Boller, K., & Zaveri, H. (2011). *Child care quality rating and improvement systems: Approaches to integrating programs for young children in two states* (OPRE Report #2011-28). Washington, DC: U.S. Department of Health and Human Services.

Malone, L., Kirby, G., Caronongan, P., Tout, K., & Boller, K. (2011). *Measuring quality across three child care quality rating and improvement systems* (OPRE Report #2011-30). Washington, DC: U.S. Department of Health and Human Services.

Metz, A., & Bartley, L. (2012). Active implementation frameworks for program success. *Zero to Three, 32*(4), 11–17.

Midgley, G. (2007). Systems thinking for evaluation. In B. Williams & I. Imam (Eds.), *Systems concepts in evaluation: An expert anthology* (pp. 11–34). Point Reyes, CA: American Evaluation Association.

Mitchell, A.W. (2005). *Stair steps to quality: A guide for states and communities developing quality rating systems for early care and education.* Alexandria, VA: United Way of America, Success by 6.

Olson, E.E., & Eoyang, G.H. (2001). *Facilitating organizational change: Lessons from complexity science.* San Francisco, CA: Jossey-Bass/Pfeiffer.

Parsons, B. (2007). *Designing initiative evaluation: A systems-oriented framework for evaluating social change efforts.* Battle Creek, MI: W.K. Kellogg Foundation.

Pianta, R.C., La Paro, K.M., & Hamre, B.K. (2008). *Classroom Assessment Scoring System.* Baltimore, MD: Paul H. Brookes Publishing Co.

Schaack, D., Tarrant, K., Boller, K., & Tout, K. (2012). Quality rating and improvement systems: Frameworks for early care and education systems change. In S.L. Kagan & K. Kauerz (Eds.), *Early childhood systems: Transforming early learning* (pp. 71–86). New York, NY: Teachers College Press.

Smith, S., Schneider, W., & Kreader, J.L. (2010). *Features of professional development and on-site technical assistance in child care quality rating and improvement systems: A survey of state-wide systems.* New York, NY: National Center for Children in Poverty, Columbia University Mailman School of Public Health.

Snow, M., & Spiker, D. (2009). *Evaluation of School Readiness Connections Pilot Project.* Menlo Park, CA: SRI International.

Step Up to Quality. (2010). *Quality Achievement Awards policy changes, 7/1/09 to 6/30/10.* Retrieved from http://jfs.ohio.gov/cdc/docs/QAAPolicyChanges7-1-09to6-30-10.pdf

Swenson-Klatt, D., & Tout, K. (2011). Measuring and rating quality: A state perspective on the demands for quality measurement in a policy context. In M. Zaslow, I. Martinez-Beck, K. Tout, & T. Halle (Eds.), *Quality measurement in early childhood settings.* Baltimore, MD: Paul H. Brookes Publishing Co.

Tout, K., & Maxwell, K.L. (2010). Quality rating and improvement systems: Achieving the promise for programs, families, and early childhood systems. In P.W. Wesley & V. Buysee (Eds.), *The quest for quality: Promising innovations for early childhood programs.* Baltimore, MD: Paul H. Brookes Publishing Co.

Tout, K., Starr, R., & Cleveland, J. (2008). *Evaluation of Parent Aware, Minnesota's quality rating system pilot: Year 1 evaluation report.* Minneapolis, MN: Child Trends.

Tout, K., Starr, R., Isner, T., Cleveland, J., Soli, M., & Quinn, K. (2010). *Evaluation of Parent Aware, Minnesota's quality rating system pilot: Year 3 evaluation report.* Minneapolis, MN: Child Trends.

Tout, K., Starr, R., Isner, T., Daily, S., Moodie, S., Rothenberg, L., & Soli, M. (2012). *Executive Summary of the Kentucky STARS for KIDS NOW Process Evaluation, Evaluation Brief #1.* Washington, DC: Child Trends. Retrieved from http:/www.kentuckypartnership.org/starsevaluation

Tout, K., Starr, R., Soli, M., Moodie, S., Kirby, G., & Boller, K. (2010). *Compendium of quality rating systems and evaluations.* Washington, DC: Child Trends.

Zellman, G.L., & Perlman, M. (2008). *Child care quality improvement systems in five pioneer states: Implementation issues and lessons learned.* Santa Monica, CA: Rand.

Zellman, G.L., Perlman, M., Le, V., & Setodji, C.M. (2008). *Assessing the validity of the Qualistar Early Learning quality rating and improvement system as a tool for improving child-care quality* (MG-650-QEL). Santa Monica: CA: Rand.

CHAPTER 15

Applications of Implementation Science to Early Care and Education Programs and Systems

Implications for Research, Policy, and Practice

Tamara Halle, Martha Zaslow, Ivelisse Martinez-Beck, and Allison Metz

This book marks and seeks to advance an important conceptual shift in early childhood research, policy, and practice. Its authors acknowledge that all of the strenuous work involved in developing and conducting rigorous evaluations of programs to strengthen early childhood development—even though it is a substantial accomplishment that we now have a body of work through such efforts identifying evidence-based practices for early childhood—is not enough. There is growing recognition that programs not only need to be demonstrated as effective in carefully controlled circumstances—or even in less controlled community settings—but also need careful preparation to plan for and assure replicability, need to assure that there will be structures and practices in place to allow for sustainability, and even early in program planning and development, need to prepare for expansion in order to be worthy of full investment by policy and in practice.

While there is growing acknowledgment of the need for such a focus on implementation—and there is a body of work summarizing the literature and providing a framework for implementation science as it might be applied to early childhood—we are at an early stage in terms of application of this work within early childhood research, policy, and practice. Though it is clear that early childhood implementation science should involve taking steps to plan for and support fidelity of implementation, sustainability, and expansion, it is much less clear at this point what measures and methods should be used to document that these steps are being taken appropriately. Furthermore, we are only at the beginning of applying implementation science within early childhood systems.

The chapters prepared for this book draw together the most advanced work in this area, seeking to apply implementation science to the early childhood field and focusing on the development of methods and measures for application of these frameworks. Because implementation science is of importance to researchers, practitioners, and policy makers, this book has been written with these multiple audiences in mind. For early childhood researchers, we wanted to present frameworks that would inform the design of program evaluations and could illuminate the many aspects of an early childhood initiative (large or small) that contribute to the successful functioning, replication, and scale-up of that initiative. For practitioners, we wanted to present concrete examples of successful early childhood initiatives at early and later stages of implementation and to share lessons learned about what contributes to the successful implementation of such initiatives. For policy makers, we wanted to raise awareness about the importance of implementation for the success of early childhood programs and systems and to provide a relatively new perspective on how to evaluate and support early childhood programs and systems so that effective practices can be sustained in real-world settings and children and families can ultimately benefit from activities and programs as intended.

The chapters in this volume have already been well summarized in the overviews to the four sections of the book, and several integrative chapters have provided important insights into emerging patterns of findings and lessons learned for researchers and decision makers actively engaged with the implementation of early childhood initiatives at both the program and policy levels. In this final chapter, we consider how the chapters in this volume collectively suggest broad implications for future early childhood research, policy, and practice. We also draw on examples from other work ongoing in the field.

Implications for Research

Early childhood researchers have long been aware of implementation issues with regard to early childhood practices and programs and their effects on intended outcomes. For example, the *selection* and *training* of program delivery staff and ongoing support from *administrators* and *leadership* have been found to be essential to the success of home visitation programs and are considered by some program evaluators of comparable importance to the *content* conveyed in the home visitation sessions or the *duration* and *intensity* of those sessions (Chapter 10; *Future of Children*, 1999). Likewise, research and evaluation regarding professional development supports for the early childhood workforce have perennially focused on developing early childhood educators' competencies through training and ongoing support, be these supports aimed at strengthening early childhood practices related to specific child outcomes (e.g., language and literacy, mathematics) or strengthening the overall quality of early childhood settings (Chapters 5 and 9; Zaslow, Tout, Halle, Vick, & Lavelle, 2010; Zaslow, Tout, Halle, Whittaker, & Lavelle, 2010).

The salience of implementation has come to the fore in recent years, however, because increasingly early childhood program developers are being asked not only to prove their program's efficacy before it is brought to scale or transported to other locations but also to articulate what components of their model, or what contexts in which the model is deployed, are essential for making the intervention a success. Up until now, the early childhood field has lacked a common framework and language with which to examine important implementation supports for successful initiatives. The frameworks proposed by implementation science offer a means by which to create a shared understanding of what it takes to have effective, replicable, and sustainable early childhood programs and systems in community-based settings. The chapters in this volume provide examples of how implementation frameworks and methodologies can be applied to early childhood practices, programs, and systems. This volume, therefore, represents a starting point for a continuing journey toward the use of common definitions, frameworks, and methodologies for studying implementation within the field of early care and education (ECE) research.

While the implementation science perspective holds much promise for ECE researchers, it can also pose challenges. Clearly, one cannot expect to achieve the desired results of an early childhood practice or intervention without faithfully adhering to the particular practice or intervention model. A focus on intervention fidelity is therefore a critical component to success. In Chapter 4, Chris S. Hulleman, Sara E. Rimm-Kaufman, and Tashia Avry provide practical guidance to researchers on how to conduct rigorous analysis of fidelity of a particular early childhood intervention model that has been sufficiently defined—for example, providing guidance on how to analyze fidelity data from multiple raters and how to determine statistically the "zone of tolerable adaptation" of the model and exploring the effects of weighting and sequencing the core components of a well-defined intervention model. In a departure from the usual way of thinking about fidelity, Chrishana M. Lloyd, Lauren H. Supplee, and Shira Kolnik Mattera in Chapter 7 suggest that researchers consider developing measures of fidelity that can be applied universally across intervention models. They provide a concrete example of an observational tool designed to measure fidelity to multiple types of early childhood curricula that are aimed at supporting children's social-emotional development in early care settings. This approach is groundbreaking and appears to have the potential for wider application within the field. However, further work is needed to explore the benefits and challenges of creating "generic" measures of intervention fidelity within early childhood research and evaluation. On the one hand, having a fidelity measure that can be used across intervention types may produce cost savings and provide the field with a uniform benchmark for achieving fidelity to a particular type of early childhood intervention. On the other hand, it is not clear how such a tool could help clarify what components of particular program models are essential for making the model a success or whether adaptations and sequencing of those essential components have differential effects on outcomes. Collectively, these two chapters suggest that there is room for both specific and more generalized performance assessment tools in future research endeavors aimed at understanding the effectiveness of particular early childhood interventions.

The implementation science perspective argues that intervention fidelity is necessary but not sufficient for articulating the essential components of a successful intervention. In particular, implementation science is interested in what it takes to both *establish* and *maintain* well-defined, scientifically proven practices (or innovative and "promising" practices) in real-world settings, what it takes to *replicate* and *disseminate* program models in different contexts (including necessary *adaptations* to the model), and how to use data and effective communication to create *feedback loops* for quality assurance and targeted program improvement (Chapters 1 and 2; Durlak & DuPre, 2008; Fixsen, Naoom, Blase, Friedman, & Wallace, 2005; Greenhalgh, Robert, Bate, MacFarlane, & Kyriakidou, 2005; Meyers,

Durlak, & Wandersman, 2012). What are some implications for researchers and evaluators who want to take this broader perspective in understanding the effectiveness of early childhood initiatives? Below, we explore a few such implications, drawn collectively from the chapters in this volume. We follow these with a consideration of some remaining challenges for the early childhood research community.

Intentionally and Consistently Incorporate Research Questions Related to Implementation into Early Childhood Studies

Early childhood researchers are used to studying complex processes for child development. For example, they often develop multivariate models to study what works, for whom, and under what conditions. But often these multivariate models developed to answer important research and policy questions fail to take into account all of the factors implementation science posits are important for successful outcomes. Early childhood researchers should make sure that their evaluations of early childhood practices, programs, and systems include specific research questions that address the process of implementation. Examples include:

- What does it take to establish or install a new practice or an innovative model in an early childhood classroom, an early childhood setting, and/or a state?

- How can we establish the competency of early childhood practitioners?

- What does it take to maintain such practices and innovations over time?

- How can we establish the organizational and systems supports needed to create hospitable environments so that early childhood innovations can thrive?

- Who is involved in establishing or maintaining such practices and innovations at the specific site, the institution, and/or the state level? What structures and processes are needed to maintain practices and innovations?

- What does it take to reach the majority of individuals who are the targets of these practices and innovations (e.g., children, early childhood providers, parents) within a program, community, and/or state?

- What adaptations are required of the particular model within specific sites or communities, and why? How are these adaptations made, and who makes them? Do these adaptations increase and enhance desired outcomes or diminish them? What does "fidelity to the model" mean within the context of adaption?

Likewise, conceptual models for early childhood initiatives should also explicitly include what Fixsen et al. (2005) call the "drivers" of effective implementation, either as core components of the intervention itself or as important contextual factors or moderators. Hulleman and colleagues (Chapter 4, pp. 68–69) note that the implementation core components identified by implementation science frameworks are most typically modeled as indirect effects on outcomes:

> These implementation core components (Fixsen et al., 2005), which include administrative support and training, selection of staff, and consulting, have an *indirect* effect on children as mediated by the intervention core components. That is, administrative

support can provide a facilitative condition for the implementation of [early childhood] practices, but it is the [early childhood] practices themselves that are theorized to directly enhance [child] outcomes. … The caveat to this distinction is the case in which the contextual level is specifically a part of the intervention model; then, those aspects become intervention core components.

When implementation components are a part of the intervention, however, they still require the full implementation supports to be installed effectively. For example, an intervention that involves coaching would still require the selection, training, and coaching of the coaches (Chapter 8). Whether modeled as a direct or indirect effect on outcomes, core implementation components should be intentionally and consistently included in our early childhood research models.

Research Measures and Methodologies
Should Address Implementation Questions

In addition to including research questions that focus on implementation into their studies, early childhood researchers also need to utilize appropriate measures for collecting implementation data. As noted in several chapters in this volume, fidelity measures are often included in ECE research and evaluation studies, but they are usually limited to measures of fidelity of a particular intervention model.

A continuing challenge from the research perspective is that the implementation science frameworks outlined in Chapters 1 and 2 are conceptual in nature and are drawn largely from literature reviews; consequently, they do not necessarily yield research measures that are available for wide use in the early childhood field. Indeed, Noreen Yazejian, Donna Bryant, and Portia Kennel (Chapter 11, p. 217) acknowledge that they have struggled to find or create an objective measure for "using research and data to guide program implementation and improvement," which is a core feature of the Educare model but incidentally is also a key driver of effective implementation. As noted by Robert P. Franks and Jennifer Schroeder (Chapter 1, p. 17):

> In some cases, good measures of the implementation process do not yet exist or have not been sufficiently validated. Self-report measures can be unreliable, and objective measures are lacking and often difficult to operationalize (requiring intensive external observation by an objective party).

Jason Downer in Chapter 8 also notes that several implementation drivers are undermeasured and understudied in the literature.

Happily, some promising inroads have been made in recent years to develop measures of readiness, climate and culture, implementation drivers, and stages of implementation (Chamberlain, Hendricks Brown, & Saldana, 2011; Lehman, Greener, & Simpson, 2002; National Implementation Research Network, 2012; Saldana, Chamberlain, Wang, & Hendricks Brown, 2012; Stamatakis et al., 2012); this represents major progress for the field. And yet, much work still needs to be done to get such measures in use routinely in ECE research.

Despite the need for further measures development, there does seem to be consensus that triangulating the analysis of information gathered on implementation from multiple sources is a good way to better understand implementation. Most of the implementation studies with which we are familiar utilize document review, key informant interviews, online surveys, and focus groups to gather important information on all aspects of implementation supports rather than relying solely on one data source or type of data. For example, individual or group interviews with program developers can identify the systems put in place for recruiting and selecting key staff, the development and use of performance assessments for key staff, and the establishment of data collection systems and how data are being used to make decisions about program improvement. Then review of the recruitment and staff assessment materials, observation of staff training sessions, and review of data from the data collection systems can confirm information gathered verbally from the informants (or provide additional information). Furthermore, surveys of early childhood providers can determine their evaluation of trainings they received, their experiences using a new tool or practice, challenges they faced in implementing a new practice, and so forth. Early childhood coaches can fill out short questionnaires about individual early childhood providers with whom they work, thereby supplying formalized assessment data on coaches' perceptions of providers' readiness to change their practice during different stages of implementation (Chapter 3). Both qualitative and quantitative data from multiple sources can be used for this process of corroboration.

Evaluation Plans for an Early Care and Education Initiative Should Be Aligned with the Initiative's Stage of Implementation

Chapter 2 outlines the different stages of implementation: exploration, installation, initial implementation, and full implementation. Many other chapters in this volume provide helpful illustrations of how to align evaluation plans with the initiative's stage of implementation. For example, Shira M. Peterson in Chapter 3 describes how formal and informal assessments of "readiness to change" are often conducted at the exploration stage of an intervention but are also important to incorporate at the installation stage to ensure that all staff are sufficiently ready to begin implementation. In addition, measures of readiness can be obtained during initial and full implementation to monitor the level of readiness of staff as they are actually implementing the intervention and as new staff are added to the initiative as it goes to scale.

Other helpful examples are the illustration of specific strategies that could be used to improve access to professional development and are matched to the stages of implementation of an ECE and school-age care professional development system (see Table 13.2) and a detailed list of research questions that could be asked at each stage of implementation for the specific components of a quality rating and improvement system (QRIS; see Table 14.1). These specific applications show that paying attention to the stage of implementation when designing and carrying out an evaluation of an early childhood initiative, regardless of its scope (i.e., an intervention in one classroom, one early childhood program, or an entire county or state early childhood system), is important and can be accomplished. Furthermore, these examples illustrate that questions that are not often asked in traditional evaluation studies can and should be included in such studies so that underlying conditions that facilitate the success of the initiative can be documented and supported, with the ultimate goal of reaching more of the targeted population for the initiative and achieving the desired goals.

Another important lesson for both researchers and policy makers is that expectations for changes in outcomes should be aligned with the stage of implementation of the intervention. In particular, Allison Metz, Tamara Halle, Leah Bartley, and Amy Blasberg in Chapter 2 emphasize that one should not expect long-term outcomes such as changes in child outcomes to be affected during the initial stage of implementation of an early childhood intervention. While it might be appropriate to monitor child outcomes across all stages of implementation, researchers and policy makers should not anticipate changes in long-term outcomes until an initiative has been fully implemented, which often takes 2–5 years (Fixsen, Blase, Timbers, & Wolf, 2001; Panzano et al., 2004; Rubin et al., 2011).

While in some ways it is clear how to incorporate implementation science in an ongoing way into ECE evaluation research, in other ways the path is less clear. A number of important challenges remain.

Research Challenges

A major challenge for early childhood researchers is that many early childhood initiatives advocate for highly individualized strategies targeted to children, parents, and early childhood practitioners. For example, home visitation programs, such as the Getting Ready model highlighted by Lisa L. Knoche in Chapter 6, require that the strategies employed during home visits be "fluid, dynamic, and individualized" (Chapter 6, p. 120). Indeed, many relationship-based interventions such as coaching and home visitation are based on the belief that a significant reason for their success is an ability to be flexible and responsive to the needs of the individual parent or ECE provider. Highly individualized intervention models pose problems for researchers who are trying to isolate the factors that lead to the desired outcomes. They also pose problems for funders who wish to replicate promising models across communities (this is discussed further below). In terms of measurement, they suggest a need to capture whether individualization is occurring appropriately.

Another research challenge involves how we operationalize the stage of implementation in our evaluation models and how we address the possibility of different components of an initiative being at different stages of implementation at the same time. As noted above and throughout this volume, aligning research and evaluation strategies to the stage of implementation of an initiative is very important. Yet, as a field, we lack ready tools to determine the stage of implementation for initiatives. When does an initiative move from initial to full implementation? What benchmarks or milestones should we be looking for? Do we need to have a standardized measure?

Furthermore, since different components of a complex initiative (or a systems model) can be at different stages of implementation at the same time (Chapter 2), it becomes all the more complicated to determine the right level of performance we should be expecting at any given time for each component of an initiative. It is not always clear what sorts of measures we need to incorporate into our studies in order to determine stage of implementation. What is a reasonable time frame for a program to move through the stages? At what point is it possible to say that a program is stuck and not progressing, or that key components are out of line with the stage of implementation of others? Is it possible to develop an understanding of "sticking points" that delay movement toward maturation? Is it possible to identify "leverage points" for moving from one stage to the next? Is it possible to understand the threshold or dosage of particular stage-based work that is necessary to move effectively to another stage?

Another research challenge is actively keeping issues of replication, sustainability, and scale in mind at all stages of research design and analysis, no matter the size of the intervention. The science of implementation has been built around the establishment, maintenance, and replication of evidence-based programs or practices (Chapter 1). The chapters in this volume collectively provide an affirmation of the importance of implementation frameworks and strategies for contributing to the evidence for new early childhood interventions. Efficacy trials help to build the evidence base for early childhood interventions, and there are several examples of how implementation frameworks can help guide early efficacy studies of early childhood models (e.g., Chapters 6 and 9). As Knoche (Chapter 6, p. 133) states, "Using the core implementation component framework at early stages in a research line is essential to knowing what will become important as evidence-based interventions are disseminated at scale."

But there are certain large-scale interventions typically executed at the community or state level that are difficult to study using the traditional randomized controlled research methods. These large-scale early childhood interventions include community-based models such as Promise Neighborhoods or Educare (Chapter 11) that are informed or based on research and theory and are therefore often referred to as "evidence-informed" or "promising" models, or even "innovations." Yazejian, Bryant, and Kennel (Chapter 11) suggest that the Educare model has been successful in its replication in multiple sites across the country because of specific features of the community-based model, including the establishment of local public–private partnerships and an emphasis on collecting data for program improvement purposes. Indeed, the political and financial wherewithal to expand to multiple sites was based on promising findings of increased cognitive outcomes for participating children but without the results of randomized controlled trials (although such trials are currently under way).

We tend to agree that the designers of the evidence-informed Educare model ensured the model's successful replication by making several key drivers of effective implementation core features of the Educare model (e.g., public–private partnerships, data-driven decision making). However, it remains an empirical question whether making implementation central to an intervention model (as opposed to a contextual element external to the core implementation model) improves the model's sustainability or replicability.

The implementation science perspective takes sustainability and replication as seriously as the initial establishment of effectiveness of a practice or program. Furthermore, implementation science claims that implementation is most successful when it is *actively* and *intentionally* a focus of an initiative at all stages within the life of that initiative. For example, even when a model is proven to be efficacious, there can still be challenges to replication of such models due to a lack of intentionality about establishing infrastructure support in the new setting and/or the failure to act in a compensatory manner when new situations pose threats to control over selection, training, and ongoing oversight of staff (see the Introduction to this volume). Thus, within a research discipline that focuses on rigorous establishment of evidence for an early childhood practice or model, implementation science has a clear place and should be built into all stages of research design and analysis.

Finally, researchers need to address how best to study the implementation of a systems-level initiative. The scientific study of early childhood systems remains a challenge, but Chapters 13 and 14 of this volume begin an important discussion that must continue in the field about the role implementation science frameworks and strategies can play in the study of early childhood systems. A major theme noted by Kathryn Tout, Allison Metz, and Leah Bartley in Chapter 13 is the importance of establishing implementation teams at all levels of a system and ensuring that there is good communication and collaboration among these teams. Another theme highlighted by Diane Paulsell, Kathryn Tout, and Kelly Maxwell in Chapter 14 is the use of implementation tools such as cascading logic models to articulate the connections among actors, activities, and outcomes at multiple levels of a system.

Both chapters consider not only implementation science frameworks but also systems theory frameworks (Coffman, 2007; Eoyang, 2007; Hargreaves, 2010) to understand and predict the successful functioning of early childhood systems. Specifically, Chapter 13 shows how Coffman's (2007) systems initiative framework can work hand in hand with a staged implementation framework to explain and actualize a well-functioning ECE professional development system. Similarly, Chapter 14 outlines three important attributes of dynamic and complex systems— boundaries, relationships, and perspectives—and posits that these system attributes are important to assess at each stage of implementation in order to understand the functioning of a QRIS.

In sum, both of these chapters illustrate the compatibility of implementation frameworks with other theoretical frameworks in the study of early childhood systems. But as Carolyn Layzer notes in Chapter 12, implementation needs to work well simultaneously at both the systems level and the practitioner level. We turn now to consider the implications of implementation science for practitioners and policy makers.

Implications for Policy and Practice

The findings from basic early childhood research can help identify the conditions under which well-defined interventions achieve successful outcomes for young children and their families. But for these interventions to have widespread influence on outcomes at a societal level, they must be disseminated and embedded within community-based settings in a way that preserves faithfulness to the key components of the intervention model but also adapts to local conditions. Federal, state, and local policies can encourage the establishment and expansion of research-based programs and practices by providing resources and incentives for states and communities to implement such programs at scale; they can also help inform the field about effective implementation by requiring ongoing evaluation of the implementation of such programs within states and local communities. In this section, we consider several examples of how implementation frameworks and strategies can support early childhood programs within communities.

First, let us consider implementation at the level of a single program. Many of the chapters in this volume describe evidence-based or evidence-informed early childhood interventions that can be implemented within a single setting (e.g., professional development targeting children's early language and literacy skills in Chapter 5 or early mathematics skills in Chapter 9, or a home visitation program targeting prenatal health and early child development in Chapter 10). What if an ECE center director decides to implement one of these interventions based on evidence of effectiveness, but it is not feasible to have the developer of the intervention come and train her staff directly? How can this center director ensure that the investments she is making in a new practice or program will lead to the desired results?

As Layzer notes, it is difficult but not impossible to ensure adherence to an evidence-based model without diluting its effectiveness, even when it is being implemented without the program developer's immediate involvement. Implementation science would suggest that if the director pays attention to staff selection and training, as well as ongoing support and monitoring, then the expected outcomes of the evidence-based model will be more likely to be realized. Furthermore, institutional structures need to be established to support the training and monitoring necessary to ensure fidelity to the model.

Knowing that these core implementation components are vital to the successful outcomes the center director seeks, she can institute policies that require staff training on the new intervention, hire trainers and coaches certified in the model who can train her staff and provide ongoing support, and ensure access to online tools that the developer created for additional ongoing support of the model. The center director can furnish institutional support for the staff training in terms of professional development time for the staff, direct financial resources toward the effort, and establish a monitoring and tracking system to determine not only whether staff are receiving the appropriate dosage of training and mentoring and are accessing the online tools but also whether the children are receiving the intervention with a high level of fidelity and quality.

Ideally, the center director would use the data gathered from the monitoring and tracking system to feed information back to mentors and staff so that meaningful and timely adjustments can be made to improve the intervention's effectiveness in this particular setting and with these particular children and staff. If adjustments are made, data from the monitoring system should be used to ensure that the adaptation is "tolerable"—that is, does not unduly decrease the model's effectiveness (Chapter 4). As Layzer (Chapter 12, p. 230) wisely notes:

> Adaptation that hews to the principles on which the model rests can increase the program's effectiveness, while changes to the program that violate the model's theory of action can be counterproductive even if the changes are made with the best intentions.

Implementation principles are also important when diffusion and scale-up of an intervention is happening on a larger scale. As discussed by Ivelisse Martinez-Beck in the Introduction to this volume, the Affordable Care Act is a recent piece of federal legislation that both created the Maternal, Infant, and Early Childhood Home Visiting Program (MIECHV), which has encouraged states to expand home visiting programs that have evidence of effectiveness from rigorous evaluation research, and required that states conduct ongoing evaluations of home visiting (as implemented through the MIECHV) in order to better understand the processes and contexts that support successful implementation of effective home visiting programs within communities.

Another example of how federal policies and programs can target improved early childhood outcomes at the local and state levels is a recent federal initiative called the Race to the Top-Early Learning Challenge (RTT-ELC), which has encouraged states to put together comprehensive plans to strengthen early childhood systems throughout the state (e.g., QRIS, professional development for the ECE workforce, kindergarten readiness assessments) and also has encouraged states to establish and strengthen integrated early childhood data systems across health, early childhood, education, and child welfare systems. The Race to the Top-Early Learning Challenge program was first launched in 2011 as a program jointly administered by the U.S. Departments of Education and Health and Human Services (see http://www.ed.gov/news/press-releases/five-more-states-secure-race-top-early-learning-challenge-grants). Thirty-five states, the District of Columbia, and the Commonwealth of Puerto Rico responded to the initial RTT-ELC funding opportunity, and nine states were initially provided federal funding in December 2011 to put their plans into action (California, Delaware, Maryland, Massachusetts, Minnesota, North Carolina, Ohio, Rhode Island, and Washington). In November 2012, five additional states were awarded RTT-ELC grants in a second phase of funding (Colorado, Illinois, New Mexico, Oregon, and Wisconsin). These states have created high-quality comprehensive plans to improve early learning and development programs around five key areas of reform: establishing successful state systems; defining high-quality, accountable programs; promoting early learning and development outcomes for children; supporting a great early childhood education workforce; and measuring outcomes and progress (see http://www2.ed.gov/programs/racetothetop-earlylearningchallenge/letter-announcing-winners.pdf). In the years to come, as these RTT-ELC grantees begin to implement their proposed plans to strengthen early childhood systems within their states, they will be collecting data to monitor progress toward the establishment and maintenance of these systems (i.e., implementation data).

To what extent are states trying to incorporate implementation frameworks and principles into their early childhood programs and systems? An examination of an RTT-ELC grantee is useful here, as grantees have been provided funding to evaluate the implementation of each early childhood system they are strengthening and are required to provide data on their progress. As one example, the state of Delaware is implementing a statewide kindergarten entry assessment called the Delaware Early Learner Survey (ELS) as part of its RTT-ELC grant. Grounded in a new state law (House Bill 317) requiring the use of a kindergarten entry assessment spanning key areas of development (language and literacy development, cognition and general knowledge, approaches toward learning, physical well-being and motor development, and social and emotional development), the ELS will be expanded over a 3-year period from an initial group of about 100 kindergarten classrooms across the state to all kindergarten classrooms in the state (approximately 500 classrooms total in 2014). Kindergarten teachers will be expected to use the ELS with only half of the students in their classrooms in their first year of using the tool; in the second year of implementation, they will be expected to use it with all of their students. Thus, there is an incremental approach to the rollout of this new practice, and the graduated strategy allows the state to use data gathered along the way to inform adjustments in training and ongoing supports offered to teachers in an effort to improve staff competency and the reliability and validity of the data collected through the ELS system.

Delaware has a three-part approach to its strategy for moving from design to sound and sustainable implementation of the survey. First, with the help of a research partner, Delaware is collecting ongoing implementation data (via observations of teacher trainings; surveys of teachers who have participated in trainings and have used the ELS; and interviews with teachers, principals, and superintendents regarding the ELS rollout) that will be used to inform adjustments to the implementation of the ELS. For example, surveys of teachers who participated in the initial ELS training indicated that they would like more practice with the tool prior to using it in their classrooms. This feedback has led the state to consider and plan for changes to the length and type of training provided to teachers prior to the start of the next school year.

Second, the state is partnering with a vendor that provides training to teachers on the ELS tool and its accompanying web-based data entry system. This vendor will also help analyze the data entered by the teachers to determine the psychometric properties of the ELS, thereby informing an understanding of the validity and reliability of the tool as it has been adapted for the state.

Third, the state, through its lead Office of Early Learning, has established an Early Learner Survey Committee that serves as a state-level implementation team and plays a critical and active role in the design and implementation of the ELS. Thus, in addition to building the competency of the practitioners who will be collecting the ELS data, state administrators are starting to build the infrastructure necessary to sustain the system over time. The ELS Committee is made up of teacher and administrative (leadership) representatives from the state's school districts and public charter schools, along with other key stakeholders such as local foundations and the teachers' union. Members helped select the assessment tool, co-lead training and professional development, and are deeply engaged in all facets of the initiative, including spearheading both regional and statewide kindergarten communities of practice.

In sum, the state of Delaware is making use of data collected on both the *process* and *outcomes* of implementation of the state kindergarten entry assessment and engaging leadership to make data-informed decisions about the tools and training needed for the ELS that will ultimately lead to the collection of comprehensive and valid data on kindergartners throughout the state.

While Delaware provides one example of how a state might incorporate implementation frameworks and principles into its early childhood programs and systems, states may also consider the role of establishing implementation teams at regional, county, school district, and/or school levels; engaging additional stakeholders such as parents; and developing intentional and productive communication pathways among all levels of the system (e.g., classroom, school, district, region, state). States and localities should consider the role of partners such as state-based or local funders, community groups, or associations that can assist in ensuring that the initiative is both financially and programmatically sustainable for the long run (Chapter 2). For example, similar to Delaware's experience, the San Francisco Unified School District has found it beneficial to engage private funders and the teachers' union as partners in its child assessment initiative that spans prekindergarten to third grade (Bryant, 2012).

States that did not receive federal RTT-ELC grants may not have the same level of support and incentives for establishing or expanding early childhood programs and systems. (RTT-ELC grants are just one of many sources of funding for state-level early childhood initiatives. Other sources include, but are not limited to, state and foundation funding.) However, the federal government does provide a strong network of technical assistance (TA) centers. The Office of Child Care (OCC) within the Administration for Children and Families, Department of Health and Human Services (ACF/HHS), funds a Child Care Technical Assistance Network (CCTAN) that offers regional and state-level support to all states for the establishment and maintenance of various early childhood programs and systems, including systems for quality improvement of the ECE sector and professional development of the ECE workforce. A similar set of TA centers funded by the Office of Head Start (OHS) ACF/HHS are directed to the Early Head Start and Head Start communities. There is also a newly established contract funded by the U.S. Department of Education that aims to deliver coordinated technical assistance primarily to RTT-ELC grantees while making TA materials and information available to all states. This TA activity will be coordinated with various entities, including but not limited to the CCTAN. From an implementation science perspective, this network of TA centers represents a federal-level implementation support team for states.

The National Center on Child Care Professional Development Systems and Workforce Initiatives (PDW Center) is a CCTAN technical assistance center that is jointly funded by OCC and OHS. This center has embedded the implementation science framework in its work with states. The PDW Center has developed and disseminated webinars that provide an overview to implementation science frameworks, an overview to the concept of "readiness to change" (Halle, 2012; see also Chapter 3, and planning tools to gauge the feasibility of building professional development systems at the local or state levels, including assessing 1) the "fit" of the professional development for community needs and 2) the level of resources and coordination already in place or that needs to be in place to carry out a systems change initiative. In addition to providing states a general orientation to the frameworks and tools of implementation science, the PDW Center also convenes "Learning Communities" that provide a forum for states to share challenges and lessons learned with regard to specific aspects of implementing professional development systems for the ECE workforce. Below are some examples of questions discussed among Learning Communities:

- What strategies can be used in the interview process to identify staff who will be successful TA professionals/coaches?

- What are strategies to successfully retrain staff transitioning to TA or coaching from other roles?

- How can supervisory structures for TA providers be strengthened?

In addition to addressing the competency of those carrying out the intervention (e.g., the technical assistance professionals such as coaches working directly with ECE providers to improve their practice), technical assistance resources developed by the PDW Center showcase "lessons learned" to establish necessary partnerships and infrastructure to sustain state and local professional development systems.

The PDW Center's planning tools address the following types of questions, also informed by the implementation science perspective:

- Are public–private partnerships needed for a TA initiative? If so, what kinds have proven to be successful? How can public–private partnerships be successfully established and maintained?

- How does a new professional development initiative align and integrate with existing state-level systems?

- Does the lead agency supporting this professional development effort have the necessary staff (in terms of number and qualifications) to oversee hiring, quality control, etc.?

- What is the best way to use existing service delivery systems while also seeking to ensure appropriate TA services are delivered? What sorts of retrofitting are possible or necessary, and when do new systems of service delivery need to be created?

- What data systems provide the necessary data to determine the effectiveness of a TA initiative?

This is just an example of the types of practical planning tools that could be developed, based on an implementation science perspective, that could address the needs of states grappling with implementation of early childhood programs and systems "on the ground." As noted by Metz, Halle, Bartley, and Blasberg (Chapter 2, a prerequisite for implementation is a clearly operationalized practice or program model. Technical assistance services are not exempt from this requirement for effective implementation. It will be important for early childhood technical assistance providers to clearly define their principles, core components, and key activities so that implementation supports such as selecting, training, and coaching technical assistance professionals, and creating organizational and systems supports for effective technical assistance delivery, can be installed. Although this example is pertinent to early childhood professional development systems, comparable tools could be developed for other early childhood programs and systems, including home visiting, quality initiatives, or the support of mathematics, language and literacy, or social-emotional competency within ECE settings.

Policy and Practice Challenges

State administrators will readily admit that the process of studying the implementation of early childhood systems is extremely complicated. Early childhood systems are multilayered and often have complex connections to other systems that may or may not be well aligned. For example, Tout, Metz, and Bartley in Chapter 13 rightly point to the complexities of integrating the current professional development system for early childhood practitioners, which does not have uniform standards across sectors (e.g., Head Start and some types of child care programs have different requirements for staff qualifications). Furthermore, as noted earlier in this chapter, states are often not starting from scratch but rather revamping an existing early childhood system that is likely to have different pieces of the system at different stages of implementation. How do we keep all the pieces of a complex, comprehensive ECE system in mind so that all segments of the system, regardless of their stage of implementation, can be implemented well? In addition, how do we strengthen a research base that provides evidence for connections between these complex early childhood systems and child outcomes?

A partial answer to these challenging questions is offered by implementation science tools such as cascading logic models. By explicitly identifying connections between levels of a system, a cascading logic model can help guide strategic implementation activities and supports by implementation teams to facilitate the successful functioning of the entire system (Chapter 14). These logic models can also be used by researchers to guide research and analysis plans that can help build the evidence for the effectiveness of ECE systems in real communities by looking incrementally first at short-term outcomes that would likely be affected at practice levels, then systematically at outcomes that would be hypothesized to be affected at organizational and systems levels once full implementation is achieved. For both implementation teams and system evaluators, breaking the system down into manageable pieces may help achieve research and practice goals. As a field, we need to develop additional tools that will help translate implementation science frameworks into practical tools for use in both research and practice.

There are multiple factors, including adequate time and funding, that pose additional challenges to actively and intentionally using implementation processes and tools. How can a program director or a state administrator make room for attending to implementation components when time and resources are limited? What if a lack of clear understanding of the core program and/or implementation components leads to adaptations that jeopardize the effectiveness of the program? Perhaps it would be helpful to have examples of what happens when states or programs do *not* attend to core implementation components, in addition to examples of recommended practices, to demonstrate the cost-effectiveness of attending to implementation components (Lee & Aos, 2011). Such studies are available in other social science research areas, such as juvenile delinquency prevention research (Jones, Bumbarger, Greenberg, Greenwood, & Kyler, 2008; Rhoades, Bumbarger, & Moore, 2012), but are not yet as common within early childhood intervention research (National Research Council & Institute of Medicine, 2009).

Another challenge from a practice perspective is connecting implementation teams across different levels of an ECE system. Implementation teams are important at all levels of a program or system. These teams need to be not only "intentional" but also somewhat guided by intrinsic motivation to be part of such a group at each level; implementation teams at all levels cannot be constructed entirely by a top-down approach, although support for their creation is important to convey from the upper levels of the system. Furthermore, it is critically important to have good communication within and across implementation teams. As noted above, there are examples of states and localities setting up effective implementation teams at the state or local level, but currently we have few good examples of implementation teams functioning well at multiple levels within a system, and few examples of effective communication among implementation teams. The field needs more concrete examples of constructive ways of connecting implementation teams in practical ways and in real time.

Finally, it is important to remember that researchers should be seen as partners in the process of continuous program improvement. The typical role of researchers is as "independent" evaluators of ECE programs or systems. An independent evaluator ensures objectivity and removes bias from the evaluation process. But an important message conveyed in this volume is that valid and reliable data are necessary in order to inform program improvement efforts, and researchers can be important partners to help program providers develop systems for collecting and analyzing data and can also aid in interpreting the data for program improvement efforts. This volume provided at least two examples of research teams being true partners in the process of continuous program improvement: Knoche (Chapter 6) highlighted researchers' roles as supporting the implementation of the Getting Ready model, and Yazejian, Bryant, and Kennel (Chapter 11) showcased the strong partnership between research and program staff within the Educare model. Key elements of good partnerships between researchers and program implementers include trust, frequent and open communication, and mutual respect. While it is clear that researchers can be critical to program improvement activities, the conditions under which the same research team can and should collect data to be used for both independent program evaluation and program improvement purposes remain open for discussion.

From the perspective of program developers (and some policy makers), the research process can take so much time that when results are actually available and presented, they are no longer of practical use for making decisions. This is as true for data gathered for program improvement purposes as it is for data gathered for independent program evaluation. A challenge, therefore, remains for researchers to provide findings in a timely manner so that they contribute to the process of data-driven decision making and continuous program improvement.

One process that has shown promise in several studies has been to provide interim memos that summarize information on specific data sources and/or targeted analyses from ongoing data collection. These memos provide important information and context as well as interpretation of findings and implications, which can feed back into contemporaneous decision making by program developers and/or deliverers. As one example, the Catawba County Child Wellbeing Project measured the strength of functioning of implementation core components for several evidence-informed and evidence-based practice models and created action plans for program improvement based on these data. Findings demonstrated that using these data for action planning strengthened fidelity to the models and consequently improved outcomes for children (Metz, Naoom, Ball, Wilson, & Redmond, 2012).

Looking to the Future

If our goal in the long term is to assure that evaluation research works hand in hand with implementation science to assure that effective early childhood practices and programs are well implemented and reach more children, then we will need to regularly incorporate implementation science into the infrastructures for training scientists, sharing research, establishing policy and practice initiatives, and developing new measures. As starting points, we provide the following suggestions.

The study of implementation science frameworks and methodologies should be incorporated into training programs for early childhood researchers. Currently, few early childhood researchers are adequately trained to conduct implementation research.

Training programs should be developed for universities (e.g., specific curricula incorporated into degrees for master's and Ph.D. students), as well as for other research organizations and institutions that conduct research on programs (e.g., workshop content developed for on-the-job training within such institutions). This will require working toward agreement on the implementation science tools and methods most important for researchers to master. Once model syllabi have been developed, it will be important to share them.

More peer-reviewed journal outlets need to feature implementation science studies and findings. There are some noteworthy examples cited throughout this volume of journal publications focusing on early childhood implementation science. It would be extremely helpful in strengthening efforts in this area for special sections or editions of journals to be devoted to implementation science. For example, a 2012 special issue of the *Journal of Behavioral Health Services and Research* featured a series of papers on fidelity of implementation, and the Evidence-Based Practice Consortium (an international group that sponsors the biennial Global Implementation Conference) has as one of its goals contributing every year one journal article specific to bridging the gap between implementation research and practice. These efforts are an important start and should be continued in social science journals that feature early childhood research.

Policy and practice initiatives should build in requirements for measurement of implementation. We have provided examples of federal TA centers and federally funded state early childhood initiatives that incorporate a focus on documenting implementation. To underscore the importance both of using evidence-based practices in early childhood and of assuring their careful implementation as they are replicated and extended, and to encourage a focus on planning for and documenting implementation efforts in early childhood systems, it will be critical to articulate implementation components when requests for proposals are prepared for early childhood policy and practice initiatives. This can be anticipated only if policy makers and practitioners continue to be educated about the importance not only of initial design but also of implementation. Just as there is a need for researchers to receive training in implementation science, there is a need for increasing the awareness of policy makers and providing explicit training for practitioners on approaches to strengthen implementation.

More measures development is needed. Even if policy makers build in requirements for measurement of implementation, it is a moot point if the tools to do so are not widely available. As noted earlier in this chapter and throughout this volume, the measurement of core implementation components is critical to understanding implementation science's influence on desired outcomes. Yet, there is currently a dearth of implementation measures in actual use within ECE research. While it is encouraging that new measures development is under way (Chapter 7; Chamberlain et al., 2011; Saldana et al., 2012), the creation and validation of such measures, and the dissemination of the measures for wider use, need to be a high priority for the ECE field.

Implementation science is important but not enough. Implementation science is, by itself, necessary but not sufficient for ensuring that effective early childhood programs are replicated and sustained. We have repeatedly articulated the need for evaluation research and implementation science to be used in a complementary manner (and indeed noted that these should not always be viewed as entirely separate, as when implementation measures are built into rigorous evaluations). Beyond this fundamentally important pairing, however, other types of research evidence are also important for garnering political support and attracting the necessary funding for the expansion and sustainability of effective early childhood practices and programs within communities. One key example is cost-benefit analysis. Analysis could be expanded to include an assessment of costs and benefits when programs are and are not implemented with strong fidelity or when they do and do not build in a requirement to prepare for and document system-wide implementation measures as programs go to scale (Lee & Aos, 2011).

Conclusion

Many researchers across disciplines have been paying attention to implementation issues for decades, as noted in several seminal literature reviews (Berkel, Mauricio, Schoenfelder, & Sandler, 2011; Durlak & DuPre, 2008; Fixsen et al., 2005; Meyers et al., 2012). In contrast, the focus on implementation supports for early childhood programs and systems has only recently gained salience to program developers, TA providers, policy makers, and early childhood researchers.

As noted throughout this volume, the field of implementation science argues that traditional implementation evaluation methodologies that assess whether program activities have been implemented as planned (referred to as "intervention fidelity" by Hulleman, Rimm-Kaufman, and Avry in Chapter 4) are necessary but not sufficient to identify what is required for achieving desired outcomes in real-world settings (Fixsen et al., 2005; Meyers et al., 2012). Additional key implementation components include improving the competency of those carrying out the initiative, supporting the infrastructure that is necessary to sustain the initiative, and marshalling different forms of leadership necessary to address challenges that emerge along the way. Other key concepts include recognizing the importance of implementation stages, recursive feedback loops for continuous program improvement, and innovations to address optimal fit of a proven model within a new context. Tools such as cascading logic models can help articulate the connections between implementation activities and outcomes at different levels of a complex system (Chapter 14; Metz & Bartley, 2012).

The extent to which early childhood researchers, policy makers, and practitioners begin to adopt common frameworks, strategies, and vocabularies regarding implementation will determine how quickly we can move the field toward an understanding of what truly underlies successful early childhood programs and systems and come to a deeper understanding of how best to support and sustain these programs and systems in communities over time so that children, families, and society can all reap the benefits. It is our hope that this book furthers this goal and thereby contributes to strengthening early childhood programs and systems over time.

References

Berkel, C., Mauricio, A.M., Schoenfelder, E., & Sandler, I.N. (2011). Putting the pieces together: An integrated model of program implementation. *Prevention Science, 12,* 23–33.
Bryant, C. (2012). Presentation as part of the PreK–3rd Grade National Work Group, *Using data to inform and improve instruction: Child assessment* (webinar), December 5, 2012.

Retrieved from http://www.prek-3rdgradenationalworkgroup.org and http://www.prek-3rdgradenationalworkgroup.org/sites/prek-3rdgradenationalworkgroup.org/files/PreK-3%20Assessment%20Webinar-12-3-12_FINAL_.pdf#overlay-context=node/15

Chamberlain, P., Hendricks Brown, C., Saldana, L. (2011). Observational measure of implementation process in community-based settings: The stages of implementation completion (SIC). *Implementation Science, 6*, 116.

Coffman, J. (2007). *A framework for evaluating systems initiatives.* Retrieved from http://www.buildinitiative.org/content/evaluation-systems-change

Durlak, J.A., & DuPre, E.P. (2008). Implementation matters: A review of research on the influence of implementation on program outcomes and the factors affecting implementation. *American Journal of Community Psychology, 41*, 327–350.

Eoyang, G. (2007). Human systems dynamics: Complexity-based approach to a complex evaluation. In B. Williams & I. Imam (Eds.), *Systems concepts in evaluation: An expert anthology* (pp. 75–88). Point Reyes Station, CA: American Evaluation Association.

Fixsen, D.L., Blase, K.A., Timbers, G.D., & Wolf, M.M. (2001). In search of program implementation: 792 replications of the Teaching-Family Model. In G.A. Bernfeld, D.P. Farrington, & A.W. Leschied (Eds.), *Offender rehabilitation in practice: Implementing and evaluating effective programs* (pp. 149–166). London, England: Wiley.

Fixsen, D.L., Naoom, S.F., Blase, K.A., Friedman, R.M., & Wallace, F. (2005). *Implementation research: A synthesis of the literature.* (FMHI Publication No. 231). Tampa, FL: University of South Florida, Louis de la Parte Florida Mental Health Institute, National Implementation Research Network.

Future of Children. (1999). Home visiting: Recent program evaluations. *Future of Children, 9*(1). Retrieved from http://futureofchildren.org/futureofchildren/publications/docs/09_01_ExecSummary.pdf

Greenhalgh, T., Robert, G., Bate, P., MacFarlane, F., & Kyriakidou, O. (2005). *Diffusion of innovations in health service organizations: A systematic literature review.* Oxford, England: BMJ Books/Blackwell.

Halle, T. (2012, May 30). *Implementation science and its applications to state-level integrated professional development systems for early care and education* (webinar). Presentation for the National Center on Child Care Professional Development Systems and Workforce Initiatives (PDW Center), Intersections of Implementation Science and Policy series.

Hargreaves, M.B. (2010). *Evaluating systems change: A planning guide.* Princeton, NJ: Mathematica Policy Research.

Jones, D., Bumbarger, B.K., Greenberg, M.T., Greenwood, P., & Kyler, S. (2008). *The economic return on PCCD's investment in research-based programs: A cost-benefit assessment of delinquency prevention in Pennsylvania.* State College, PA: Prevention Research Center for the Promotion of Human Development, Pennsylvania State University.

Lee, S., & Aos, S. (2011). Using cost-benefit analysis to understand the value of social interventions. *Research on Social Work Practice, 21*(6), 682–688.

Lehman, W.E.K., Greener, J.M., & Simpson, D.D. (2002). Assessing organizational readiness for change. *Journal of Substance Abuse Treatment, 22*(4), 197–209.

Metz, A., & Bartley, L. (2012). How to use implementation science to improve outcomes for children. *Zero To Three, 32*(4), 11–18.

Metz, A., Naoom, S., Ball, H., Wilson, D., and Redmond, P. (2012). *Measuring, assessing and improving implementation at multiple levels of the service delivery system.* Paper presented at the Australian Implementation Conference, Melbourne, Victoria, Australia.

Meyers, D.C., Durlak, J.A., & Wandersman, A. (2012). The quality implementation framework: A synthesis of critical steps to the implementation process. *American Journal of Community Psychology, 50*(3-4), 462–480.

National Implementation Research Network. (2012). *Implementation measures.* Retrieved from http://nirn.fpg.unc.edu/learn-implementation/measures

National Research Council & Institute of Medicine. (2009). *Strengthening benefit-cost analysis for early childhood interventions: Workshop summary.* Washington, DC: National Academies Press.

Panzano, P.C., Seffrin, B., Chaney-Jones, S., Roth, D., Crane-Ross, D., Massatti, R., & Carstens, C. (2004). The Innovation Diffusion and Adoption Research Project (IDARP). In D. Roth &

W. Lutz (Eds.), *New research in mental health* (Vol. 16, pp. 78–89). Columbus, OH: Ohio Department of Mental Health, Office of Program Evaluation and Research.

Rhoades, B.L., Bumbarger, B.K., & Moore, J.E. (2012). The role of a state-level prevention support system in promoting high-quality implementation and sustainability of evidence-based programs. *American Journal of Community Psychology, 50,* 1–16.

Rubin, D.M., O'Reilly, A.L.R., Luan, X., Dai, D., Localio, A.R., & Christian, C.W. (2011). Variation in pregnancy outcomes following statewide implementation of a prenatal home visitation program. *Archives of Pediatric and Adolescent Medicine, 165*(3), 198–204.

Saldana, L., Chamberlain, P., Wang, W., & Hendricks Brown, C. (2012). Predicting program start-up using the stages of implementation measure. *Administration and Policy in Mental Health and Mental Health Services Research, 39,* 419–425.

Stamatakis, K., McQueen, A., Filler, C., Boland, E., Dreisinger, M., Brownson, R., & Luke, D. (2012). Measurement properties of a novel survey to access stages of organizational readiness for evidence-based interventions in community chronic disease prevention settings. *Implementation Science, 7,* 65.

Zaslow, M., Tout, K., Halle, T., Vick, J., & Lavelle, B. (2010). *Towards the identification of features of effective professional development for early childhood educators: A review of the literature.* Washington, DC: U.S. Department of Education. Retrieved from http://www2.ed.gov/rschstat/eval/professional-development/literature-review.pdf

Zaslow, M., Tout, K., Halle, T., Whittaker, J.V., & Lavelle, B. (2010). Emerging research on early childhood professional development. In S. Neuman & M. Kamil (Eds.), *Preparing teachers for the early childhood classroom* (pp. 19–47). Baltimore, MD: Paul H. Brookes Publishing Co.

Index

Tables and figures are indicated by *t* and *f*, respectively.

Ability to change, 45
Academic Choice, Responsive Classroom
    (RC) approach, 66, 79, 81, 86
Achieved relative strength, 69, 78
Achieved relative strength indices (ARSI),
    78–81
Action stage of change, 51*t*
Active implementation frameworks
    core implementation components, 28–33
    implementation drivers, 28–33
    overview, 24
    stages of implementation, 24–28
Active ingredients, 68
Adaptation
    Educare model, 223–224
    overview, 6, 12
    technology-enhanced, Research-
        based, Instruction, Assessment, and
        professional Development (TRIAD)
        scale-up model, 181, 184, 185
    using fidelity tools in decisions regarding,
        152–153
    zone of tolerable adaptation, 85–86
Adaptive challenges, 39
Adaptive leadership, 33
Adherence
    diffusion versus, 230–231
    during replication, 231–232
Administration
    facilitative, 32, 60, 278
    fostering positive staff behaviors, 234
    increasing readiness, 60–61
    in scale-up models, 177
    support from, 47
Adoption, 11, 25
Affordable Care Act, 304
Aligning stage-appropriate evaluation with
    stages of implementation, 228–229
Anchors, 143–144, 145–147, 151
ARSI, *see* Achieved relative strength indices
Assigning ratings, quality rating and
    improvement systems (QRIS), 271–272,
    281–283*t*, 287

Attachment experiences, effect on
    readiness, 49
Audiotape transcripts of coaching sessions,
    105
Autonomy, 49, 53
Average achieved relative strength index
    (ARSI), 78–80
Awareness, raising, 54–55

BBLT, *see* Building Blocks Learning
    Trajectories
BECF, *see* Buffett Early Childhood Fund
Behavioral processes, 51
Binary complier index, 80–81, 82*t*
Bounce Learning Network, 209
Boundaries, quality rating and
    improvement systems (QRIS), 284–285
Buffett Early Childhood Fund (BECF), 209,
    212–213
Building Blocks, 171, 181–185
Building Blocks Learning Trajectories
    (BBLT), 184
Buy-in, 11, 55

Capacity, 8, 11
CARES demonstration project, *see* Head
    Start Classroom-Based Approaches
    and Resources for Emotion and Social
    skill promotion demonstration project
Cascading logic models, 309
Case studies
    The Incredible Years, 15–16
    Learning Collaborative methodology,
        13–15
    readiness to change, 45–47
CCDF, *see* The Child Care and
    Development Fund
CCTAN, *see* Child Care Technical
    Assistance Network
Center for Effective Practice at the Child
    Health and Development Institute, 14

Change beliefs, 45
Change processes, managing, 27
Chicago School Readiness Project, 159
Child assessments, 38–40
The Child Care and Development Fund
    (CCDF), 244
Child Care Technical Assistance Network
    (CCTAN), 307
Child FIRST, 13–15
Children, in scale-up models, 179
Children's Institute, 58–59
Circle process, in meetings, 58
Classroom Assessment Scoring System
    (CLASS) observation measure, 235
Classroom Links to Early Literacy, 98,
    108–109
Classroom Links to Sounds and Words
    program, 98, 107, 109
Classroom Practice Frequency Survey
    (CPFS), 75, 77–78
Classroom Practices Observation Measure
    (CPOM), 75, 77–78
Classroom Practices Teacher Survey
    (CPTS), 75, 77–78
Coach, in Head Start Classroom-Based
    Approaches and Resources for
    Emotion and Social skill promotion
    (CARES) demonstration project, 142t
Coaching
    component of successful implementation,
        30–31
    defined, 9
    in early care and education (ECE),
        158–161
    increasing readiness, 59–60
    of professionals in Getting Ready
        intervention, 127–128
    structure of sessions, 101
Coaching-based professional development
    (PD) program
    determining feasibility with
        implementation data, 106–108
    identifying correlates of coaching
        implementation, 111–112
    identifying dimensions of coaching,
        100–102
    identifying patterns of variation with
        implementation data, 109–110
    interpreting outcomes with
        implementation data, 108–109
    measuring implementation of coaching,
        103–105
    overview, 97–98
    predicting strength and type of outcomes
        with implementation data, 110–111
    research on coaching in early childhood
        programs, 98–100

Collaboration
    in development of fidelity measures, 150
    spirit of, 53
Collaborative (conjoint) consultation
    models, 120
Colorado
    Early Childhood Council Health
        Integration Initiative, 16
    The Incredible Years program, 15–16
Common characteristics of implementation
    research, 10–11
Communication
    linking communication protocols,
        262–263
    in scale-up models, 178
    Technology-enhanced, Research-
        based, Instruction, Assessment, and
        professional Development (TRIAD)
        scale-up model, 179, 182, 185, 186
Competence, 49
Competence of early care and education
    (ECE) practitioners, developing, 26, 29
Competency components, Getting Ready
    intervention, 126
Competency drivers, 28, 29–31, 34–35t,
    56–57, 276–277
Components
    in integrated professional development
        (PD) system, 253–254
    systems initiative framework, 245, 246t,
        248–249
Composite fidelity indices, 73–74, 77
Compromise, in Nurse–Family Partnership
    (NFP), 202–203
Conceptual framework
    for implementation analysis, 229–230
    for Nurse–Family Partnership (NFP), 199f
Conceptual logic model, 70–71
Confidence, raising, 56
Confidence of early care and education
    (ECE) practitioners, developing, 26, 29
Connecticut, implementation of learning
    collaboratives in, 13–15
Connections
    in integrated professional development
        (PD) system, 254
    systems initiative framework, 245, 246t,
        249–250
Construct validity, 65, 68–70
Consultant Evaluation Form, 131
Consultation, see Coaching
Consumer education, quality rating and
    improvement systems (QRIS), 274,
    281–283t, 288
Contemplation stage of change, 51t
Content
    coverage in coaching sessions, 102

of early childhood preparation programs, 248

Context
in integrated professional development (PD) system, 253
systems initiative framework, 245, 246t, 247–248

Contextual factors affecting readiness, 48–50

Contextual variables, Network of Influences framework, 176, 177f

Continuous improvement, 27, 264–265, 309–310

Continuum of motivation, 55

Core implementation components
competency drivers, 29–31
driver integration, 33
Educare model, 214, 215f
Getting Ready intervention, 126–131
including in conceptual models for early childhood initiatives, 298–299
intervention fidelity, 68–69
leadership drivers, 33
organization drivers, 31–33
overview, 2, 10, 24, 28–29
quality rating and improvement systems (QRIS), 276

Correlates of coaching implementation, identifying, 111–112

Correlational analyses of fidelity measures, 82–84

CPFS, *see* Classroom Practice Frequency Survey

CPOM, *see* Classroom Practices Observation Measure

CPTS, *see* Classroom Practices Teacher Survey

Cross-quality rating and improvement systems (QRIS) analyses, 275

Cultural diversity, 47–48, 49, 249

Current stressors, 49–50

Curriculum, Educare model, 224

Data
collection in Educare model, 220
review process in Educare model, 222–223
sources for coaching implementation, 103–104
use of, Educare model, 221–222

Data-driven decision making, 161–163

Decision-support data systems, 32–33, 277–278

Delaware Early Learner Survey (ELS), 305–306

Descriptive statistics of fidelity measures, 83

Designation Renewal System, 38

Diffusion, 25, 174–175, 230–231

Discrepancy, 45

Dissemination, 7

Diversity, 47–48, 49, 249

Early care and education (ECE)
aligning stage-appropriate evaluations, 300–301
fully operationalized programs or initiatives, requirements for, 22–24
future evaluation and research, 16–17, 310–312
implementation drivers, 28, 29f
implementation science perspective on, 296–298
implications of implementation for, 37–40, 303–308
integration of key implementation components into, 5, 13
overview, 295–296
policy and practice challenges, 308–310
questions related to implementation into, 298–300
readiness to change, 45–47
research challenges, 301–303
workforce, 47–48

Early care and education (ECE) practitioners
coaching and supervision, 30–31
developing competence and confidence of, 26, 29
performance assessments of, 23, 31, 129–130
professional development in Getting Ready intervention, 126–128
registries for, 251
regulations for education and training of, 247
role in Getting Ready intervention, 120–122, 123, 124
selection of, 30
training, 30
see also professional development

Early Childhood Councils (ECCs), 16

Early Head Start (EHS)
Educare model, 210
Getting Ready intervention, 123

Early Learner Survey Committee, 306

Early Learner Survey (ELS), 305–306

EBP, *see* Evidence-based practice

ECCs, *see* Early Childhood Councils

ECE, *see* Early care and education

ECE practitioners, *see* Early care and education practitioners

Edna McConnell Clark Foundation, 204

Educare Implementation Study, 215–217, 218–223
Educare Learning Network (ELN), 209, 228
Educare model
　core implementation components, 214, 215f
　core practices, 210–213
　ensuring adherence without dilution in, 232
　evaluating from implementation science perspective, 223–224
　general discussion, 210
　issues encountered in, 218–223
　lessons from, 224–225
　measuring implementation, 215–217
　overview, 172, 209–210
　phase and level of implementation, 217–218
　replication, 302
Educare Program Implementation Checklist, 217
Educating stakeholders on quality rating and improvement systems (QRIS) implementation, 290
Educational interactions, in scale-up models, 177
Educational qualifications of practitioners, 247
Effectiveness
　evaluating in replication, 233
　of professional development systems, 251, 253
Efficacy, 45
Efficacy and Replication phase, 217–218
Efficacy trial of Getting Ready intervention, 132
EHS, see Early Head Start
ELN, see Educare Learning Network
ELS, see Early Learner Survey
Empathy, spirit of, 52–53
Empirical investigation, 7
Enduring personal characteristics, effect on readiness, 50
Engagement, 11
Environment Rating Scales, 273
Equity, promoting in Technology-enhanced, Research-based, Instruction, Assessment, and professional Development (TRIAD) scale-up model, 180, 183
Essential functions, 23, 68
Evaluations
　of implementation in replication, 233–234
　implications of implementation for, 37–40
Evidence-Based Practice Attitude Scale, 57
Evidence-Based Practice Consortium, 311
Evidence-based practice (EBP), 6, 157
Experiential processes, 51

Exploration stage
　general discussion, 25–26
　implementation teams during, 36
　integrated professional development (PD) system, 256–257, 259t, 263
　quality rating and improvement systems (QRIS), 279, 281t
　questions about implementation drivers in, 34t
　readiness assessments, 44

Facilitative administration, 32, 60, 278
Family Resource Centers of Crestwood Children's Center, 60
Family support, Educare model, 212
Family-based providers, 247
Feasibility, determining with coaching implementation data, 106–108
Feedback, 12, 101
Fidelity
　defined, 8
　linking to outcome measures, Responsive Classroom Efficacy Study (RCES), 82–85
　monitoring, 12
　see also Implementation fidelity; Intervention fidelity
Fidelity indicators
　Responsive Classroom Efficacy Study (RCES), 75–77
　weighting and combining components, 86–87
Fidelity logs, Head Start Classroom-Based Approaches and Resources for Emotion and Social skill promotion (CARES) demonstration project, 143, 148, 162
Financial incentives, quality rating and improvement systems (QRIS), 273–274, 281–283t, 288
Financial model, Nurse–Family Partnership (NFP), 204
Financial sustainability, 28
Financing for Nurse–Family Partnership (NFP), changes in, 202
Five-step intervention fidelity assessment model, 73–74
　see also Responsive Classroom Efficacy Study
Flexible fidelity tools, 152
Frank Porter Graham Child Development Institute (FPG), 212, 220
Full implementation stage
　implementation teams during, 37
　integrated professional development (PD) system, 257–258, 260t, 263

overview, 27
quality rating and improvement systems (QRIS), 279, 282*t*
questions about implementation drivers in, 35*t*
readiness monitoring, 44
Fully operationalized programs or initiatives, requirements for, 22–24
Funding, Educare model, 213
Future evaluation and research, 16–17

Gestaltists, 65
Getting Ready intervention
  core implementation components, 126–131
  general discussion, 117–118
  key features of, 120–122
  lessons from, 131–133
  level of intervention, 124–126
  overview, 117
  research support for parent–child relationship, 118–119
  research support for parent–professional partnerships, 119–120
  significant outcomes, 124
  site and participant characteristics, 122–124
  stage of implementation, 124–126
Glows and grows mentoring tool, 101
Grantee supervisor, in Head Start CARES (Classroom-Based Approaches and Resources for Emotion and Social skill promotion) demonstration project, 142*t*
Guided Discovery, Responsive Classroom (RC) approach, 66
Guides, implementation frameworks as, 13

Head Start Classroom-Based Approaches and Resources for Emotion and Social skill promotion (CARES) demonstration project
  anchors, 143–144, 145–147
  considerations for early childhood field, 150–153
  creating fidelity measures, 141–143
  fidelity documentation and measurement challenges, 149–150
  intervention documentation, 148
  key players, 142*t*
  multiple reporters, 148
  overview, 140–141
  thresholds for ratings, 147–148
  training, 149
  universal and specific measures of fidelity, 143–147
Head Start programs
  Educare model, 210
  effective use of early childhood assessments in, 38–40

monitoring, 250
Research-based, Developmentally Informed (REDI), 165–166
  see also Head Start Classroom-Based Approaches and Resources for Emotion and Social skill promotion demonstration project
Home visiting programs
  Getting Ready intervention, 123
  Parents as Teachers, 60
  Partners in Family Child Care project, 59–60
  readiness to change, 48
Honesty during collaboration, 53
Host organizations for Nurse–Family Partnership (NFP), 201–202, 205
How, of implementation, 38
Hypermedia coaching resource, 109–110

IA teams, Ounce of Prevention Fund, *see* Implementation assistance teams, Ounce of Prevention Fund
iFidelity form, 186
IHI, *see* Institute for Healthcare Improvement
Implementation, defined, 7
Implementation assistance (IA) teams, Ounce of Prevention Fund, 212–213
Implementation dip, 88–89
Implementation drivers
  for coaching implementation, 160–161
  competency drivers, 29–31
  driver integration, 33
  leadership drivers, 33
  organization drivers, 31–33
  overview, 24, 28–29, 69
  quality rating and improvement systems (QRIS), 276
  in stages of implementation, 33–35
Implementation fidelity
  defined, 8
  Educare model, 215–217
  versus intervention fidelity, 158
  overview, 68
  technology-enhanced, Research-based, Instruction, Assessment, and professional Development (TRIAD) scale-up model, 186–187
Implementation frameworks
  core implementation components, 28–33
  implementation drivers, 28–33
  overview, 24
  potential challenges, 12–13
  stages of implementation, 24–28
Implementation process, structure of, 11

Implementation processes that support readiness to change
administration, 60–61
coaching, 59–60
overview, 56–57
selection, 57
training, 58–59
Implementation science
applying to quality rating and improvement systems (QRIS), 275–280
common terms defined, 7–10
defined, 5–7
potential challenges of frameworks, 12–13
themes in literature, 10–12
Implementation science framework, Educare model, 215*f*
Implementation Study, Educare model, 215–217, 218–223
Implementation teams
connecting across different levels of systems, 309
during exploration stage, 36
during full implementation stage, 37
general discussion, 35–36
Head Start programs, 39–40
during initial implementation stage, 37
during installation stage, 36
integrated professional development (PD) system, 260–263
quality rating and improvement systems (QRIS), 289–290
Implementation variables, Network of Influences framework, 176, 177*f*
Importance, raising, 55–56
Improving Head Start for School Readiness Act of 2007 (PL 110-134), 38
The Incredible Years, 15–16
The Incredible Years Teacher Training, 141
Index validity and reliability, Responsive Classroom Efficacy Study (RCES), 77–82
Individualized interventions, challenges of, 131–132
Infrastructure
in integrated professional development (PD) system, 254–255
systems initiative framework, 245, 246*t*, 250–251
Initial implementation stage
implementation teams during, 37
integrated professional development (PD) system, 257, 259–260*t*, 263
overview, 26–27
quality rating and improvement systems (QRIS), 279, 282*t*

questions about implementation drivers in, 34*t*
readiness monitoring, 44
Innovation, 12, 235, 280, 283*t*
In-service training, Getting Ready intervention, 127
Installation, defined, 11
Installation stage
implementation teams during, 36
increasing readiness, 44
integrated professional development (PD) system, 257, 259*t*, 263
overview, 26
quality rating and improvement systems (QRIS), 279, 281*t*
questions about implementation drivers in, 34*t*
Institute for Healthcare Improvement (IHI), 14
Institutional infrastructure, 39
Integrated professional development (PD) system
components in, 253–254
connections in, 254
context in, 253
guide to action for achieving, 260–265
infrastructure in, 254–255
overview, 245, 253
scale in, 255
stage-based framework for, 255–260
Integration of implementation drivers, 33
Intent-to-treat analysis, 68
Interagency School Readiness Consortium, 124–125
Interdisciplinary services, Educare model, 212
Interim memos, 310
Intermediary organization, 9–10, 35–36
Internal motivation, 55–56
Interpersonal relationship between coach and teacher, 101–102
Interpretation of results, Educare model, 222
Intervention core components, 68, 214, 215*f*
Intervention documentation, Head Start Classroom-Based Approaches and Resources for Emotion and Social skill promotion (CARES) demonstration project, 148
Intervention fidelity
aligning initial program development with later at-scale applications, 167–168
coaching, 158–161
data-driven decision making, 161–163
defined, 8, 68
development of measurements, 139–140, 150–153, 163–166

versus implementation fidelity, 158
at replication, 234–235
see also Head Start Classroom-Based
    Approaches and Resources for
    Emotion and Social skill promotion
    demonstration project
Intervention fidelity assessment
    construct validity, 68–70
    fidelity definitions, 68–70
    five-step process, 72–73
    issues within, 85–89
    logic models, 70–73
    overview, 2–3, 65–66
    Responsive Classroom approach, 66–68
    see also Responsive Classroom Efficacy
        Study
Intimate partner violence (IPV), 203
Invest in Kids, 15
Issues within, 83

Kentucky's Stars for Kids Now quality
    rating system, 57
Knowledge translation, 7

Language development, coaching
    programs focused on, 106–107
Leadership, Educare model, 212
Leadership drivers, 28–29, 33
Learning Collaborative methodology, 13–15
Learning organization, creating support
    implementation at scale, 203–204
Learning trajectories, 178–179
Levels of implementation, 72–73, 124–126
Linked teaming structure, 261, 262f
Linking communication protocols, 262–263
Listening meetings, 58
Literacy, coaching programs focused on,
    106–107
Literature on implementation, themes in,
    10–12
Local evaluation, Educare model, 212
Local implementation teams, 36
Logic models, 70–73, 74–75, 309
Logs
    fidelity, 143, 148, 162
    online coaching, 103

Maintenance stage of change, 51t
"Making it happen" category, 35
Managing change processes, 27
Marketing, quality rating and
    improvement systems (QRIS), 274, 288
Maternal, Infant, and Early Childhood
    Home Visiting Program (MIECHV), 304

Mathematics education, 175
MDRC research and technical assistance
    team, 142t
Measures development, 311
Mentoring, *see* Coaching
Mentoring intervention study, readiness to
    change in, 48
MIECHV, *see* Maternal, Infant, and Early
    Childhood Home Visiting Program
Mindfulness, 52–53
Model-specific training, 30
Monitoring
    fidelity, 12
    Head Start, 250
    quality rating and improvement systems
        (QRIS), 250
Morning Meeting, Responsive Classroom
    (RC) approach, 66, 67, 79, 80–81, 86
Motivation for change, 43, 55–56
MST, *see* Multisystemic Therapy
MTP, *see* MyTeachingPartner program
Multiple reporters, Head Start Classroom-
    Based Approaches and Resources for
    Emotion and Social skill promotion
    (CARES) demonstration project, 148
Multisystemic Therapy (MST), 8
MyTeachingPartner (MTP) program,
    159–160, 162

The National Association for the Education
    of Young Children (NAEYC) Policy
    Blueprint, 244
National Center on Child Care Professional
    Development Systems and Workforce
    Initiatives (PDW Center), 307–308
National level implementation teams, 39–40
The National Professional Development
    Center on Inclusion (NPDCI), 244
NEFC, *see* Northeast Foundation for
    Children
Network of Influences framework, 176–179
NFP, *see* Nurse–Family Partnership
NFP National Service Office (NSO),
    199–200, 204
Northeast Foundation for Children (NEFC),
    66
NPDCI, *see* The National Professional
    Development Center on Inclusion
Nurse home visitor turnover, Nurse–
    Family Partnership (NFP), 201
Nurse–Family Partnership (NFP)
    creating learning organization to support
        implementation at scale, 203–204
    development of intervention, 194–196
    ensuring adherence without dilution in,
        232

Nurse–Family Partnership
    (NFP)—continued
  lessons from, 206–207
  overview, 172, 193–194
  preparing to support installation in
    community settings, 196–200
  program quality data system, 228
  reflective supervision model, 234
  resources and commitments at multiple
    levels, 204–206
  sustainability, 200–203

Observation measures, quality rating and
    improvement systems (QRIS), 277
Observational home visit data, Getting
    Ready intervention, 130
Office of Special Education Programs, 250
Online coaching logs, 103
On-site coaching visits, 98, 108
Open-ended questioning skills, 53–54
Operational logic model, 70, 71–72
Organization drivers, 28, 29f, 31–33, 34–35t,
    57, 60
Organizational selection, Getting Ready
    intervention, 129
Ounce of Prevention Fund, 209, 212–213
Outcomes
  evaluation, 12
  interpreting with coaching
    implementation data, 108–109
  predicting with coaching implementation
    data, 110–111

Parents
  Getting Ready outcomes on, 124
  parent–child relationship, research
    support for, 118–119
  parent–professional partnerships,
    research support for, 119–120
  in scale-up models, 179
Parents as Teachers home visiting
    program, 60
Participant characteristics, Getting Ready
    intervention, 122–124
Partners in Family Child Care project, 59–60
Partnerships, Educare model, 212
Path modeling, 84–85
PATHS, see Preschool Promoting
    Alternative Thinking Strategies
Patterns of variation, identifying with
    coaching implementation data, 109–110
PD, see Professional development
PDSA cycle, see Plan, do, study, act cycle
PDW Center, see National Center on Child
    Care Professional Development
    Systems and Workforce Initiatives

Peer-reviewed journals, implementation
    science studies in, 311
Performance assessment, 31, 277
Persistence, 174
Persistent stressors, 49–50
Personal characteristics, effect on
    readiness, 50
Perspectives, in quality rating and
    improvement systems (QRIS),
    285–286
Phonological awareness skills, coaching
    programs focused on, 107
PL 110-134, see Improving Head Start for
    School Readiness Act of 2007
Plan, do, study, act (PDSA) cycle, 264
Policies
  challenges in early care and education
    implementation, 308–310
  integrated professional development
    system, 253
  for Nurse–Family Partnership (NFP),
    202, 205
  policy–practice feedback loops, 265
  requirements for measurement of
    implementation, 311
  targeting improved early childhood
    outcomes, 303–308
Population served by Nurse–Family
    Partnership (NFP), changes in, 201
Practice profiles, 23
Practice–policy feedback loops, 265
Precontemplation stage of change, 51t
Predicting strength and type of outcomes
    with coaching implementation data,
    110–111
Preparation stage of change, 51t
Preschool Curriculum Evaluation Research
    Consortium (2008) study, 99, 164
Preschool Curriculum Evaluation Research
    Initiative, 151
Preschool Promoting Alternative Thinking
    Strategies (PATHS), 141
Presentation review process, Educare
    model, 222–223
Problem solving, rapid-cycle, 264–265
Process domain of coaching, 101–102
Professional development (PD)
  Educare model, 211
  in Getting Ready intervention, 126–128,
    132–133
  improving systems initiatives, 239–240
  MyTeachingPartner (MTP) program,
    159–160
  in scale-up projects, 175, 178
  technology-enhanced, Research-
    based, Instruction, Assessment, and
    professional Development (TRIAD)
    scale-up model, 180, 183–184, 186

see also Coaching-based professional development program; Statewide professional development systems
Professional standards for high-quality practice, 250, 254
Program fidelity, *see* Intervention fidelity
Program Implementation Checklist, Educare, 217
Program installation, 11
Program level implementation teams, 39
Program model, 231
Programmatic sustainability, 28
Project Literacy, 98
Promising practices, 6
Psychometrically testing fidelity measures, 151
Purveyor organization
    defined, 9–10
    Educare model, 212
    Getting Ready intervention, 125
    interactions with during exploration stage, 26
    Invest in Kids, 15

QRIS, *see* Quality rating and improvement systems
Quality assurance, 9
Quality awards, 274
Quality improvement
    defined, 9
    overview, 12
    quality rating and improvement systems (QRIS), 273, 281–283*t*, 287
Quality measures of intervention fidelity, 165
Quality of coaching implementation, 104
Quality rating and improvement systems (QRIS)
    applying implementation science to, 275–280
    applying systems theory to, 280, 284–286
    assigning ratings, 271–272
    emergence of, 270–271
    financial incentives, 273–274
    future directions for researchers, 290–291
    future directions for stakeholders, 288–290
    ideal components of, 286–288
    marketing and consumer education, 274
    monitoring processes, 250
    overview, 240, 269–270
    quality improvement, 273
    quality standards, 271–272
    research literature, 275
    researchers, 290–291
    stakeholders, 288–290
Quality standards, quality rating and improvement systems (QRIS), 271–272, 281–283*t*

Quantity and quality of curriculum implementation, 110
Questionnaires in coaching interventions, 103–104
Questions to address during stages of implementation, 263

Race to the Top-Early Learning Challenge (RTT-ELC), 305–307
Raising
    awareness, 54–55
    confidence, 56
    importance, 55–56
Randomized clinical trial, Educare model, 225
Rapid-cycle problem solving, 264–265
Ratings, quality rating and improvement systems (QRIS), 271–272, 281–283*t*, 287
RC approach, *see* Responsive Classroom approach
RCES, *see* Responsive Classroom Efficacy Study
Readiness
    assessing, 11
    case studies, 45–47
    contextual factors affecting, 48–50
    creating, 36
    defined, 8, 44–45
    early care and education workforce, 47–48
    implementation processes that support, 56–61
    overview, 2, 43–44
    spirit and skills for increasing, 51–56
    stages of change, 50–51
Recommended practices
    for coaching, 31
    for decision-support data systems, 33
    overview, 6
    for performance assessment, 31
    in staff selection, 30
    for systems interventions, 32
    for training, 30
Record-keeping systems, coaching-based professional development (PD) programs, 103
Reflective listening skills, 53–54
Regional level implementation teams, 39
Registries for practitioners, 251
Regulations for education and training of practitioners, 247
Relatedness, 49
Relationships
    between coach and teacher, 101–102
    effect on readiness, 49
    in quality rating and improvement systems (QRIS), 285

Reliability
    considerations in coaching
        implementation, 105
    of fidelity measures, 73
Replication
    aligning stage-appropriate evaluation
        with stages of implementation,
        228–229
    conceptual framework for implementation
        analysis, 229–230
    defined, 7
    diffusion versus adherence, 230–231
    Educare model, 217–218, 223–224, 302
    ensuring adherence without dilution,
        231–232
    evaluating effectiveness, 233
    evaluating implementation in, 233–234
    importance of intervention fidelity at,
        234–235
    issues with, 235–236
    overview, 227–228
Research-to-practice gap, 21–22
Resources, Nurse–Family Partnership
    (NFP), 204–206
Responsive Classroom Efficacy Study
    (RCES)
    determining index validity and reliability,
        77–82
    developing fidelity indicators, 75–77
    linking fidelity measures to outcome
        measures, 82–85
    model specification, 74–75
    overview, 74
Responsive Classroom (RC) approach
    conceptual logic model, 70–71
    general discussion, 66–68
    operational logic model, 71–72
    see also Responsive Classroom Efficacy
        Study
RTT-ELC, see Race to the Top-Early
    Learning Challenge
Rule Creation, Responsive Classroom (RC)
    approach, 66

Scalability, defined, 8
Scale
    in integrated professional development
        (PD) system, 255
    systems initiative framework, 245, 246t,
        251–252
Scale-up
    ensuring adherence without dilution in,
        231–232
    evaluating effectiveness, 233
    importance of intervention fidelity at,
        234–235

overview, 171, 173–174
of quality rating and improvement
    systems (QRIS), 290–291
see also Nurse–Family Partnership;
    Technology-enhanced, Research-
    based, Instruction, Assessment, and
    professional Development scale-up
    model
School readiness interventions, see Getting
    Ready intervention
School-level leaders, in scale-up models,
    177
SCITS, see South Carolina Infant/Toddler
    Specialist Network
Selection, increasing readiness, 57
Self-concept, 54
Self-determination theory, 49
Self-efficacy, 56
Self-reporting, 88, 105
Sense of autonomy, 53
Sequencing of components, 87
Silos, 249, 252
Site characteristics, Getting Ready
    intervention, 122–124
Skills
    open-ended questioning, 53–54
    reflective listening, 53–54
Social systems, effect on readiness, 49
Social-emotional development, 141
South Carolina Infant/Toddler Specialist
    Network (SCITS), 60–61
Specific measures of fidelity, 143–147
Spirit and skills for increasing readiness
    open-ended questioning skills, 53–54
    overview, 51–52
    reflective listening skills, 53–54
    spirit of empathy and collaboration,
        52–53
    support strategies, 54–56
Staff performance assessment, Getting
    Ready intervention, 129–130, 132
Staff selection, 30, 160–161
The Stage of Change Approach to Early
    Education Professional Development
    seminar, 61
The Stage of Change Scale for Early Care
    and Education, 57
Stage-based framework for professional
    development (PD), 255–260
Staged implementation framework, 244
Stages of change, 50–51
Stages of Concern Questionnaire, 57
Stages of implementation
    aligning evaluation plans with, 228–229,
        300–301
    dealing with components in different
        stages within initiatives, 301

exploration, 25–26
full implementation stage, 27
implementation drivers in, 33–35
initial implementation, 26–27
installation, 26
overview, 24–25
quality rating and improvement systems
    (QRIS), 279, 281–283*t*
sustainability, 27–28
Stakeholder groups, 26
Standards, in quality rating and
    improvement systems (QRIS), 286–287
State level implementation teams, 39
Statewide professional development (PD)
    systems
  guide to action for achieving integrated
      systems, 260–265
  overview, 243–244
  stage-based framework for, 255–260
  see also Integrated professional
      development system; System as is,
      professional development systems
Stressors, current and persistent, 49–50
Structural domain of coaching, 101
Structuralism, 65
Structure of implementation process, 11
Successful implementation, components of
  fully operationalized programs or
      initiatives, requirements for, 22–24
  implementation driver framework, 28–33
  implementation teams, 35–37
  implications for early care and education
      (ECE), 37–40
  integration of frameworks, 33–35
  overview, 21–22
  stages of implementation framework,
      24–28
Supervision, 30–31
Support for installation of Nurse–Family
    Partnership (NFP), 196–200
Support strategies for increasing readiness,
    54–56
Sustainability
  defined, 9
  Getting Ready intervention, 125
  Nurse–Family Partnership (NFP), 200–203
  planning, 9
  quality rating and improvement systems
      (QRIS), 280, 283*t*
  scale-up projects, 174
  in stages of implementation, 27–28
System as is, professional development
    (PD) systems
  components, 248–249
  connections, 249–250
  context, 245, 247–248
  infrastructure, 250–251

overview, 245
scale, 251–252
strengths and challenges in, 251–252
targets, 246*t*
System boundaries, quality rating and
    improvement systems (QRIS), 284–285
Systems initiative framework
  components, 248–249
  connections, 249–250
  context, 245, 247–248
  infrastructure, 250–251
  overview, 244, 245, 246*t*
  scale, 251–252
Systems interventions, 32, 278, 279*t*
Systems theory, applying to quality rating
    and improvement systems (QRIS), 280,
    284–286

Teachers
  in Head Start Classroom-Based
      Approaches and Resources for
      Emotion and Social skill promotion
      (CARES) demonstration project, 142*t*
  in scale-up models, 178
  teacher–coach relationship quality,
      101–102
Technical assistance
  defined, 9
  quality rating and improvement systems
      (QRIS), 273
Technical challenges, 39
Technical leadership, 33
Technologically mediated delivery of
    coaching, 98, 101, 104, 108, 109–110
Technology-enhanced, Research-
    based, Instruction, Assessment, and
    professional Development (TRIAD)
    scale-up model
  background, 173–175
  Building Blocks, 181–185
  empirical evaluation, 181–182
  ensuring adherence without dilution in,
      231–232
  lessons from, 185–187
  overview, 173
  research-based guidelines, 179–181
  theoretical framework for, 176–179
Terminology, 7–10
TF-CBT, *see* Trauma-Focused Cognitive-
    Behavior Therapy
Theoretical base for implementation, 12
Theoretical framework for Technology-
    enhanced, Research-based,
    Instruction, Assessment, and
    professional Development (TRIAD)
    scale-up model, 176–179

Thresholds for ratings, Head Start Classroom-Based Approaches and Resources for Emotion and Social skill promotion (CARES) demonstration project, 147–148

Tiered reimbursement, 273–274

Timelines for quality rating and improvement systems (QRIS) implementation, 290

Timing, influence on construct validity of intervention fidelity measures, 88–89

Tolerable adaptation, zone of, 85–86

Tools of the Mind, 141, 144–145

Trainer, in Head Start CARES (Classroom-Based Approaches and Resources for Emotion and Social skill promotion) demonstration project, 142*t*

Training
coaches, 161
defined, 9
Head Start CARES (Classroom-Based Approaches and Resources for Emotion and Social skill promotion) demonstration project, 149
increasing readiness, 58–59
overview, 30
of professionals in Getting Ready intervention, 127

Training and Technical Assistance Network, 39–40

Transtheoretical Model (TTM) of change spirit and skills for increasing readiness, 51–56
stages of change, 50–51

Trauma history, effect on readiness, 50

Trauma-Focused Cognitive-Behavior Therapy (TF-CBT), 13–15

TRIAD scale-up model, *see* Technology-enhanced, Research-based, Instruction, Assessment, and professional Development scale-up model

Triadic intervention, 120

TTM, *see* Transtheoretical Model of change

Type III error, 6, 68, 140

Unintentional program drift, 153

Universal measures of fidelity, 143–147

University of Rhode Island Change Assessment (URICA), 57

Valence, 45

Validity of fidelity measures, 73

Variation patterns, identifying with coaching implementation data, 109–110

Video-based coaching, 98, 101, 104, 108, 109–110

Videotaping coaching sessions, 105

Web, data collection and use through, 163

Weighting fidelity indicators, 86–87

What, of implementation, 38

Who, of implementation, 38

Willingness, 45

Work plans for quality rating and improvement systems (QRIS) implementation, 290

Zero-order correlations, 83

Zone of tolerable adaptation, 85–86